CCNA Certification: Routing Basics for Cisco Certified Network Associates Exam 640-407

ISBN 0-13-086185-5

90000

9 780130 861856

Cisco Technology Titles from Prentice Hall PTR

- *Cisco Certification: Bridges, Routers and Switches for CCIEs,* Caslow

- *CCNA Certification: Routing Basics for Cisco Certified Network Associates Exam 640-407,* Myhre

CCNA Certification:
Routing Basics for Cisco Certified Network Associates Exam 640-407

Robert N. Myhre

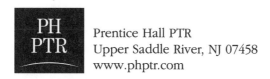

Prentice Hall PTR
Upper Saddle River, NJ 07458
www.phptr.com

Library of Congress Cataloging-in-Publication Data

Myhre, Robert N.
  CCNA certification: routing basics for Cisco certified network associates exam
640-407 / Robert N. Myhre.
    p. cm.
  ISBN 0-13-086185-5 (hc.)
  1. Electronic data processing personel--Certification. 2. Computer
networks--Examinations--Study guides. I. Title.
QA76.3.M95   1999
004.6--dc21   99-055011

Editorial/Production Supervision: Benchmark Productions, Inc.
Acquisitions Editor: *Mary Franz*
Cover Design Director: *Jerry Votta*
Cover Design: *Talar Agasyan*
Manufacturing Manager: *Maura Goldstaub*
Editorial Assistant: *Noreen Regina*
Marketing Manager: *Lisa Konzelmann*
Project Coordinator: *Anne Trowbridge*

 © 2000 Prentice Hall PTR
Prentice-Hall, Inc.
Upper Saddle River, NJ 07458

The Exam Objectives have been reproduced by Prentice Hall with the permission of Cisco Systems, Inc.
COPYRIGHT © 1999 CISCO SYSTEMS, INC. ALL RIGHTS RESERVED.

Prentice Hall books are widely used by corporations and government agencies for training, marketing, and resale.

The publisher offers discounts on this book when ordered in bulk quantities.
For more information, contact: Corporate Sales Department, Phone: 800-382-3419;
Fax: 201-236-7141; E-mail: corpsales@prenhall.com; or write: Prentice Hall PTR,
Corp. Sales Dept., One Lake Street, Upper Saddle River, NJ 07458.

Printed in the United States of America

10 9 8 7 6 5 4 3 2 1

ISBN 0-13-086185-5

Prentice-Hall International (UK) Limited, *London*
Prentice-Hall of Australia Pty. Limited, *Sydney*
Prentice-Hall Canada Inc., *Toronto*
Prentice-Hall Hispanoamericana, S.A., *Mexico*
Prentice-Hall of India Private Limited, *New Delhi*
Prentice-Hall of Japan, Inc., *Tokyo*
Pearson Education Asia Pte. Ltd.
Editora Prentice-Hall do Brasil, Ltda., *Rio de Janeiro*

I would like to dedicate this book to my wife, Kelly, who has given me a direction in life these past 13 years. Without her constant stability in my otherwise constantly changing world, I would have been nothing but a whisper. My daughters, Pamela and Jacquelyn, have also been a constant in this world as they continue to grow into wonderful young adults right in front of my eyes. I love them all dearly.

Contents

x   Contents

Introduction

As an instructor in a classroom environment, I have learned there are two types of instructors. The first type, whether likable or not, is proud to show off his or her knowledge, but dislikes anyone learning anything. This type of instructor is more concerned with being better than everyone else. The second type of instructor, again whether likable or not, actually enjoys teaching. This person likes to share knowledge and does so in an informative way. I like to think of myself as the latter type.

When I began researching the material for this book, I looked into the various books on CCNA certification in the marketplace. I found a majority of these books to be either from a noninstructor, or from an instructor of the first type. The information lacking in these books was the actual step by step, how to configure a Cisco router. While these books gave you the commands to use, I didn't feel there was any continuity to actually seeing the routers configured and placed into action. To me, this is more important than simply certification. My goal was to take the information needed to pass the CCNA exam and put it in the format needed to perform actual work on the Cisco routers.

Who Is This Book For?

This book is for anyone with at least a small amount of networking experience; roughly equivalent to six months' experience. As an MCSE myself, I found a need to learn new technologies, and since Windows 2000 was delayed, it became apparent that the new technology to learn was not in the Microsoft field yet. Since Cisco products account for a vast majority of the routers and switches in the field, it lent itself to being the technology to learn. I saw a large number of MCSEs and CNEs start examining the Cisco products, and it became clear this was an ideal direction. Even if you do not wish to pursue the coveted CCIE certification, knowing the basics of routing and switching that you will gain in this book will help you greatly in the field. You never know, it may get you that pay raise you have been looking for.

If you are new to networking and still wish to pursue the CCNA certification, you may wish to pick up a book on networking to fill in the small holes you will find in this book. Use that book in conjunction with this book.

How This Book Is Laid Out

The first part of the book (Chapters 1–4) is all knowledge and theory material. Chapter 1 begins with a more thorough look at the OSI model and is relevant to the test. It is also good material to help build your troubleshooting skills. Chapters 2 and 3 are not so much test material as they are for getting everyone up to speed on the basics of LAN technologies. If you have years of experience, you may wish to simply browse through the chapters and pick up any small pieces of information that you do not have. Chapter 4 is a quick look at the TCP/IP protocol suite.

The second part of the book (Chapters 5–14) is the essence of the Cisco router configuration. Chapter 5 starts with a look at the various models of the Cisco product line. It then continues with an in-depth look at the Cisco 2500 model, which can be considered the staple of the products. Chapter 6 looks at TCP/IP addressing and how to configure the Cisco router with addresses. Chapter 7 is a look at subnetting, including what it is and how to do it. There can be many questions about this on the CCNA test, and this should be a chapter that is thoroughly understood. The benefit to you is that this chapter has been a work in progress for over two years and has been class tested. I hope that you find it an easy lesson on subnetting. Chapters 8 and 9 begin the routing portion of the Cisco routers. You will learn static, RIP, and IGRP as the methods to enable routing. Chapter 10 is a quick look at the different methods needed to configure, save, and restore the Cisco router. Chapter 11 is a look at IPX/SPX and how to configure the router to work in these environments. Chapter 12 is about AppleTalk, and although there are no official exam objectives at this time, it is highly possible that AppleTalk will appear on your test when Cisco changes the exam. It is also important to understand because AppleTalk is still encountered in the field, and you should have a basic understanding of how it works. Chapter 13 is a look at access lists and how to set up the router to filter packets for AppleTalk, IPX/SPX, and, most important (to the test), TCP/IP. Chapter 14 is a look at WAN technologies and how Cisco routers can be used in these environments. This is only a brief review of WAN technologies, and should you decide to pursue more certifications in Cisco, you will be introduced to more WAN technologies and in more depth.

The final part of the book (Chapter 15) is not on the test, but it is extra material that you may find useful. This chapter is an accumulation of questions from students on "How do I do this?"

The appendices have the answers to the review questions, and also a flowchart of the commands used in this book.

Recommended Strategies When Reading This Book

I have three simple strategies for you as you read this book. The first is to get your hands on at least one Cisco router to try the various commands. There are places on the Net where you can rent time on a router or two. If you have access to a router at work, make sure you can change the configurations before doing these exercises. Also, if you would like to purchase a router, there are a few auction sites on the Internet where you will find good bargains for used Cisco routers.

The second strategy is for you to write down each command as you learn it. Most people learn better by writing items down. I found this to be true in the classroom environment, and it may be the same with you. After Chapter 7, you will find that you have a large list of commands, and you may be tired of writing them down. At that point, you are certainly welcome to use Appendix C for the remainder of the book, where I have laid out the commands in a hierarchical fashion for you.

The final strategy involves the Scenario questions at the end of each chapter. These questions have no right or wrong answers, but are more for you to review each of the chapters' materials. Please take a moment to try to answer each of the questions. Imagine that you are the consultant and have to report to the individual listed in the scenario. If you have the time and inclination, write down the answers in a report format. If you do this, I would love to see your reports. E-mail them to me at ccna@uswestmail.net.

Why and How to Obtain the CCNA Certification

Certification is becoming a large part of the corporate world. Sometimes it appears that you cannot even get a new job unless you have the certification to prove you know a little something. This does change depending on the certification (some certifications are required, and then the company will pay you to learn the technologies—these are known as *paper certifications*), but nonetheless, it may be vital for any career advancement. Cisco certification indicates that you are able to operate a Cisco router in a LAN or small WAN environment. It also means you understand the different protocols such as IPX/SPX and TCP/IP, and how to integrate the routers into these various environments. By becoming a CCNA, you are advertising yourself to your boss or your prospective employer as an individual who can perform these functions.

To become a CCNA, you must pass a single test that is offered through Sylvan Prometric. You can reach them at (800) 204-EXAM (3926). The current version of the CCNA test is 604-407. The cost to take the exam is $100, and although you can pay in advance, it is easier to pay with a credit card. One suggestion I would offer you as a person who has taken more than a few tests through Sylvan Prometric, is to call them 24 hours in advance and confirm your test. You cannot take a Cisco test the same day that you register. Remember to bring some form of identification with you to the test.

Other Cisco Certifications

The best way to get a feel for the different certifications is to visit Cisco's Web site at www.cisco.com and explore the training and certification paths. You will find there are many other certifications, including:

- CCDA (Cisco Certified Design Associate) for designing small LAN and WAN networks.
- CCNP (Cisco Certified Network Professional) for building and configuring bigger and more complex LANs and WANs.
- CCDP (Cisco Certified Design Professional) for designing bigger and more complex LANs and WANs.
- CCIE (Cisco Certified Internetworking Expert). The biggest and probably the most coveted certification in the industry. It requires a minimum of $1200 to pass the exams, and that doesn't include airfare.

How to Contact the Author

You can reach me at ccna@uswestmail.net. Questions about this book, scenario reports, and misprints are always welcome. I also have a class that I offer if you have more than a couple of people interested in this certification.

Acknowledgments

I would like to thank the many people who helped make this book a reality. It all started with Karen Moen, who forwarded me e-mail from Prentice Hall. It turns out that they were looking for a TCP/IP book for the Microsoft certification. The contact for them was Mary Franz. Although Mary and I talked, the timing was not truly right for me to commit to such a large undertaking.

Beginning in April, I again contacted Mary (never throw out those old contacts!) and asked her if she was interested in a book for the Cisco Certified Network Associate. She was most excited because Prentice Hall was looking for someone to do just that. I spent the next Sunday creating a formal outline of a course I was developing at the time.

After submitting the outline to Mary, I waited . . . and waited . . . and waited some more. Finally, I received a response: Mary and Prentice Hall were giving me a chance! After the paperwork (legal contracts, and so forth) was completed, I began writing the book.

If you are reading this and want to write a manual yourself, pay heed to the next couple of sentences. As I was writing the book, technical nightmares started plaguing me. Problems with FTP servers, and Word itself started acting strange. It turns out that I reused each chapter to start the next chapter to keep the formatting consistent. DO NOT DO THIS! My Word files got larger and larger (on the order of

10MB!). Files were not saving to the FTP directory, and they were too large to e-mail. After splitting my files in half and then putting them back together again, the size went back to the respectable 1MB (including the graphics, which are very tedious to create for someone who is graphically challenged—like me). Mary was most patient with my troubles (more so than *I*, anyway). I must thank her for all her work and help teaching a new author the things *not* to do. There are so many small pieces to producing a book.

Anyway, as soon as a chapter was finished, I had my own proofreaders read it and make any corrections. My wife, Kelly (who has learned more about Cisco router configuration than she ever wanted to!), read it first. After she was finished, my mother, Connie, read a few of the chapters. Finally, a former student, current consultant, and friend of mine, Mia Less, read the chapters. Amazingly enough, the three of them could not find all the simple little mistakes. Even after *I* read the chapters again, I found *more* mistakes! To make matters even worse for my ego (after all, I am a perfectionist), students in my many classes found little typos or incoherent statements—I thank those who pointed them out to me. In fact, I thank each of the students in each of the classes for helping me make the course, and subsequently the book, better.

As the technical reviewers from Prentice Hall completed scouring the chapters (and finding yet *more* errors), I made the changes. My thanks go to the many reviewers for their insights and suggestions. Finally, Beth Roberts, the copy editor, received the chapters and made even *more* corrections, but most of those were formatting changes (and would you believe I found a couple more grammatical errors after this?).

So, after many hours and much work, the book is now a reality (and I no longer have any misconceptions about you not finding any grammatical errors. For any that you may find, I apologize). My heart and my instruction are now in your hands, and may you succeed in your CCNA certification.

Changes can be e-mailed to me at ccna@uswestmail.net with a subject heading of "Even More Errors."

About the Author

Robert N. Myhre is an independent trainer and consultant living in the Minneapolis, Minnesota area. He currently teaches a variety of courses for Mind Sharp, including Windows 2000, Windows NT, Networking, and Visual Basic. Working with Mind Sharp, he has developed custom curriculums, including a CCNA course on which this book is based. He is also an instructor for Learning Tree International, where his primary focus is on Windows NT, Windows Security, and Windows 2000. Because of the many courses he teaches, he has amassed a large number of certifications, including CCNP, CCDP, MSCE + I, MCSD, and MCT. When not training, he is consulting with small to medium-sized businesses offering services including networking, security, and development. He can be reached at ccna@uswestmail.net.

Introduction to Networking and the OSI Model

In This Chapter

- ◆ Local Area Networks
- ◆ Wide Area Networks
- ◆ Internetworking
- ◆ The Seven Layers of the OSI Model

In this chapter, we begin our journey toward the CCNA certification by examining some networking concepts key to working with Cisco routers. The most important concept is a discussion of the OSI model and how data flows across a network. Once the OSI model is understood, it will be easier to design, use, and especially, troubleshoot Cisco networks.

Introduction to Networking

In the early days of computing, there were mainframe computers. These computers were large and centrally located, usually in a very cold and climate-controlled environment.

Although processing was performed on the mainframe, the average user did not walk up to it and start an application. Instead, he or she would sit at a terminal that was connected to the mainframe by some type of cabling. This terminal, located in a remote location, was the gateway to the processing power of the mainframe. The terminal performed very little work on its own. In fact, it merely displayed data on the monitor and processed keystrokes to send back to the mainframe.   For this reason, these terminals were often called *dumb* terminals.

As time progressed, more and more users were connecting to the mainframe computer through the terminals. This increased the load on the mainframe, thereby slowing productivity. The mainframe computers were continually being enhanced and upgraded to keep up with the processing demand.

Technology started producing smarter terminals to decrease the load on the mainframe. When the personal computer (PC) became a reality in the late 1980s, the paradigm began to shift. PCs could connect to the mainframe in place of the dumb terminals, but more importantly, they could process data on their own. The PC revolution began, and the increasing importance of the home and office computer was realized.

As PCs began to work in conjunction with the mainframe, new technology was required to efficiently connect them. Local Area Networks, or LANs, became the term used to describe the way in which computers were connected together to share data. LANs were implemented in a business using technologies such as Ethernet and Token Ring to connect computers together using Network Interface Cards, or NICs. LAN connectivity became a new industry market, and new businesses worldwide started operations.

As more and more LANs became operational, it became necessary to link these networks together across floors, buildings, cities, and even countries; hence, the introduction of the Wide Area Network, or WAN. A WAN is a means of connecting LANs together across a distance boundary. Typical WAN connectivity was accomplished through phone lines.

Today, computers throughout the world are connected through WANs, LANs, and various combinations of the two. Perhaps the most well-known network is the Internet. The means of connecting all these networks together to achieve a desired goal is called *internetworking*, and this is where Cisco has positioned itself as the world leader.

The OSI Model

Networking evolved from the basic principle of moving data from one computer to another. The first method involved copying data to a storage media such as a floppy disc and then taking that storage media to another computer and copying the data. This was charmingly referred to as *sneaker-net*. As more efficient means were discovered—namely, electricity on a copper wire—networking became more popular. However, there were no standards in place. This meant that one network manufacturer implemented a different means of data transfer than another. If you had an IBM network, you purchased only IBM network devices.

In 1984, a group known as the International Organization for Standardization (ISO) created a model called the Open Systems Interconnect (OSI). This model defined guidelines for interoperability between network manufacturers. A company could now mix and match network devices and protocols from various manufacturers in their own network without being locked into using a single vendor. It also had a great side effect: competition meant lower prices.

Although the OSI model defined a set of standards, it is important to note that it is merely a model. Many other models exist in the networking industry; however, understanding a single model gives us the capability of understanding other models in the future. The OSI model is the most widely taught as the foundation for this knowledge.

Why Use a Layered Model?

By using a layered model, we can categorize the procedures that are necessary to transmit data across a network. Let's explore this in more detail. Imagine that we are developers and we are about to create a new protocol for communication across a network.

First, we need to define the term *protocol*: A protocol is a set of guidelines or rules of communication. Some think of a protocol as a dialect of a language; this is erroneous. The British and the Americans both speak the same language: English. However, certain words differ in meaning between the two countries. The timing of the exchange of words between the two cultures can also lead to difficulties in complete understanding. A protocol, then, is more than just the "words" of computers. It also includes the timing and the same dictionary so that at any time, both computers using the same protocol have an exact, complete understanding of each other.

Developing a new protocol without a model would be a tedious and time-consuming task. We would need to reinvent the wheel by recreating work that has already been done by other developers. We could save time by cutting and pasting the code, but we would still need to do extensive testing. Further, when we needed to update the protocol, we would have to redesign and retest the entire protocol.

However, if we were to use a layered design, we could separate the processes into specific layers. We could then design, enhance, and test each individual layer. As the process continued, we would have a complete protocol based on a layered model. When we needed to update code, we would only have to modify the one layer that needed the updating; the rest of the layers would not be affected. This allows us to enhance specific functions easier and quicker.

Further, by using a layered model, we could then license our protocol to other developers for use in their own networks. If the protocol did not work on their chosen hardware platform, they could replace one of the layers with their own version, thereby creating multivendor compatibility.

If we did decide to enhance one of the layers, we could take just that specific layer and redistribute it to all the developers, thereby making our protocol even better.

To summarize, layered modeling allows us to:

- Create a protocol that can be designed and tested in stages, which, in turn, reduces the complexity
- Enhance functionality of the protocol without adversely affecting the other layers
- Provide multivendor compatibility
- Allow for easier troubleshooting by locating the specific layer causing the problem

How Does a Model Work?

Before defining how a model works, we must clarify one thing. The OSI model defines what each layer should do, it does *not* tell you how to do it. This allows developers the freedom to choose the best method they can design.

The OSI model is divided into seven layers. Figure 1–1 lists the name and order of each layer. Notice that the bottom layer is identified as the first layer.

Application	Layer 7
Presentation	Layer 6
Session	Layer 5
Transport	Layer 4
Network	Layer 3
Data Link	Layer 2
Physical	Layer 1

FIGURE 1–1   The seven layers of the OSI model

It is important to remember the order of the layers in the OSI model. By doing so, it creates a better understanding of the network data flow. It is also needed to pass the exam. Many acrostics can be used to remember the order, but possibly, the most common is

Please	(**P**hysical	Layer 1)
Do	(**D**ata Link	Layer 2)
Not	(**N**etwork	Layer 3)
Throw	(**T**ransport	Layer 4)
Sausage	(**S**ession	Layer 5)
Pizzas	(**P**resentation	Layer 6)
Away	(**A**pplication	Layer 7)

If we wish to use this acrostic to remember the order of the OSI model, there are two important items to note. First, this acrostic starts from the bottom (Layer 1) and moves toward the top. Second, there are two Ps, so we have to remember which is the Physical and which is the Presentation.

FIGURE 1–2   Virtual link between application layers

Each layer is separated, or encapsulated, from each other layer. This means that each layer can function on its own. Each layer thinks it is talking directly to the same layer on the remote computer (see Figure 1–2) through a "virtual" link. Furthermore, each layer can only communicate with the layers above and below it. In fact, the layer doesn't know that any other layers even exist. For example, notice in Figure 1–3 that the Transport layer can communicate only with the Network and the Session layers.

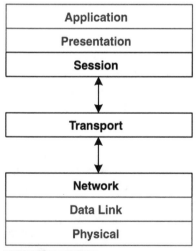

FIGURE 1–3   Each layer knows only about the layer above and below

Finally, the flow of data starts at the Application layer of the sending computer, flows down the layers, across the wire to the receiving computer, and then back up the layers to the Application layer (see Figure 1–4).

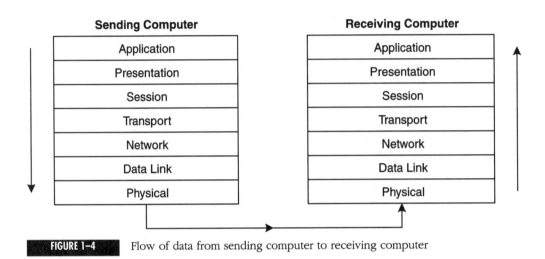

FIGURE 1–4 Flow of data from sending computer to receiving computer

Each layer has a specific function for which it is responsible. Although the layers start at the bottom, we will examine the layers starting at the top.

Application Layer (Layer 7)

The Application layer is a buffer between the user interface (that which the user uses to perform work) and the network application. The network application may be a part of the user application or an Application Programming Interface (API) that is called by the user's application.

The Application layer is responsible for finding a communication partner on the network. Once a partner is found, it is then responsible for ensuring that there is sufficient network bandwidth to deliver the data.

This layer may also be responsible for synchronizing communication and providing error checking between the two partners. This ensures that the application is either sending or receiving, but not both, and that the data transmitted is the same data received.

Typical applications include a client/server application, an e-mail application, and an application to transfer files using FTP or HTTP.

Presentation Layer (Layer 6)

The Presentation layer is responsible for the presentation of data to the Application layer. This presentation may take the form of many structures.

For example, when communicating from a PC to a mainframe, data may need to be converted between ASCII and EBCDIC (a different character formatting method used on many mainframes).

Another structure of data includes multimedia formats used for enhancing our computer experiences. The World Wide Web (WWW) is a fantastic exchange of information that uses many types of multimedia. The Presentation layer must ensure that the Application can view the appropriate data when it is reassembled. Graphic files such as PICT, JPEG, TIFF, and GIF, and video and sound files such as MPEG and Apple's QuickTime are examples of Presentation layer responsibilities.

One final data structure is *data encryption*. Sometimes, it is vital that we can send data across a network without someone being able to view our data, or "snoop" it. Data encryption is the method that allows us to accomplish this.

Session Layer (Layer 5)

The Session layer sets up communications between the two partners. This layer decides on the method of communication: *half-duplex* or *full-duplex*. Half-duplex is the method of sending data only when the other computer is finished. We can use the telephone to illustrate these methods. As a polite person (note the word *polite*), we wait until the other person is finished speaking before we respond. This is an example of half-duplex. If we were to both start speaking at the same time, it would take a trained ear to actually listen to the conversation. This is an example of full-duplex, where both sides communicate as fast as they are able, at the same time.

The Session layer starts a session by establishing the initial connection to the communication partner. This initial dialog allows the partners to decide on the communication method and the protocol to use. When this is finished, data transfer can occur between the partners. Finally, after all data has been transferred, the partners disconnect. Using our example of the telephone, this would be similar to me calling you. The initial "Hello" establishes the protocol (roughly equivalent to speaking English versus Spanish) and the method of communication, half-duplex. After we discuss the new products that Cisco is introducing and how they will make our lives better (the data transfer), we then conclude our conversation by saying "Good-bye."

In the early days of communication, reliability of data across the network was a major concern. With today's technology, this is less of a concern, but the Session layer has some error checking included. In order to ensure that the data has been transferred correctly, the Session layer sets up a checkpoint in the data stream. This checkpoint is a means for the receiving computer to acknowledge to the sender that the data has been received. If data is missed, the checkpoint acknowledgment back to the sender would indicate that data is missing, and the sender would then decide what data was missed, and re-send it.

When the sender and receiver negotiate the use of checkpoints in the data stream, this is called *connection–oriented service*. We use this method when reliable delivery of data is required. However, there are times when reliable data is not needed, so to reduce network bandwidth, the checkpoints will not be used. The sender sends the data through the network and does not wait for any acknowledgments from the receiver. It is the responsibility of the Application layer to decide if data is missing. Although less reliable, it is a quicker method of sending data.

Examples of the Session layer protocol include:

- **SQL** (Structured Query Language). A database language originally developed by IBM.
- **RPC** (Remote Procedure Call). A method of running routines on a server called from the client.
- **X Windows**. A graphical-based system used to communicate with Unix servers.
- **NFS** (Network File System). A method of accessing resources on servers.

Transport Layer (Layer 4)

Although the Session layer is responsible for deciding on the communication method, the Transport layer implements it. This layer implements the functions necessary to send data to the communication partner. These mechanisms include multiplexing data from different applications, establishing data integrity, and management of virtual circuits.

Multiplexing is the method of combining data from the upper layers and sending them through the same data stream. This allows more than one application to communicate with the communication partner at the same time. When the data reaches the remote partner, the Transport layer then disassembles the segment and passes the correct data to each of the receiving applications.

Virtual circuits are the methods of setting up a communication path to the receiver. This path may physically change depending on the network, but the path remains open through a virtual link. The Transport layer is responsible for establishing, maintaining, and disconnecting the virtual circuits.

Data integrity is essential to passing data across a network. There are three methods that the Transport layer can use in order to ensure the integrity: buffering, source quench, and windowing. These three methods are implementations of flow control.

Buffering is maintained on the receiving computer. As data flows in faster than can be processed, some data is placed in a buffer and held until the computer has the time to process it. Unfortunately, if the speed of the data flow is too fast, the buffer will overflow and data will be lost.

Source quench is a technique where the receiving computer can send a control message back to the sending computer when too much data is being received. The sending computer then will delay sending any more data until the receiving computer can finish processing the current data. At this point, the receiving computer will send another control message back to the sender telling it to start sending data again.

The last method, *windowing*, works on the principle that the receiver tells the sender how much data it can send at one time. This amount sets the window size. After the receiver receives the data, it will send back an acknowledgment to the sender. This acknowledgment tells the sender which data segments have been received. The sender will remove the data from the window and fill it with new data. This process in sometimes referred to as a *sliding window*. Any data that has not been received will be re-sent. In fact, the sender has a timer on each segment that it sends, so it knows if the data has not been received. After the timer expires, it will re-send the data and wait for the acknowledgment. This method is known as *Positive Acknowledgment With Retransmission*.

To illustrate window control, let's look at Figure 1–5.

1. The Sender sends a message asking to speak with the Receiver.
2. The Receiver decides on a window size and replies. The reply includes an acknowledgment to speak with the Sender and the size of the window to use; in this case, 4 bytes.
3. The Sender then creates a 4-byte window (shown in gray) and places the first data into it. The data "DATA" is sent across the network. The Receiver only receives the first two bytes, or "DA", and sends back a positive acknowledgment. This packet tells the Sender that it has received bytes 1 and 2.
4. The Sender then slides the window to start with the third and fourth bytes and adds two more bytes to the free space. The data "TA12" is sent across the network. The Receiver again sends back a positive acknowledgment to the Sender that the third, fourth, fifth, and sixth bytes have been received. Both partners will now slide the window four more bytes, and the Sender will send the seventh through eleventh bytes. This continues until all data has been sent and the two partners agree to stop communications.

Note that this is a simple example and more communication may be taking place between the Sender and the Receiver.

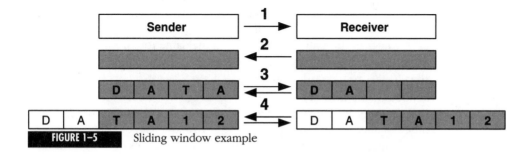

FIGURE 1–5 Sliding window example

Network Layer (Layer 3)

The bottom two layers allow the communication partners to communicate only if they are on the same segment. A *segment* is defined as all network devices, or nodes, that are directly connected together. Hubs and MAUs

(Multi-station Access Units) are part of the same segment. If we were to have all the computers in the world on a single segment, there would be no Internet. Either there would be far too many broadcasts, or the time for a single node to communicate with another via a token would be ridiculously slow. The function of the Network layer is to identify a remote network and deliver the data to it. This allows us to have *segmentation*. These concepts are explored in more detail in later chapters.

The Network layer enables us to send data to any computer in the world, as long as there is a physical network connection. However, since we can't have a single segment, we must divide these segments up and yet keep them communicating. The device that allows us to accomplish this spectacular feat is the *router*, sometimes referred to as a *Layer 3 device*. The majority of this book is centered on this specific layer.

A router may know more than one way to get data to its final destination. Again, this is the function of the Network layer. In order for the router to succeed in this endeavor, it must be able to identify the source segment and the final destination segment. This is done through network addresses, also called *logical addresses*.

A network address consists of two parts, the network portion and the host portion. As a simple example, suppose the number 1.2 was assigned to your specific machine. The 1 would identify the network segment and the 2 would identify you as a specific host on that network. Another computer on your segment would have an address of 1.x, where x would be a unique number. A computer on a different segment might have an address of 2.2, or 3.49. To connect these two segments together, we would need to place a router.

It is important to note that routers work only with the network address. They really don't want to know your specific host address. When a router receives data, it examines the Layer 3 data to determine the destination network address. It then looks up the address in a table that tells it which route to use to get the data to its final destination. It places the data on the proper connection, thereby routing the packet from one segment to another. The data may need to travel through many routers before reaching its destination host. Each router in the path would perform the same lookup in its table.

Examples of network protocols include:

- **IP** (Internet Protocol). A routed protocol used in the TCP/IP suite, made famous by the Internet.
- **IPX** (Internet Packet eXchange). A routed protocol used in the IPX/SPX protocol suite usually used in Novell environments.
- **RIP** (Routing Information Protocol). One of the many routing protocols implemented on Cisco routers.
- **OSPF** (Open Shortest Path First). Another routing protocol used by Cisco routers.

We discuss the difference between routed protocols and routing protocols later in this book.

Data Link Layer (Layer 2)

The Data Link layer is the layer that connects the software protocols to the hardware protocols. It is responsible for taking the data from the upper layers and converting it to the bits needed to send across the physical wire, and vice versa.

The Data Link layer is split into two sublayers, the Logical Link Control (LLC) and the Media Access Control (MAC). As you can see in Figure 1–6, the MAC sublayer is closer to the Physical layer.

The MAC sublayer defines a physical address, called a *MAC address* or *hardware address*, which is unique to each individual network interface. This allows a way to uniquely identify each network interface on a network, even if the network interfaces are on the same computer. More importantly, though, the MAC address can be used in any network that supports the chosen network interface (Ethernet or Token Ring, for example). This allows us to take a computer from one network running TCP/IP and connect it to another network running IPX/SPX by changing just the Network layer protocol. Remember that the network address, or logical address, is specific to the Network layer protocol that is being used. This address may be a unique numbering scheme, as in TCP/IP, or it may be the MAC address, as in IPX/SPX.

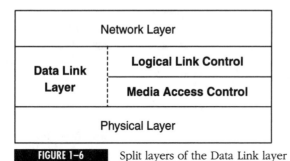

Network Layer		
Data Link Layer	Logical Link Control	
	Media Access Control	
Physical Layer		

FIGURE 1–6   Split layers of the Data Link layer

A MAC address is a 6-byte value that is usually created by the network interface manufacturer. The first three bytes are assigned by the IEEE (Institute of Electrical and Electronics Engineers) and are specific to each vendor. The vendor generates the last three bytes. Examples are shown here where X can be any hex value from 0 to F.

- 00-00-0C-XX-XX-XX   Cisco
- 00-E0-98-XX-XX-XX   LinkSys
- 00-10-5A-XX-XX-XX   3Com

The MAC layer on the receiving computer will take the bits from the Physical layer and put them in order into a frame. It will also do a CRC (Cyclic Redundancy Check) to determine if there are any errors in the frame. It will check the destination hardware address to determine if the data is meant for it, or if it should be dropped or sent on to the next machine. If the data is meant for the current computer, it will pass it to the LLC layer.

The MAC layer can be referred to as the *hardware layer*. This implies that the software protocols above it are hidden from the physical media.

The LLC layer is the buffer between the software protocols and the hardware protocols. It is responsible for taking the data from the Network layer and sending it to the MAC layer. This allows the software protocols to run on any type of network architecture, including Ethernet and Token Ring.

When the LLC receives data from the MAC layer, it must determine which software protocol in the Network layer to send it to. In order to do this, the LLC includes service access points (SAP) in the header. The Source SAP (SSAP) identifies the sending protocol and the Destination SAP (DSAP) identifies the receiving protocol. When the LLC receives the frame from the MAC sublayer, it can then strip off the header and examine the DSAP. Using this information, the LLC can now forward the data to the correct Network layer protocol.

Examples of Data Link protocols include:

- **HDLC** (High-Level Data Link Control). A serial communication that is usually vendor specific.
- **X.25**. A packet-switching network.
- **PPP** (Point-to-Point Protocol). A low-speed serial protocol.
- **ISDN** (Integrated Services Digital Network). A digital communication method used over copper wire.
- **Frame Relay**

Physical Layer (Layer 1)

The Physical layer does only two things, yet these two things are vital to the network. It is responsible for sending data and receiving data across a physical medium. This data is sent in bits, either a 0 or a 1. The data may be transmitted as electrical signals (that is, positive and negative voltages), audio tones, or light.

This layer also defines the Data Terminal Equipment (DTE) and the Data Circuit-Terminating Equipment (DCE). The DTE is often accessed through a modem or a Channel Service Unit/Data Service Unit (CSU/DSU) connected to a PC or a router. The carrier of the WAN signal provides the DCE equipment. A typical device would be a packet switch, which is responsible for clocking and switching.

Typical interfaces of this layer include:

- **HSSI** (High Speed Serial Interface). A point-to-point connection over copper wires.
- **V.35**. A synchronous communication method developed by the International Telecommunication Union-Telecommunication Standardization Sector (ITU-T). All the V.xx standards have been created by the ITU-T.

- **EIA/TIA-232**. A serial port interface using the RS-232 port.
- **X.21**

Data Encapsulation Using the OSI Model

As we read through the description of the OSI layers, a question may arise: Since there may be more than one application using more than one communication partner using more than one protocol, how does the data get to its destination correctly?

		User Data
Application	**Application Header**	**User Data**
Presentation	**Presentation Header**	A	**User Data**
Session	**Session Header**	P A	**User Data**
Transport	**Transport Header**	**Message**
Network	**Network Header**	**Segment**
Data Link	**Frame Header**	**Packet**
Physical	0010110101000101011110

FIGURE 1-7   Data encapsulation flow

This is accomplished through a process called *data encapsulation* (see Figure 1–7). Basically, it works like this:

1. A user is working on an application and decides to save the data to a remote server. The application calls the Application layer to start the process.
2. The Application layer takes the data and places some information, called a *header*, at the beginning. The header tells the Application layer which user application sent the data.
3. The Application layer then sends the data to the Presentation layer, where the data conversion takes place. The Presentation layer places a header on all of the information received from the Application layer (including the Application layer header). This header identifies which function in the Application layer to pass it back.
4. The Presentation layer then sends the complete *message* to the Session layer. The Session layer sets up the synchronized communication information to speak with the communication partner and appends the information to another header.

5. The Session layer then sends the *message* to the Transport layer, where information is placed into the header identifying the source and the destination hosts and the method of connection (connectionless versus connection-oriented).

6. The Transport layer then passes the *segment* to the Network layer, where the network address for the destination and the source are included in the header.

7. The Network layer passes the *packet* (connection-oriented) or the *datagram* (connectionless) to the Data Link layer. The Data Link layer then includes the SSAP and the DSAP to identify which Transport protocol to return it to. It also includes the source and the destination MAC addresses.

8. The Data Link layer then passes the *frame* to the Physical layer for transmitting on the physical medium as individual bits.

9. Finally, the receiving computer receives the bits and reverses the process to get the original data to the source application; in this case, a file server service.

In summary:

1. Data encapsulation takes the data from the user.

2. Packages it as a message at the Session layer to send to the receiver.

3. Encapsulates the segment inside a packet at the Network layer with the network addressing information.

4. Encapsulates this packet into a frame at the Data Link layer with the MAC addresses.

5. Sends the frame across the wire as individual bits at the Physical layer.

Summary

The OSI model is a tool used to provide a standard set of rules for communication across multivendor hardware. Each layer of the OSI model has a function it must accomplish, but the method to perform this function is left to the developer. As data flows down each of the layers, encapsulation takes place allowing for reassembly of the data on the receiving machine. Each layer is responsible in part for the complete data transfer from the source host to the destination host. Knowing the OSI model will help in troubleshooting Cisco networks.

Scenario Lab 1.1

You have been asked to begin a large design and implementation project with Network Solutions, Inc. (a fictional company). However, before you are allowed to proceed, the project manager wants to be sure that you are the correct person for the job. This person asks you to list the layers of the OSI model and describe in brief the functions of each layer. Can you prove you are the correct person for the job?

Exam Objective Checklist

By working through this chapter, you should have sufficient knowledge to answer these exam objectives:

- Identify and describe the functions of each of the seven layers of the OSI reference model.
- Describe data link addresses and network addresses, and identify the key differences between them.
- Define and describe the function of a MAC address.
- Identify at least three reasons why the industry uses a layered model.
- Define and explain the five conversion steps of data encapsulation.
- Define flow control and describe the three basic methods used in networking.
- List the key internetworking functions of the OSI Network layer and how they are performed in a router.

Practice Questions

1. The technology used to connect multiple computers together in a single office is called:

   a. LAN
   b. WAN
   c. MAN
   d. Internet

2. Connecting multiple networks together using an outside carrier's signal, such as the telephone service is known as:

   a. LAN
   b. WAN
   c. Protocol
   d. Internet

3. Why should we use layered models in a network architecture? (Select all that apply)

   a. It tells us exactly how to perform a specific function.
   b. It allows us to take a complex method and break it into smaller, more manageable methods.
   c. A change to one layer has no affect on any other layer.
   d. A change to one layer affects all other layers.

    e. It restricts us to using only one network vendor.

    f. It makes troubleshooting networks easier by being able to locate the exact layer causing the problem.

4. Which layer is responsible for finding a communication partner on the network?

    a. Transport

    b. Data Link

    c. Application

    d. Physical

5. What is the correct order for the shown layers? (Bottom to top)

    a. Presentation

    b. Transport

    c. Application

    d. Network

    e. Data Link

    f. Physical

    g. Session

6. True or False: The Transport layer can communicate directly with the Network and Presentation layers?

7. Which of the following are performed at the Presentation layer? (Choose two)

    a. Presents data to the Application layer

    b. Sets checkpoints in the data stream for reliability

    c. Provides character conversion between dissimilar operating systems (such as PC to mainframe)

    d. Adds the network addresses to the header

8. The Presentation layer protocols include? (Choose two)

    a. PICT

    b. SQL

    c. TCP

    d. IPX

    e. JPEG

9. The function of the Session layer is? (Choose two)

    a. Determines if half-duplex or full-duplex is being used

    b. Presents data to the Network layer

    c. Places checkpoints into the data stream for reliability

    d. Provides flow control

10. The Session layer protocols include? (Choose three)

    a. PICT
    b. SQL
    c. TCP
    d. X Windows
    e. NFS

11. Which layer is responsible for multiplexing data from upper layers and placing the data into a segment?

    a. Transport
    b. Network
    c. Data Link
    d. Physical

12. Windowing is performed at the Transport layer. What is windowing?

    a. A method of buffering
    b. A method of session establishment
    c. A method of flow control
    d. A method of character conversion

13. The Network layer's primary function is to:

    a. Add MAC addresses to the packet
    b. Establish a communication path to the communication partner
    c. Provide connection-oriented service
    d. Route data between different network segments

14. What are the two parts to a network address? (Choose two)

    a. Source Service Access Point
    b. Host Identifier
    c. MAC address
    d. Network Identifier

15. The Data Link layer is split into two sublayers. Name them. (Choose two)

    a. Local Link Control
    b. Logical Link Control
    c. Machine Address Code
    d. Media Access Control

16. List the functions of the MAC sublayer. (Choose three)

    a. Unique hardware addresses allow us to switch between different networks and still be uniquely identified
    b. Provides SSAP and DSAP for passing frame to proper Transport protocol

c. Provides error checking through CRC

    d. Provides an interface to the physical medium

    e. Acts as a buffer between software and hardware protocols

17. List the functions of the LLC sublayer. (Choose two)

    a. Unique hardware addresses allow us to switch between different networks and still be uniquely identified

    b. Provides SSAP and DSAP for passing frames to the proper Network protocol

    c. Provides error checking through CRC

    d. Provides an interface to the physical medium

    e. Acts as a buffer between software and hardware protocols

18. Which layer is responsible for creating and disconnecting virtual circuits?

    a. Presentation

    b. Session

    c. Transport

    d. Network

19. Which of the following terms describes the address used at the Network layer?

    a. Physical

    b. Logical

    c. MAC

    d. Host

20. Place the following in the correct order of data encapsulation for the sending node.

    a. Encapsulates this packet or datagram into a frame with the MAC addresses

    b. Packages it as a message to send to the receiver

    c. Sends the frame across the wire as individual bits

    d. Data encapsulation takes the data from the user

    e. Encapsulates the segment inside a packet or datagram with the network addressing information

LAN
Technologies

In This Chapter

Before we start working with Cisco routers, it is important to explore the different topologies and architectures that may be encountered in local area networks (LANs). This chapter describes the workings of Ethernet, Token Ring, FDDI, and ATM networks. We also examine the Physical and Data Link layers as they pertain to each of the architectures.

Ethernet

Ethernet is the most-used network architecture in the world. Xerox created the first implementation in the 1970s. In 1980, Digital Equipment Corporation and Intel joined Xerox, the joint venture referred to as DIX, in formalizing Ethernet. In 1984, the group upgraded the specification of Ethernet I, and it became known as Ethernet II. After Ethernet II was finalized, the IEEE created a group to define Ethernet as a standard. They created the IEEE 802.3 specifications, which are almost identical to Ethernet II.

CSMA/CD

Ethernet describes a process to pass data called CSMA/CD, or Carrier Sense, Multiple Access, Collision Detection. If we examine a typical Ethernet design, we can see that all nodes are directly attached to the physical media (see Figure 2–1). This design is referred to as *multiple access*. More important to this design, though, is that all nodes will see the data as it is transmitted by a single node. Since only one node can safely transmit data at a time, each node must contend with all other nodes. For this reason, Ethernet is described as a *contention-based* system.

If each node transmitted when it wanted to, without regard for the other nodes, there would be mass chaos on the wire. As each node transmitted, it would collide with the data sent by the other nodes at the same time, thereby corrupting the data. To eliminate this problem, Ethernet uses a method called *Carrier Sense*.

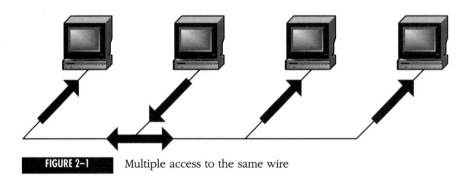

| FIGURE 2–1 | Multiple access to the same wire |

Before each node actually transmits data, it checks the wire to detect if any data is currently being transmitted. If data is currently being transmitted by another node, the first node will wait a short interval and then sense the line again. Once the line is clear, the node will then send its own data through the wire. A problem can occur, however, when there are too many nodes on the wire. It is possible that the other nodes can effectively block out a single node that is trying to send data. A node will only attempt to send data for a short period of time before it gives up and times out.

An additional problem can occur when two nodes transmit data at the same time. For this to occur, both nodes would have to sense that the line is clear and then begin sending data. However, as the data moves down the wire it would collide with the data from the other sending node, causing the data to be corrupted. When this occurs, one of the nodes will discover that there has been a collision. This is known as *collision detection*. When a collision is detected, the node will send out a special packet known as an *extended jam signal* that will tell all nodes to stop sending. The nodes will all wait a random interval and then start the process of sensing and sending data again.

Physical Layer

Ethernet is connected through the Physical layer by a single cable connection, otherwise known as a *bus*. Examining Figure 2–2, we can see that the bus connects all nodes. This architecture type is known simply as a *bus topology*.

Bus topology has certain limitations, one of which is that it is difficult to scale well. As we try adding another node into this network, we may have to rearrange cables to make everything work correctly. To remove this problem, a new method of connecting nodes together was created using a device called a *hub*. In its simplest form, a hub is a device that contains the bus inside it. Nodes are then attached to the hub in any order. If we examine Figure 2–2 again, we can see an example of using a network with a hub. This topology is referred to as a *star bus* or simply a *star* network.

The Physical layer also determines the speed of Ethernet. As we will see later in this chapter, the speed of Ethernet changes depending on the type of physical media and specifications that can be used.

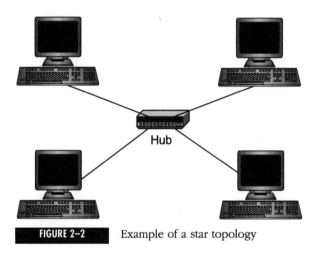

FIGURE 2–2 Example of a star topology

Data Link Layer

The Data Link layer is subtly different depending on if we are talking about Ethernet or IEEE 802.3. However, for this discussion we will assume they are identical.

At the Data Link layer, if we recall from Chapter 1, "Introduction to Networking and the OSI Model," the physical address of the device is described here. For Ethernet, that physical address is known as the *MAC address*. A MAC address is 48 bits in length, or 6 bytes, and it uniquely identifies a node on the network. When data is transmitted onto the physical media, the data actually travels to all nodes. However, unless it is a broadcast or multicast, the data is intended for only one node. Therefore, network interfaces contain code implemented in the hardware to examine each packet and decide if it should interrupt the CPU of the computer for processing.

For example, in Figure 2–3 we can see a star network. Although MAC addresses are 6 bytes in length, we have made it easier by using only 1 byte. Imagine that node A is sending data to node C. Node A transmits data (remember our CSMA/CD definition) and the data travels down the wire. All nodes then receive the data. However, only node C cares because the packet identifies it as being the intended target. The other nodes drop (discard) the packet and wait for data to arrive that is intended for them. Node C, now having data it needs to process, interrupts the CPU of the computer to indicate that work now needs to be done. Without a method of using the NIC to determine if the data is intended for that node, every node would have to interrupt the CPU to identify if the logical address is its own. This would cause heavy performance hits on the CPU, and networking wouldn't really be possible.

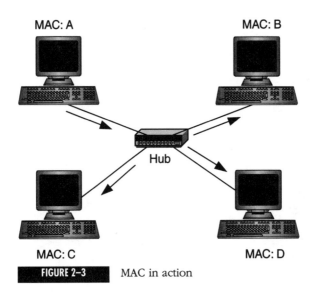

FIGURE 2–3   MAC in action

A broadcast packet is a packet that is intended for all nodes on the network. Since the packet is intended for all nodes, due to the nature of Ethernet, the packet is only sent once. Every node will receive the data, determine that it is a broadcast packet, and then interrupt the CPU to process the information. Although this appears to be efficient, we need to think about what would happen if we had 1000 nodes all broadcasting data. Every CPU would be extremely busy. For this reason, *segmentation*, or the act of splitting nodes into separate collision domains, becomes a major factor in network design. We examine this in more detail in the next chapter.

Types of Ethernet

There are many types of Ethernet, so we will examine the most common types. Ethernet is typically described in such terms as "10Base2" or "100BaseTX." The breakdown of the term is as follows:

- Base stands for baseband. This is a method of signaling in which only one frequency carrier is being transmitted.
- The first number stands for the speed of the network. 10 stands for 10 Mbps and 100 stands for 100 Mbps.
- The last part stands for the physical media that is being used.

THICKNET OR 10BASE5 • 10Base5 uses a thick coax cable for transmitting data. This is an older method that is slowly being phased out. It is difficult to work with because of the inflexible nature of the cable. Thicknet has a maximum single segment distance of 500 meters. It operates at 10 Mbps.

THINNET OR 10BASE2 • 10Base2 uses a thinner coax cable that is similar to, but not the same as, television cable. This is used with a bus topology and has a maximum single segment distance of 185 meters. It operates at 10 Mbps.

10BASET • 10BaseT uses a telephone-type cable. There are different categories of the cable, but today most installations have a category 5 cable that will allow for signals up to 100 Mbps. This cable can either be shielded or unshielded against EMI (electromagnetic interference). 10BaseT is predominately the most common type of architecture found in today's networks. It is easy to work with, easy to implement, and easy to troubleshoot. It uses the star topology and operates at 10 Mbps. It has a maximum distance of 100 meters.

10BASEFL • 10BaseFL is similar to 10BaseT except that it uses fiber optics instead of copper wire. It has a maximum distance of 2000 meters and uses a point-to-point architecture.

100BASETX OR FAST ETHERNET • This architecture is one of the newer ones being implemented in networks today. The IEEE created it in 1995 under the 802.3u implementation. There are different versions of it running on category 3 cable, fiber, and copper. Standard 100BaseTX runs on category 5 cable.

One of the benefits of using 100BaseT, besides the obvious speed increase of nearly tenfold over 10BaseT, is the fact that it can be migrated into an existing installation of 10BaseT. The cost of getting 100BaseT network interface cards is only slightly higher with today's prices. The most expensive part of the migration would be to upgrade the hubs to 100-Mbps switches. Switches are covered in more detail in the next chapter. The maximum distance for 100BaseT is 100 meters.

FULL-DUPLEX AND HALF-DUPLEX • Although not a real architecture type, full- and half-duplex Ethernet describes the way data flows through the physical wire. Half-duplex data can be described as a narrow, one-way bridge. Just as a single car can only go over the bridge in one direction at a time, data can only be trans-mitted in one direction. This is the most common type of network.

Full-duplex Ethernet is the four-lane divided highway. Data can flow in both directions, typically on different pairs of wires. However, both the NIC and the switch need to support full-duplex for this to work. In essence, with a 100BaseT with the appropriate NICs and switches, a network can flow at 200 Mbps!

Token Ring

Token Ring architecture was created by IBM. Token Ring architecture includes a repeater in every network interface. The result of this is that implementing a Token Ring network is more costly than Ethernet. However, Token Ring net-works are predominately more stable, reliable, and faster than similar archi-tectures using Ethernet.

The IEEE did create a standard version of Token Ring, IEEE 802.5. This is even closer in specifications than Ethernet is to IEEE 802.3. In fact, the IEEE maintains both sets of specifications today.

Physical Layer

Token Ring uses a ring architecture with each node directly connected to an "upstream" neighbor and a "downstream" neighbor. Figure 2–4 is an example of a Token Ring network.

This Token Ring architecture has been moved inside a device similar to the way the bus was moved into the hub. This device is known as a MAU (Multi-station Access Unit) or MSAU (Multi-Station Access Unit). Different from Ethernet, however, is the fact that there is a single frame being passed around the ring. This frame is referred to as the *token*. As the frame circles the ring, each node removes the token and examines it. If the token is free for use, a node may then modify the token, indicating that it is sending data. The frame is then sent back onto the ring to the next node. The benefit to this is that there are no collisions on the network. Token Ring works at 4, 16, or 100 Mbps.

Data Link Layer

Token Ring uses a similar concept for the MAC address. Each Token Ring card has a burned-in factory address. However, it is quite possible for an adminis-trator to manually change the factory address.

If we examine the network in Figure 2–4, we can see how the data flows around a ring. Node A wants to transmit data to node C. When the token arrives at node A, it examines the frame to determine if another node is sending data. Seeing that the token is available, it modifies the frame to indicate

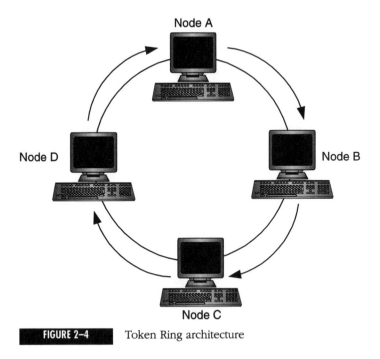

FIGURE 2–4 Token Ring architecture

to the rest of the network that it is sending data. It appends the data to the frame, marks the frame for the destination of node C, and then places it onto the wire. The frame is examined by node B, determined that data is being sent, and puts the frame back onto the wire. Node C now receives the frame, examines it, and determines that the data is meant for it. It removes the data, modifies the frame to let node A know that it has successfully received the data, and then places the frame back onto the wire. When node A is finished sending data, it releases the token back onto the ring.

Fault Tolerance

In the event that a node was to crash after sending some data onto the ring, it is possible that the frame could circle forever. Token Ring elects a node identified as the *active monitor*. The active monitor can be any of the currently running nodes. Its purpose is to examine the frame for such an occurrence of a perpetual loop and remove it from the ring. It will then replace it with a new token.

Another method of fault tolerance is to use dual rings. If one ring should fail, it is possible to wrap the frame back onto the second ring in the opposite direction. FDDI uses this method.

FDDI

Fiber Distributed Data Interface, or FDDI, is a specification for a 100-Mbps LAN. This LAN uses token passing similar to Token Ring, but runs on fiber cable. It is, therefore, extremely fast and reliable. The specification, standardized by the ISO in the 1980s, allows for longer cable runs between nodes reaching up to 2 kilometers, or approximately 1.2 miles, in a single segment. Additionally, since fiber uses light to transmit the data, FDDI is not susceptible to EMI and RFI (radio frequency interference). Copper also emits electrical signals that can be tapped, thereby reducing security. FDDI does not suffer from this problem.

FDDI design includes two rings in counter-rotating directions. The dual rings include the primary and the secondary rings. The primary is used for data transmission and the secondary is idle, used only for fault tolerance.

Data transmission can occur either through single-mode or multimode fiber. A *mode* is the light that is emitted through the fiber. A single-mode fiber uses a single point of light, typically a laser, to transmit. A multimode fiber connection uses LEDs as the points of light. The lights are directed at a slight angle into the fiber. Because of this angle, light arrives at different times at the end of the fiber cable. Multimode suffers from modal dispersion that weakens the signal being transmitted. For this reason, multimode is used in small locations, while single mode is used for longer distances.

Three types of devices are connected to an FDDI network: single attachment stations (SAS), dual attachment stations (DAS), and concentrators.

SAS are connected to an FDDI network through a concentrator. Since they are not directly connected to the ring itself, powering off or removing an SAS does not adversely affect the network. The token will be passed to the next SAS or DAS downstream.

The DAS, on the other hand, will affect the network in the event of a failure. A DAS is directly connected to both the primary and the secondary rings. If the DAS is removed, a network break will occur. However, since there are two rings, fault tolerance will prevail.

Suppose, for example, that we have the network shown in Figure 2–5. As we can see, there are two rings, the P and the S rings. If a DAS station were to fail, the stations on each side would put the token onto the other ring, a process known as *wrapping*. This allows data to flow to all devices even if one device fails.

Additionally, if the cable segment between two stations failed, wrapping can still occur, keeping the FDDI in operation. Note, however, that if two stations fail, it can result in multiple, isolated rings.

Physical and Data Link Layers

FDDI roughly corresponds to the Physical layer and the MAC sublayer of the Data Link layer. The MAC sublayer then communicates with the LLC layer to

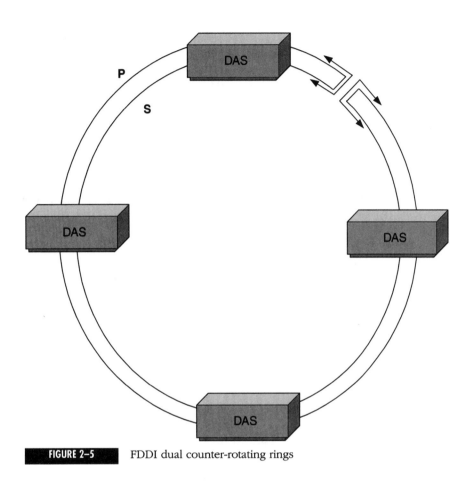

FIGURE 2-5   FDDI dual counter-rotating rings

use the various transport protocols available, such as IP and IPX. FDDI uses a
four-layer model at this level, but the equivalence is shown in Figure 2–6.

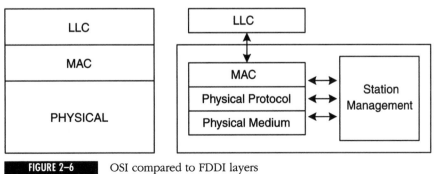

FIGURE 2-6   OSI compared to FDDI layers

Although FDDI uses fiber, by definition, there is a specification to run 100 Mbps on copper wires. This specification is commonly known as CDDI (Copper Distributed Data Interface), or, not as common, Twisted Pair Distributed Data Interface (TP-DDI).

ATM

Asynchronous Transfer Mode (ATM) is a method of data transfer that includes data types of voice, video, and data through the same media. This is known as *multiplexing*, where more than one type of data can be present in a single packet.

Although ATM is more of a WAN protocol, there is a specification referred to as LANE (LAN Emulation) that can emulate an Ethernet or Token Ring network over ATM. The price of converting to a LANE network is very prohibitive, thereby limiting the LANs that actually run this.

ATM uses an asynchronous method of transferring data so that no single station monopolizes the bandwidth. This makes it highly efficient to transfer various types of data. Bandwidth can range in the gigabits per second (Gbps).

Since voice and video data can be extremely large, it is necessary to break the data down into smaller bytes to allow them to be sent immediately. Data is sent through fiber cable using fixed-sized cells, instead of packets. The cells that are used to carry the data are 53 bytes in total length; 48 of which are used for the data (also called the *payload*), and the remaining 5 are used for the ATM header.

Network devices include the ATM switch and the ATM *endpoint*. Endpoints can be PCs, routers, switches, and other devices. Note that ATM networks can either be completely private, belonging only to the organization, or mixed with a public carrier.

Finally, ATM is a connection-oriented network. Virtual connections are made from point to point using virtual channels inside virtual paths. These virtual paths may get switched at every ATM switch to find an available path to the destination (see Figure 2–7).

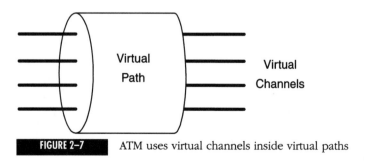

FIGURE 2–7   ATM uses virtual channels inside virtual paths

Physical and Data Link Layers

The ATM model has more of a 3-D look, than the flat, linear look of the OSI model. Briefly, the Physical layer is responsible for converting bits into cells, and then transmitting the cells on the ATM media. There are functions to synchronize the data, perform error checking, and handling of connection-oriented services.

LAN Emulation (LANE)

LANE provides a mechanism of using either IEEE 802.3 or 802.5 as a network architecture, while gaining the benefits of using ATM as the Physical and Data Link carrier. This process is accomplished through resolving MAC addresses to ATM addresses. Additionally, the upper layers of the OSI model are transparent to ATM, and vice versa.

A number of LANE components must be present in order for this to be implemented:

1. **LEC** (LANE Client). This is the end system such as a PC with an ATM NIC installed.
2. **LES** (LANE Server). The LEC will forward information upon initialization to the LES.
3. **BUS** (Broadcast and Unknown Server). This server is responsible for handling broadcasts and multicasts.
4. **LECS** (LANE Configuration Server). This server maintains the list of ATM addresses and which Emulated LAN each LEC belongs.

Once these components are implemented, Ethernet or Token Ring can work with ATM infrastructures to provide extremely fast and reliable local area networks.

Summary

Four types of LAN architectures may be encountered in the field. The most common types are Ethernet and Token Ring. Ethernet uses a method referred to as CSMA/CD, a broadcast-based protocol that uses MAC addresses to specify source and destination. As more hosts are added to an Ethernet segment, more broadcast traffic is generated, thereby degrading the performance of the network. Token Ring uses a method of token passing instead of broadcasting. The only node that is allowed to transmit data is the one that has control of the token. Token Ring networks are more reliable and do not suffer from blocking, but are more costly to implement. FDDI and ATM are newer technologies that use fiber to transmit data. FDDI uses a method similar to Token Ring, but operates at a much faster rate and is more reliable and secure. ATM is not itself a LAN architecture, but with LAN Emulation it can emulate an Ethernet or Token Ring network over ATM media.

Scenario Lab 2.1

Now that you have successfully indicated to the project manager that you are perfect for the project of designing and implementing a network, it is time to start designing the network. The CIO would like a network consisting of two buildings in downtown Minneapolis, Minnesota. The buildings have separate functions associated with them. One building is for the Research and Development division. This building hosts 180 Windows Hosts, 5 Windows NT Servers, and 5 HP Network printers. The second building is for the business office. It consists of 6 NT Servers, 2 Novell Servers, 150 Windows hosts, 10 Macintoshes, and 2 Apple Laser-Writer Printers. Based on this information, and knowing that the CIO is concerned about costs, what basic recommendations of LAN architecture will you propose?

Exam Objective Checklist

By working through this chapter, you should have sufficient knowledge to answer these exam objectives:

- Describe data link addresses and network addresses, and identify the key differences between them.
- Describe the features and benefits of Fast Ethernet.
- Describe the guidelines and distance limitations of Fast Ethernet.
- Describe full-duplex and half-duplex Ethernet operation.

Practice Questions

1. When a collision is detected in an Ethernet network, a special packet is sent out. What is the name of that packet?

    a. Collision Packet
    b. Token Packet
    c. Extended Jam Signal
    d. Collision Jam Signal

2. 10Base5 operates at what speed?

    a. 5 Mbps
    b. 10 Mbps
    c. 100 Mbps
    d. 16 Mbps

3. The most common type of LAN network today is:

    a. 10BaseT
    b. Token Ring
    c. ATM
    d. FDDI

4. What are two benefits of using Fast Ethernet?

    a. Cheaper to upgrade equipment
    b. Can migrate into an existing network
    c. 10 times faster than 10BaseT
    d. Uses a token for increased reliability

5. Which of the following describes full-duplex? (Select all that apply)

    a. A fast moving four-lane highway
    b. A method of sending data only in one direction
    c. A narrow, one-way bridge
    d. A method of sending data in both directions

6. What is the correct order for a node to transmit data on a Token Ring network?

    a. Destination node receives frame, copies data, and returns frame to sender
    b. Source node grabs frame and checks to see if it can transfer data
    c. Source node modifies frame and appends data
    d. Source node receives frame and releases token onto the network

7. What is the maximum distance of FDDI?

    a. 100 meters
    b. 200 meters
    c. 1000 meters
    d. 2000 meters

8. Multimode fiber uses what as its data source?

    a. Laser
    b. LED
    c. Electricity
    d. Radio waves

9. How is data packaged for transmission over ATM media?

    a. Frames
    b. Packets
    c. Cells
    d. Datagrams

10. Which two of the following are needed in a LANE network?

    a. LANE client
    b. Active monitor
    c. Hub
    d. BUS

11. ATM uses a connection-oriented path established by creating:

    a. Virtual channels through virtual paths
    b. Virtual paths through virtual channels
    c. Virtual tokens through virtual channels
    d. Virtual paths through virtual modes

12. If a DAS fails in an FDDI network, what is the result?

    a. There is no effect on the network.
    b. The entire network will crash.
    c. The token will be wrapped around by the upstream and downstream DAS.
    d. The token will be passed through the DAS.

13. Single-mode fiber uses what as its data source?

    a. Laser
    b. LED
    c. Electricity
    d. Radio waves

14. What is the term used to describe the node that removes unused frames on a Token Ring network?

    a. MAU
    b. Active monitor
    c. BUS
    d. Token

15. What device is used to connect nodes to a Token Ring network?

    a. Repeater
    b. DMAU
    c. MAU
    d. LECS

16. Which of the following describe half-duplex? (Select all that apply)

    a. A fast moving four-lane highway
    b. A method of sending data only in one direction
    c. A narrow, one-way bridge
    d. A method of sending data in both directions

17. What is a disadvantage of using Fast Ethernet?

    a. Costs may be higher to upgrade equipment
    b. Can't migrate into an existing network
    c. Slower than 10BaseFL
    d. Uses a token similar to Token Ring

18. What is the maximum distance of a 10Base2 network?

    a. 200 meters
    b. 500 meters
    c. 185 meters
    d. 476 meters

19. A packet that is destined for all nodes on a network is known as what?

   a. Multicast

   b. Unicast

   c. Broadcast

   d. Bandcast

20. What does the acronym CSMA/CD stand for?

   a. Collision Sense, Multiple Access, Carrier Division

   b. Carrier Sense, Multiple Access, Carrier Division

   c. Carrier Sense, Multistation Access, Collision Detection

   d. Carrier Sense, Multiple Access, Collision Detection

Repeaters, Switches, Bridges, and Routers

In This Chapter

♦ Segmentation

♦ Network Devices

♦ VLAN

♦ Spanning Tree

In Chapter 2, "LAN Technologies," we examined Ethernet and some of the limitations associated with it. As more and more nodes are added to a segment, the chances of collisions increase substantially. Furthermore, broadcasts can also decrease the available bandwidth. Ethernet segments have some distance limitations, so we will examine ways to increase the distances. We also examine ways to decrease the size of both collision and broadcast domains using various network devices.

LAN Segmentation

One of the worst calls a network administrator can receive is one from a user complaining that the network is slow. Trying to determine why the user thinks it is slow is worse than finding the needle in the haystack. Since Ethernet networks degrade in performance as more nodes are added, some method is needed to help reduce collisions. In order to understand this and to develop a foundation on which to find the answer to the user's complaint, we must examine some definitions.

The first definition is *collision domain*. All the nodes that are directly connected together and must contend with the Ethernet bus are considered in the same collision domain. Since larger collision domains decrease bandwidth, it becomes necessary to break up these collision domains.

The second definition is *broadcast domain*. A broadcast domain is a logical grouping of computers that all receive the same broadcasts.

Amazingly enough, it is possible to have separate collision domains while still having the same broadcast domain. Various network devices can accomplish this.

If we can reduce the size of each of our collision domains, we can substantially increase the throughput of data through our network. This means we will not get those frustrating "network is slow" calls. This allows users to increase their productivity, which increases the business' profits, which means bigger pay raises for us!

Another way to increase throughput is to increase the bandwidth that the network runs on. Upgrading from a 10BaseT network to a 100BaseT network would decrease the number of collisions for the same number of nodes, but this doesn't really solve the problem. As we add more nodes to a faster network, collisions increase and we are back to where we were before upgrading. Additionally, network cards and CPUs may not be fast enough to adequately process the data on the network. Additional hardware upgrades then become necessary. A good design today is substantially better than "patching" network problems tomorrow.

Repeaters

Repeaters are devices that can extend the cable lengths of a single Ethernet network. Referring to Figure 3–1, we can see that the cable length for the left side has reached 90 meters. In a normal segment using 10BaseT, we would only have 10 meters left and that would be under ideal conditions. However, by placing the repeater at the end of the segment, we can extend the cable segment another 100 meters (ideal conditions).

A repeater connects two or more segments together, thereby increasing the maximum distance of the segment. *Attenuation* is the loss of electrical signal strength over distance. As the distance increases, the signal deteriorates to the point where it cannot be correctly identified. In order to eliminate attenuation, the repeater will boost the signal strength. As the bits arrive on the first port, the repeater will amplify the signal and then place it back onto the next segment as if it had originated from the repeater. Since the repeater only works with the electrical signals converted to bits, it is a Layer 1 device. Remember that the first layer of the OSI model is the Physical layer, which deals only with the cables and the actual signals being transmitted.

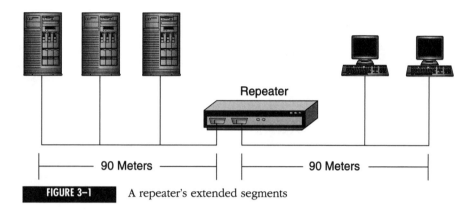

FIGURE 3-1   A repeater's extended segments

Although this does increase our segment lengths, there are disadvantages to this. First, since the repeater removes the signal to regenerate it, and then places it on the destination segment, there is *latency* associated with it. Latency is the time it takes for the leading edge of the data signal to enter one port until the trailing edge of the signal leaves the destination port.

Additionally, the timing of the 10BaseT is such that the maximum number of segments you could extend is five using four repeaters. Of those five segments, only three of them can actually be populated with nodes. This is referred to as the "5-4-3" rule.

When dealing with LAN segmentation, since the repeater works at the Physical layer, it does not reduce the number of signals being transmitted. Therefore, a repeater does not decrease the size of a collision domain nor a broadcast domain.

It is important to note that most Ethernet hubs today are multiport repeaters.

Bridges

Bridges are Layer 2 devices, or Data Link layer devices that work on the principle of a forwarding table using MAC addresses. Although there are different kinds of bridging, they essentially work the same. We will concern ourselves with the type of bridging referred to as *transparent bridging*.

Transparent bridging is so-called because hosts are unaware that any bridge may be in the direct path to another node. These bridges work by dynamically building a table of MAC addresses and defining on which network segment they belong. As a frame is received on a port, the source MAC address is identified and then added to the table.

For example, using Figure 3–2, Node 1 wants to send to Node 4. When the frame arrives at Bridge A, the source address (Node 1) is found in the header and placed into the table as coming from Segment 1. It then identifies

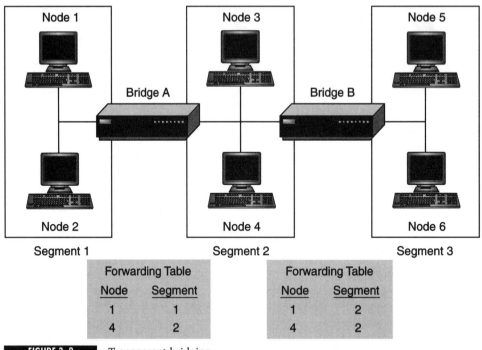

Forwarding Table	
Node	Segment
1	1
4	2

Forwarding Table	
Node	Segment
1	2
4	2

FIGURE 3–2   Transparent bridging

the destination MAC address (Node 4), looks it up in the table, and since it has not added it to the table yet, the bridge sends the frame out all ports except for the one that it was received on. Node 4 will then receive the frame, as will Bridge B. Bridge B performs the same decisions as Bridge A, and determines that Node 1 is on Segment 2. This occurs because Bridge B thinks everything to its left is on Segment 2. It does not even know that Segment 1 exists. Since it does not know where Node 4 is, Bridge B will forward the frame onto Segment 3.

At this point, Node 4 is likely to respond to Node 1. Node 4 places the data onto the physical media, and both Bridges A and B will receive the frame. Bridge A will determine that Node 4 is on Segment 2 and modify its table. Looking up the destination MAC address of Node 1, it finds it and forwards the frame to Segment 1. Bridge B will receive the frame, examine the source address of Node 4, and place it into the table. The destination address of Node 1 is looked for in the table and this time it is found. Since the source and the destination are on the same segment (Segment 2, according to its table), it will not forward the packet onto Segment 3. In this instance, we have our first example of segmentation.

As nodes send data through the network, the table will build up to a complete state as shown in Figure 3–3.

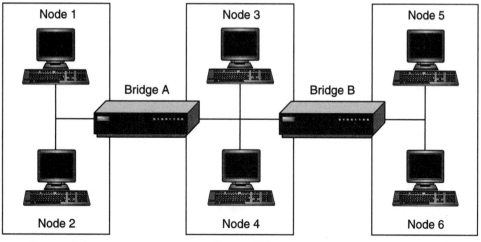

Forwarding Table

Node	Segment
1	1
2	1
3	2
4	2
5	2
6	2

Forwarding Table

Node	Segment
1	2
2	2
3	2
4	2
5	3
6	3

FIGURE 3-3   Final view of forwarding tables

Since bridges only forward frames onto the segment where the destination exists, bridges effectively separate collision domains. Our previous example had three collision domains, thereby increasing the bandwidth available to the nodes on the same segment.

Another advantage to bridging is that a node may be moved at any time. When the node is moved to another segment, the bridges will update as frames are sent from the node in its new destination. There is a possibility that packets will be lost until all the bridges update the tables correctly.

By using bridging, networks are more maintainable and easier to scale. As more nodes are added to a network, the number of collision domains can be kept constant.

There are a couple of disadvantages to bridges, though. Since broadcasts are sent to all MAC addresses, all nodes will receive the broadcast. When a bridge receives a broadcast packet, it forwards it to all other segments to which it is connected. This means that a bridged network still has a single broadcast domain.

Because bridges must examine the MAC addresses of each frame as it is received, there is additional latency introduced into the network. This disadvantage can cause a 20–30 percent latency. Again, latency is the time it takes from the first signal to reach the incoming port until the trailing signal is sent out the destination port. In essence, it slows the network.

A third disadvantage can occur when a bridging loop is created. A loop may be created because we would like to include fault tolerance in our network. If one bridge should fail, we would like a backup path to continue forwarding frames.

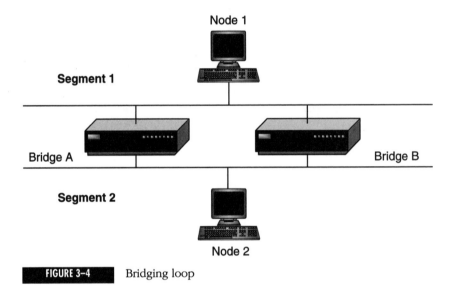

FIGURE 3-4   Bridging loop

In Figure 3–4, we can see an example of a bridging loop. If Node 1 were to send to Node 2, both bridges would receive the frame, determine that Node 1 is on Segment 1, and forward the frame to Segment 2. Although Node 2 would receive two copies of the frame, each bridge also receives the frame from the other bridge. They each update their tables to indicate that Node 1 came from Segment 2, since this is on the port from which they last heard the frame. When Node 2 replies to Node 1, both bridges think that Node 1 is on Segment 2 and therefore will not forward the frame.

Imagine the same scenario using a broadcast frame. The broadcast frame would be received by each bridge and forwarded to each other. The broadcast would circle endlessly. This results in a broadcast storm, which could bring down the entire network.

The IEEE modified an earlier version of DEC's bridging protocol and it was published as IEEE 802.1d. This specification defines a protocol that

bridges can use to prevent bridging loops, called Spanning Tree Protocol (SPT). More appropriately, the IEEE 802.1d defines a Spanning Tree Algorithm (SPA) that the SPT uses.

The SPA defines a method that puts a port that would cause a loop into a blocked mode. Once in a blocked mode, the bridge will not process any frames it receives on that port. This configuration is done at initialization and when a bridge fails. The bridges communicate through a message called *bridge protocol data unit*, or BPDU. These BPDUs are exchanged upon boot up and periodically after that. Once all bridges have exchanged data, a root bridge is elected. After the root bridge is determined, each bridge then will translate a value of what it would cost to get to the root bridge. The bridges then compare the values to determine which bridge has the best route, and all other bridges will disable one or more ports to prevent any looping.

Typically, the bridge with the lowest MAC address will be designated as the root. In our example, we can assume that Bridge A becomes the root and Bridge B defines the cost associated with getting to Bridge A through each of its ports.

If the costs are identical, then the SPA further defines which port loses and becomes blocked. When the port becomes blocked, and as shown in Figure 3–5, there is now only one route from Segment 1 to Segment 2.

If Bridge A were to fail, the BPDU from Bridge A would not arrive at Bridge B. Bridge B would then activate its port to enable a path from Segment 1 to Segment 2, allowing data to once again flow and ensuring any redundancy requirements.

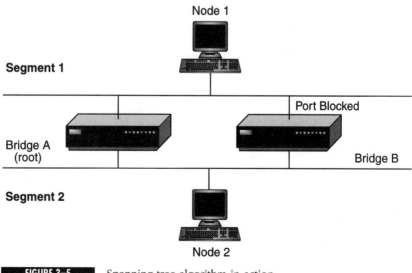

FIGURE 3–5 Spanning tree algorithm in action

Routers

Routers operate at the Network layer of the OSI model. Because of this, they are often referred to as Layer 3 devices. The Network layer is responsible for routing data between networks. This is accomplished using network addresses. Each protocol that supports routing uses it own method of defining network addresses (we examine TCP/IP and IPX/SPX later in this book).

The goal of a router is to help quiet our network by completely separating not only the collision domains, but also the broadcast domains. To meet this goal, routers will not forward broadcasts.

Another way to help achieve this goal is referred to as the 80–20 rule. This rule simply states that if the traffic from Node A to Node B occupies 80 percent of the total traffic sent from Node B, then the two nodes should be placed within the same segment. The other 20 percent of data traffic could occur on other segments. In other words, keep the users (demand nodes) close to the servers (resource nodes) that they typically use.

In Figure 3–6, a router has been positioned between two separate networks. A Layer 3 address, or simply a network address, uniquely identifies these networks. When Node A wants to communicate with Node B, the data will be sent to the MAC address of Node B. Although the router will receive the frame, it will see that the MAC address is not its own, and therefore will not forward the data to Network 2.

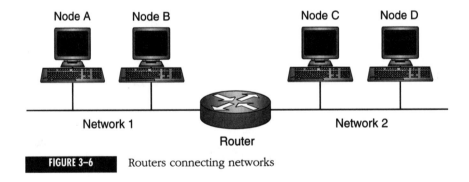

FIGURE 3–6   Routers connecting networks

If Node A sends a broadcast out, both Node A and the router will receive the broadcast, and will perform any actions as necessary. However, the router will not forward the broadcast to Network 2.

If Node B wants to communicate with Node D, Node B will perform some calculations and determine that Node D is on a different network. In order to get the data to the destination, it must send it through the router. In this instance, the destination network address will identify Node D, but the destination MAC address will identify the router. When the router receives the data addressed to it, it will examine the network address and see that the data is actually meant for Node D. It will modify the packet to include the destination MAC address of Node D and then forward the packet out the correct router port. Node D will receive the packet and by reading the source network address it can determine that the data came from Node B.

Advantages to routing include network isolation, which is good for keeping small broadcast and collision domains as well as ease of trouble-shooting. If one side of a router crashes, the rest of the network will be unaffected. Additionally, manageability and scalability of the network are much easier. Routers can be configured to not only include fault tolerance, but also actual *load balancing*. Load balancing is the act of using two or more routers to get the stream of data to its final destination. The router chosen is the router with the lowest cost or, in essence, the router with the least amount of work currently being performed.

In the early days of routers, some routers included the capability to be bridges as well. The drawback to routers is that not all protocols are capable of being routed. If the design specifications did not include a Network layer, they can't be routed. Protocols such as SNA and NetBEUI are examples of nonroutable protocols. However, by including a bridge and a router in the same device, we can then route the routable protocols and bridge the non-routable protocols. These devices were sometimes referred to as *brouters*. Most of today's routers include the capability to bridge and are still referred to as *routers*, and not *brouters*.

Switches

Switches are similar to bridges, but they operate at a much faster rate. We typically describe switches as operating at wire speed, which means the latency through switches is dramatically reduced to the point where it almost appears as if the switch does not exist. In essence, switches work by internally creating connections between two or more ports.

The memory location that is used to store the MAC addresses and the ports they are connected to is referred to as the CAM, or Content Addressable Memory. Like the bridge, it is dynamically created upon reboot and lost when powered off.

A switch is at its most efficient when a single node is connected to a port. This is often referred to as *microsegmentation*. When this occurs, the node has full use of the bandwidth available. If both the switch and the NIC support full-duplex, the bandwidth is effectively doubled. This means a 100BaseT network could have throughput equal to 200 Mbps! Since each port has only one node, it is in its own collision domain, and no collisions can occur.

There are several modes that a switch can operate in. The first mode is called *Store-and-Forward switching*. When a switch begins to receive a frame, it stores it in a buffer until the full frame arrives. When this occurs, a CRC check is performed to ensure that the frame has not been corrupted. If the CRC check fails, the packet is less than 64 bytes (a runt), or the packet is greater than 1518 bytes (a giant), then the frame is discarded. Although this ensures that bad frames do not get forwarded, there is additional latency involved due to the buffering. This method is required when switching between a 10-Mbps port and a 100-Mbps port. A side benefit is that if any filtering of frames needs to be done, Store-and-Forward switching will apply the filter. Filtering can be used to decide which packets are allowed through the switch.

The next method is called *Cut-Through* switching. When the switch begins to receive a frame, it examines the destination MAC address and immediately switches the frame onto the destination port. This switching actually occurs before the full frame has arrived. There is little latency involved with this method. Disadvantages are that bad frames will be forwarded, and filters cannot be applied to the frames.

Another method is referred to as *FragmentFree* switching. This type of switching buffers the frame until the first 64 bytes have been received. Interestingly, most frames are corrupted within these first 64 bytes. Once the 64 bytes have been detected for collisions and the frame is detected as being good, the frame will be forwarded out the correct port and the source and destination ports are then switched, ensuring the rest of the frame is sent directly to the final destination.

Some switches can be configured to use the Cut-Through switching and to fail over to Store-and-Forward when a predefined error detection threshold has been reached. When another threshold has been reached, Cut-Through can be reactivated.

Switches provide many benefits, including minimal size collision domains, low latency, full-duplex communication between the NIC and the switch port, and the ability to work in a mixed 10/100 Mbps network. Because of the low latency, it is beneficial to design a network to use as much switching as possible, and to use routers only when needed to route between networks.

There are versions of switches that operate at the Network layer (Layer 3) and can use network addresses to act upon. These switches are beyond the scope of this book.

Virtual LANs, or VLANs

A switch must still send all broadcasts and multicasts to each port. Like a bridge, a switch can create individual collision domains, but only one broadcast domain. There are instances when it would be nice to separate out some of the ports and isolate them as if they were in a separate broadcast domain. This can be accomplished with switches that support VLAN. An example of this would be a "chatty" protocol such as NetBEUI. This protocol is a multicast protocol and is not routable. Because of these limitations, it has a limited use. However, there are instances when two or more nodes need to communicate using it; access to an SNA mainframe would be an example. Instead of forwarding these multicast packets to each port, a VLAN can be created to isolate the NetBEUI nodes.

VLANs are a logical segment that can be created through the IOS on Cisco switches. Essentially, a VLAN acts as if it is a separate broadcast domain, so that only those ports that are configured to be part of that VLAN can receive frames from other members of the VLAN.

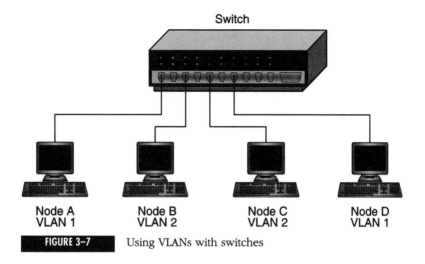

FIGURE 3–7   Using VLANs with switches

In Figure 3–7, we can see that two VLANs have been created. Nodes A and D are on VLAN 1, and Nodes B and C are on VLAN 2. When Node A sends out a broadcast, the switch will be able to determine by examining the frame header that the broadcast should only be sent to other members of VLAN 1. In this case, the frame will only go to Node D.

An additional benefit of using VLANs is the ability to create VLANs across multiple switches. This is accomplished through a VTP, Virtual Trunking Protocol. Using this method, it is possible to group nodes that are physically separated into a logical grouping. This allows geographically separated nodes to belong to the same segment through VLANs even across different switches.

To communicate across VLANs it becomes necessary to use routers. In this instance, switches are replacing routers for internal networks. The routers are then being used only when necessary. Since switches are much faster than routers, network speeds can dramatically increase.

Summary

LAN segmentation is necessary because of the amount of collisions and broadcasts that can occur as more nodes are added to the physical wire. Two types of segmentation can be performed: collision domain segmentation and broadcast domain segmentation. Repeaters are Layer 1 devices that increase the signal strength, thereby increasing the maximum distance of an Ethernet bus. Bridges are Layer 2 devices that create separate collision domains, but still maintain a single broadcast domain. Bridges use forwarding tables that are built as network traffic is processed. Using multiple bridges can increase fault tolerance, but only if a bridging protocol is used to prevent bridging loops. The Spanning Tree Algorithm was adopted by the IEEE and defined as 802.1d. Routers operate at the Network layer and are sometimes referred to as Layer 3 devices. Routers do not pass broadcasts, and therefore can segment a network on both collision and broadcast domains. Finally, switches are a faster version of a bridge that operate at wire speeds. Switches have several modes that can be used, including Cut-Through, Store-and-Forward, and FragmentFree. Switches, by default, separate a collision domain into a single port but still maintain a single broadcast domain. Using VLANs, a switch can create multiple broadcast domains.

Scenario Lab 3.1

The project plan is coming along at a rapid pace. The initial network diagram is currently being drawn up, but some questions remain. You have been asked to describe the cost versus benefits of using switches in the final network design. A specific document should be created that describes the advantages and disadvantages of switching versus bridging and routing. Are you up to the task? If so, what will be your final recommendations and why?

Exam Objective Checklist

By working through this chapter, you should have sufficient knowledge to answer these exam objectives:

- Describe the advantages of segmentation using bridges.
- Describe LAN segmentation using bridges.
- Describe LAN segmentation using routers.
- Describe LAN segmentation using switches.
- Name and describe two switching methods.
- Describe network congestion problems in Ethernet networks.
- Describe the benefits of network segmentation with bridges.
- Describe the benefits of network segmentation with routers.
- Describe the benefits of network segmentation with switches.
- Distinguish between Cut-Through and Store-and-Forward LAN switching.
- Describe the operation of the Spanning Tree Protocol and its benefits.
- Describe the benefits of virtual LANs.

Practice Questions

1. When segmenting a network, it is essential to:

   a. Limit the number of routers in a segment
   b. Decrease the size of the collision domain
   c. Increase the number of nodes in a segment
   d. Use repeaters whenever possible

2. Which method of switching has less latency through the switch?

   a. VLAN
   b. Cut-Forward
   c. Cut-Through
   d. Store-and-Forward

3. Which device works at the Physical layer?

   a. Repeaters
   b. Bridges
   c. Switches
   d. Routers

4. Which two devices work at the Data Link layer?

   a. Repeaters
   b. Bridges
   c. Switches
   d. Routers

5. What method is used to prevent bridging loops?

   a. Manually disable the ports
   b. Spanning Tree Algorithm
   c. VLAN
   d. IEEE 802.10

6. What is the name of the messages that bridges use to communicate with each other?

   a. SPT
   b. SPA
   c. BPDU
   d. MAC

7. Which device always works at the Network layer?

   a. Repeaters
   b. Bridges
   c. Switches
   d. Routers

8. Which method of switching has the best error checking?

   a. FragmentFree
   b. Cut-Through
   c. Store-and-Forward
   d. Cut-Forward

9. You want to place a demand node on the same segment as a resource node. At what percentage of traffic leaving the demand node going to the resource node do you want before making this change?

   a. 50%
   b. 60%
   c. 70%
   d. 80%

10. Which protocol cannot be routed?

   a. NetBEUI
   b. TCP/IP
   c. IPX/SPX
   d. AppleTalk

11. Which method of switching has a variable latency?

   a. VLAN
   b. Cut-Forward
   c. Cut-Through
   d. Store-and-Forward

12. What is the name of the packet that has less than 64 bytes?

   a. BPDU

   b. Giant

   c. Runt

   d. Stunted

13. Which method of switching can be used with filters?

   a. VLAN

   b. Cut-Forward

   c. Cut-Through

   d. Store-and-Forward

14. What method can switches use to create smaller broadcast domains?

   a. Spanning Tree Protocol

   b. Virtual Trunking Protocol

   c. Virtual Local Area Networks

   d. Routing

TCP/IP

In This Chapter

Although we discussed the OSI model in the examples in the previous chapter, TCP/IP itself does not follow the OSI model. We will examine the TCP/IP model and the different protocols that make up each layer. After gaining a general understanding of TCP/IP, we will be ready to tackle the act of TCP/IP addressing and subnetting that will be presented in future chapters.

The OSI Model versus the TCP/IP Model

In the 1960s, the Department of Defense (DoD) became interested in a protocol that was being used by universities to connect their computers together using a packet-switching technology. The DoD was interested in using this technology to maintain communications with all their systems around the world in the event of a nuclear disaster. The Advanced Research Projects Agency (ARPA), a branch of the DoD and later added the prefix Defense (DARPA), became involved in the development. The result is what we know as the Internet, which evolved from the earlier version known as ARPANET. The protocol suite that was created is TCP/IP, which stands for Transmission Control Protocol/Internet Protocol. The real reason for the worldwide acceptance of TCP/IP, however, is due to Berkeley's version of Unix including the TCP/IP protocol and being released into the public domain where anyone could use and modify it.

Many organizations have sprung up from the development of TCP/IP, but most notably is probably the Internet Engineering Task Force (IETF). This committee is responsible for maintaining and helping establish standards for the Internet and TCP/IP in general through a series of documents referred to as Request for Comments (RFC). These documents describe the way technologies should be or must be developed to work in conjunction with other technologies. To learn more about the IETF, visit the Web page at http://www.ietf.org, and specifically http://www.ietf.org/tao.html.

As TCP/IP evolved into a structured set of protocols, developers' trials and tribulations were taken into account when the OSI model was developed. This is to say that the OSI model could be considered a child model of the TCP/IP model. The TCP/IP model is a four-layered model, and can be roughly equated to the OSI model as shown in Figure 4–1.

OSI Model	TCP/IP Model
Application	Application / Process
Presentation	
Session	
Transport	Host-Host / Transport
Network	Network
Data Link	
Physical	Physical

FIGURE 4–1   How the TCP/IP model compares to the OSI model

Each of the layers functions in much the same way as the OSI model, but there are exceptions. Whereas the OSI model exclusively precludes any layer other than the one directly above or below it to be accessed from any other layer (for instance, the Session layer cannot access the Network layer), this does happen on occasion with the TCP/IP model. For example, ping is a utility (Application layer) that may talk directly to the ICMP protocol (Network layer).

The Application layer, or Process Level, is responsible for allowing applications to communicate across hardware and software over different operating systems and platforms. This process is generally referred to as *client/server architecture*. The client application typically runs on the end user's computer and facilitates the user interface. The client application will send requests to the server application that is typically run on a different and more powerful computer. The server handles all the requests that arrive from different clients, and must process information in a quick and timely manner. The server will then return the results back to the client. This type of architecture is often referred to as a *two-tier* architecture.

The Host-Host (pronounced "Host to Host") layer, sometimes called the Transport layer, is very similar to the OSI Transport layer. This layer is responsible for setting up and taking down communication channels to the communication partner. It is also responsible for maintaining some type of flow control and other mechanisms for error checking and correction.

The Network layer is responsible for the largest part of networking: routing. This layer is used to assign network addresses to hosts and to route data to the correct network. This layer is also the shield from the upper-layer protocols to the hardware protocols used to communicate over the chosen physical medium. In essence, without this layer there would have to be an application written for each type of network architecture, such as Ethernet and Token Ring.

The final layer, the Physical layer, was not defined in TCP/IP but is used by vendors to access TCP/IP through the Network layer. This layer is responsible for the physical bits, the frames, and the MAC addresses associated with each network interface.

Let's now examine the protocols that are associated with the various layers.

Internet Protocol (IP)

The Internet Protocol is defined at the Network layer. The Network layer is responsible for routing data to and from other networks; this is accomplished through IP. IP defines a network address that is given to each host. This addressing is examined in detail in Chapter 6, "TCP/IP Addressing." The address can be broken into a network portion and a host portion. Using the network portion, IP can decide on the best route to get the data to its destination by using a routing table.

IP receives data from the Host-Host layer in the form of *segments*. The data received may be too large to actually send to the host, so IP will separate the segment into datagrams. This process is known as *fragmentation*. These fragments are then encoded and sent to the Physical layer for distribution onto the physical medium.

An IP datagram can be examined with software known as *protocol analyzers*. The important parts for our discussion are summarized in Figure 4–2.

The 32 bits that make up the *header* contain various information, such as the version number of IP and the Type of Service (ToS), a field that is

32 bits Header	16 bits Length	16 bits Fragment	8 bits TTL	8 bits Protocol	16 bits Checksum	32 bits Source IP	32 bits Dest. IP	??? bits Data

FIGURE 4–2   IP datagram structure

commonly used in Quality of Service (QoS). The actual header is all of the information up to but not including the data section. The 16 bits for the length identify the total length including the entire header and the data. The 16 bits used for the Fragment field tell IP how to reassemble this datagram if it was received in a fragmented state. The 8-bit TTL field identifies the Time To Live for this datagram. This TTL value will be decremented as this datagram passes through routers. If the TTL should ever reach zero, the router will discard the datagram. The 8-bit protocol field identifies to which Host-Host layer to pass the data. If the value is 6, it will be passed to TCP; if it is 17, it will be passed to UDP. (These two protocols are examined later.) The next 16 bits identify a Cyclical Redundancy Check (CRC) or a Frame Check Sequence (FCS) value used for checking for errors. The next 64 bits are used to store the source IP address and the destination IP address. In Chapter 6, we will see that TCP/IP addresses are 32 bits in length, and here is where the addresses are actually stored. The rest of the datagram is the data that was sent down from the Host-Host layer, or the data that should be sent up to that layer, depending on the direction flow of the datagram.

All of this information is required for IP to effectively communicate with the rest of the network. However, for us, the most important part is the Source and Destination IP address fields. Remember that the Network layer uses logical addresses to define the networks that exist and how to get data to them. How does the data actually get to the host? This is accomplished through the MAC address. TCP/IP defines a protocol, ARP, to do this translation from TCP/IP address to MAC address.

Address Resolution Protocol (ARP)

When IP is ready to send the datagram out onto the wire bound for the final destination host, it needs to find the MAC address to send it to. This is where ARP comes in.

Using Figure 4–3 as an example, suppose an application on Node A wanted to send data to Node B. As the data is sent down to the IP layer, the requested IP address is included. IP then formats the datagram for transmitting onto the network. Using an algorithm discussed in Chapter 6, IP determines that Node B is on the same network as Node A. In order to send the data to the final host, IP asks ARP to request the MAC address of Node B. ARP will send out a broadcast across the local segment asking for the owner of IP

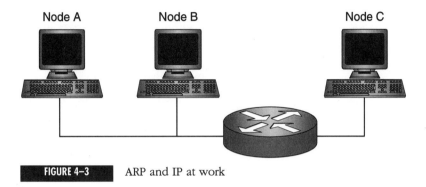

| FIGURE 4–3 | ARP and IP at work |

address Node B to respond with its MAC address. Node B will then respond with a broadcast stating its MAC address. Node A will put Node B's IP address and MAC address into a cache that will be held for a predetermined amount of time. The response being sent back as a broadcast allows other hosts on the segment to also add Node B's IP address and MAC address to their cache. The next time that a node on the same segment as Node B needs to send data to Node B, it will check its ARP cache and, finding an entry, will not need to broadcast again. Finally, Node A will send the frame out onto the wire destined for Node B. Both Node B and the router will receive the frame, but only Node B will process it because the destination MAC address matches its own.

What happens when Node A wants to send data to Node C? We have already discussed that broadcasts do not pass routers, and therefore Node C will not respond to an ARP request. Actually, IP will determine through its algorithm that Node C is on a different network from Node A. In order for the data to get to the different network, Node A knows that it has to send the data to a router. Once again, IP asks for ARP to broadcast a request. This time, the request is for the MAC address of the router. The router will respond with its MAC address, which allows IP to forward the data to the router.

When the router receives the data, it strips off the data link header and examines the IP datagram. Inside the datagram are the destination and source IP addresses. The router examines the destination IP address, looks up the address in its routing table, and then determines that the data needs to be sent to the next segment. The router then will use ARP to request the MAC address of Node C. Node C will hear the request since the router and Node C are on the same segment, and will respond with its MAC address. The router then creates a new data link header that includes its own MAC address as the source MAC and Node C's MAC address as the destination. Note, however, that the router does not touch the source and destination IP addresses. Once Node C finally receives the data and strips off the data link header, IP can correctly deduce that the sender was originally Node A.

ARP has a partner known as RARP that works in a similar fashion. When a diskless machine boots, it knows its MAC address and sends out a RARP request asking for an IP address. If there is a computer within broadcast range that is a RARP server, it will give the booting machine an address.

BootP and DHCP are two similar protocols. When a workstation configured for BootP boots up, it will not only get an IP address, but it will be given a network location from which to load a file or operating system. DHCP clients already have an operating system, but can be given more information than just the IP address. Additional information that can be granted could include a DNS server, a Time server, or a WINS server for Microsoft clients.

Although our example has ARP sending out a broadcast at each step, there is actually an ARP table that is maintained and checked first. When a MAC-to-IP address has been resolved, it will be placed into the table. This speeds up communications because the initial broadcast and response are not required.

Internet Control Message Protocol (ICMP)

The final protocol that we will discuss that runs in the Network layer is ICMP. ICMP is the control messaging protocol that nodes use to communicate messages to other nodes. These messages include information for flow control and other status messages.

For instance, when a router is processing data and more data is flowing in too fast, the router could use flow control to decide to issue a *source quench* message. Source quench is used to indicate to the source to stop or slow down its sending. ICMP is the protocol used to send that message.

Another example is the use of the TTL in the datagrams. If the datagram passes too many routers on its way to the final destination and the TTL is incremented to zero, the router that discards the datagram will send back a message indicating it is using ICMP.

One final example is the ICMP Redirect message. When a router receives a datagram from a source and the router determines that a better path exists, it will forward the packet, but it will also send the ICMP Redirect message to the sending host telling it of the better path. It is up to the host protocol implementation to use the new information. Some operating systems will ignore the message and keep sending to the less efficient route.

Transmission Control Protocol (TCP)

TCP is the reliable protocol of the TCP/IP suite. While IP sends data out to the network, it does not care if the datagram arrives or not. It is sometimes described as a "best effort" protocol. It is the Host-Host layer—specifically, the TCP protocol—that defines how to handle datagrams when they are lost or corrupted.

Besides ensuring data delivery, TCP is also responsible for setting up the initial connections with the receiving host and multiplexing data from multiple Application layer protocols into a single connection. This multiplexing allows multiple applications to communicate with the same destination node more efficiently.

TCP uses a *three-way handshake* to initiate a connection to a remote host. The sender will decide on a sequence number to start with when sending the segments. The sender then initiates a SYN connection to the receiver. This lets the sender know what sequence number to expect next, allows the sender and receiver to both indicate they are ready to send and receive, and allows the receiver to send its own sequence number for communication to the sender. This response is known as the *Acknowledgment,* or the ACK. Once the sender receives the ACK, it can respond with its own ACK, indicating that transmission will now occur.

This process of the three-way handshake sets up a connection, which makes TCP a connection-oriented protocol. The entire process can be likened to that of the telephone. A person (sender) picks up the telephone and dials (SYN) the number of the person to whom they wish to speak (receiver). The receiver answers with a "Hello" (ACK). The sender hears the answer and responds with some data by beginning a conversation.

TCP uses the sliding window concept to speed communications across a network. Remember that the sliding window is a method of receiving more than 1 byte of data before needing to send an ACK back to the sender. The receiver can indicate the last number of the data that it received, and the sender would then know if it could send new data, or if it needed to re-send data that may have been lost.

Like IP, TCP needs to know to which Application layer protocol to give the data. This is also accomplished with numbers similar to what IP uses. These numbers are referred to as *ports*. Port numbers are either well-known ports that have been assigned, or ephemeral ports that are dynamically assigned. Well-known ports range from 0 to 1023, and ephemeral ports range from 1024 to 65535. Note that although the well-known ports have been assigned, there are ports greater than 1024 that have also been assigned and cannot be dynamically assigned. We will examine ports in more detail when we discuss FTP.

User Datagram Protocol (UDP)

There are times when communication with a remote node does not need to have guaranteed delivery. UDP is the protocol that can be used for just such instances. UDP is a connectionless protocol, which means it does not need to set up a connection before sending data. In fact, it does not even verify if the receiver is online. UDP packages data and sends it to IP for delivery. Although it numbers the segments before sending them off, any guarantee of delivery is up to the Application layer. If TCP is like the telephone, then UDP is like the mail. We put a stamp on a letter, drop it into the mailbox, and hope that it arrives at its destination. UDP, like TCP, is part of the Transport layer.

Application Layer Protocols

There are many protocols that run at the Application layer, and it would be unfeasible to list them all here. We will discuss the more common ones, and the ones that we will have a need for further understanding Cisco routers later in this book.

File Transfer Protocol (FTP)

FTP is a protocol used to transfer files in either binary or ASCII format. Most of us are familiar with FTP because of the Internet. However, there are some important considerations to keep in mind.

FTP uses TCP to establish a connection with a remote server. FTP applications are a kind of client/server application. The end user uses an FTP client to access an FTP server that is running on a central server. Authentication may be required, or the default authentication of the user "anonymous" or "ftp" may be accepted. In either event, the name and password are sent as clear text across the network, and protocol analyzers can intercept these. We need to keep this in mind the next time we want to log on an FTP server.

When an initial connection from the client is made, it dynamically chooses an ephemeral port and sends that to the FTP server. FTP servers default to listening to connections on port 20. When a request is heard from the client, the FTP server will send data out its own port 21 to the port number that the client sent in the initial request. By using the port numbers, we can have multiple FTP sessions open to the same FTP server and the data will arrive at each client session correctly, even if the client sessions are on the same computer.

Trivial File Transfer Protocol (TFTP)

Similar to FTP, TFTP is used to transfer files and to configure routers and printers. TFTP uses UDP, which has an added benefit in that it can increase the chance of getting through to configure a critical router when the network bandwidth won't support any more TCP connections. TFTP servers have no authentication mechanism, which makes them vulnerable to unsolicited damage from hackers. In Chpater 10, "Managing the Cisco Router," we will use TFTP to configure Cisco routers.

Telnet

Telnet is a connection-oriented protocol that uses TCP. Like FTP, it is also a client/server application. A telnet terminal is used to connect up to a telnet server and run applications remotely. This is a common protocol that is used to connect to mainframe computers to perform work. Telnet can also be used to connect to Cisco routers and configure them from remote locations. However, Telnet cannot transfer files, so it is often used in conjunction with FTP.

Simple Network Management Protocol (SNMP)

SNMP is a protocol that uses UDP to manage networks. Using SNMP, a network administrator can configure and maintain a network from a remote console. Version 1 of SNMP has poor security standards, and is thus a prime protocol for hackers to infiltrate a network. Despite this major disadvantage, SNMP remains the management protocol of choice. Products such as HP OpenView and CiscoWorks 2000 can be used to graphically map a network, be alerted when a node fails, and configure devices.

SNMP works on the principle that nodes are polled on a regular interval, and information is retrieved from that node. This information that can be retrieved, and possibly even configured, is stored in a database called the Management Information Base (MIB). Additionally, nodes can be configured to watch for occurrences of trouble such as bad ports, illegal attempts at management, and high bandwidth. When this type of condition occurs, the node can then issue a trap that will alert the SNMP manager and we can then be notified at 2:00 A.M. that a problem has occurred with our network.

Other Protocols and Applications

There are many other protocols, including Simple Mail Transfer Protocol (SMTP), Domain Name System (DNS), Rlogin, X Windows, and Network File System (NFS). Each of these protocols/applications can be used to enhance TCP/IP in some way.

There are a couple of troubleshooting tools that should also be mentioned. *Ping* (although not originally an acronym, ping has come to be known as Packet InterNet Groper) is an application that can be used to verify connectivity from one TCP/IP node to another. We will use ping throughout the remaining chapters in this book as a method of testing configurations. Ping works by using the ICMP protocol to return status messages to indicate if a node is alive. ICMP will also be used when ping (and other applications) cannot reach a destination because IP itself does not know how to route the datagram to the final destination. In this case, ICMP will respond with a Destination Host Unreachable message.

Another application that is useful in troubleshooting is *traceroute*. Traceroute uses the TTL and ICMP protocols to trace the actual path a datagram takes to reach its final destination. When dealing with routing tables, traceroute can be a valuable asset in finding problems in a network.

Summary

TCP/IP is not a single protocol, but a collection of protocols that operate at various layers of the DoD or TCP/IP model. The TCP/IP model is composed of four layers: Application, Host-Host, Network, and Physical. The Physical layer is not actually described in the TCP/IP architecture, but is needed to establish connections between the network applications and the network itself. IP is the mainstay of the TCP/IP suite. IP is used to assign logical addresses to hosts and to networks, and can use the network addresses to effectively map the path to reach a given destination. TCP and UDP are two protocols that operate at the Transport layer. TCP is a connection-oriented protocol that is used to ensure data integrity. UDP is a connectionless protocol that is not concerned with ensuring reliable or guaranteed delivery. There are many additional protocols and applications that make use of the TCP/IP or UDP/IP connections.

Scenario Lab 4.1

The hardware requirements are in place for the design of Network Solutions, Inc. TCP/IP will be used as the primary protocol for this network, but the project manager would like to understand the protocol in a little more detail. Can you describe the functions of TCP/IP and how it is used to transfer data across the network? Be sure to include in the discussion the various applications that may use TCP/IP.

Exam Objective Checklist

By working through this chapter, you should have sufficient knowledge to answer these exam objectives:

- Describe connection-oriented network service and connectionless network service, and identify the key differences between them.
- Describe data link addresses and network addresses, and identify the key differences between them.
- Identify the functions of the TCP/IP Transport-layer protocols.
- Identify the functions of the TCP/IP Network-layer protocols.
- Identify the functions performed by ICMP.

Practice Questions

1. What is the name used for the list of documents that describe TCP/IP in detail?

   a. IETF
   b. ARPA
   c. RFC
   d. DNS

2. Which order is the correct order (from top to bottom) of the DoD or TCP/IP model?

   a. Application
   b. Network
   c. Physical
   d. Host-Host

3. Which protocol resolves MAC addresses from TCP/IP addresses?

   a. TCP
   b. ICMP
   c. ARP
   d. DNS

4. Which layer of the DoD model defines flow control and error checking?

   a. Application
   b. Network
   c. Physical
   d. Host-Host

5. Which protocol does the value 17 in the Protocol field of the IP packet refer to?

   a. TCP
   b. IP
   c. ARP
   d. UDP

6. Which TCP/IP protocols operate at the Network layer? (Choose two)

   a. TCP
   b. UDP
   c. IP
   d. ICMP

7. The router will route a datagram after changing which two fields in the IP header? (Choose two)

   a. Source MAC address
   b. Source IP address
   c. Destination MAC address
   d. Destination IP address

8. Which TCP/IP protocols operate at the Host-Host layer? (Choose two)

   a. TCP
   b. UDP
   c. IP
   d. ICMP

9. Which protocol is the messaging and control protocol?

   a. TCP
   b. ICMP
   c. ARP
   d. DNS

10. Which of the following is a connection-oriented protocol?

   a. TCP
   b. UDP
   c. IP
   d. ICMP

11. Which protocol uses the three-way handshake?

    a. TCP
    b. ICMP
    c. ARP
    d. DNS

12. Which of the following is a connectionless protocol?

    a. TCP
    b. UDP
    c. Telnet
    d. FTP

13. Which protocol is used to transfer files?

    a. Telnet
    b. FTP
    c. DNS
    d. SNMP

14. Which protocol is used to manage networks with the aid of MIBs?

    a. Telnet
    b. FTP
    c. DNS
    d. SNMP

15. Which protocol can be used to log in and configure Cisco routers?

    a. Telnet
    b. FTP
    c. DNS
    d. SNMP

Introduction to Cisco Routers

In This Chapter

◆ Cisco Products

◆ Cisco 2500 Series Routers

◆ IOS

◆ Configuring Cisco Routers

Cisco Systems, Inc. evolved from a project started by Len and Sandy Bossack, a married couple who worked at Stanford University. The need for communication between the two departments they worked for gave them the inspiration to create a hardware device using TCP/IP. The original name of the company spawned from this new-generation hardware was cisco Systems with the small "c" The name has since been changed to the capital "C" and Cisco Systems, Inc. is now the leading hardware and software vendor for internetworking. In this chapter, we examine a few of the types of network devices that are sold, as well as the operating system that runs on the devices. We then examine the Cisco 2500 series in more detail. Finally, we start to configure the routers using the command-line interface.

Cisco Products Overview

There are many products currently being sold worldwide that Cisco has engineered. There are many new products being released, and it seems as if they are being released

75

daily. We will examine some of the more popular devices in brief, and then examine the 2500 series routers in more detail. This book focuses on the 2500 throughout the remaining chapters.

Switches—Catalyst 1900 Series

The 1900 series switches include 10BaseT ports of various densities (the number of ports that are available for each model) and two 100BaseT ports for connecting to a backbone network. They use the command-line interface to configure the routers, as well as Web-based interface. These switches are used for low-cost connectivity by replacing hubs and connecting to desktops.

Switches—Catalyst 2820 Series

These switches include 24 10BaseT ports for connecting to desktops and two modular ports that can be configured with various modules. Using these switches allows a business to integrate into existing 100BaseT, 100BaseFX, FDDI, and/or ATM networks.

Switches—Catalyst 2900 Series

These switches are 10/100 Mbps autosensing to allow a mix of 10BaseT and 100BaseT to work together. The port density varies with the model. In addition, the 2916MXL has two modular ports that can be used to custom configure the switch to a business's environment. Modules that can be used include 100BaseFX, Gigabit Ethernet, ATM, and others as they are developed by Cisco. Figure 5–1 shows the 2916MXL without any modular devices added.

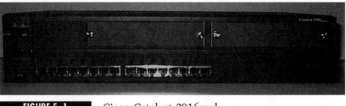

FIGURE 5–1   Cisco Catalyst 2916mxl

Switches—Catalyst 5000 Series

The Catalyst 5000 and 5500 models are the workhorses of enterprise switching. These switches have so many features that Cisco has required this as one of the tests to become a CCNP, and we wouldn't even want to think about trying for the CCIE without becoming intimately familiar with this product. Technologies include redundant power supplies, redundant Supervisor engines, 10/100 Base T support, Token Ring, 100Base FX, CDDI, FDDI, ATM, LANE, Load sharing,

Remote management, and VLANs. The list continues as Cisco develops new technologies to run on these models. Figure 5–2 shows the Catalyst 5000. The picture shows the dual power supplies for redundancy. It also has two 12-port 10/100 Autosensing cards, which will be used to connect various devices, including computers, printers, and routers onto the same segment.

FIGURE 5–2   Cisco Catalyst 5000

Routers—Cisco 700 Series

These routers are used to connect ISDN to a small office or to the home. Some models include 10BaseT hubs integrated into the router.

Routers—Cisco 1600 Series

These routers are used for small businesses to access WAN connections of various types. Using one of these routers, a small business can connect its LAN to a WAN using ISDN, X.25, T1, Fractional T1, and Switched 56K lines.

Routers—Cisco 2600 Series

These routers provide modular upgrades for remote offices to connect to the central office. The 2600 series router offers one or two Ethernet ports and module slots for connecting to typical WAN networks. This router is ideal for creating VPNs, or Virtual Private Networks, for security through the Internet.

Routers—Cisco 3600 Series

These models are for those companies that require extensive dial-in or dial-out services. The 3600 series routers offer modular upgrades to increase the number of modems, integrated digital modems, or ISDN connections available. In addition, these routers can be used for connecting to Ethernet and/or Token Ring networks.

Routers—Cisco 4000 Series

The 4000 series routers are also a modular platform. They can connect Ethernet, Token Ring, and Fast Ethernet networks into a single, manageable network. In addition, they can be used to connect FDDI, ISDN, and asynchronous modems for WAN connectivity.

Routers—Cisco 7000 Series

Like the Catalyst 5000 series, the Cisco 7000 Series routers are the workhorse for network connectivity. This router has just as many features as the Catalyst, and we should be very familiar with this product before taking the CCIE test.

Learning More

The preceding is just a brief introduction to some of the Cisco models of switches and routers. There are many more products, and many more being developed and released. To learn more about these or any other Cisco products, we have a couple of resources at our disposal. Using the phonebook, we can find the name of the nearest Cisco distributor and talk to their sales and technical people. In addition, up-to-date information can be found in the product section of the Cisco Web site.

Cisco 2500 Series Access Routers

The 2500 series routers could be considered the staple of the Cisco product line. This series has the largest abundance of models that can quickly connect two or more networks together and route between them. Each model can contain one or more of the following interface types and special features:

Ethernet ports. Used for connecting to 10 Mbps Ethernet networks. Most ports use an AUI, which requires an external transceiver device to convert from the 15-pin port to the proper 10Base2 or 10BaseT network connections. Others, however, include both an AUI port and a standard 10BaseT port.
Token Ring ports. Used for connecting to Token Ring networks.
Synchronous serial ports. Used for connecting to WANs.
Asynchronous serial ports. Used for connecting terminals or modems for asynchronous communications.
ISDN ports. Used for connecting to ISDN.

Hub ports. Used to integrate a 10BaseT hub with the router for low-cost, one-device connectivity.

Modular ports. Used to upgrade connectivity to WAN, including ISDN, T1, Fractional T1, and Switched 56.

Auxiliary port. Used for asynchronous communications. Typically used for connecting modems for remote configuration of routers.

Console port. Used to connect a PC or terminal to a router for local configuration.

Using the information in Table 5.1, we can match up the requirements for a router to the correct model. Following the table are a few pictures that show different models of the 2500 series.

In Table 5.1, S.Serial stands for synchronous serial ports; A.Serial stands for asynchronous serial ports; Aux is the auxiliary port; Cons is the console port; and M stands for Modular upgrade available.

TABLE 5.1 Various models of the Cisco 2500 series

Model	Ethernet	Token	S.Serial	A.Serial	ISDN	Hub	Aux	Cons
2501	1	0	2	0	0	0	1	1
2502	0	1	2	0	0	0	1	1
2503	1	0	2	0	1	0	1	1
2504	0	1	2	0	1	0	1	1
2505	1	0	2	0	0	8	1	1
2507	1	0	2	0	0	16	1	1
2509	1	0	2	8	0	0	1	1
2511	1	0	2	16	0	0	1	1
2512	0	1	2	16	0	0	1	1
2513	1	1	2	0	0	0	1	1
2514	2	0	2	0	0	0	1	1
2515	0	2	2	0	0	0	1	1
2516	1	0	2	0	1	14	1	1
2520	1	0	2	2	1	0	1	1
2521	0	1	2	2	1	0	1	1
2522	1	0	2	8	1	0	1	1
2523	0	1	2	8	1	0	1	1
2524	1	0	M	M	M	0	1	1
2525	0	1	M	M	M	0	1	1

The Cisco 2513 shown in Figure 5–3 has a single Ethernet port and a single Token Ring port. This router can be used to connect two disparate systems together as well as connecting to two separate WANs. Moving from left to right, the ports are Token Ring, Ethernet AUI, Serial 0, Serial 1, console, auxiliary, power switch, and power connection.

FIGURE 5–3   Cisco 2513

The Cisco 2520 shown in Figure 5–4 can be used as a low-cost access server to allow users to dial in to a business's network. From left to right it includes the ports Serial 0, Serial 1, Serial 2 (Asynchronous or Synchronous), Serial 3 (Asynchronous or Synchronous), Ethernet AUI or 10BaseT (only 1 of the two can be used), ISDN, console, auxiliary, power switch, and power connection.

FIGURE 5–4   Cisco 2520

The Cisco 2503 shown in Figure 5–5 is a low-cost router that can be used to connect a LAN to a WAN through ISDN. This can be used to provide Internet access, or for remote branch offices for faster than modem connections. From left to right, the ports are Ethernet AUI, Serial 0, Serial 1, ISDN, console, auxiliary, power switch, and power connection.

FIGURE 5–5   Cisco 2503

The Cisco 2505 shown in Figure 5–6 combines a 10BaseT 8-port hub with connectivity to a WAN network in a single package. This was designed for small businesses that need a small network and WAN connectivity, but price is an issue. From left to right, the ports include 8 10BaseT ports, Serial 0, Serial 1, console, auxiliary, power switch, and power connection. There is also an internal Ethernet port that can be configured to route between the hub and the serial ports.

FIGURE 5–6   Cisco 2505

These are just a few of the various models, but upon examining the pictures we should be able to identify other routers when actually seen. Note that at one time there was a smaller, cheaper version of some of these models known as the CiscoPro. These routers came packaged in a white case instead of the standard charcoal gray. While these routers were functional, some of the internals were downgraded to decrease the costs. These routers are no longer made, but if we need to install one in a network we must make sure that the memory, FLASH, and ROM are upgraded to run the current software, otherwise known as the IOS.

Router Architecture

In this section, we examine the router architecture in brief. More detail is presented in Chapter 10, "Managing the Cisco Router," but for now, we need to know enough to actually start using the routers.

The routers maintain a ROM (Read-Only Memory) on the system boards for booting up. Once the router boots up, it reads the operating system that is found in FLASH memory. The operating system is called Internetwork Operating System, or IOS. There are many versions of the IOS available and we examine them in more detail in the next section. FLASH memory is a type of memory that acts like ROM, but can be erased and reprogrammed by us. The IOS sits in the FLASH memory and is run by the Cisco router. This is similar to booting a PC and having Windows 98 loaded and running.

While the router is running, it may need routing tables and buffers for the incoming and outgoing packets. All of this information is stored in RAM (Random Access Memory). This RAM is almost identical to the type of RAM in a PC. It is sometimes referred to as DRAM or SIMMs.

As the router boots, it needs to be configured. This configuration includes such items as the hostname, TCP/IP addresses, routing information, interface information, and other information. This initial configuration, or startup configuration, is stored in a small memory chip called the NVRAM. NV stands for *non-volatile*, which means the contents of the memory will be preserved between reboots. In essence, it is similar to FLASH memory. NVRAM is only 32K in size, but it is sufficient to hold all the configuration information. Once the router is booted, the startup configuration is loaded into memory. At this point, there is now a running configuration that the router uses dynamically.

All of this may sound wonderful, but what does it really have to do with us? There are times when the routers have to be upgraded. Perhaps the routing tables have grown too large, or the traffic is flowing at a heavy pace and we are running out of the packet buffers. We might be upgrading the IOS and new system requirements to include adding more FLASH and more DRAM.

So now, the real question becomes, "How do we actually change these items?" In order to do this, we have to remove the cover of the router. When the router is placed upside down, we will find two slots that are typically marked "Pry Slot." Refer to Figure 5–7 for the location of these slots. First, we need to remove the single screw that is in the middle of these two slots. Once that is removed, we can then use a flat-bladed screwdriver to twist the pry slots and open the case. The case is two pieces and is shaped into an "L" and will have to be physically separated when we can't pry the slots open any further. Once the cover is off, we can then see the system board see Figure 5–8.

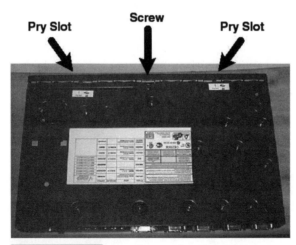

FIGURE 5–7   Pry slots on the Cisco 2500 series

IOS

The IOS is the brains of the routers. Without this software, the router is no more than a doorstop. There are many versions of the IOS in production and there is no correct one to have. If our router is performing its job well and we don't have any need for the newer features that are being sold, then we don't need to upgrade. However, if we did wish to upgrade our IOS to the latest and greatest

FLASH Memory   **Memory**

FIGURE 5-8   Location of FLASH and DRAM inside a Cisco 2500 series

version, we would need to contact our Cisco supplier and order a Feature Pack, or possibly download a newer version if we have a support contract.

Feature Pack is the term used for the packaging of the IOS. There are at least three versions of the IOS: Base, Plus, and Encryption. The Base version has just the basics needed to run the router. The Plus version includes some additional support for IBM connectivity, as well as some extra features. The Encryption version can be either 40-bit or 56-bit encryption. The 56-bit encryption is not available outside the United States.

There are many additional configurations that can be added to one of these standard versions. For example, we could order Desktop edition, which has support for IPX/SPX and AppleTalk (and many other protocols). We could order the Plus version of this and include 56-bit encryption as well. There is even a firewall product that can be installed to turn the Cisco 2500 into a firewall for security. A firewall is a product that can filter, or block, specific ports to add additional security to our TCP/IP network. We can check out the Cisco Web site for any additional information on the various versions and flavors of each version.

Once the correct version has been loaded (we will see how to do this in Chapter 10), we can then begin configuring the router to work in our network. If we had purchased a new router and it did not have an IOS installed, there is a software program that comes with the Feature Pack that can run on Windows 95/98/NT that can be used to automatically load the IOS for us.

It's now time to start configuring the router. We will assume that the IOS has already been loaded for us, and that the version is 11.3.

Configuring the Cisco Router

There are three ways to configure the router. We can Telnet to a router, but this requires that the router can be reached over the network. This option is

most useful for reconfiguring a router. If we had a modem attached to the
AUX port, we could dial in and configure the router. Again, this option
requires the router to be preconfigured for a mode. Finally, we can use a
direct connection to the console cable. For brand new routers, the only
option is the last one.

In order to directly connect to the router, we need the console cable that
comes with it. In addition, we need the DB9-to-RJ45 converter (or if the serial
port we will be connecting with is a 25-pin port, we would need the DB25-to-
RJ45 converter). Next, connect the console cable to the console port on the
router, and the serial converter into the serial port on the back of the PC.
Finally, load up HyperTerm or some other terminal program and set the
parameters to 9600 baud, 8 bits, and no parity, using the COM port that you
plugged the console cable into. Once this is done, we can begin configuring
the routers.

But wait! We shouldn't just go configuring routers haphazardly. We need
a plan. It just so happens that we have been contacted by IC, Inc. to configure
their three routers. Figure 5–9 is a look at their network.

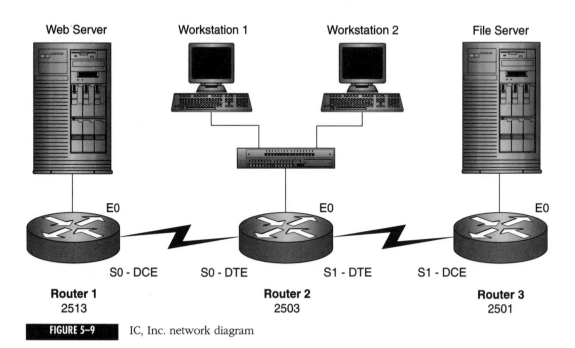

FIGURE 5–9   IC, Inc. network diagram

Okay, so IC stands for Imaginary Company, and this is a really small and
unusual network, but it is perfect for learning about routers, and it makes it
seem like we are actually building up the work experience. This doesn't mean
that we should list IC, Inc. on our résumés, though.

Looking at the diagram, we can see that each router has an E0 listed at the top. This is the Ethernet port. All the numbering of interfaces start at 0, not 1. The S0 listed is the first Serial port, and the S1 is the second interface port. These two ports are actually listed on the back of the router as Serial 0 and Serial 1. We cover the DCE and DTE information later in this chapter.

Configuration Script Install

Router 1 is the 2513 router. Suppose that Router 1 has never been configured before. Once the IOS is loaded, when we connect to the router it will start up an initial configuration script. Let's examine the router boot-up in more detail.

```
System Bootstrap, Version 5.2(5), RELEASE SOFTWARE
Copyright (c) 1986-1994 by cisco Systems
2500 processor with 16384 Kbytes of main memory

F3: 6158796+80664+401524 at 0x3000060


                 Restricted Rights Legend

Use, duplication, or disclosure by the Government is
subject to restrictions as set forth in subparagraph
(c) of the Commercial Computer Software - Restricted
Rights clause at FAR sec. 52.227-19 and subparagraph
(c) (1) (ii) of the Rights in Technical Data and Computer
Software clause at DFARS sec. 252.227-7013.


                 cisco Systems, Inc.
                 170 West Tasman Drive
                 San Jose, California 95134-1706
```

The initial information displayed lists the bootstrap version that is used to start the boot routing. It lists the address of Cisco Systems, Inc., but notice the small "c" in Cisco. It also shows us the size of our main memory that is used to store the routing tables and the running configuration parameters. In this case, it is 16MB.

```
Cisco Internetwork Operating System Software
IOS (tm) 2500 Software (C2500-D-L), Version 11.3(3)T, RELEASE SOFTWARE (fc1)
Copyright (c) 1986-1998 by cisco Systems, Inc.
Compiled Mon 20-Apr-98 17:49 by ccai
Image text-base: 0x03033A04, data-base: 0x00001000
```

The router then continues to boot and displays the version of the IOS that this router is running. In this example, we can see that this router is running 11.3(3) T, and the actual image name itself is 2500-D-L.

```
cisco 2500 (68030) processor (revision D) with 16384K/2048K bytes of memory.
Processor board ID 02009581, with hardware revision 00000000
```

```
Bridging software.
X.25 software, Version 3.0.0.
1 Ethernet/IEEE 802.3 interface(s)
1 Token Ring/IEEE 802.5 interface(s)
2 Serial network interface(s)
32K bytes of non-volatile configuration memory.
8192K bytes of processor board System flash (Read ONLY)
```

The next part of the screen shows us the breakdown of our primary or main memory, and the shared memory. Shared memory is used for the packet buffering. Our example shows that again we have 16MB for primary memory and an additional 2MB in shared memory. This memory actually is built onto the system board.

The screen continues by showing us what interfaces this router supports, as well as any additional features of the IOS. This one has Bridging and X.25 that we can use. There is one Ethernet, one Token Ring, and two Serial interfaces.

Finally, it tells us the size of the NVRAM, which is 32K. Again, this NVRAM contains the startup configuration. The last line tells us the size of our FLASH memory, and here we have 8MB.

```
Notice: NVRAM invalid, possibly due to write erase.


          --- System Configuration Dialog ---

Would you like to enter the initial configuration dialog? [yes/no]:
```

The last couple of lines tell us that whatever is in NVRAM is invalid. This is true because this is the first time the router has been booted, and so the NVRAM is empty. Because it is, we are asked if we would like to enter an initial configuration script. Let's do just that.

```
Would you like to enter the initial configuration dialog? [yes/no]: y

At any point you may enter a question mark '?' for help.
Use ctrl-c to abort configuration dialog at any prompt.
Default settings are in square brackets '[]'.

First, would you like to see the current interface summary? [yes]: y

Any interface listed with OK? value "NO" does not have a valid
configuration
```

Interface	IP-Address	OK?	Method	Status	Protocol
Ethernet0	unassigned	NO	unset	up	up
Serial0	unassigned	NO	unset	up	down

```
Serial1          unassigned    NO  unset  down              down

TokenRing0       unassigned    NO  unset  reset             down
```

At this point, we were asked if we would like to view the current interface settings. We said "yes" and now we can see the four interfaces. None of them have TCP/IP addresses yet. We will do this in the next chapter. Under the OK method, they are listed as NO. This means they have not been set up yet. The status of the interfaces varies, but since Ethernet 0 and Serial 0 are both plugged in, their status is currently up. Finally, it lists the protocols either being up or down. We will examine this more later.

```
Configuring global parameters:

  Enter hostname [Router]: Router1

  The enable secret is a password used to protect access to
  privileged EXEC and configuration modes. This password, after
  entered, becomes encrypted in the configuration.
  Enter enable secret: secret

  The enable password is used when you do not specify an
  enable secret password, with some older software versions, and
  some boot images.
  Enter enable password: enable

  The virtual terminal password is used to protect
  access to the router over a network interface.
  Enter virtual terminal password: virtual
```

Next, we enter a name for the router. This is referred to as the host name, but this script also changes the prompt at the Command Line Interface (CLI) to the name of the router. Although the script doesn't check, spaces in the hostname are not allowed.

We were then asked to enter some passwords. There is a secret password that is needed to configure the router, an enable password in case the secret doesn't exist. Only one of the two is used, and secret always wins if it is configured. This is because the secret password is actually encrypted. There is also a virtual password that is required if we use Telnet to configure our router.

The next few steps ask us if we want to configure various settings. At this point, we will not do that.

```
Configure SNMP Network Management? [yes]: n
  Configure DECnet? [no]: n
  Configure AppleTalk? [no]: n
  Configure IPX? [no]: n
  Configure IP? [yes]: n
```

```
Configuring interface parameters:

Do you want to configure Ethernet0  interface? [yes]: n

Do you want to configure Serial0  interface? [yes]: n

Do you want to configure Serial1  interface? [yes]: n

Do you want to configure TokenRing0  interface? [yes]: n
```

The next section is the actual list of the configuration commands. As you can see, it is pure text. In fact, almost everything is clear text, including the enable and virtual passwords. Now we can see why the secret password is used if it is configured. At least the secret password is encrypted.

This configuration file is then written to the NVRAM where it is stored for use upon rebooting the router. Again, this is called the *startup configuration*. Additionally, the configuration file is stored in the primary memory and is being used while the router is running. This is the running configuration.

```
The following configuration command script was created:

hostname Router1
enable secret 5 $1$v79G$dPv3mIwgXtNpffY2ihMvW.
enable password enable
line vty 0 4
password virtual
no snmp-server
!
no decnet routing
no appletalk routing
no ipx routing
no ip routing
!
interface Ethernet0
shutdown
no ip address
!
interface Serial0
shutdown
no ip address
!
interface Serial1
shutdown
no ip address
!
interface TokenRing0
shutdown
no ip address
dialer-list 1 protocol ip permit
```

```
dialer-list 1 protocol ipx permit
!
end


[0] Go to the IOS command prompt without saving this config.
[1] Return back to the setup without saving this config.
[2] Save this configuration to nvram and exit.

Enter your selection [2]: 2
Building configuration...
Use the enabled mode 'configure' command to modify this
configuration.


Press RETURN to get started!
```

The script has been written to NVRAM and the router is now in operation. However, since we really haven't configured much of it yet, it isn't doing anything important. We will add functionality as we continue through the remaining chapters.

Let's go ahead and configure Router 2 the same way.

```
Would you like to enter the initial configuration dialog? [yes/no]: y

At any point you may enter a question mark '?' for help.
Use ctrl-c to abort configuration dialog at any prompt.
Default settings are in square brackets '[]'.

First, would you like to see the current interface summary? [yes]: y

Any interface listed with OK? value "NO" does not have a valid
configuration
```

Interface	IP-Address	OK?	Method	Status	Protocol
BRI0	unassigned	NO	unset	up	down
BRI0:1	unassigned	YES	unset	down	down
BRI0:2	unassigned	YES	unset	down	down
Ethernet0	unassigned	NO	unset	up	up
Serial0	unassigned	NO	unset	down	down
Serial1	unassigned	NO	unset	up	up

```
Configuring global parameters:

  Enter hostname [Router]: Router2

  The enable secret is a password used to protect access to
  privileged EXEC and configuration modes. This password, after
  entered, becomes encrypted in the configuration.
  Enter enable secret: secret

  The enable password is used when you do not specify an
  enable secret password, with some older software versions, and
  some boot images.
  Enter enable password: enable

  The virtual terminal password is used to protect
  access to the router over a network interface.
  Enter virtual terminal password: virtual
  Configure SNMP Network Management? [yes]: n
  Configure DECnet? [no]: n
  Configure AppleTalk? [no]: n
  Configure IPX? [no]: n
  Configure IP? [yes]: n

  BRI interface needs isdn switch-type to be configured
  Valid switch types are :
    [0]  none.........Only if you don't want to configure BRI.
    [1]  basic-1tr6....1TR6 switch type for Germany
    [2]  basic-5ess....AT&T 5ESS switch type for the US/Canada
    [3]  basic-dms100..Northern DMS-100 switch type for US/Canada
    [4]  basic-net3....NET3 switch type for UK and Europe
    [5]  basic-ni......National ISDN switch type
  [6]  basic-ts013...TS013 switch type for Australia
  [7]  ntt..........NTT switch type for Japan
  [8]  vn3..........VN3 and VN4 switch types for France
  Choose ISDN BRI Switch Type [2]: 0

Configuring interface parameters:

Do you want to configure BRI0 (BRI d-channel) interface? [yes]: n

Do you want to configure Ethernet0  interface? [yes]: n

Do you want to configure Serial0  interface? [yes]: n

Do you want to configure Serial1  interface? [yes]: n

The following configuration command script was created:

hostname Router2
enable secret 5 $1$60Xg$upCs8Esi49tXDFSsPRt0L.
enable password enable
```

```
line vty 0 4
password virtual
no snmp-server
!
no decnet routing
no appletalk routing
no ipx routing
no ip routing
isdn switch-type  none
!
interface BRI0
shutdown
no ip address
!
interface Ethernet0
shutdown
no ip address
!
interface Serial0
shutdown
no ip address
!
interface Serial1
shutdown
no ip address
dialer-list 1 protocol ip permit
dialer-list 1 protocol ipx permit
!
end


[0] Go to the IOS command prompt without saving this config.
[1] Return back to the setup without saving this config.
[2] Save this configuration to nvram and exit.

Enter your selection [2]: 2
Building configuration...
Use the enabled mode 'configure' command to modify this
configuration.


Press RETURN to get started!
```

This script configuration is slightly different because Router 2 is a 2503 with an ISDN interface. Some of the commands are for the ISDN port configuration.

Manual Configuration Using CLI

We have one more router to configure, but this time we are going to do it manually using the Command Line Interface (CLI). This is the normal way we would configure our routers once they are in operation.

```
Would you like to enter the initial configuration dialog? [yes]:n
```

```
Press RETURN to get started!
```

After stopping the configuration script, the router prompts us to press Return, after which we see the following:

```
Router>
```

At this point, we are in user mode. The router actually interprets any commands that we enter into something that the router can use. This interpreter is referred to as the EXEC. Now that we actually have a prompt, we can perform some configurations. But, what can we do? In order to answer that, we need to understand the help system. To access help, we use the ? character.

```
Router>?
Exec commands:
  access-enable    Create a temporary Access-List entry
  clear            Reset functions
  connect          Open a terminal connection
  disable          Turn off privileged commands
  disconnect       Disconnect an existing network connection
  enable           Turn on privileged commands
  exit             Exit from the EXEC
  help             Description of the interactive help system
  lock             Lock the terminal
  login            Log in as a particular user
  logout           Exit from the EXEC
  mrinfo           Request neighbor and version information from a multicast
                   router
  mstat            Show statistics after multiple multicast traceroutes
  mtrace           Trace reverse multicast path from destination to source
  name-connection  Name an existing network connection
  pad              Open a X.29 PAD connection
  ping             Send echo messages
  ppp              Start IETF Point-to-Point Protocol (PPP)
  resume           Resume an active network connection
  rlogin           Open an rlogin connection
   --More-- <space>
  show             Show running system information
  slip             Start Serial-line IP (SLIP)
  systat           Display information about terminal lines
  telnet           Open a telnet connection
  terminal         Set terminal line parameters
  traceroute       Trace route to destination
  tunnel           Open a tunnel connection
  where            List active connections
  x3               Set X.3 parameters on PAD

Router>
```

There are three things worth mentioning at this point:

- When we hit the ?, the command was interpreted immediately and a list of all the available commands returned.
- During a long list such as this one, we may see the line **-- More --**. This is a page separator so that the list of commands will not scroll off before we see it. By pressing the Enter key at this point, it will scroll one more line. Instead, if we press the space bar, it will scroll an entire page. Finally, if we don't need to see the rest of the pages, hitting q will quit the output.
- The commands that are shown above are only used in this user mode. There are other modes as we configure the router, and the commands will change. Also, not all commands are actually listed here. There may be others, and the only way to find out is to read the documentation or ask another person who configures routers.

Now that we understand the use of the help system, we can examine it in more detail. What is the difference between the following commands?

```
Router>sh?
show

Router>sh ?
  clock          Display the system clock
  history        Display the session command history
  hosts          IP domain-name, lookup style, nameservers, and host table
  location       Display the system location
  modemcap       Show Modem Capabilities database
  ppp            PPP parameters and statistics
  rmon           rmon statistics
  sessions       Information about Telnet connections
  snmp           snmp statistics
  tacacs         Shows tacacs+ server statistics
  terminal       Display terminal configuration parameters
  traffic-shape  traffic rate shaping configuration
  users          Display information about terminal lines
  version        System hardware and software status
```

The first command, **sh?**, listed all the commands that start with the letters sh. The second command, **sh ?**, listed the next argument for the show command.

This brings up another interesting point about the CLI. These commands that we are entering only have to have enough characters to distinguish the command we want from another command. In the preceding example, we did not need to type the entire word **show** because there are no other commands that begin with sh at this level of EXEC.

Let's examine a couple of the show commands because some of them are the most used commands you will use configuring routers.

```
Router>show clock
*08:30:15.997 UTC Mon Mar 1 1993
```

```
Router>show users
    Line     User     Host(s)              Idle Location
*   0 con 0           idle                 0

Router>show version
Cisco Internetwork Operating System Software
IOS (tm) 2500 Software (C2500-I-L), Version 11.2(3)P, SHARED PLATFORM, RELEASE
SOFTWARE (fc1)
Copyright (c) 1986-1996 by cisco Systems, Inc.
Compiled Tue 31-Dec-96 16:18 by tamb
Image text-base: 0x03021B38, data-base: 0x00001000

ROM: System Bootstrap, Version 5.2(8a), RELEASE SOFTWARE
ROM: 3000 Bootstrap Software (IGS-RXBOOT), Version 10.2(8a), RELEASE SOFTWARE
(fc1)

Router uptime is 8 hours, 31 minutes
System restarted by reload
System image file is "flash:80135403.bin", booted via flash

cisco 2500 (68030) processor (revision L) with 2048K/2048K bytes of memory.
Processor board ID 03848080, with hardware revision 00000000
Bridging software.
X.25 software, Version 2.0, NET2, BFE and GOSIP compliant.
1 Ethernet/IEEE 802.3 interface(s)
2 Serial network interface(s)
32K bytes of non-volatile configuration memory.
8192K bytes of processor board System flash (Read ONLY)

Configuration register is 0x2102

Router>show aliases
Exec mode aliases:
    h                help
    lo               logout
    p                ping
    r                resume
    s                show
    u                undebug
    un               undebug
    w                where

Router>
```

The first command shows us the date and time in reference to the UTC (Coordinated Universal Time). The second command shows us if the console port is active, and if there are any users connected to the router via Telnet. The third command shows us the same basic information as we see when the router is rebooted. The final one is an example of a command that is not listed in the help. This command shows the default (alias) commands to use for the chosen letters.

If at any time you forget how to use the ? character, typing **h** at the router prompt will provide the directions.

If we go back and examine the list of commands, we don't see any commands to actually configure the router. Remember, this is the user mode, so we don't want to expose any of this to a user who stumbles upon our router. Later, we will examine a way to put up a password just for logging in to the router.

Now it's time to start configuring the router. To do this, we need to elevate our status to the next level, called *privileged mode*. The command we want is **enable**.

```
Router>enable
Router#
```

Notice the router prompt has changed. The # sign indicates that we are now in privileged mode. We could also have just typed **en** instead of the entire word **enable**. Again, all we have to type is enough of the command to differentiate it from any other command. At this point, there was no password prompt, so anyone could alter this router. To get back to user mode, we would just use the command **disable** and it would take us back.

Now that we are in privileged mode, we can modify the router. Let's examine the commands.

```
Router#?
Exec commands:
  access-enable     Create a temporary Access-List entry
  access-template   Create a temporary Access-List entry
  bfe               For manual emergency modes setting
  clear             Reset functions
  clock             Manage the system clock
  configure         Enter configuration mode
  connect           Open a terminal connection
  copy              Copy configuration or image data
  debug             Debugging functions (see also 'undebug')
  disable           Turn off privileged commands
  disconnect        Disconnect an existing network connection
  enable            Turn on privileged commands
  erase             Erase flash or configuration memory
  exit              Exit from the EXEC
  help              Description of the interactive help system
  lock              Lock the terminal
  login             Log in as a particular user
  logout            Exit from the EXEC
  mbranch           Trace multicast route down tree branch
  mrbranch          Trace reverse multicast route up tree branch
  mrinfo            Request neighbor and version information from
                    a multicast router
```

```
--More--<space>
  mstat              Show statistics after multiple multicast
                     traceroutes
  mtrace             Trace reverse multicast path from destination
                     to source
  name-connection    Name an existing network connection
  no                 Disable debugging functions
  pad                Open a X.29 PAD connection
  ping               Send echo messages
  ppp                Start IETF Point-to-Point Protocol (PPP)
  reload             Halt and perform a cold restart
  resume             Resume an active network connection
  rlogin             Open an rlogin connection
  rsh                Execute a remote command
  send               Send a message to other tty lines
  setup              Run the SETUP command facility
  show               Show running system information
  slip               Start Serial-line IP (SLIP)
  start-chat         Start a chat-script on a line
  systat             Display information about terminal lines
  telnet             Open a telnet connection
  terminal           Set terminal line parameters
  test               Test subsystems, memory, and interfaces
  traceroute         Trace route to destination
  tunnel             Open a tunnel connection
--More--<space>
  undebug            Disable debugging functions (see also 'debug')
    verify             Verify checksum of a Flash file
    where              List active connections
    write              Write running configuration to memory,
                       network, or terminal
  x3                 Set X.3 parameters on PAD

Router#
```

As we can see, there are many more commands at this level. In fact, there are more commands here than we really need for this first test. We will examine only a few of the available commands, but if we had a question on a command, the Cisco documentation would tell us what it's used for. It's time for our first configuration change. We will change the clock to reflect the current date and time.

```
Router#cl ?
% Ambiguous command:   "cl "
```

Hey, we encountered our first problem. We wanted to see what the parameters were for the clock command, but instead we received an "Ambiguous command" error message. This occurs because there is more than one command that starts with cl.

```
Router#cl?
clear   clock
```

As we can see here, clear is a command also. We need to differentiate three letters in this case. We will make it easy and just use the full command this time.

```
Router#clock ?
  set   Set the time and date
```

```
Router#clock set ?
  hh:mm:ss   Current Time
```

```
Router#clock set 04:24:00 ?
  <1-31>  Day of the month
  MONTH   Month of the year
```

```
Router#clock set 04:24:00 28 ?
  MONTH   Month of the year
```

```
Router#clock set 04:24:00 28 June ?
  <1993-2035>   Year
```

```
Router#clock set 04:24:00 28 June 1999 ?
  <cr>
```

```
Router#clock set 04:24:00 28 June 1999
```

```
Router#show clock
04:24:37.391 UTC Mon Jun 28 1999
Router#
```

We successfully set the clock by using the ? command each step of the way until we saw that there were no arguments left. This was indicated by the <cr> parameter, which stands for carriage return, or Enter. We performed the show clock command, and sure enough, we did set the clock!

We should change our router prompt so that we know at any time which router we are currently configuring. It just so happens that the command we want to use is the hostname command.

```
Router#hostname ?
% Unrecognized command
```

Our second problem has just occurred! It appears that the hostname command is not available at this stage. In reality, in order to change most of the important router configurations, we need to switch to a configuration mode. The privileged mode is not enough for us. To change to the configuration mode, we need to issue the command **configuration**, or just enough letters to differentiate it from the other commands. In this case, **conf** is enough, but **config** is more readable.

```
Router#config ?
  memory              Configure from NV memory
  network             Configure from a TFTP network host
  overwrite-network   Overwrite NV memory from TFTP network host
  terminal            Configure from the terminal
  <cr>
```

There are many options that can be configured, but we are interested in the terminal configuration. This allows us to make changes directly by using the CLI instead of loading the changes from a file.

```
Router#config term
Enter configuration commands, one per line.   End with CNTL/Z.
Router(config)#
```

Again, notice the change in the router prompt. This time we can see we are in a configuration mode. Actually, this is the global configuration mode. All commands that apply to the router as a whole are entered here. Later, we will enter commands that are specific to each interface.

To leave configuration mode, we just press the Ctrl and Z keys at the same time. This is a great time to mention one of the annoying things about the CLI. When we type ^Z to exit the global configuration, Cisco will send us a message stating that the router has just been configured. For example:

```
Router(config)#^Z
Router#
%SYS-5-CONFIG_I: Configured from console by console
```

This in itself is not annoying, but the status message can come after we are already entering the next command. It appears as if our typing has been interrupted. But the truth is the status message does not have any effect on our typing, so ignore it. If it really bothers us, we can always type ^r to refresh the display.

There are some additional features that are associated with the editing. For instance, there is a history buffer that lists all the commands we have entered in this session.

```
Router#show history
  show clock
  show users
  show version
  show aliases
  enable
  clock set 04:24:00 28 June 1999
  show clock
  config term
  show history
Router#
```

Here we can see the list of commands that we have typed since we started this chapter. There are a couple of hot keys that we can use for working with the history buffer and the command line:

- Ctrl-p or Up Arrow—Repeat previous command in buffer
- Ctrl-n or Down Arrow—Repeat most recent command
- Ctrl-a—Move to the beginning of the command line
- Ctrl-e—Move to the end of the command line

In addition, there are some enhanced editing features that we can use. For instance, when we are typing in a command line and the line exceeds 78 characters for a standard HyperTerm session, the command will scroll to the left 10 characters so that we can keep working on the same line. The following line is the entire line typed.

```
Router(config)#access-list 100 permit ip 192.168.0.0 0.0.255.255
192.168.2.0 0.0.0.255 log
```

However, when we hit the address 192.168.2.0, the line shifts left 10 characters and displays like this:

```
Router(config)#$t ip 192.168.0.0 0.0.255.255 192.168.2.0 0.0.0.255
```

Notice the $ character after the # sign. This tells us that we are in a long string and that it has shifted to the left.

If we really didn't like this feature, we could turn it off by using the **terminal no editing** command. This would cause the command line to wrap to the next line. To turn it back on, we would use the command **terminal editing**.

There is one additional feature that we have with the editing of commands. Using the Tab key, the EXEC will write the entire command word out in full. For instance, the command access-list can be abbreviated to ac but, if after typing the characters ac and then pressing the Tab key, the EXEC will fill the line out to include access-list.

Now that we have covered the basics of using the router configuration commands, we need to change a couple of things. Establishing passwords would be a good first choice, so let's do that. First, enter global configuration mode.

```
Router#config term
Enter configuration commands, one per line.  End with CNTL/Z.
Router(config)#
```

Let's try changing the hostname again. Enter configuration mode first.

```
Router#config term
Enter configuration commands, one per line.  End with CNTL/Z.
Router(config)#hostname ?
  WORD  This system's network name
```

```
Router(config)#hostname Router3
Router3(config)#
```

Notice the prompt changed as well. We could actually have a different prompt than our hostname for the router using the **prompt** command, but this works for us. It is an easy way to remember what router we are working on. This is especially beneficial when we telnet to multiple routers at the same time.

Now that we are in global configuration mode, we can set passwords. The first password we should set is the encrypted password that we saw earlier in the chapter. To do this, we use the following command to set the password to *cisco*.

```
Router3(config)#enable secret cisco
Router3(config)#
```

We can test this by leaving both configuration mode and privileged mode. The easiest way is to use the **exit** command, which completely logs us off the router. Next, we can try entering privileged mode again.

```
Router3(config)#^Z
Router3#exit

Router con0 is now available

Press RETURN to get started.
<enter>

Router3>enable
Password:cisco
Router3#
```

The password *cisco* would not show up on the terminal screen. It is shown here just for our benefit. We can see that we now have to know the password in order to configure our router.

There are other passwords that we can set as well. Remember that during the configuration script we were also asked for the enable password. This password is used for older IOS images that did not support the encrypted password. If the encrypted password is used, the enable password will not be used. We can verify this by doing the following:

```
Router3(config)#enable password cisco2
Router3(config)#^Z
Router3#exit

Router3 con0 is now available

Press RETURN to get started.
<enter>

Router3>enable
```

```
Password:cisco2
Password:cisco
Router3#
```

We can see that it did not allow us to enter the password cisco2 because the encrypted password, cisco, is in effect.

Additional passwords include passwords for using Telnet and the Auxiliary port for modem access. Also, we may want a password for just logging in to the router. The three methods are displayed next.

```
Router3#config term
Enter configuration commands, one per line.  End with CNTL/Z.
Router3(config)#line vty 0 4
Router3(config-line)#login
Router3(config-line)#password virtual
Router3(config-line)#^Z
Router3#


Router3#config term
Enter configuration commands, one per line.  End with CNTL/Z.
Router3(config)#line aux 0
Router3(config-line)#login
Router3(config-line)#password aux
Router3(config-line)#^Z


Router3#config term
Enter configuration commands, one per line.  End with CNTL/Z.
Router3(config)#line con 0
Router3(config)#login
Router3(config-line)#password console
Router3(config-line)#^Z
```

While we are on the subject of using passwords for logging in to a router, it may also be nice to display a login message. This can be accomplished through the **banner** command.

```
Router3(config)#banner ?
  LINE      c banner-text c, where 'c' is a delimiting character
  exec      Set EXEC process creation banner
  incoming  Set incoming terminal line banner
  login     Set login banner
  motd      Set Message of the Day banner

Router3(config)#banner motd ?
  LINE  c banner-text c, where 'c' is a delimiting character

Router3(config)#banner motd #
Enter TEXT message.  End with the character '#'.
You have accessed Router 3 and this is the MOTD banner
#
```

The preceding commands have created an MOTD (Message Of The Day) banner that users will see when logging in to the router. The format of the **banner** command requires a delimiter character that can be anything we want. When we type our message, we can keep typing until we enter the delimiter character, at which point the command finishes. In fact, we can enter the entire command in a single line like this:

```
Router3(config)#banner motd $ This is on router 3 $
```

The motd parameter could be replaced with login, or in addition to the motd banner, we could have a second banner with the **banner login** command. Notice the different delimiter character. This time we used the $ character.

Let's test out our banner and our console password.

```
Router3 con0 is now available

Press RETURN to get started.
<enter>

You have accessed Router 3 and this is the MOTD banner

User Access Verification

Password: console
Router3>
```

As we can see, the motd banner displayed before we logged in. This banner would display even if we had used Telnet to access the router. When we pressed the Enter key to log in, we were asked to enter a password, and in this case, it was *console*.

We have set up security now, but what if we don't want to use these passwords anymore? Simply reissue the command and the password will be changed. However, if we want to turn off the passwords, we would use the following method:

```
Router3(config)#line con 0
Router3(config-line)#login
Router3(config-line)#no password
Router3(config-line)#^Z
```

In fact, most commands that we want to perform the opposite with, we just put the word "no" before the command.

At this point, we have configured this router like the other two. Although this process has been a little more involved, some of it was because we examined other commands. However, when we need to do some real configurations on the router, the configuration script won't be enough. Using the CLI becomes the only alternative, and the quickest once we learn the commands and the command structure.

Connecting Routers to Each Other

In a normal environment, we would be connecting our routers to a device called a CSU/DSU (Channel Service Units/Data Service Units). This CSU/DSU would then connect to the Central Office (CO) through the WAN signal carrier. The CO is a hub of equipment that links to other COs. These other offices then distribute the WAN signal to other companies. The CSU/DSU is needed because it provides a clock so that the signal can maintain synchronization between end nodes. Incidentally, the CSU/DSU is stored on the customer's site and looks like a medium-sized modem. The equipment stored on the customer's site is typically the responsibility of the customer and is commonly referred to as Customer Premise Equipment, or CPE.

In our network that we are using as a test lab, we do not have the luxury of using CSU/DSUs and T1 links. Instead, we can simulate the link using a special cable called a DCE (Data Communication Equipment) cable. This cable connects to the standard V.35 DTE (Data Terminal Equipment) cable that comes with the Cisco router.

As shown in Figure 5–9, we can see that Router 1 and Router 3 have a DCE cable connected to their serial ports. Router 2 is directly connected to each of the other routers and uses the DTE cable to complete the connection. In order for communications to take place, we must tell the serial interfaces on Routers 1 and 3 that they are DCE cables.

This leads to a new form of the configuration command. In global configuration, we make changes for the entire router. However, there are certain commands that only pertain to certain interfaces. In order to change the interface, we need to give the command **interface** and the name of the interface we wish to configure. For example, the following commands configure Router 1's serial 0 interface.

```
Router1(config)#interface serial 0
Router1(config-if)#clock rate 56000
Router1(config-if)#no shutdown
Router1(config-if)#^Z
```

In this example, we entered the serial 0 configuration mode and specified a clock rate of 56000 bps. This tells the router that it needs to set up a clocking signal for a 56K leased line.

In addition, we issued the command **no shutdown**, which turns the interface on. This is known as the *administrative state*. Although the administrative state is turned on, until both routers are completely configured correctly, the link will not come up. We can also turn the interface administratively down by using the command **shutdown**.

There are instances where we need to further define which interface we are working with. For example, the Cisco 7000 series routers use interface cards called VIPs (Versatile Interface Processor). These cards can have multiple slots for port adapters, and each adapter can have multiple interfaces.

This allows us to greatly expand the port density of the router. However, when choosing the port we want to work with, it is not enough to just identify the port and number like we have been doing. We need to choose the VIP/Port/Interface. For example, to use the VIP card in the first slot with the second port and the third Ethernet interface on that port, we would issue the command **interface ethernet 0/1/2**. Remember that all interfaces start numbering at zero.

We need to issue the same commands on Router 3. At this point, we are assuming that we will have a 56K link between them both. If it was something else, like a 128K link, we can use the **clock rate ?** command to choose an appropriate number for the bps.

```
Router3(config)#int s0
Router3(config-if)#description 56K WAN link between Router2 and 3
Router3(config-if)#clock rate 56000
Router3(config-if)#no shut
Router3(config-if)#^Z
```

In the previous example, we abbreviated the commands for faster entry. We also introduced a new command. The **description** command is used to assign some type of description to the interfaces. We could use it to remember the circuit numbers or other specific interface configuration information, or we could use it just to remind us what the general purpose of the interface is.

What if we don't remember which cable is connected to the interface? We can use the command **show controller serial x** to list the details of the serial *x* port.

```
Router3>show controller serial 1
HD unit 1, idb = 0x97F28, driver structure at 0x9BB68
buffer size 1524   HD unit 1, V.35 DCE cable
cpb = 0x22, eda = 0x3140, cda = 0x3000
RX ring with 16 entries at 0x223000
00 bd_ptr=0x3000 pak=0x09E6E4 ds=0x22CDB0 status=80 pak_size=0
01 bd_ptr=0x3014 pak=0x09E518 ds=0x22C6F8 status=80 pak_size=0
02 bd_ptr=0x3028 pak=0x09E34C ds=0x22C040 status=80 pak_size=0
03 bd_ptr=0x303C pak=0x09E180 ds=0x22B988 status=80 pak_size=0
04 bd_ptr=0x3050 pak=0x09DFB4 ds=0x22B2D0 status=80 pak_size=0
05 bd_ptr=0x3064 pak=0x09DDE8 ds=0x22AC18 status=80 pak_size=0
06 bd_ptr=0x3078 pak=0x09DC1C ds=0x22A560 status=80 pak_size=0
07 bd_ptr=0x308C pak=0x09DA50 ds=0x229EA8 status=80 pak_size=0
08 bd_ptr=0x30A0 pak=0x09D884 ds=0x2297F0 status=80 pak_size=0
09 bd_ptr=0x30B4 pak=0x09D6B8 ds=0x229138 status=80 pak_size=0
10 bd_ptr=0x30C8 pak=0x09D4EC ds=0x228A80 status=80 pak_size=0
11 bd_ptr=0x30DC pak=0x09D320 ds=0x2283C8 status=80 pak_size=0
12 bd_ptr=0x30F0 pak=0x09D154 ds=0x227D10 status=80 pak_size=0
13 bd_ptr=0x3104 pak=0x09CF88 ds=0x227658 status=80 pak_size=0
14 bd_ptr=0x3118 pak=0x09CDBC ds=0x226FA0 status=80 pak_size=0
15 bd_ptr=0x312C pak=0x09CBF0 ds=0x2268E8 status=80 pak_size=0
```

```
16 bd_ptr=0x3140 pak=0x09CA24 ds=0x226230 status=80 pak_size=0
cpb = 0x22, eda = 0x3800, cda = 0x3800
TX ring with 2 entries at 0x223800
00 bd_ptr=0x3800 pak=0x000000 ds=0x000000 status=80 pak_size=0
01 bd_ptr=0x3814 pak=0x000000 ds=0x000000 status=80 pak_size=0
02 bd_ptr=0x3828 pak=0x000000 ds=0x000000 status=80 pak_size=0
0 missed datagrams, 0 overruns
0 bad datagram encapsulations, 0 memory errors
0 transmitter underruns
0 residual bit errors

Router3>
```

Notice on the second line that it shows that a DCE cable has been detected. Using the command **show interface serial x** can list more information, such as if the serial interface is up and running. Any of the interface commands can also be used with Ethernet, Token Ring, ISDN, and so forth.

```
Router3>show interface serial 1
Serial1 is administratively down, line protocol is down
  Hardware is HD64570
  MTU 1500 bytes, BW 1544 Kbit, DLY 20000 usec, rely 255/255,
load 1/255
  Encapsulation HDLC, loopback not set, keepalive set (10 sec)
  Last input never, output never, output hang never
  Last clearing of "show interface" counters never
  Input queue: 0/75/0 (size/max/drops); Total output drops: 0
  Queueing strategy: weighted fair
  Output queue: 0/64/0 (size/threshold/drops)
    Conversations  0/0 (active/max active)
    Reserved Conversations 0/0 (allocated/max allocated)
  5 minute input rate 0 bits/sec, 0 packets/sec
  5 minute output rate 0 bits/sec, 0 packets/sec
    0 packets input, 0 bytes, 0 no buffer
    Received 0 broadcasts, 0 runts, 0 giants
    0 input errors, 0 CRC, 0 frame, 0 overrun, 0 ignored, 0 abort
    0 packets output, 0 bytes, 0 underruns
    0 output errors, 0 collisions, 22 interface resets
    0 output buffer failures, 0 output buffers swapped out
    0 carrier transitions
    DCD=down  DSR=down  DTR=down  RTS=down  CTS=down
Router3>
```

At this point, we have successfully configured each of our routers. However, if we examine the end of the configuration script, there is something worth noting there. A configuration script was generated and we were prompted to save it to NVRAM. However, when we do this configuration manually, we are modifying the running configuration. We can view this configuration information by running the command **show running-config**, or **show run** for short.

```
Router3#show run
Building configuration...

Current configuration:
!
! Last configuration change at 06:09:09 UTC Mon Jun 28 1999
!
version 11.2
!
hostname Router3
!
enable secret 5 $1$HqSP$wgqrQSvFqI00v.kX9KsYI/
enable password cisco2
!
!
interface Ethernet0
 ip address 192.168.3.254 255.255.255.0
!
interface Serial0
 description 56K WAN link between Router 2 and 3
 clockrate 56000
!
interface Serial1
 no ip address
 shutdown
!
no ip classless
access-list 100 permit ipinip 192.168.0.0 0.0.255.255 192.168.2.0 0.0.0.255
banner motd ^C
You have accessed Router 3 and this is the MOTD banner
^C
!
line con 0
 login
line aux 0
 password aux
 login
line vty 0 4
 password virtual
 login
!

end
```

We can see the different information that we configured is actually in the running configuration. However, it has not been saved to NVRAM. As a side note, we can see the passwords stored in the configuration file. Because of this, the prior command and the next command cannot be executed in user mode. Again, we can verify this by using the command **show startup-config**, or **show start**.

```
Router3#show start
%% Non-volatile configuration memory has not been set up
```

In order to save the changes so that they will persist across reboots, we will use the **copy** command. The format of the copy command is **copy source destination**. Here we want to copy the running configuration to the startup configuration.

```
Router3#copy run start
Building configuration...
[OK]
Router3#show start
Using 700 out of 32762 bytes
!
! Last configuration change at 06:09:09 UTC Mon Jun 28 1999
! NVRAM config last updated at 06:44:18 UTC Mon Jun 28 1999
!
version 11.2
!
hostname Router3
!
enable secret 5 $1$HqSP$wgqrQSvFqI00v.kX9KsYI/
enable password cisco2
!
!
interface Ethernet0
 ip address 192.168.3.254 255.255.255.0
!
interface Serial0
 description 56K WAN link between Router 2 and 3
 no ip address
 clockrate 56000
!
interface Serial1
 no ip address
 shutdown
!
no ip classless
access-list 100 permit ipinip 192.168.0.0 0.0.255.255 192.168.2.0 0.0.0.255
banner motd ^C
You have accessed Router 3 and this is the MOTD banner
^C
!
line con 0
 login
line aux 0
 password aux
 login
line vty 0 4
 password virtual
```

```
 login
 !
end

Router3#
```

This time, we can see the configuration stored in NVRAM. Now we can safely power off our router, and when we turn it back on, the router will configure itself safely. This is perhaps the most important command to remember. If we just spent the last 30 minutes configuring our router, we do not want to forget this command. If we do, we will be spending another 30 minutes the next time we reboot or lose power to the router.

In the next chapter we will learn about TCP/IP addresses and then configure our routers to do some actual work.

Summary

Cisco makes many models of routers for small businesses up to enterprise networks. The most common model is the 2500 series router, and there are various models to adapt to the needs of a business. Configuring the router can be accomplished through Telnet, the auxiliary port using a modem, or through the console port. To configure the router when the NVRAM is empty requires the console connection. A router can be configured using the configuration script that executes upon logging in to the router for the first time, or it can be done manually through the Command Line Interface (CLI). When the configuration is done through the CLI, it is imperative to remember to write the configuration back to the NVRAM for persistence across reboots.

Scenario Lab 5.1

The network diagram is just about finished. The requirements for Building 1 include two separate segments for the internal LAN. These segments are both Ethernet 10BaseT. There is a connection to the Internet using a 56KB leased line, but there needs to be a way to upgrade this connection in the future. Building 2 has similar design constraints. Again, both networks are Ethernet, and there is a connection to the Internet. Finally, both remote sales sites need a connection to the buildings, and this will be accomplished through a frame relay connection. The remote sites will then be able to connect to the Internet through the Minneapolis network. The Project Manager would like to know what Cisco routers you would recommend for these sites. As always, cost is an issue. Deciding to go with the Cisco 2500 series routers, which model or models would you place into the various sites (see Figure 5-10)?

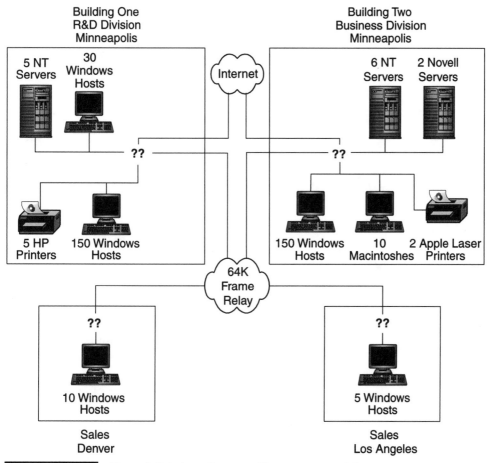

FIGURE 5–10 Network Solutions diagram without router models

Practice Lab 5.1

Using Figure 5–11, perform the following steps. If you need help, re-read the chapter for the correct answers.

If you have already configured your router before this, at the privileged mode prompt, type **erase start**, confirm, and then reboot the router.

- Using the initial configuration script, set up Router 1 with the following:
  - Hostname: Router1
  - Secret password: secret
  - Enable password: enable
  - Virtual password: virtual

  Do not configure any other options at this time.

- Using the CLI, change the secret password to cisco.
- Enable an motd banner.
- Examine the Serial port to determine if the DCE cable has been connected. Use the command **show controller**.
- Set up serial 0 with a clock rate of 56 Kbps.
- Save your configuration.
- Perform steps 1–6 with Router 2, but this time do not use the configuration script. Use privileged mode commands for each step.

- Save your configuration.
- Examine some of the other commands that have been shown in this chapter.

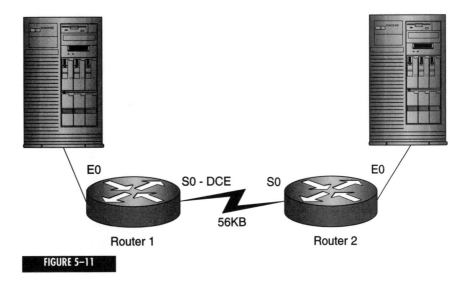

FIGURE 5–11

Practice Lab 5.2

Use the CLI to configure each of the routers in Figure 5–12. Include the following:

- Passwords for privileged and user mode.
- DCE settings for 56 Kbps and 512 Kbps.
- Hostnames for each router.
- Set the time for each router.
- Examine the running configuration as you make changes.
- Examine the amount of Main/Shared memory.
- Examine the interface details.

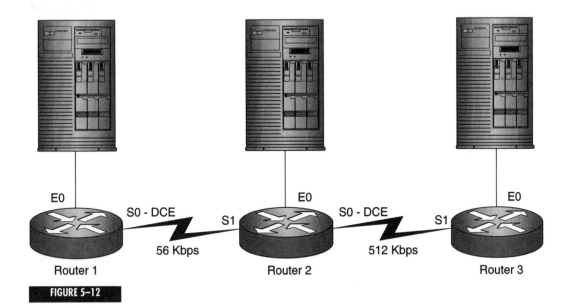

FIGURE 5-12

Exam Objective Checklist

By working through this chapter, you should have sufficient knowledge to answer these exam objectives:

- Log in to a router in both user and privileged modes.
- Use the context-sensitive help facility.
- Use the command history and editing features.
- Examine router elements (RAM, ROM, CDP, show).
- Manage configuration files from the privileged exec mode.
- Control router passwords, identification, and banner.

Practice Questions

1. Which method would you use to find all the commands that start with "cl"?

    a. Help cl
    b. Help cl?
    c. cl ?
    d. cl?

2. What command causes us to exit privileged mode back to user mode?

    a. User mode
    b. exit
    c. disable
    d. user

3. What ports can a Cisco 2500 series router have? (Choose all that apply)

    a. Ethernet
    b. ISDN
    c. Token Ring
    d. ATM
    e. 10/100 switch
    f. Serial

4. A user can run any number of commands at the user mode. Which command must be run in privileged mode?

    a. Show version
    b. Show startup-config
    c. Show users
    d. Show interface

5. The size of the NVRAM is _____?

    a. 16KB
    b. 32KB
    c. 16MB
    d. 32MB

6. Which command will turn on a banner that users will see when logging in?

    a. Banner Welcome to Router 3
    b. Banner #Welcome to Router 3#
    c. Banner motd Welcome to Router 3
    d. Banner motd %Welcome to Router 3%

7. What are some of the features that the IOS software can have? (Choose all that apply)

    a. Firewall
    b. Encryption
    c. TCP/IP
    d. IBM Connectivity
    e. AppleTalk
    f. IPX/SPX

8. Which commands will require a password when trying to enter privileged mode? (Pick two)

    a. Enable password cisco
    b. Enable cisco password
    c. Enable cisco secret
    d. Enable secret cisco

9. What command will enter privileged mode?

    a. Press the Enter key
    b. privileged
    c. privilege
    d. enable

10. What keystroke takes you to the end of the line?

    a. Ctrl-A
    b. Ctrl-N
    c. Ctrl-U
    d. Ctrl-E

11. What action does the command banner motd perform?

    a. Displays a message when a terminal server logs in
    b. Displays a message when entering privileged mode
    c. Displays a message when logging in
    d. Displays a message after entering user mode

12. Which command will save you hours of work by saving the configuration to NVRAM?

    a. Copy running configuration NVRAM
    b. Copy run NVRAM
    c. Copy run to start
    d. Copy run start

13. What causes an ambiguous command message?

    a. The command entered does not contain enough parameter information.
    b. The command entered does not have enough characters to differentiate it from another command.
    c. The command entered does not exist.
    d. The command entered cannot be used in the current EXEC mode.

14. When using a DCE cable to emulate a WAN, what command must you use?

    a. Clock rate 56000
    b. Bandwidth 56000
    c. Clock rate 56
    d. Enable clock rate 56000

15. Which command allows you to modify the Ethernet port?

    a. Config ethernet 0
    b. Enable ethernet
    c. Interface ethernet 0
    d. Config terminal

16. Which command will show you the same information as the opening boot screen?

    a. Show boot
    b. Show version
    c. Show run
    d. Show start

17. Which set of commands will require a password to log in to the console?

    a. line con 0
            password console
    b. line user 0
            login
            password console
    c. line con 0
            login
            password console
    d. line aux 0
            login
            password console

18. Which command will administratively disable an interface?

    a. Shutdown
    b. Disable
    c. No disable
    d. No shutdown

TCP/IP Addressing

In This Chapter

- ◆ Binary Counting
- ◆ Classes
- ◆ Subnet Masking
- ◆ Planning
- ◆ Implementing

TCP/IP uses a binary method of addressing at the Network layer. Knowing how to convert binary to decimal, and vice versa, will greatly aid in your understanding of designing, configuring, and troubleshooting a network. Once the binary counting is understood, it is relatively easy to break a TCP/IP address down into its Network ID and Host ID using a subnet mask. Determining which class of address to use is crucial to designing and troubleshooting a network, and binary can aid us in this endeavor.

Binary Counting

All digital electronics use a binary method for communication. This communication can be from hardware to hardware, software to hardware, or software to software. Binary can be expressed using only two values: on or off, 0 or 1, positive voltage or negative voltage, true or false. TCP/IP addresses are based on a binary method of 0s and 1s.

In order to count in binary, it is important to remember that there are only two numbers: 0–1. In the decimal fashion that humans have used for generations, there are 10 numbers: 0–9. Since we are so used to these larger numbers, we usually represent binary by converting it to a decimal number. Here is how we can do it.

First, moving from right to left, create a chart that starts at the decimal number 1 and then double it 7 times. The chart should look like the following:

128	64	32	16	8	4	2	1

Now, given a binary number, place the number under the chart (right justified). Add up the decimal values of the chart in any column that you placed a binary 1. For example, convert the binary number 1101 to decimal.

128	64	32	16	8	4	2	1
				1	1	0	1

Add the numbers 8 + 4 + 1 to arrive at the final decimal result of **13**. That's all there is to converting from binary to decimal. For practice, let's try to convert the following binary numbers to decimal:

1. 10100   =
2. 111   =
3. 11001101 =
4. 10011011 =
5. 11111111 =

If we used our chart correctly, we should have come up with the decimal numbers of 20, 7, 205, 155, and 255.

What about converting decimal to binary? We just use the chart in reverse. Let's convert the number 58 to binary. First, create your chart again. We need to remember to start at the right-most column, and starting with the number 1, double each number after that.

128	64	32	16	8	4	2	1

1. Now, find the largest number that is equal to or less than the number you are converting to binary. The largest number in our example that is equal to or less than 58 is 32. Place a 1 under that space on the chart.

128	64	32	16	8	4	2	1
		1					

2. Next, subtract that number from the original decimal number. Subtracting 32 from 58 gives us 26.

Repeat steps 1 and 2 until we have a subtracted result of 0. The next largest number that is less than or equal to 26 is 16. Place a 1 in that position. Subtract 16 from 26 to get a result of 10. Place a 1 under the 8 in the chart. Subtract 8 from 10. The result is 2. Since 4 is greater than our current result of 2, place a 0 in the 4 column. Place a 1 under the 2, and then subtract 2 from 2 to get a result of 0. Now, fill in 0s for the remaining numbers in the column. In our example, place a 0 in the 1 column.

128	64	32	16	8	4	2	1
		1	1	1	0	1	0

Our final answer is 111010. Here are a couple of practice examples for us to try:

1. 76 =
2. 134 =
3. 240 =
4. 101 =
5. 255 =

If we used the chart correctly, we should have arrived at the numbers of 1001100, 10000110, 11110000, 1100101, and 11111111.

Notice that the largest number that we can convert in this chart is 255. What if we needed to convert a larger number, say 510? The answer is simple, just extend your chart out further.

256	128	64	32	16	8	4	2	1
1	1	1	1	1	1	1	1	0

One final concept to understanding binary is to learn to actually count in binary. If we start with the smallest binary number of 0 and add 1 to it, we get a result of 1. But what happens when we add 1 and 1? We can't use the number 2 because that is not a valid binary number. So instead we would do the same as if we were adding 5 and 5 in decimal. Place a 0 and carry the 1. The result of 1+1 is 10. Add 1 to this and we would have an answer of 11. Finally, 11 + 1 again results in two carries:

Carry	1	1	
		1	1
			1
Sum	1	0	0

If we examine Table 6.1, we should see the pattern emerging when we add 1 to each number. Getting comfortable with this pattern will help us in the future when we start subnetting.

TABLE 6.1	Binary counting charts		
Decimal	**Binary**	**Decimal**	**Binary**
1	1	11	1011
2	10	12	1100
3	11	13	1101
4	100	14	1110
5	101	15	1111
6	110	16	10000
7	111	17	10001
8	1000	18	10010
9	1001	19	10011
10	1010	20	10100

Addressing Principles

Now that we have a basic understanding of binary, we can move on to the more appropriate principles of addressing in a TCP/IP environment.

Recalling from a prior chapter, the Network layer uses logical addresses to differentiate hosts on a network. It is the Network layer that is responsible for determining if the host that we are trying to communicate with is on the same segment as ours, or on a different segment. If it is on a different segment, we must have a router configured to get the data to its final destination.

Each logical address in TCP/IP is 32 bits in length. Each bit can either be a 0 or a 1, meaning it is a binary address. The act of remembering a 32-bit address for each computer is beyond the capabilities of most of us mere humans. Luckily, there is a method of converting the binary address to a decimal address. For example, if we wanted to convert the 32-bit address 11001010110011000010111100101001 to a decimal number, we would break the 32 bits into smaller pieces. The 32 bits are broken into four 8-bit chunks, called *octets*. If we rewrite the address, now it would be 11001010.11001100.00101111.00101001. Notice that we separate the octets by the use of a period symbol. Now, using our chart from the prior section, we can convert each of the 8-bit octets to decimal to arrive at

202.204.47.41. This is referred to as the *dotted decimal notation*, and this number is much easier to remember than 32 1s and 0s.

At this point, we need to define the term *host*. A host is any device that has a network interface connected to a network. Examples of hosts include computers with NICs, routers, and network printers. If a computer has two NICs in it, we should consider that as two hosts.

One further point with defining a host is that every host in a connected TCP/IP environment must have a unique TCP/IP address. If two hosts had the same address, there would be confusion about which host we were actually trying to talk to. To help prevent this problem, most implementations of TCP/IP will display an error message telling you that it has detected a host with a duplicate TCP/IP address.

Every TCP/IP address can be broken down into two parts. The first part determines on which network the host resides. This is referred to as the *network ID*, or Net ID. This would be analogous to our zip code, which specifies the specific city in a specific state. The second part of the address refers to the actual host. This would be similar to the street address for our home.

By being able to identify both a Net ID and a Host ID, TCP/IP addresses are described as a *hierarchical addressing scheme*. This means that given a TCP/IP address, we can define where it exists in the world. This method will be examined in detail in the next section. The opposite of this would be a *flat address*. An example of a flat address would be the MAC address of the network card. How can we tell where 000030A456FE exists in the world? There is no mechanism for this.

Classes of Addresses

A class of a TCP/IP address helps identify the Net ID from the Host ID. There are five classes of addresses defined in TCP/IP, and it is important to be able to identify them.

Class A

Looking at the first octet of a Class A address in binary, the first bit will always be a 0. The last 7 bits in the first octet can be either 0s or 1s. This means that the range of a Class A address is from 00000000.x.y.z to 01111111.x.y.z. Converting to decimal shows us that a Class A address always starts with a number from 0.x.y.z to 127.x.y.z, where the values x, y, and z can be any number from 0 to 255.

However, there are certain rules that must be adhered to. The first rule states that a network address can never be all 0s. This means that a Class A address really starts with 1, and not 0. The third rule (we will come back to the second later) states that the address of 127.x.y.z is referred to as a *loopback* address. Every host refers to itself for diagnostics as 127.x.y.z. Most implementations of the loopback address are 127.0.0.1. It is interesting to note that we do not actually have to have a network card installed. If we use the ping command to test connectivity to the loopback address, we are in essence testing just the TCP/IP protocol stack itself. These rules mean that a Class A address actually runs from 1.x.y.z to 126.x.y.z.

A Class A address also defines the network portion of the address as consisting of the first octet. The last three octets are used by us to assign unique addresses to our hosts. The x.y.z represents this notation. However, we need to finish our rules that we started earlier.

The first rule should be modified to say that no network OR host ID can be all 0s. If we choose a Class A Net ID of 100.x.y.z and we try assigning the host ID of 0.0.0, we would have an address of 100.0.0.0. However, this address actually refers to the Net ID. This identifies the entire network and not a specific host on that network. The first valid host address would then be 100.0.0.1.

Rule number two states that no network or host ID can be all 1s. If we make one of our octets all 1s, what number is represented in decimal? The answer is 255 (eight 1s in a row converted to decimal). The address 100.255.255.255 is actually a broadcast address for the logical network of 100.0.0.0. Therefore, the last valid host that is available is 100.255.255.254.

To give another example, if we decided to use a Class A address that started with 15, we could then assign our host addresses like 15.10.95.96 and 15.10.96.95. Remember that each host must have a unique address. These 24 bits, or three octets, can be anything that we want, with the exceptions of the rules above. In other words, we can use the 24 bits to build our network of unique host addresses. The address of 15.0.0.0 specifies the entire network, and 15.255.255.255 specifies the broadcast address for this network

Determining the number of networks for a Class A is easy. There are only 126 networks that can be created. However, the last three octets are used for the hosts, so we need to determine how many hosts each network can have. If we use our previous example of a Class A Net ID of 15.x.y.z, or more appropriately, 15.0.0.0, then we are allowed to change the remaining 24 bits to any value except all 0s and all 1s. This leads to a calculation of $2^{24} \times 2 = 16,777,214$. We can have 16 million hosts on a single network segment! Of course, this would be a serious disaster because of all the broadcasts.

Class B

A Class B address will always begin with 10 in binary in the first octet. This means that the first octet will range from 10000000 to 10111111. Converting this to decimal would give us a range of 128–191.

The first two octets of a Class B are used to identify the network portion of the TCP/IP address. This means that the range of networks is from

128.0.y.z to 191.255.y.z. If we were to figure out the number of possible combinations, it would be (192–128) × 256. This would be similar to subtracting 1 from 11 to show that there are actually 10 combinations. For every number in the first octet, there are 256 possible combinations (0 to 255) in the second octet, for a total of 16,384 network IDs. In other words, we have 14 bits available for the network address and this leads to $2^{14} \times 2 = 16,384$.

The last two octets, or 16 bits, are the 1s that we can use for anything we want. Remembering that a host cannot have all 0s for the Host ID, nor can it have all 1s, we have a total of $2^{16} \times 2 = 65,534$ combinations. In other words, we have more networks to use, but less hosts per each network when compared to a Class A address. Still, with 65,534 hosts on a single segment, we are still going to suffer from severe broadcast traffic.

Class C

The third class of addresses, and the last one we use for identifying unique hosts in a network, uses a binary number of 110XXXXX for the first octet. Replacing the Xs with 0s gives us 11000000, or 192. Replacing the Xs with 1s gives us 11011111, or 223. Therefore, a Class C address ranges from 192.0.0.z to 223.255.255.z, where z can be any number from 1–254.

The first three octets are used to identify the network. For every first octet, there are 256 possible second octets, and for every second octet, there are 256 possible third octets. Running through our possible combinations once again, we have (224–192) × 256 × 256 = 2,097,152 possible network IDs. There are over 2 million Net IDs available in the world!

Since we can only work with the fourth octet for our host IDs though, we only have 8 bits to use. $2^8 = 256$ possible combinations. However, don't forget to remove the combinations of all 0s and all 1s. Our final number of host IDs per network is then 254.

Class D and Class E

The last two octets are used for special purposes. Class D addresses range from 224 to 239.x.y.z. The first octet in binary is defined as 1110XXXX, again replacing the Xs with whatever number we wish. This address class is used for *multicasting*. Multicasting is a method of sending a single data packet to multiple hosts. This is accomplished by having each of the hosts subscribe to a multicast address. An analogy for multicasting, although not in TCP/IP addressing, would be a distribution e-mail list. We can send one e-mail out, and it would be sent to multiple individuals that have subscribed. It is important to note that this address is not used for hosts.

The final class of address, Class E, ranges from 240.x.y.z to 255.x.y.z, or in binary, the first octet is 1111XXXX. This is an experimental address range and is not used in any actual networks.

Class Summary

Review Table 6.2 for the exact numbers for each of the first three classes. We need to keep in mind the beginning numbers for each class address so that we can identify a given network ID. Also keep in mind the number of bits that are available for the Host IDs. These are the bits that we can work with.

TABLE 6.2	Class address summary					
Class	**First Octet in Binary**	**First Octet in Decimal**	**# bits in Net ID**	**Total Networks**	**# bits in Host ID**	**Total Hosts**
A	00000001–01111110	1–126	8	126	24	16,777,214
B	10000000–10111111	128–191	16	16,384	16	65,534
C	11000000–11011111	192–223	24	2,097,152	8	254

Subnet Masks

A subnet mask is a binary number that can be used to perform some calculations on a TCP/IP address to determine the Net ID from the Host ID. A subnet mask is required for every host, and most implementations of TCP/IP on vendor platforms will prompt you for this during configuration.

Classful addressing, or using Class A, B, and C addresses, has default subnet masks already created for us. Class A addresses have a default subnet mask of 255.0.0.0. Likewise, Class B addresses have a subnet mask of 255.255.0.0, and Class C addresses have 255.255.255.0. If we convert 255 to binary it is eight 1s.

So, just what is a subnet mask then? To answer this question, we need to understand something called a *truth table*. Truth tables are great for some arithmetic and digital theory. Since this book is about passing the CCNA test, and learning some useful skills in the field, we will just have to accept the following shown in Table 6.3 without questioning it:

TABLE 6.3	Truth table			
0	AND	0	=	0
0	AND	1	=	0
1	AND	0	=	0
1	AND	1	=	1

Notice that the only time that a value of 1 is calculated is when we AND two 1s. Also note that this is called ANDing, and it is quite different from mathematical adding. Let's examine what happens when we AND two binary numbers that are larger than 1 number. For example, 1010 AND 1111 =

1	0	1	0
1	1	1	1
1	**0**	**1**	**0**

The statement 1010 AND 1111 results in an answer of 1010. If we examine the first value again, we will notice that it is identical to the answer. In fact, any number that is ANDed with all 1s, results in an answer identical to the first value. As another example, the statement 11001100 AND 11111111 results in an answer of 11001100. By the way, if we convert 11111111 to decimal, we will arrive at the number 255.

Now that we understand the concept of binary ANDing, let's examine how it works with TCP/IP addresses. In Figure 6–1, we have a simple network with two hosts attached to the same segment. Notice that they are both Class C addresses. Host A would like to send to Host B. Will it be able to?

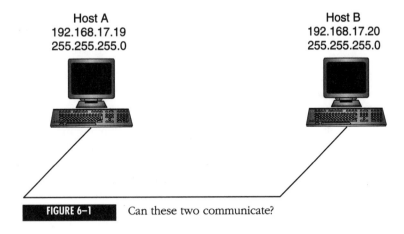

Host A
192.168.17.19
255.255.255.0

Host B
192.168.17.20
255.255.255.0

FIGURE 6–1   Can these two communicate?

Once Host A has decided to send some data to Host B, an algorithm is performed at the Network layer to determine if these two hosts are on the same segment. This algorithm is the ANDing process.

First, Host A computes the AND result with the Host A address and the subnet mask. The decimal numbers are converted to binary. The TCP/IP address of 192.168.17.19 in binary is 11000000.10101000.00010001.00010011, and the subnet mask of 255.255.255.0 is 11111111.11111111.11111111.00000000. The result is 11000000.10101000.00010001.00000000, or in decimal 192.168.17.0. Remember that a Host ID cannot be all 0s because that represents the network address. Here is the proof of that statement. The subnet mask has effectively stripped off, or masked, the Host ID from the Net ID.

Next, the sending computer ANDs the destination TCP/IP address with the subnet mask. Again, the decimal numbers are converted to binary such that the TCP/IP address is 11000000.10101000.00010001.00010100, and the subnet mask is again 11111111.11111111.11111111.00000000. The result is 11000000.10101000.00010001.00000000, or in decimal 192.168.17.0.

Finally, the results are compared, and 192.168.17.0 for the Net ID of Host A and 192.168.17.0 for the Net ID of Host B are the same. Therefore, these two computers can communicate directly.

One more example can be seen in Figure 6–2.

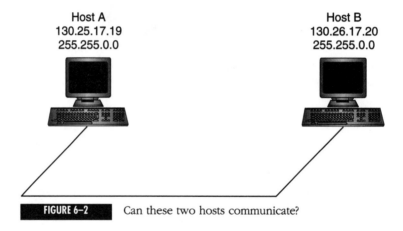

Host A
130.25.17.19
255.255.0.0

Host B
130.26.17.20
255.255.0.0

FIGURE 6–2   Can these two hosts communicate?

Host A again wants to send to Host B. Running through the algorithm once again, the sending computer ANDs the source TCP/IP address with the subnet mask. 130.25.17.19 AND 255.255.0.0 (Class B subnet mask) results in 130.25.0.0.

Next, the destination address of 130.26.17.20 is ANDed with the subnet mask of 255.255.0.0, and the result is 130.26.0.0.

Finally, the two results are compared. 130.25.0.0 and 130.26.0.0 are different; therefore, these two computers are logically on different networks. Host A will forward the data to a router to route to the appropriate network.

In this example, Host A will be unable to communicate with Host B.

Assigning TCP/IP Addresses

For a long time, the Internet was running out of TCP/IP addresses. Although this is still happening, it is not nearly at such an alarming rate. The reason behind this apparent problem was due to the fact that the Internet was suddenly hailed as the greatest resource a business could use to succeed. As more and more businesses wanted to go online, more and more TCP/IP addresses were given out.

Choosing a TCP/IP address range for our organization entails some planning. Remember that every host in a network has to have a unique TCP/IP address. The largest network in the world is, of course, the Internet. In order for a business or an individual to get onto the Internet, they had to have a valid TCP/IP address.

So, how was this address chosen without conflicting with another node somewhere else in the world? An organization was created that was responsible for tracking and assigning these unique TCP/IP addresses. This entity is known as IANA, or Internet Assigned Numbers Authority. A person who wanted to be on the Internet would contact IANA and ask for a TCP/IP address. If approved, a TCP/IP address would be given to the requester and then marked as being used. This ensured that there would be no duplicate TCP/IP addresses on the Internet.

Many companies would request TCP/IP addresses for their entire network. Every single node in the organization could have a valid TCP/IP address, and as more companies wanted to join the Internet community, the addresses started disappearing rapidly. Imagine companies with thousands or tens of thousands of computers all taking valid Internet addresses!

There is a serious problem to this however. If we examine Figure 6–3, we can see that there are quite a few addresses that need to be given to this network. The good news is that it can be accomplished with a single Class A or B address. Every node on the network can get out to the Internet. The bad news, however, is that every node on the Internet can get back into the company's network as well. It becomes very difficult to implement good security on this network.

So what if the company had no plans for being on the Internet? The company could then choose any of the valid TCP/IP addresses in the entire range. Since there is no connection to the Internet, there would be no outside TCP/IP address conflicts. Problem solved—don't connect to the Internet!

In this given scenario, we could choose any TCP/IP address that we wanted to use. But what happens when we merge with another company? It is possible that this new company may have TCP/IP addresses that conflict with our own addresses. What if our company wanted to connect to the Internet at a later date? We would then have to apply for valid Internet addresses and restructure our entire network. This is also not a good solution.

The answers to most of these problems were solved in RFC 1918. This document defines a subset of valid TCP/IP addresses as being reserved for internal use only. This means these addresses will not be found on the Internet, nor assigned by IANA. The addresses are:

IC, Inc.

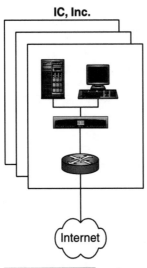

1500 NT Servers
3500 NT Workstations
5300 Windows 98
40 Unix Servers
3 Mainframes

Internet

FIGURE 6–3   A large network gaining access to the Internet

1. 10.0.0.0 to 10.255.255.255—Class A
2. 172.16.0.0 to 172.31.255.255—Class B
3. 192.168.0.0 to 192.168.255.255—Class C

If we should decide to set up a network with TCP/IP addresses we can choose any or all of the private addresses to use in our internal organization. However, since these addresses do not exist on the Internet, we cannot use them to access the Internet. In order to get around this, we would install a proxy server or a firewall. This firewall would have a valid Internet address assigned by IANA, and the firewall would route traffic from our internal network to the Internet (see Figure 6–4). We now have saved all those valid Internet addresses for other companies to use on their firewalls, we have Internet access, and we have some additional security installed.

It should be noted that the one problem this does not solve is the company merger. Two companies could have conflicting private addresses, and restructuring would then still be necessary.

There is also an Internet Draft (ID) that is in progress that lists some additional addresses that should be considered reserved. These addresses include:

1. 0.0.0.0 to 0.255.255.255—A special block of addresses with limited use
2. 192.0.2.0—Called the TEST-NET, it is reserved for documentation and sample code.
3. 169.254.0.0 to 169.254.255.255—Used for operating systems that automatically assign addresses in the event a DHCP server is unavailable.

One final detail to mention is that most companies will implement some type of convention for addresses. This convention may be something like have the first 20% of the addresses on a network used for servers, the next 50% for workstations, the next 10% for printers, and the last 20% for routers and other network devices. The address convention used is not as important as it is to create one and use it.

Now that we have an understanding of the addressing of TCP/IP, let's examine how to set up addresses on Cisco routers.

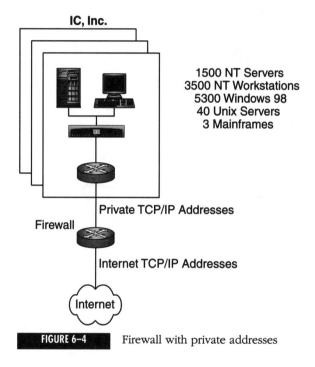

IC, Inc.

1500 NT Servers
3500 NT Workstations
5300 Windows 98
40 Unix Servers
3 Mainframes

Private TCP/IP Addresses

Firewall

Internet TCP/IP Addresses

Internet

| FIGURE 6–4 | Firewall with private addresses |

Setting Up Cisco Routers

Before we start configuring our routers, let's review our network diagram (see Figure 6–5). IC, Inc. has three routers between three remote sites. Each router is a Cisco 2500 series with a minimum of two serial connections and one Ethernet connection. Each Ethernet connection connects to the internal LAN. Counting up the networks (or segments), we can see that we have five networks in use. These five networks need to be assigned a unique TCP/IP Net ID, and each node needs a unique host address. We decided to use a Class C address for each of the segments, and we are using the private address of 192.168.0.0. We will use the default Class C subnet mask, which is 255.255.255.0.

Notice the layouts of the DCE and the DTE connections. If we recall from Chapter 5, "Introduction to Cisco Routers," routers are connected together either through a CSU/DSU or by using a special cable to emulate the DCE connection. For our example we have the special cables, but in a real network, the DCE configurations shown in Figure 6–5 would not be necessary.

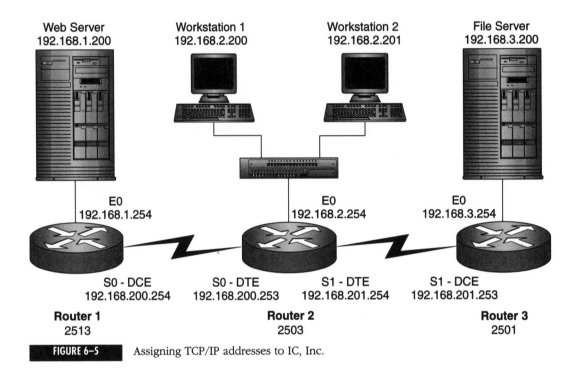

Web Server	**Workstation 1**	**Workstation 2**	**File Server**
192.168.1.200	192.168.2.200	192.168.2.201	192.168.3.200

E0
192.168.1.254

E0
192.168.2.254

E0
192.168.3.254

S0 - DCE
192.168.200.254

S0 - DTE
192.168.200.253

S1 - DTE
192.168.201.254

S1 - DCE
192.168.201.253

Router 1
2513

Router 2
2503

Router 3
2501

FIGURE 6–5   Assigning TCP/IP addresses to IC, Inc.

Now it's time to configure the routers. Our assistant has already configured the TCP/IP addresses on each of the workstations and servers.

To configure Router 1, we will use the script install. There are two ways that we can run the script. We can erase the startup-config and reboot the router, or we can simply type **setup** at the configuration prompt. In our case, we will erase the startup-config to simulate configuring a router for the first time.

```
Router1#erase start
[OK]
Router1#reload

Proceed with reload? [confirm]<enter>

%SYS-5-RELOAD: Reload requested
System Bootstrap, Version 5.2(5), RELEASE SOFTWARE
```

```
Copyright (c) 1986-1994 by cisco Systems
2500 processor with 16384 Kbytes of main memory
```

After the router finishes rebooting, we can then enter the configuration script. Here we will assign the TCP/IP addresses to each of the interfaces.

```
Notice: NVRAM invalid, possibly due to write erase.


    --- System Configuration Dialog ---

Would you like to enter the initial configuration dialog? [yes/no]: y

At any point you may enter a question mark '?' for help.
Use ctrl-c to abort configuration dialog at any prompt.
Default settings are in square brackets '[]'.

First, would you like to see the current interface summary? [yes]: y

Any interface listed with OK? value "NO" does not have a valid configuration

Interface    IP-Address  OK? Method Status    Protocol

Ethernet0    unassigned  NO unset up         up

Serial0      unassigned  NO unset down       down

Serial1      unassigned  NO unset down       down

TokenRing0   unassigned  NO unset reset      down
```

In the preceding example, we viewed the current interface configurations. We can see that there are no currently assigned addresses, and that only the Ethernet interface is administratively up.

```
Configuring global parameters:

  Enter host name [Router]: Router1

  The enable secret is a password used to protect access to
  privileged EXEC and configuration modes. This password, after
  entered, becomes encrypted in the configuration.
  Enter enable secret: secret

  The enable password is used when you do not specify an
  enable secret password, with some older software versions, and
  some boot images.
  Enter enable password: password

  The virtual terminal password is used to protect
```

```
access to the router over a network interface.
Enter virtual terminal password: virtual
```

Depending on the version of the IOS that we are currently running, some of the following configuration options may not appear, or there may be more than shown.

```
Configure SNMP Network Management? [yes]: n
 Configure DECnet? [no]: n
 Configure AppleTalk? [no]: n
 Configure IPX? [no]: n
 Configure IP? [yes]: y
  Configure IGRP routing? [yes]: n
  Configure RIP routing? [no]: n
```

Finally, we arrive at the TCP/IP configuration. Now is a good time to point out that saying "TCP/IP" over and over is likely to have serious effects on your tongue. So, as with many terms in the IT industry, we can abbreviate it. The quicker way is to say just "IP."

IGRP and RIP are two routing protocols. We will examine these in more detail in Chapter 9, "Dynamic Routing." Next, we assign IP addresses to the Ethernet and to the Serial 0 port.

```
Configuring interface parameters:

Do you want to configure Ethernet0 interface? [yes]: y
 Configure IP on this interface? [yes]: y
  IP address for this interface: 192.168.1.254
  Subnet mask for this interface [255.255.255.0] <enter>
  Class C network is 192.168.1.0, 24 subnet bits; mask is /24

Do you want to configure Serial0 interface? [yes]: y
 Configure IP on this interface? [yes]: y
 Configure IP unnumbered on this interface? [no]: n
  IP address for this interface: 192.168.200.254
  Subnet mask for this interface [255.255.255.0] <enter>
  Class C network is 192.168.200.0, 24 subnet bits; mask is /24

Do you want to configure Serial1 interface? [yes]: n

Do you want to configure TokenRing0 interface? [yes]: n
```

Notice the designation where it defines the mask as /24. This is referred to as CIDR (pronounced cider) notation. Remember that there are 8 bits in an octet and, that we used three octets for the subnet mask. Eight times three is 24, so we can abbreviate the subnet mask 255.255.255.0 to /24.

We are now finished, and a configuration file will be created and stored in NVRAM for us.

The following configuration command script was created:

```
hostname Router1
enable secret 5 $1$7hdG$e1NYz1DkjLdwRYxYWxb7n1
enable password password
line vty 0 4
password virtual
no snmp-server
!
no decnet routing
no appletalk routing
no ipx routing
ip routing
!
interface Ethernet0
ip address 192.168.1.254 255.255.255.0
no mop enabled
!
interface Serial0
ip address 192.168.200.254 255.255.255.0
no mop enabled
!
interface Serial1
shutdown
no ip address
!
interface TokenRing0
shutdown
no ip address
dialer-list 1 protocol ip permit
dialer-list 1 protocol ipx permit
!
end

[0] Go to the IOS command prompt without saving this config.
[1] Return back to the setup without saving this config.
[2] Save this configuration to nvram and exit.

Enter your selection [2]: 2
Building configuration...
Use the enabled mode 'configure' command to modify this
configuration.


Press RETURN to get started!
```

We are not quite finished configuring this router yet. The first thing we should do is log in to the router and try pinging the Web server to see if we have connectivity.

```
Press RETURN to get started.
<enter>

Router1>enable
Password: secret
Router1#ping 192.168.1.200

Type escape sequence to abort.
Sending 5, 100-byte ICMP Echos to 192.168.1.200, timeout is 2 seconds:
!!!!!
Success rate is 100 percent (5/5), round-trip min/avg/max = 1/2/4 ms
Router1#
```

Next, we use ping to test our network connections. We received five exclamation points for 100% success. This tells us that both the sender and the receiver are configured correctly and are communicating.

Next, we need to configure the DCE information on the serial 0 port.

```
Router1#config term
Enter configuration commands, one per line. End with CNTL/Z.
Router1(config)#int serial 0
Router1(config-if)#clockrate 56000
Router1(config-if)#dce-terminal-timing-enable
Router1(config-if)#no shutdown
Router1(config-if)#^Z
Router1#
%SYS-5-CONFIG_I: Configured from console by console
Router1#copy run start
Building configuration...
[OK]
Router1#
```

There are a couple of important things to note here. Again, we can abbreviate commands by using enough characters to differentiate other commands. This can be seen with the next command **int serial 0**. We can abbreviate it down even more to **int s0**, which is the notation that we will use throughout the remaining chapters.

The command **dce-terminal-timing-enable** identifies this interface as a DCE interface and that it should use a clock signal for the serial communication. This command helps with phase shifting that can occur between two serial devices that have long distances or high speeds being used.

The next command turns the interface on. The command **shutdown** disables the interface administratively. This is how we turn off interfaces. By using the **no** in front of it, we turn it on. The **no** command can be used to negate almost all of the configuration commands.

Finally, we copy the running configuration into NVRAM by using the command **copy run start**.

To examine the status of the interfaces, we can use the command **show interface**, or **sho int**.

```
Router1#sho int
Ethernet0 is up, line protocol is up
 Hardware is Lance, address is 0000.0c47.b113 (bia 0000.0c47.b113)
 Internet address is 192.168.1.254/24
 <lines deleted>

Serial0 is down, line protocol is down
 Hardware is HD64570
 Internet address is 192.168.200.254/24
 <lines deleted>

Serial1 is administratively down, line protocol is down
 Hardware is HD64570
 <lines deleted>

TokenRing0 is administratively down, line protocol is down
 Hardware is TMS380, address is 0000.30e2.8d48 (bia 0000.30e2.8d48)
 Hardware is TMS380, address is 0000.30e2.8d48 (bia 0000.30e2.8d48)
  <lines deleted>

Router1#
```

We can see that Ethernet0 is up and running, Serial0 is down because there is no link currently on that connection, and Serial1 and TokenRing0 are both administratively down (meaning that the **shutdown** command is in effect).

One last command would be to examine the cable connecting Serial0. Is it DTE or DCE? Remember, to determine this, we just issue the command **show controllers serial 0**.

```
Router1#show controllers s 0
HD unit 0, idb = 0xA4498, driver structure at 0xA97D8
buffer size 1524 HD unit 0, V.35 DCE cable, clockrate 56000
```

Here we can see that a DCE cable is connected, and that the clock rate has been specified at 56000 bits per second.

At this point, Router 1 has been configured. There is one more thing to note about using the configuration script. If we reload at this point, we may see some annoying messages about trying to load a configuration file. This continues for quite some time. The reason has to do with the initial configuration script. Occasionally, the command **service config** gets written to the configuration file. This typically occurs if the configuration script is aborted in some fashion. This command instructs the router to try to load a configuration file from a TFTP server. This will be explored in more detail in Chapter 10, "Managing the Cisco Router." However, it can be disabled by using the **no** command.

```
cisco 2500 (68030) processor (revision D) with 16384K/2048K bytes of memory.
Processor board ID 02009581, with hardware revision 00000000
Bridging software.
X.25 software, Version 3.0.0.
1 Ethernet/IEEE 802.3 interface(s)
1 Token Ring/IEEE 802.5 interface(s)
2 Serial network interface(s)
32K bytes of non-volatile configuration memory.
8192K bytes of processor board System flash (Read ONLY)

Loading network-confg ... [timed out]

Loading cisconet.cfg ... [timed out]

Loading router1.cfg ... [timed out]

Press RETURN to get started!
<enter>

Router1>enable
Password: secret
Router1#conf t
Enter configuration commands, one per line. End with CNTL/Z.
Router1(config)#no service config
Router1(config)#^Z
%SYS-5-CONFIG_I: Configured from console by cons
Router1#copy run start
```

> This will stop the auto configuration trying to occur.
> Now it is time to configure the second router. This time, however, we will skip the initial script configuration and do the commands manually at the CLI.

```
Router2>enable
Router2#erase start
[OK]
Router2#reload

System configuration has been modified. Save? [yes/no]: n
Proceed with reload? [confirm]<enter>

%SYS-5-RELOAD: Reload requested
System Bootstrap, Version 5.2(8a), RELEASE SOFTWARE
Copyright (c) 1986-1995 by cisco Systems

<lines deleted>

    --- System Configuration Dialog ---

Would you like to enter the initial configuration dialog? [yes/no]: n
```

```
Press RETURN to get started!
<enter>

Cisco Internetwork Operating System Software
IOS (tm) 2500 Software (C2500-D-L), Version 11.3(3)T, RELEASE SOFTWARE (fc1)
Copyright (c) 1986-1998 by cisco Systems, Inc.
Compiled Mon 20-Apr-98 17:49 by ccai
Router>enable
Router#conf t
Enter configuration commands, one per line. End with CNTL/Z.
Router(config)#hostname Router2
Router2(config)#enable secret secret
```

We entered privileged mode and then configuration mode. Notice that we were not prompted for a password to enter configuration mode. Since this is a router with no configuration information, it has not been set up. For security reasons, it is a good idea to enable one. We wouldn't like the first person to come through our router to start changing our configurations! We change the name of the router using the **hostname** command and then set the enable password. We do this with the last line and we set the password to *secret*.

To configure the interfaces manually, we have to enter the interface command **int e0**. Instead of using e0, we may use something else like e1, s0, s1, and so forth. We can tell we are in an interface configuration mode because the prompt changes to include the *if* letters. Once inside the interface configuration command we can set the IP address. We will use the ? character to determine the correct commands to use.

```
Router2(config)#int e0
Router2(config-if)#ip ?
Interface IP configuration subcommands:
 access-group    Specify access control for packets
 accounting      Enable IP accounting on this interface
 address         Set the IP address of an interface
 <lots of commands deleted>

Router2(config-if)#ip address ?
 A.B.C.D IP address

Router2(config-if)#ip address 192.168.2.254 ?
 A.B.C.D IP subnet mask

Router2(config-if)#ip address 192.168.2.254 255.255.255.0 ?
 secondary Make this IP address a secondary address
 <cr>

Router2(config-if)#ip address 192.168.2.254 255.255.255.0 <enter>
Router2(config-if)#no shut
Router2(config-if)#
%LINEPROTO-5-UPDOWN: Line protocol on Interface Ethernet0, changed state to up
```

```
%LINK-3-UPDOWN: Interface Ethernet0, changed state to up
Router2(config-if)#exit
```

After configuring the IP address and turning the interface on, a status message appears that tells us the interface has changed to an up state. Next, we need to set the serial interfaces so we issue the **exit** command to get us out of the interface configuration mode and back to the global configuration mode. We then continue with the next interface.

The secondary command allows us to have multiple IP addresses on the same interface. This is useful if we have two different logical networks on the same physical segment. Another reason is that if we are in the process of changing our IP addresses, we can migrate slowly without affecting the current network.

```
Router2(config)#int s0
Router2(config-if)#ip addr 192.168.200.253 255.255.255.0
Router2(config-if)#no shut
Router2(config-if)#
%LINK-3-UPDOWN: Interface Serial0, changed state to up
%LINEPROTO-5-UPDOWN: Line protocol on Interface Serial0, changed state to up
Router2(config-if)#int s1
Router2(config-if)#ip addr 192.168.201.254 255.255.255.0
Router2(config-if)#no shut
Router2(config-if)#^Z
Router2#
%SYS-5-CONFIG_I: Configured from console by console
%LINK-3-UPDOWN: Interface Serial1, changed state to up
%LINEPROTO-5-UPDOWN: Line protocol on Interface Serial1, changed state to up
Router2#copy run start
Building configuration...
[OK]
Router2#
```

We configured both serial interfaces, and since neither one of them is a DCE interface, we saw the interfaces come online. It is possible that the status message will not appear if the cables are not connected or the connecting router does not have its interface enabled. All pieces have to be in place before an interface will come online.

This time through the interface menu, we went directly from serial 0 to serial 1 without exiting back to the global configuration command. It is a nice shortcut to use, but the prompt does not tell us which interface we are actually modifying, so we need to be careful when doing this.

Finally, everything we have been doing has been modifying the running configuration. If we lost power during this configuration, we would lose all changes. To eliminate this problem, we used the **copy run start** command to copy the changes to the startup configuration file in NVRAM.

At this point, we can use ping to test connectivity to Router 1 and to the two workstations.

```
Router2#ping 192.168.200.254

Type escape sequence to abort.
Sending 5, 100-byte ICMP Echos to 192.168.200.254, timeout is 2 seconds:
!!!!!
Success rate is 100 percent (5/5), round-trip min/avg/max = 32/34/36 ms
Router2#ping 192.168.2.201

Type escape sequence to abort.
Sending 5, 100-byte ICMP Echos to 192.168.2.201, timeout is 2 seconds:
.!!!!
Success rate is 80 percent (4/5), round-trip min/avg/max = 1/2/4 ms
Router2#ping 192.168.2.200

Type escape sequence to abort.
Sending 5, 100-byte ICMP Echos to 192.168.2.200, timeout is 2 seconds:
.!!!!
Success rate is 80 percent (4/5), round-trip min/avg/max = 1/2/4 ms
Router2#ping 192.168.1.200

Type escape sequence to abort.
Sending 5, 100-byte ICMP Echos to 192.168.1.200, timeout is 2 seconds:
.....
Success rate is 0 percent (0/5)
```

We have good connectivity to everything that we are directly connected to. However, when we tried to ping the Web server, we were unable to get a response. The reason behind this is that there is no route information about how to get a packet to that network. The ANDing process worked correctly, but it now has to send the packet to a router, and we have not configured one. We will examine how to do that in Chapter 8, "Static TCP/IP Routing," and Chapter 9.

If something didn't work at this point, we could use the commands **show interfaces** and **show controllers** to examine the settings.

We will configure the last router manually as well. The commands are almost identical, with the exceptions that serial 1 is a DCE connection and serial 0 is not being used.

```
Router3>enable
Router3#erase start
[OK]
Router3#reload
Proceed with reload? [confirm]

%SYS-5-RELOAD: Reload requested
<lines deleted>
Notice: NVRAM invalid, possibly due to write erase.
```

```
    --- System Configuration Dialog ---

At any point you may enter a question mark '?' for help.
Use ctrl-c to abort configuration dialog at any prompt.
Default settings are in square brackets '[]'.
Would you like to enter the initial configuration dialog? [yes]: n


Press RETURN to get started!
<enter>
Router>enable
Router#conf t
Enter configuration commands, one per line. End with CNTL/Z.
Router(config)#hostname Router3
Router3(config)#enable secret secret
Router3(config)#int e0
Router3(config-if)#ip addr 192.168.3.254 255.255.255.0
Router3(config-if)#no shut
Router3(config-if)#
%LINEPROTO-5-UPDOWN: Line protocol on Interface Ethernet0, changed state to up
%LINK-3-UPDOWN: Interface Ethernet0, changed state to up
Router3(config-if)#int s1
Router3(config-if)#ip addr 192.168.201.253 255.255.255.0
Router3(config-if)#dce-terminal-timing-enable
Router3(config-if)#clockrate 56000
Router3(config-if)#no shut
Router3(config-if)#
%LINK-3-UPDOWN: Interface Serial1, changed state to up
%LINEPROTO-5-UPDOWN: Line protocol on Interface Serial1, changed state to up
Router3(config-if)#^Z
Router3#
%SYS-5-CONFIG_I: Configured from console by console
Router3#copy run start
Building configuration...
[OK]
Router3#sho int
Ethernet0 is up, line protocol is up
 Hardware is Lance, address is 0000.0c91.a1ed (bia 0000.0c91.a1ed)
 Internet address is 192.168.3.254/24
 <lines deleted>
Serial0 is administratively down, line protocol is down
 Hardware is HD64570
 <lines deleted>
Serial1 is up, line protocol is up
 Hardware is HD64570
 Internet address is 192.168.201.253/24
 <lines deleted>
Router3#ping 192.168.3.200


Type escape sequence to abort.
```

```
Sending 5, 100-byte ICMP Echos to 192.168.3.200, timeout is 2 seconds:
.!!!!
Success rate is 80 percent (4/5), round-trip min/avg/max = 1/3/4 ms
Router3#ping 192.168.201.254

Type escape sequence to abort.
Sending 5, 100-byte ICMP Echos to 192.168.201.254, timeout is 2 seconds:
!!!!!
Success rate is 100 percent (5/5), round-trip min/avg/max = 32/34/36 ms
Router3#
```

After configuring and saving the router, we tested the changes by pinging the fileserver and Router2. Both replied which indicates that at this point everything is working correctly. We also looked at the interfaces so that we could verify the configuration. Note that if we only wanted to examine one interface we could use the command **show int** *interface* where interface would be **s0**, for example.

Summary

TCP/IP addresses are 32 bits in length and are in binary coding. It is more efficient for us to work with these addresses in dotted decimal notation. Identifying TCP/IP addresses can be accomplished through examining the values in the first octet. Each address is broken into the network ID and a host ID. Every host in a connected TCP/IP environment must have a unique address. A subnet mask is used to identify the Net ID from the Host ID.

Configuring the routers to use TCP/IP entails giving each interface a valid TCP/IP address through the command **ip address**. Each interface must then be turned on, and once there is a connection between the router and another host, the interfaces and protocols will change to an up state. Interfaces that will use clocking to control the serial communications must have a clock rate enabled.

Finally, troubleshooting basic TCP/IP connectivity can be accomplished by using the **ping** command. However, connectivity cannot be established beyond directly connected nodes because a routing table is required.

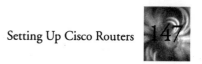

Class	First Octet Range	Default Subnet Mask	# bits in Net ID	# bits in Host ID
A	1–126	255.0.0.0	8	24
B	128–191	255.255.0.0	16	16
C	192–223	255.255.255.0	24	8

Scenario Lab 6.1

The project manager has laid out a rough network diagram based on the locations of the two buildings previously identified, as well as the two remote sales locations (see Figure 6–6). You have been asked to design a TCP/IP addressing scheme. The company wants to maintain some security by using the two 2514 routers as firewalls to the Internet. What solution can you arrive at for the addresses? Your solution should identify a common convention for giving addresses to workstations, servers, printers, and routers.

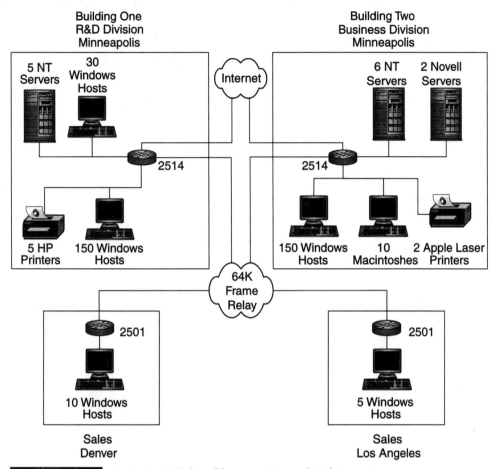

Building One
R&D Division
Minneapolis

Building Two
Business Division
Minneapolis

5 NT
Servers

30
Windows
Hosts

Internet

6 NT
Servers

2 Novell
Servers

2514

2514

5 HP
Printers

150 Windows
Hosts

150 Windows
Hosts

10
Macintoshes

2 Apple Laser
Printers

64K
Frame
Relay

2501

2501

10 Windows
Hosts

5 Windows
Hosts

Sales
Denver

Sales
Los Angeles

FIGURE 6–6 Assigning TCP/IP addresses to Network Solutions, Inc.

Practice Lab 6.1

In this lab, you will configure each of the routers in Figure 6–7 using a Class C network address. You will verify connectivity by using the ping command.

- Using the configuration script, set up the passwords, hostname, and the following IP addresses on the interfaces. Remember, if you need to wipe out the configuration from the last lab, use the command **erase start** while logged into privileged mode. Reboot or use the command **reload** to force the router to reboot.

    Router 1–E0–192.168.1.254
    Router 1–S0–192.168.2.254

    The subnet mask is the default for a Class C. Hopefully, you don't have to look it up, but just in case, it is 255.255.255.0

- Set up the serial 0 port to enable the clocking. Make sure you turn the interface on.
- Save your configuration changes.
- Try pinging the workstation connected to E0. If you haven't changed that IP address, you can use 192.168.1.1.
- Next, configure Router 2 using the CLI. Use the following settings:

    Router 2–E0 192.168.3.254
    Router 2–S0 192.168.2.253

- Enable the interface on serial 0.

- Save your changes.
- Try pinging the workstation connected to Router 2's Ethernet port. If you need an address for the workstation, you can use 192.168.3.1. You should be successful at pinging it.
- Try pinging Router 1's serial interface. Again, you should be successful. If not, examine the interface settings with the show interface command. Make sure that both ports are administratively up as well as the line protocol.
- Try pinging the workstation on Router 1's Ethernet port. At this point, you should be unsuccessful because Router 2 does not know how to get the packets to the correct network. The same would be true if you tried to ping Router 2's workstation from Router 1.

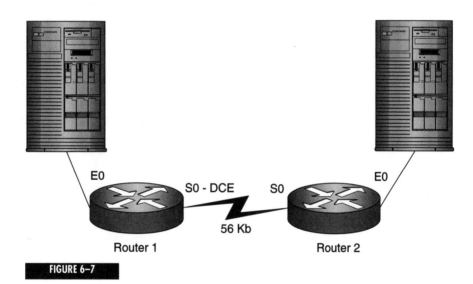

FIGURE 6–7

Practice Lab 6.2

In this lab, you will configure the three routers in Figure 6–8 using different classes of Addresses. You will then use ping to test the connectivity between them. Use the CLI to configure each of the routers.

- Configure Router 1 with the following IP addresses and subnet masks:
    Router 1 E0–192.168.1.254 / 24
    Router 1 S0–159.19.15.254 / 16
- Set up the serial interface to communicate at 56 Kbps (clock rate 56000) with the DCE cable.
- Test connectivity to the workstation on the Ethernet LAN.
- Configure Router 2 with the following IP addresses and subnet masks:
    Router 2 E0–192.168.2.254 / 24
    Router 2 S1–159.19.22.254 / 16
    Router 2 S0–121.1.1.254 / 8
- Set up serial interface 0 to communicate at 512 Kbps (clock rate 56000) using a DCE cable.
- Test the connectivity to the workstation and to Router 1. If there is no response, remember to check the status of the interfaces. If the interface is administratively down, bring it up.
- Remember to save changes!

- Configure Router 3 with the following IP addresses and subnet masks:
  Router 3 E0–192.168.3.254 / 24
  Router 3 S1–121.254.254.254 / 8
- Test the connectivity to the workstation on Ethernet 0 and to Router 2. There should be connectivity with each.
- Save your configurations
- Verify that you cannot ping pass the next router in line. For example, from Router 1 verify that you cannot reach the workstations connected to Routers 2 and 3.

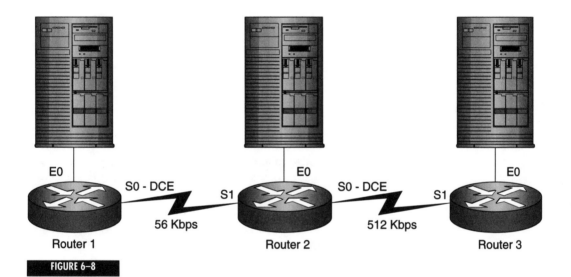

FIGURE 6–8

Exam Objective Checklist

By working through this chapter, you should have sufficient knowledge to answer these exam objectives:

- Log in to a router in both user and privileged modes.
- Use the context-sensitive help facility.
- Manage configuration files from the privileged exec mode.
- Identify the main Cisco IOS commands for router startup.
- Check an initial configuration using the setup command.
- Describe the two parts of network addressing, then identify the parts in specific protocol address examples.
- Describe the different classes of IP addresses.
- Configure IP addresses.
- Verify IP addresses.
- Prepare the initial configuration of your router and enable IP.

Practice Questions

1. What is the number 11001010 in decimal?

    a. 202
    b. 203
    c. 201
    d. 200

2. What number is 177 in binary?

    a. 10110010
    b. 10100001
    c. 10110001
    d. 10100010

3. What command would show you if serial 0 were administratively down?

    a. Show controllers s 0
    b. Show interface s0
    c. Show start
    d. Show run

4. Identify the Class A address

    a. 192.168.17.34
    b. 131.15.45.120
    c. 125.76.133.234
    d. 191.234.56.34

5. Identify the Class C address

    a. 192.168.17.34
    b. 131.15.45.120
    c. 125.76.133.234
    d. 191.234.56.34

6. What series of commands are used to configure an IP address on serial 0?

    a. config terminal
        Ip address 192.168.17.0 255.255.255.0
    b. config terminal
        int s0
        ip addr 192.168.17.17 mask 255.255.255.0
    c. config terminal
        ip addr 192.168.17.17 mask 255.255.255.0
    d. config terminal
        int s0
        ip addr 192.168.17.17 255.255.255.0

7. What is a Class D address used for?

    a. Assigning IP addresses to hosts
    b. Assigning IP addresses to networks
    c. Assigning IP addresses for multicasting
    d. Class D is not used

8. Identify the Class B address

    a. 192.168.17.34
    b. 101.17.43.20
    c. 125.76.133.234
    d. 191.234.56.34

9. What is the correct subnet mask for a Class A address?

    a. 255.0.0.0
    b. 255.255.0.0
    c. 255.255.255.0
    d. 255.255.255.255

10. Which statement is correct?

    a. 192.168.17.34
        Net ID = 192.168.17.0
    b. 125.73.133.234
    c. .234.79.65
        Net ID = 191.234.79.0
    d. 225.16.54.58
        Net ID = 225.16.0.0

11. How many bits are available for Host IDs with a Class B network?

    a. 8
    b. 16
    c. 24
    d. 32

12. How many bits are available for Host IDs with a Class C network?

    a. 8
    b. 16
    c. 24
    d. 32

13. Which command will start the configuration script?

    a. reload
    b. config script
    c. auto script
    d. setup

14. Which two hosts are on the same segment?

    a. 192.168.1.254
    b. 192.168.2.254
    c. 192.168.1.17
    d. 192.168.3.253

15. What is the broadcast address for a node 131.15.46.59

    a. 131.15.46.255
    b. 131.15.255.255
    c. 131.255.255.255
    d. 255.255.46.59

16. Which two hosts are on the same segment?

    a. 191.19.15.255
    b. 191.18.15.255
    c. 191.19.79.202
    d. 192.19.15.254

17. Which of the following are considered private addresses? (Choose all that apply)

    a. 11.0.0.0
    b. 10.0.0.0
    c. 172.19.0.0
    d. 162.198.0.0
    e. 16.172.0.0
    f. 192.168.0.0

18. Which command will set up a second address of 192.168.17.101 on an interface?

    a. Ip address 192.168.17.101 secondary

    b. Ip secondary address 192.168.17.101 255.255.255.0

    c. Ip secondary-address 192.168.17.101 255.255.255.0

    d. Ip address 192.168.17.101 255.255.255.0 secondary

TCP/IP
Subnetting

In This Chapter

◆ Subnetting

◆ Supernetting

Subnetting may be the most difficult concept to learn. There are many network engineers to date who still do not understand it. Understanding subnetting will not only help us pass the CCNA test, but also make us better network engineers and designers.

What Is Subnetting?

Subnetting is the process of dividing a network address into smaller groups. It is perhaps best expressed in this fashion: When we are given an IP address range from the InterNIC, we are given a large group of host addresses within one class of network. We cannot touch the Net ID, but we can do anything we want with the Host IDs that make up that network. For example, in Figure 7-1 we have been given the network address of 192.168.17.0. Since this is a Class C network, we cannot touch the first three octets. However, we can use the fourth octet, or the last 8 bits, in any fashion. In Figure 7–1, we have 18 hosts showing, but we can use all 254 hosts (Don't forget that the first Host ID of 0 is used to identify the network itself, and the last Host

159

ID of 255 is the broadcast address for this network). These hosts are all defined within the Class C address.

Class C Network Address
192.168.17.0

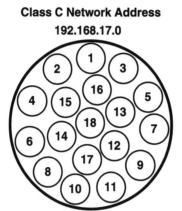

FIGURE 7–1   Nonsubnetted Class C network address consists of 254 hosts

In the last chapter, we used an entire network address for the WAN link between two routers. In essence, we were committed to using all 254 hosts in a Class C network, even though there were never more than two hosts. However, if we were to create subgroups within the network group, we could then use the subgroups for different segments. For example, refer to Figure 7–2.

Class C Network Address
192.168.17.0

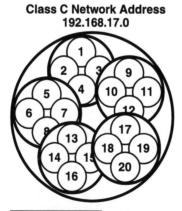

FIGURE 7–2   Subgrouping within a network address

Here we can see that we have created the subgroups within our network address of 192.168.17.0. We can then take this subgroup and assign it to a network. Each subgroup has its own subnetwork address to identify it within the larger network. This address is defined by having all the host bits set to 0. In our example, we could assign one of the groups to our WAN link and instead of wasting 254 host addresses, we wouldn't waste any addresses. Two of them would be used for the hosts, one for the network address for routing, and one for the broadcast between the two nodes.

These subgroups are created from the host bits that we are allowed to work with. We use some of those bits to represent a subgroup, we leave less bits for the Host IDs. This is shown in Figure 7–3. We have a Class B network, which means that the first two octets are defined as the Net ID. We borrow bits from the host and give to the subgroup, or Subnet ID.

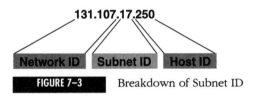

FIGURE 7–3   Breakdown of Subnet ID

There is a tradeoff though. When we subgroup, we do lose our total number of hosts. Before, we had 254 hosts total for the network address. As we further create subgroups, we lose from the 254 hosts because we are borrowing from the host bits. This will become clearer as we continue.

Why Subnet?

There are many reasons to subnet a network. We have already seen one reason, and that is having wasted addresses. We may ask ourselves, "Who cares since we have all those private addresses that we can use?" The truth is, we may not care. However, anyone with a need for addresses on the Internet definitely cares. If we were an Internet Service Provider (ISP), for instance, we would be given a network address so that we can host people dialing in from home. However, if we also wanted to sell some of the address space to businesses, it would be a waste to sell them an entire Class C network when they only need five or six actual host addresses. Remember, the Internet hasn't run out of addresses yet because people are getting smarter at using them. This is one of those cases.

Keeping this in mind, the rest of the reasons are secondary. By decreasing the number of hosts on a network, we can reduce the size of our collision and broadcast domains. Further, manageability of smaller networks is easier than giant networks. It is also easier to troubleshoot smaller networks, and if a smaller network crashes, it does not have any effect on the larger infrastructure.

Finding the Subnet Mask

The first thing about this method is to realize that the more we practice, the easier it becomes. In fact, with enough repetition, we can use this method in our heads when asked a subnetting question. We will not have to reach into our pocket and pull out a battered and torn chart, nor will we need to reach for paper and pencil. However, putting it on paper for the final design is definitely recommended!

There are four steps used to arrive at the correct subnet mask for a given scenario. We will walk through each of the steps one at a time.

Step #1

Recite the given scenario and determine what we know.
Example #1:

We are given a Class C network address of 192.168.10.0. We need 13 subnets instead of 13 isolated networks. What subnet mask do we need?

Step #1:

We know that we have a Class C network. We need 13 subnets. It is important to note this because later we may be asked for 13 hosts instead. We always need to keep in mind what we are working with. Since we have a Class C address, we know that we cannot touch the first three octets, but that we can do anything that we want to the remaining 8 bits. We also know that the default subnet mask is 255.255.255.0

Summary:

Class C – 8 bits to work with – 13 subnets required – 255.255.255.0 default mask

At this point, it may be helpful to review Chapter 6, "TCP/IP Addressing," to remember how many bits we have to work with, and the default subnet masks for each of the Classes.

Class of Address	# Bits to Work With (Host bits)	Default Subnet Mask
A	24	255.0.0.0
B	16	255.255.0.0
C	8	255.255.255.0

Step #2

Convert the number of subnets (hosts) to binary.
Example #1 *(Continued)*:

We are given a Class C network address. We need 13 subnets instead of 13 isolated networks. What subnet mask do we need?

Step #2:

Convert the number of subnets (or hosts) required into binary. Remember to keep in mind what we are working with. To do this, we reuse the table we learned in the last chapter.

128	64	32	16	8	4	2	1
				1	1	0	1

We need to add something to this step, and this is very important. If we had created our number in binary and the resultant was all 1s, we would need to add a leading 0 to the number. For example, if we convert 15 to binary, the resultant is 1111. Since this is all 1s, we need to add a leading 0, so the resultant is now 01111. This MUST be performed before the next step. This is done to account for the broadcast address (remember that a broadcast address is all 1s).

Step #3

Count the number of bits used.
Example #1 *(Continued)*:

We are given a Class C network address. We need 13 subnets instead of 13 isolated networks. What subnet mask do we need?

Step #3

Count the number of bits used. Here we used 4 bits to create the number 13 in binary. However, these bits are used for subnets, since that is the number we converted. If we had converted host bits, we would then need to subtract the number of host bits from the number of bits we have to work with. This number was found in the first step. For example, if this number had been 13 hosts, we would have converted to binary and used 4 bits. Next, we would have to subtract the 4 bits from the number of bits we have to work with, which in this case is 8 bits. Our answer would then be 4 bits, but these 4 bits are for the subnets. Remember that the subnet is created by taking bits from the hosts.

Step #4

Using our chart, count the number of bits found in step #3 from left to right. Read the subnet mask.

Before this makes any sense, we need to add to our binary counting chart. Remember, to create the chart we start on the right with the number 1 and continue counting to the left seven more places, and each time we double the previous number.

128	64	32	16	8	4	2	1

At this point, we are going to change direction. First, we place the number 128 above the 128 in our chart.

128							
128	64	32	16	8	4	2	1

Next, we add the 128 to the next number in the column, 64. The result is 192.

128	192						
128	64	32	16	8	4	2	1

We continue adding the new number to the next number in the lower half of the chart. The next number is 192 + 32 = 224. The next is 224 + 16 = 240, and so on. The final chart should look like the following:

128	192	224	240	248	252	254	255
128	64	32	16	8	4	2	1

Now that we have the chart, we can follow our step #4 rule. Moving from left to right, place the number of bits found in step #3.

1	**1**	**1**	**1**				
128	192	224	240	248	252	254	255
128	64	32	16	8	4	2	1

The final number is 240, and since we are working with the fourth octet (because this is a Class C and that is all that we can work with), our final answer becomes 255.255.255.240! This is the subnet mask required for a Class C network to have at least 13 subnets.

That didn't seem so bad. Let's try it again.

Example #2:
We are given the network address of 192.168.15.0. We need to subnet our network into 31 different networks. What is the subnet mask that will be required?

Step #1: *Recite the given scenario and determine what we know.*
Class C address – 8 bits to work with – 31 subnets – 255.255.255.0 default subnet mask

Step #2: *Convert the number of subnets (or hosts) to binary.*

128	64	32	16	8	4	2	1
			1	1	1	1	1

(Since our answer is all 1s, we need to add a leading 0.)

128	64	32	16	8	4	2	1
		0	1	1	1	1	1

Step #3: *Count the number of bits used.*
  Six bits have been used for the subnets required.
Step #4: *Using our chart, count the number of bits found in step #3 from left to right. Read the subnet mask.*

1	1	1	1	1	1		
128	192	224	240	248	252	254	255
128	64	32	16	8	4	2	1

  To create at least 31 subnets with a Class C address, the subnet mask is
  255.255.255.252.
  This doesn't seem to be so bad. Let's try one more, though, just to be sure.

Example #3:
  We are given the network address of 192.168.15.0. We need 15 hosts per
  subnet. What is the subnet mask that will be required?
Step #1: *Recite the given scenario and determine what we know.*
  Class C address – 8 bits to work with – 15 hosts required – 255.255.255.0
  default subnet mask
Step #2: *Convert the number of subnets (or hosts) to binary.*

128	64	32	16	8	4	2	1
			1	1	1	1	

(Since our answer is all 1s, we need to add a leading 0.)

128	64	32	16	8	4	2	1
		0	1	1	1	1	

Step #3: *Count the number of bits used.*

Five bits are created. However, these bits are for the hosts. We need to get the number of bits needed for the subnets. To get this number, we subtract the number of bits above (5) from the number of bits we have to work with (8). The result is 8–5=3 bits for the subnet. Three bits have been used for the subnets required.

Step #4: *Using our chart, count the number of bits found in step #3 from left to right. Read the subnet mask.*

1		1		1			
128	192	224	240	248	252	254	255
128	64	32	16	8	4	2	1

The exact bits used do not matter. We could write 000 or 011 or 101, as long as we used 3 bits that were calculated in the last step.

To create at least 15 hosts per subnet with a Class C address, the subnet mask is 255.255.255.224

For more practice on these four steps, refer to Practice Exercise 7.1.

Finding the Number of Hosts/Subnets

Up to this point, we have been assuming that the number of hosts or subnets we need has been exactly what we get. However, what we have really been determining is the minimum number of hosts or subnets.

Finding the Number of Subnets

To find the number of subnets, we just need to find out how many possible combinations exist with the number of subnet bits we determined. For example, in Example #1, we needed 13 subnets, and calculated that we needed 4 bits to get this number. If we run through the possible number of combinations, we have the following:

0000	0100	1000	1100
0001	0101	1001	1101
0010	0110	1010	1110
0011	0111	1011	1111

Counting the number of combinations, we have 16. If we remember correctly, a network address cannot be all 0s or all 1s. The same is true here with subnets. Therefore, we have to remove the first and last combinations. This leaves us with 14 possible combinations, or 14 subnets. We needed 13, and we actually have 14. In this example, our needs were met, although there isn't much room for future growth.

Counting the number of combinations is fine with 4 bits, but what if we have 7 or 8 bits. This gets to be a tedious chore. It turns out there is a quicker way to do this. If we use the calculation of $2^{\# \text{ of network bits}} - 2$, we will arrive at the same answer. Using Example #1 again, $2^4 - 2 = 14$ subnets.

Example #2 states that we need 31 subnets. We determined that it takes 6 bits to arrive at this number. If we list all the possible combinations, we might go mad. So instead, $2^6 - 2 = 62$ subnets. We needed 31 and got 62 total subnets. There is definite room for future growth with this choice. However, why wouldn't 5 bits have worked? The number of subnets for 5 bits is $2^5 - 2 = 30$ subnets. Remember that we needed to remove the first and last possible combinations, and therefore we did not create enough subnets.

Our final example stated that we need 15 hosts per subnet. Converting 15 to binary resulted in 1111, and since this was all 1s, we added a leading 0. The final resultant is 5 bits long, but these 5 bits are used for the hosts! In order to determine the number of bits for subnets, we need to subtract these bits from the total that we have to work with. The answer, then, is 8–5=3 bits for the subnet. Using our calculation again, $2^3 - 2 = 6$ subnets that were created.

Suppose that we wanted to use a subnet mask of 255.255.255.128 for a Class C subnetted address. To arrive at the 128 number in our chart requires 1 bit. However, using our calculation of $2^1 - 2 = 0$, we can see that it is invalid. The smallest number of subnet bits that we can use for a Class C network is 2. This example could happen if we required 120 hosts for a subnet. By running through our steps we would determine that we would need 7 bits for the number 120. This would then leave only 1 bit for the subnet bits, and therefore we would not be able to subnet this address.

There is a slight mistruth to this method. Although we have been throwing out the first and last subnets (all 0s and all 1s combinations), the truth is that we can actually use these subnets as long as all the hardware and software in our network supports it! However, it is not recommended to use these two subnets in any environment, and as far as the CCNA test is concerned, they are not usable.

Finding the Number of Hosts per Subnet

Now that we know how to find the number of subnets that have been created, it is only a slight change to find the number of hosts per subnet. All we have to do is remember which bits we are working with. Once we know the number of bits we have left over for the hosts, we can use the same calculation as we used for the number of subnets. Again, we have to remove the first Host ID because it references the network itself and not an actual host. We also have to remove the final Host ID because this is the subnet or network broadcast address.

In Example #1, we needed 4 bits for the subnet. To determine the number of bits for the hosts, we subtract from the total number of bits that we have to work with. In this example, $8 - 4 = 4$ bits left for the Host IDs. Using our calculation, we then determine that we have $2^4 - 2 = 14$ hosts for each subnet. This is similar to having a Class C address and having all 8 bits in the fourth octet available for us to use. Now we have taken bits from those 8 bits to create our subgroups, and inside each subgroup (subnet) we have 4 bits left to work with.

In Example #2, we needed 6 bits for the total number of subnets required. Remember that we created 62 subnets. But that only leaves 2 bits for the hosts ($8 - 6 = 2$ bits), which means we have a total of $2^2 - 2 = 2$ hosts per each subnet!

Finally, in Example #3, we actually already figured out the number of bits for the hosts. In this case, we needed 5 bits, so $2^5 - 2 = 30$ hosts per subnet. We needed 15 but we have 30 addresses available.

All of this may seem simple, but repetition is the key. Practice Exercise 7.2 can be used for more practice.

Populating the Subnets

Now that we know how many subnets, hosts per subnet, and the subnet mask, we can actually start assigning addresses to subnets and to hosts themselves. Class C addresses are perhaps the most difficult to understand, because we are only working with the last 8 bits. Remember that some of these bits are being used to create the subgroups (subnets), so that leaves even fewer bits available.

Calculating the Subnet Addresses

The best way to show this is to use an example. We will return to Example #1. We needed 13 subnets and determined that the proper subnet mask was 255.255.255.240 (or 192.168.10.0/28). This in turn gave us 14 subnets with 14 hosts on each subnet. In order to start defining the subnet addresses that can be assigned to network segments, we will use a magic number of 256. This number isn't so magic, it is the total number of combinations in 8 bits. Take the number determined as our subnet mask in step #4 (240) and subtract it from 256. The result is 16. Now, starting at 0, add 16 to the previous number to create a chart. Stop when the number reached is the same as the subnet mask value. Our chart should look like this:

0	128
16	144
32	160
48	176
64	192
80	208
96	224
112	240

Notice that we stopped at 240. If we added 16 to that, we would have 256, which is a number that cannot be represented with 8 bits in binary. Remember that we throw away the first and the last subnets? Let's do that now. The final chart, then, has 14 values (14 subnets) and ranges from 16 to 224. Since we were given the network address of 192.168.10.0, we can now further define the subnets within this network. The result is shown in Table 7.1.

TABLE 7.1	Subnet ranges for 192.168.10.0/28
16 →	192.168.10.16
32 →	192.168.10.32
48 →	192.168.10.48
64 →	192.168.10.64
80 →	192.168.10.80
96 →	192.168.10.96
112 →	192.168.10.112
128 →	192.168.10.128
144 →	192.168.10.144
160 →	192.168.10.160
176 →	192.168.10.176
192 →	192.168.10.192
208 →	192.168.10.208
224 →	192.168.10.224

We have just defined each of the subnets, so we can now start assigning Host IDs. This process is a logical progression, but we will wait to cover that in the next section. First, let's finish Examples #2 and #3.

Example #2 gave us a network address of 192.168.15.0 and required 31 subnets. Remember that it took 6 bits to do this, which gave us 62 actual subnets. Our subnet mask was determined to be 255.255.255.252. We then take the number 252 from 256 (our magic number), and the result is 4. Listing our chart out, and remembering to remove the first and the last subnets, results in Table 7.2.

TABLE 7.2	Subnet ranges for 192.168.15.0/30				
0 →	Not Available	84 →	192.168.15.84	168 →	192.168.15.168
4 →	192.168.10.4	88 →	192.168.10.88	172 →	192.168.10.172
8 →	192.168.10.8	92 →	192.168.10.92	176 →	192.168.10.176
12 →	192.168.10.12	96 →	192.168.10.96	180 →	192.168.10.180
16 →	192.168.10.16	100 →	192.168.10.100	184 →	192.168.10.184
20 →	192.168.10.20	104 →	192.168.10.104	188 →	192.168.10.188
24 →	192.168.10.24	108 →	192.168.10.108	192 →	192.168.10.192
28 →	192.168.10.28	112 →	192.168.10.112	196 →	192.168.10.196
32 →	192.168.10.32	116 →	192.168.10.116	200 →	192.168.10.200
36 →	192.168.10.36	120 →	192.168.10.120	204 →	192.168.10.204
40 →	192.168.10.40	124 →	192.168.10.124	208 →	192.168.10.208
44 →	192.168.10.44	128 →	192.168.10.128	212 →	192.168.10.212
48 →	192.168.10.48	132 →	192.168.10.132	216 →	192.168.10.216
52 →	192.168.10.52	136 →	192.168.10.136	220 →	192.168.10.220
56 →	192.168.10.56	140 →	192.168.10.140	224 →	192.168.10.224
60 →	192.168.10.60	144 →	192.168.10.144	228 →	192.168.10.228
64 →	192.168.10.64	148 →	192.168.10.148	232 →	192.168.10.232
68 →	192.168.10.68	152 →	192.168.10.152	236 →	192.168.10.236
72 →	192.168.10.72	156 →	192.168.10.156	240 →	192.168.10.240
76 →	192.168.10.76	160 →	192.168.10.160	244 →	192.168.10.244
80 →	192.168.10.80	164 →	192.168.10.164	248 →	192.168.10.248
				252 →	Not Available

In Example #3, We were given the network address of 192.168.15.0, and determined that the subnet mask is 255.255.255.224 (or 192.168.15.0/27). We needed 31 hosts per subnet and ended up with 62. This left us with 3 bits for the subnet. Taking 224 from our magic number of 256 leaves us with 32. We then start at 0 and continue adding 32 until we reach 224, which is the subnet mask value. Table 7.3 shows us the subnet ranges.

TABLE 7.3	Subnet ranges for 192.168.15.0/27			
0	→ Not Available	128	→	192.168.15.128
32	→ 192.168.15.32	160	→	192.168.15.160
64	→ 192.168.15.64	192	→	192.168.15.192
96	→ 192.168.15.96	224	→	Not Available

Calculating the Host IDs

Now that we know what the subnet network addresses are, we can use these when we start routing. However, we still need to know how to assign the Host IDs. First though, let's review what we have been doing at the bit level.

For each of the Class C addresses we have been working with, we are not allowed to touch the first three octets by definition. This leaves us the last octet, or 8 bits to do with as we please. In a normal network, we would use all 8 bits for the Host IDs. However, we want to break these Class C addresses into smaller groups known as subnets. To do this, we take bits from the hosts and create subgroups. Let's look at a single subnet from Example #1. We will look at 192.168.10.48. This address breaks down as shown in Figure 7–4.

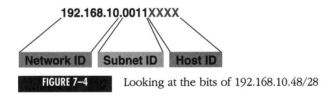

| FIGURE 7–4 | Looking at the bits of 192.168.10.48/28 |

Here we have broken the last octet down into the bits. We can see that the subnet ID of 48 would be equal to 00110000. Since the last 4 bits are being used for the Host ID, they can be almost anything we want. To define the Host IDs, we need to show the possible combinations of 0011XXXX. Looking at Table 7.4, we can see the possible combinations and the decimal equivalent of the fourth octet.

Table 7.4 tells us that our valid hosts range from 192.168.10.48 to 192.168.10.63. But wait! Remember that we cannot have all 0s for the host. This means that the Host ID of 192.168.10.48 is really the subnet address (the subgroup address within the network itself), and not a valid host. The same rule states that we cannot have all 1s for the Host ID. This is the broadcast address. So, 192.168.10.63 is the broadcast address for the subnet of 192.168.10.48. The valid host ranges are then 192.168.10.49 to 192.168.10.62.

TABLE 7.4	Binary breakdown of Host IDs		
0011**0000**	48	0011**1000**	56
0011**0001**	49	0011**1001**	57
0011**0010**	50	0011**1010**	58
0011**0011**	51	0011**1011**	59
0011**0100**	52	0011**1100**	60
0011**0101**	53	0011**1101**	61
0011**0110**	54	0011**1110**	62
0011**0111**	55	0011**1111**	63

Remembering to remove the first and last subnets, and the first and last Host IDs of each subnet, we would have the valid Host IDs for each of the subnets created in Example #1, shown in Table 7.5.

TABLE 7.5		Subnet address, Host IDs, and broadcast address for 192.168.10.0/28		
Value	→	Subnet Address	Starting Host	Ending Host	Broadcast
---	---	---	---	---	---
16	→	192.168.10.16	192.168.10.17	192.168.10.30	192.168.10.31
32	→	192.168.10.32	192.168.10.33	192.168.10.46	192.168.10.47
48	→	192.168.10.48	192.168.10.49	192.168.10.62	192.168.10.63
64	→	192.168.10.64	192.168.10.65	192.168.10.78	192.168.10.79
80	→	192.168.10.80	192.168.10.81	192.168.10.94	192.168.10.95
96	→	192.168.10.96	192.168.10.97	192.168.10.110	192.168.10.111
112	→	192.168.10.112	192.168.10.113	192.168.10.126	192.168.10.127
128	→	192.168.10.128	192.168.10.129	192.168.10.142	192.168.10.143
144	→	192.168.10.144	192.168.10.145	192.168.10.158	192.168.10.159
160	→	192.168.10.160	192.168.10.161	192.168.10.174	192.168.10.175
176	→	192.168.10.176	192.168.10.177	192.168.10.190	192.168.10.191
192	→	192.168.10.192	192.168.10.193	192.168.10.206	192.168.10.207
208	→	192.168.10.208	192.168.10.209	192.168.10.222	192.168.10.223
224	→	192.168.10.224	192.168.10.225	192.168.10.238	192.168.10.239

If we look at Table 7.5, specifically at a single column, we can see the patterns emerge. For instance, the broadcast address is simply the number before the start of the next range. The last Host ID is 1 less than that.

Using this method, we should be able to determine the ranges for Examples #2 and #3. For more practice, we can refer to Practice Exercise 7.3.

Supernetting

Supernetting is a process where we actually combine multiple class addresses into a single address with a subnet mask. This is useful when we have been given many Class C addresses, and we would like to consolidate them into a single address for defining our routing tables with.

For example, suppose we had been given the Class C addresses of 202.15.20.0, 202.15.21.0, 202.15.22.0, and 202.15.23.0. Since the first two octets are identical, there is no need to consolidate them. However, our third octet varies with each address. To consolidate them, we need to convert the third octets into binary. Our result is then:

202.15.20.0	00010100
202.15.21.0	00010101
202.15.22.0	00010110
202.15.23.0	00010111

If we look closely, we can see that the four addresses share the same first 6 bits. Since only the last 2 bits are different, we can take those 2 bits off of our default subnet mask so that the final subnet mask is 255.255.252.0. Using this method, we can reduce our routing table from four separate entries into a single entry. This would only be done on the router that is routing packets into our organization. The rest of our routers would have standard routing tables.

Configuring IC, Inc.

We can now start putting our subnetting skills in action. We have our network diagram of IC, Inc., and we would like to use a single Class C address for our network, and subnet it. The address we have chosen arbitrarily is 192.168.50.0.

First, we need to decide how many subnets are required. Referring to Figure 7–5, we can see that we have a total of five subnets. Running through our steps, we can calculate the following:

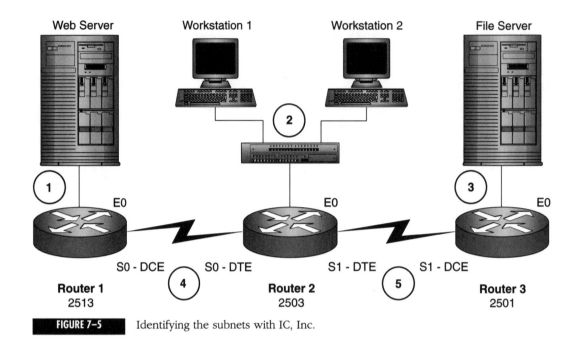

FIGURE 7–5   Identifying the subnets with IC, Inc.

Step #1

Step #1:

> Recite the given scenario and determine what we know.
>> Class C – 8 bits to work with – 5 subnets required – 255.255.255.0 default subnet mask

Step #2:

> Convert the number of subnets (hosts) to binary.
>> 5 in binary is 101

Step #3:

> Count the number of bits used.
>> 3 bits were used for the subnet.

Step #4:

> Using our chart, count the number of bits found in step #3 from left to right. Read the subnet mask.

1	0	1					
128	192	224	240	248	252	254	255
128	64	32	16	8	4	2	1

Our subnet mask is then 255.255.255.224.

Step #2

In Table 7.6 we list out our chart of subnets. 256 − 224 = 32 is our range.

TABLE 7.6	Valid hosts and subnet ranges for IC, Inc.			
Value →	**Subnet Address**	**Starting Host**	**Ending Host**	**Broadcast**
0 →	Not Valid	Not Valid	Not Valid	Not Valid
32 →	192.168.50.32	192.168.50.33	192.168.50.62	192.168.50.63
64 →	192.168.50.64	192.168.50.65	192.168.50.94	192.168.50.95
96 →	192.168.50.96	192.168.50.97	192.168.50.126	192.168.50.127
128 →	192.168.50.128	192.168.50.129	192.168.50.158	192.168.50.159
160 →	192.168.50.160	192.168.50.161	192.168.50.190	192.168.50.191
192 →	192.168.50.192	192.168.50.193	192.168.50.222	192.168.50.223
224 →	Not Valid	Not Valid	Not Valid	Not Valid

Here we can see our numbers match up. We used 3 bits for the subnet, so $2^3 - 2 = 6$ subnets. That is exactly what we have come up with.

Step #3

Now we can actually assign subnets and IP addresses. Using Table 7.6, we can fill in the values:

Subnet 1: 192.168.50.32 / 27
      Web Server IP : 192.168.50.33
      Router 1 E0: 192.168.50.62
Subnet 2: 192.168.50.64 / 27
      Workstation 1 IP: 192.168.50.65
      Workstation 2 IP: 192.168.50.66
      Router 2 E0: 192.168.50.94
Subnet 3: 192.168.50.96
      File Server IP: 192.168.50.97
      Router 3 E0: 192.168.50.126
Subnet 4: 192.168.50.128
      Router 1 S0: 192.168.50.129
      Router 2 S0: 192.168.50.158
Subnet 5: 192.168.50.160
      Router 2 S1: 192.168.50.190
      Router 3 S1: 192.168.50.161

We will assume that the WAN links between the routers are both 56K leased lines. The final diagram is shown in Figure 7–6. Let's start configuring the routers now.

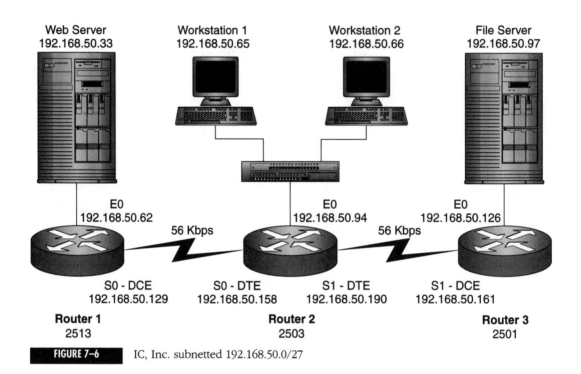

FIGURE 7–6   IC, Inc. subnetted 192.168.50.0/27

Router 1

```
Router>enable
Router#conf term
Enter configuration commands, one per line.  End with CNTL/Z.
Router(config)#hostname Router1
Router1(config)#int e0
Router1(config-if)#ip addr 192.168.50.62 255.255.255.224
Router1(config-if)#no shut
%LINEPROTO-5-UPDOWN: Line protocol on Interface Ethernet0, changed state to up
%LINK-3-UPDOWN: Interface Ethernet0, changed state to up
Router1(config-if)#int s0
Router1(config-if)#ip addr 192.168.50.129 255.255.255.224
Router1(config-if)#clockrate 56000
Router1(config-if)#no shut
%LINK-3-UPDOWN: Interface Serial0, changed state to up
%LINEPROTO-5-UPDOWN: Line protocol on Interface Serial0, changed state to up
Router1(config-if)#^Z
```

```
Router1#
%SYS-5-CONFIG_I: Configured from console by console
Router1#copy run start
Building configuration...
[OK]
Router1#ping 192.168.50.33
Type escape sequence to abort.
Sending 5, 100-byte ICMP Echos to 192.168.50.33, timeout is 2 seconds:
.!!!!
Success rate is 80 percent (4/5), round-trip min/avg/max = 1/2/4 ms
Router1#
```

As we can see, everything was configured correctly. There really is no difference in configuring a router to use a subnet. We just have to specify the correct subnet mask. Also note that the subnet mask is the same mask throughout the entire network.

Next, we configure Router 2 and test its connectivity.

Router 2

```
Router>enable
Router#conf term
Enter configuration commands, one per line.  End with CNTL/Z.
Router(config)#hostname Router2
Router2(config)#int e0
Router2(config-if)#ip addr 192.168.50.94 255.255.255.224
Router2(config-if)#no shut
Router2(config-if)#
%LINEPROTO-5-UPDOWN: Line protocol on Interface Ethernet0, changed state to up
%LINK-3-UPDOWN: Interface Ethernet0, changed state to up
Router2(config-if)#int s0
Router2(config-if)#ip addr 192.168.50.158 255.255.255.224
Router2(config-if)#no shut
Router2(config-if)#int s1
Router2(config-if)#ip addr 192.168.50.190 255.255.255.224
Router2(config-if)#no shut
Router2(config-if)#
%LINK-3-UPDOWN: Interface Serial1, changed state to up
%LINEPROTO-5-UPDOWN: Line protocol on Interface Serial1, changed state to up
Router2(config-if)#^Z
Router2#
Router2#copy run start
Building configuration...
[OK]
Router2#ping 192.168.50.65

Type escape sequence to abort.
Sending 5, 100-byte ICMP Echos to 192.168.50.65, timeout is 2 seconds:
!!!!!
```

```
Success rate is 100 percent (5/5), round-trip min/avg/max = 1/2/4 ms
Router2#ping 192.168.50.66

Type escape sequence to abort.
Sending 5, 100-byte ICMP Echos to 192.168.50.66, timeout is 2 seconds:
.!!!!
Success rate is 80 percent (4/5), round-trip min/avg/max = 1/3/4 ms
Router2#ping 192.168.50.129

Type escape sequence to abort.
Sending 5, 100-byte ICMP Echos to 192.168.50.129, timeout is 2 seconds:
!!!!!
Success rate is 100 percent (5/5), round-trip min/avg/max = 32/35/36 ms
Router2#ping 192.168.50.161

Type escape sequence to abort.
Sending 5, 100-byte ICMP Echos to 192.168.50.161, timeout is 2 seconds:
.....
Success rate is 0 percent (0/5)
Router2#
```

We set up each of the interfaces with the subnet mask of
255.255.255.224. We made sure that the interfaces were administratively
turned on with the **no shut** command, and then we tested connectivity.

The address of 192.168.50.161 failed in returning a response, but then
since we haven't configured Router 3 yet, we shouldn't have expected one.

Time to configure the final router.

Router 3

```
Router>enable
Router#config term
Enter configuration commands, one per line.  End with CNTL/Z.
Router(config)#hostname Router3
Router3(config)#int e0
Router3(config-if)#ip addr 192.168.50.126 255.255.255.224
Router3(config-if)#no shut
Router3(config-if)#
%LINEPROTO-5-UPDOWN: Line protocol on Interface Ethernet0, changed state to up
%LINK-3-UPDOWN: Interface Ethernet0, changed state to up
Router3(config-if)#int s1
Router3(config-if)#ip addr 192.168.50.161 255.255.255.224
Router3(config-if)#clockrate 56000
Router3(config-if)#no shut
Router3(config-if)#
%LINK-3-UPDOWN: Interface Serial1, changed state to up
%LINEPROTO-5-UPDOWN: Line protocol on Interface Serial1, changed state to up
Router3(config-if)#^Z
Router3#
```

```
Router3#copy run start
Building configuration...
[OK]
Router3#ping 192.168.50.97

Type escape sequence to abort.
Sending 5, 100-byte ICMP Echos to 192.168.50.97, timeout is 2 seconds:
.!!!!
Success rate is 80 percent (4/5), round-trip min/avg/max = 1/3/4 ms
Router3#ping 192.168.50.190

Type escape sequence to abort.
Sending 5, 100-byte ICMP Echos to 192.168.50.190, timeout is 2 seconds:
!!!!!
Success rate is 100 percent (5/5), round-trip min/avg/max = 36/36/36 ms
Router3#ping 192.168.50.94

Type escape sequence to abort.
Sending 5, 100-byte ICMP Echos to 192.168.50.94, timeout is 2 seconds:
.....
Success rate is 0 percent (0/5)
Router3#show int e0
Ethernet0 is up, line protocol is up
  Hardware is Lance, address is 0000.0c91.a1ed (bia 0000.0c91.a1ed)
  Internet address is 192.168.50.126/27
  MTU 1500 bytes, BW 10000 Kbit, DLY 1000 usec, rely 255/255, load 1/255
  <lines deleted>
Router3#show int s1
Serial1 is up, line protocol is up
  Hardware is HD64570
  Internet address is 192.168.50.161/27
  MTU 1500 bytes, BW 1544 Kbit, DLY 20000 usec, rely 255/255, load 1/255
```

Again, we specified the correct subnet mask and then tested connectivity with all the interfaces. Additionally, we verified our IP addresses with the **show interface** commands. It shows us our subnet mask in the CIDR notation; in this case, /27.

Notice that we did not get a response from the 192.168.50.94 interface on Router 2. The interface is working, it's just that there is no route listed, so Router 3 does not know where to send the packet for that subnet. This is the topic of the next chapter.

Summary

Subnetting is the process of creating subgroups within a network address. This subgroup is referred to as a *subnet*. Creating subnets allows us to manage our network in a more efficient manner. It also allows us to create smaller broadcast and collision domains (in an Ethernet network). The concept of creating a subnet is by taking some bits from the number of bits that we would normally use to assign Host IDs. The disadvantage to this is the loss of the total number of hosts. This is due to the fact that we cannot use the first and the last subnets, and that each subnet requires a subnet address and a broadcast address. This causes us to lose two more Host IDs for each subnet.

To determine the subnet mask, we use the following steps:

1. Recite the given scenario and determine what we know.
2. Convert the number of subnets (hosts) to binary.
3. Count the number of bits used.
4. Using our chart, count the number of bits found in step #3 from left to right. Read the subnet mask.

128	192	224	240	248	252	254	255
128	64	32	16	8	4	2	1

Scenario Lab 7.1

Your previous solution for network addresses was perfect. Unfortunately, the CIO has decided she would like to use a single network address and have it subnetted (see Figure 7–7). It is up to you to choose a class of address and subnet it. Include in your report the number of subnets actually created, the number of hosts for each subnet, the subnet address and the broadcast address, the valid host ranges, and a recommendation on the numbering scheme for each segment. Remember to allow for future growth for both subnets and hosts on each subnet.

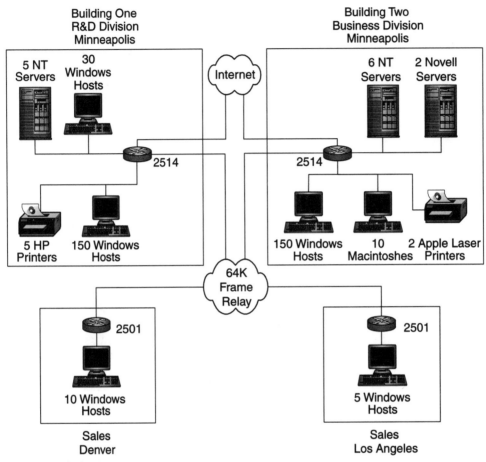

FIGURE 7–7   Subnetting Network Solutions, Inc.

Practice Exercise 7.1

1. You have a Class C address. You need to create 11 subnets. What is the subnet mask?
2. You have a Class C address. You need to create 15 subnets. What is the subnet mask?
3. You have a network address of 202.17.19.0. You need three subnets now and four additional subnets in the future. What is the subnet mask that should be used?
4. You have a Class C address. You need a maximum of 30 hosts on each subnet. What is the subnet mask?
5. You have a network address of 191.160.0.0. You need a maximum of 12 hosts on each subnet. What is the subnet mask?
6. You require 20 hosts per subnet using a Class B network address. What is the subnet mask needed?
7. Given the address of 191.15.0.0 and needing 20 subnets, what is the correct subnet mask to use?
8. Given the address of 202.15.78.0 and needing 20 hosts per subnet, what is the correct subnet mask?
9. You have a Class A address of 11.0.0.0. You need a maximum of 400 subnets. What is the subnet mask that is needed?
10. You have a class A address of 121.0.0.0. You need a maximum of 400 hosts. What is the subnet mask that is needed?

Practice Exercise 7.2

1. You have a Class C address. You need to create 13 subnets. What is the subnet mask? How many subnets and hosts per subnet are created?
2. You have a Class C address. You need to create 14 subnets. What is the subnet mask? How many subnets and hosts per subnet are created?
3. You have a network address of 202.17.19.0. You need three subnets now and will have three additional subnets in the future. What is the subnet mask that should be used? How many subnets and hosts per subnet are created?
4. You have a Class C address. You need a maximum of 40 hosts on each subnet. What is the subnet mask? How many subnets and hosts per subnet are created?
5. You have a network address of 191.160.0.0. You need a maximum of 20 hosts on each subnet. What is the subnet mask? How many subnets and hosts per subnet are created?
6. You require 50 hosts per subnet using a Class B network address. What is the subnet mask needed? How many subnets and hosts per subnet are created?
7. Given the address of 191.15.0.0 and needing 40 subnets, what is the correct subnet mask to use? How many subnets and hosts per subnet are created?

8. Given the address of 202.15.78.0 and needing 40 hosts per subnet, what is the correct subnet mask? How many subnets and hosts per subnet are created?

9. You have a Class A address of 11.0.0.0. You need a maximum of 200 subnets. What is the subnet mask that is needed? How many subnets and hosts per subnet are created?

10. You have a Class A address of 121.0.0.0. You need a maximum of 600 subnets. What is the subnet mask that is needed? How many subnets and hosts per subnet are created?

For more practice determine the number of hosts and subnets for Practice Exercise 7.1.

Practice Exercise 7.3

Using Practice Exercise 7.1, define the subnet ranges, valid Host IDs, and the broadcast and network addresses for each of the questions.

Practice Lab 7.1

In this lab you will configure each of the routers in
Figure 7–8. You have been given a Class C address of
192.168.10.0 and must subnet it appropriately. Once you
have subnetted it, you can configure the routers.

- Step #1: Identify what you already know:
    Class of Address:
    # Subnets Desired:
    Default Subnet Mask:
    # Bits to work with:
- Step #2: Convert to binary. Make sure to check for all 1s!
- Step #3: Count the number of bits. What are these bits
  used for (host or subnet?)
- Step #4: Use the chart to arrive at the new subnet mask.
- Create a chart that lists the subnet ranges, valid Host
  IDs, and the broadcast address for each subnet.

    Use the following to check your work:
        Class of Address: C
        # Subnets Desired: At least three
        Default Subnet Mask: 255.255.255.0
        # Bits to work with: 8

    Converting 3 to binary gives us 11. Since we cannot
    have all 1s, we must add a leading 0 to give us a result
    of 011. Our final subnet mask in this example would
    be 255.255.255.224.

Use the following chart to verify your own. This is one example using 3 bits. If you used more bits for the subnet, this chart will not match yours.

Value	→	Subnet Address	Starting Host	Ending Host	Broadcast
0	→	Not Valid	Not Valid	Not Valid	Not Valid
32	→	192.168.50.32	192.168.50.33	192.168.50.62	192.168.50.63
64	→	192.168.50.64	192.168.50.65	192.168.50.94	192.168.50.95
96	→	192.168.50.96	192.168.50.97	192.168.50.126	192.168.50.127
128	→	192.168.50.128	192.168.50.129	192.168.50.158	192.168.50.159
160	→	192.168.50.160	192.168.50.161	192.168.50.190	192.168.50.191
192	→	192.168.50.192	192.168.50.193	192.168.50.222	192.168.50.223
224	→	Not Valid	Not Valid	Not Valid	Not Valid

- Assign addresses to the workstations and to the routers. Configure the routers and verify connectivity using the **ping** command. For help with the configuration, refer to Chapters 6 and 7.

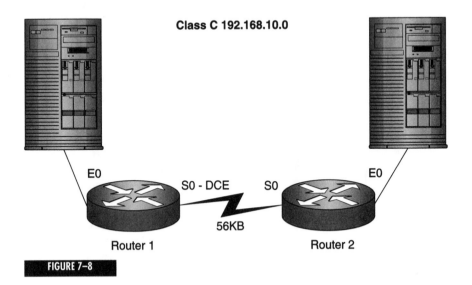

Class C 192.168.10.0

E0   S0 - DCE   S0   E0

56KB

Router 1   Router 2

FIGURE 7-8

Practice Lab 7.2

In this lab, you will configure a network using a Class C address and subnetting it. Allow for future growth of seven more subnets in the future. Create a chart listing the subnet ranges, valid Host IDs, and the broadcast and network addresses.

Configure each of the routers in Figure 7–9 and test connectivity using **ping**. For help on configuring the routers, refer to Chapters 6 and 7.

Refer to Table 7.5 for a completed chart for one way to design this network.

Class C - 192.168.10.0

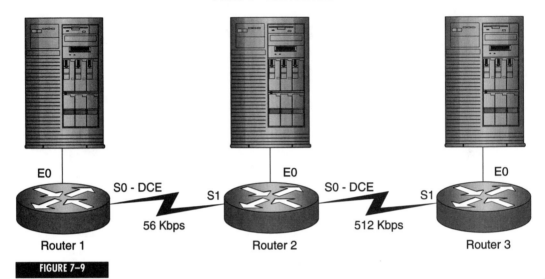

FIGURE 7–9

Exam Objective Checklist

By working through this chapter, you should have sufficient knowledge to answer these exam objectives:

- Describe the two parts of network addressing, then identify the parts in specific protocol address examples.
- Describe the different classes of IP addresses (and subnetting).
- Configure IP addresses.
- Verify IP addresses.

Practice Questions

1. The subnet mask of 255.255.255.240 can be expressed in CIDR notation as _____ ?

   a. /24
   b. /26
   c. /28
   d. /30

2. You have been given a Class C address and need to subnet it to five subnets. What is the correct subnet mask?

   a. 255.255.255.240
   b. 255.255.255.224
   c. 255.255.255.192
   d. 255.255.255.128

3. What is the correct broadcast address for a host with the IP address of 192.168.50.50 using a subnet mask of 255.255.255.240?

   a. 192.168.50.15
   b. 192.168.50.48
   c. 192.168.50.63
   d. 192.168.50.51

4. Which two hosts are on the same subnet, given the address of 192.168.50.0/27?

   a. 192.168.50.33
   b. 192.168.50.95
   c. 192.168.50.44
   d. 192.168.50.96

5. Which one of the following is a valid host using the address of 172.16.0.0/19?

   a. 172.16.32.0
   b. 172.16.64.0
   c. 172.16.63.255
   d. 172.16.80.255

6. How many subnets are created when using a Class C network with a subnet mask of 255.255.255.248?

   a. 32
   b. 30
   c. 16
   d. 14

7. You have been given a Class B address of 172.16.0.0. You need to subnet it to 14 subnets. Which subnet mask will give you the most hosts per subnet?

   a. 255.255.240.0
   b. 255.255.228.0
   c. 255.255.248.0
   d. 255.255.255.240

8. You have been given a Class B address of 172.16.0.0. You have subnetted it to 255.255.240.0. How many hosts and how many subnets are created?

   a. 14 hosts, 254 subnets
   b. 14 hosts, 4094 subnets
   c. 14 subnets, 4094 hosts
   d. 14 subnets, 254 hosts

9. You have been given a Class C address of 192.168.10.0/28. Which of the following lists a valid host range?

   a. 192.168.10.16 to 192.168.10.31
   b. 192.168.10.33 to 192.168.10.47
   c. 192.168.10.65 to 192.168.10.80
   d. 192.168.10.81 to 192.168.10.94

10. You have been given a Class C address of 192.168.10.0/29. Which of the following lists a valid host range?

 a. 192.168.10.225 to 192.168.10.230
 b. 192.168.10.233 to 192.168.10.239
 c. 192.168.10.240 to 192.168.10.246
 d. 192.168.10.249 to 192.168.10.254

Static TCP/IP Routing

In This Chapter

- ◆ Static Routing
- ◆ Default Routing

In order to use segment network traffic and reduce network collision, there needs to be a way to deliver the network traffic to the correct segment. This is the job of the router. A router must have a routing table built in order to decide on the path to deliver the datagram. We do this in this chapter.

Static Routing Concepts

By default, a router does not care where the datagram it receives originated from, nor does it care what the destination is. All a router really cares about is the network address.

By using the ANDing process, a router can determine the destination Net ID and then can look it up in the routing table. If an entry is found that matches the Net ID, it will forward the datagram appropriately.

Let's review Chapter 4, "TCP/IP." If we refer to Figure 8–1, we can see there are two nodes on the E0 side of the router, and one node on the E1 side of the router. When Node A wants to communicate with Node B, ARP will broadcast a request for the MAC address of the host that has 192.168.10.2

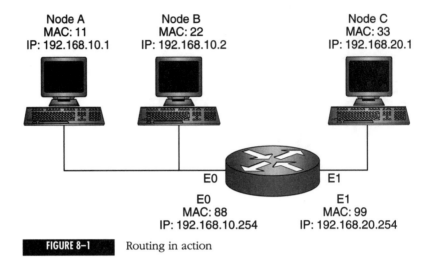

FIGURE 8-1   Routing in action

as its IP address. This assumes that the mapping of MAC to IP is not already in the ARP table. Node B will reply with the MAC address of 22. Node A will then send datagrams directly to Node B by filling in the Data Link header with the destination MAC address of 22.

If Node A wants to send to Node C, the Network layer will deduce (using the ANDing method) that the destination node is on a different network. In this instance, Node A knows that it has to send the data to the router. It will ARP for the router's MAC address and will receive the reply of 88. Next, Node A will send the datagram to the router by using the destination MAC address of 88 in the Data Link header. However, the destination IP address in the Network header indicates the true recipient is 192.168.20.1. When the router receives the data, it determines that the data is meant for it. It then looks up the destination IP address and sees that the data really belongs to Node C. The router then looks in its routing table and determines that the network address of 192.168.20.0 is directly connected to E1. The router then ARPs for the destination host, receives a reply with the MAC address of 33, modifies the Data Link header, and sends off the data onto the network. Node C will receive the data and correctly interpret that the originator of the data was Node A. This is accomplished because the router never modified the Network header, and this header included Node A's IP address as the source.

What happens when there are two routers? Examine Figure 8–2 for the answer. Here we can see two routers. If Node A wants to talk to Node B, or Node B wants to talk to Node C, then there is no difference from what was discussed for the previous figure. However, what happens when Node A wants to communicate with Node C?

In this case, Node A forwards the data to Router RA. This router then determines that the data is meant for the network 192.168.30.0. It looks in its

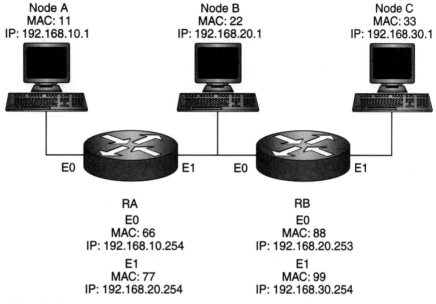

Node A
MAC: 11
IP: 192.168.10.1

Node B
MAC: 22
IP: 192.168.20.1

Node C
MAC: 33
IP: 192.168.30.1

EO   E1   EO   E1

RA
EO
MAC: 66
IP: 192.168.10.254

E1
MAC: 77
IP: 192.168.20.254

RB
EO
MAC: 88
IP: 192.168.20.253

E1
MAC: 99
IP: 192.168.30.254

FIGURE 8–2   Multiple router environment

routing table, but doesn't find a match. This is because the router is not directly connected to that network. At this point, the router gives up and drops the data. Doesn't make for a very efficient network, does it?

At this point, we would need to define a routing table. In order to do this, we need to remember two things. First, the router does not care who the destination host is, it only cares about the destination network. Second, a router can only communicate with another router that it is directly connected to. This is because ARP is a broadcast, and broadcasts do not pass routers.

To set up the routing table, we need to specify that in order for router RA to get the data to the final network of 192.168.30.0, it has to forward the data to the next router, RB. That is all that Router RA cares about. If Router RB does not know how to get the data to the final network, it is the fault of Router RB, not RA.

Let's walk through the steps to get the data from Node A to Node C and back.

1. Node A determines that Node C is on a different network, namely 192.168.30.0. In order to get the data there, it has to send it to Router RA.
2. Node A sends out an ARP request for the MAC address of Router RA (note that the MAC address may already be in the cache of Node A and thus a broadcast would be unnecessary).
3. Router RA responds with the MAC address of 66.
4. Node A sends the data to the router with the following information:
    Source MAC: 11
    Destination MAC: 66

Source IP: 192.168.10.1
Destination IP: 192.168.30.1

5. Router RA receives the data and determines that it is supposed to forward the data. It knows this because the destination IP address does not match its own. Router RA then looks in the routing table and finds the newly discovered entry that we created. Router RA knows to send the data to the next router, RB.

6. Router RA ARPs for the MAC address of Router RB.

7. Router RB responds with the MAC address of 88.

8. Router RA sends the data to Router RB with the following information:
   Source MAC: 77
   Destination MAC: 88
   Source IP: 192.168.10.1
   Destination IP: 192.168.30.1

9. Router RB receives the data. Router RB notes that the destination IP address is not its own, and therefore must forward the data. Router RB looks in its routing table for 192.168.30.0 and finds it. It finds the network because it is part of that network, or it is directly connected.

10. Router RB ARPs for the MAC address of the final destination IP address of 192.168.30.1.

11. Node C responds with the MAC address of 33.

12. Router RB forwards the data with the following information:
    Source MAC: 99
    Destination MAC: 33
    Source IP: 192.168.10.1
    Destination IP: 192.168.30.1

13. Node C receives the information. Now Node C wants to respond. Node C knows that Node A sent the information, because the source IP address told it this. Node C determines that Node A is on a different network and so forwards it to the router.

14. Router RB receives the data and determines that the destination network is 192.168.10.0. It looks in its table, and doesn't find an entry! We forgot to add an entry here telling router RB how to get to the network 192.168.10.0! Router RB gives up and drops the data. It never reaches Node A.

Not only do we have to tell a router how to get to a given destination, but we have to tell all routers how to get to all destinations. If not, the preceding scenario happens.

To fix this problem, we need to add an entry to router RB that states that the network 192.168.10.0 is reachable through the next router, RA. Specifically, we tell it the IP address of 192.168.20.254, because this is the address that Router RB can directly communicate with.

Routing tables are like the Pony Express. The Pony Express filtered out the mail for the local town and then forwarded the rest of the mail to the next

Pony Express station. It was up to the next station to perform the same filtering and forwarding steps to ensure the mail got to its final destination.

Now that we have a grasp on the routing concept, let's configure our routers.

Configuring Routers for Static Routes

In Figure 8–3, we have our network diagram of IC, Inc. We have set up a standard network using five different Class C addresses. We will use **ping** to verify that we have connectivity with each of the local hosts.

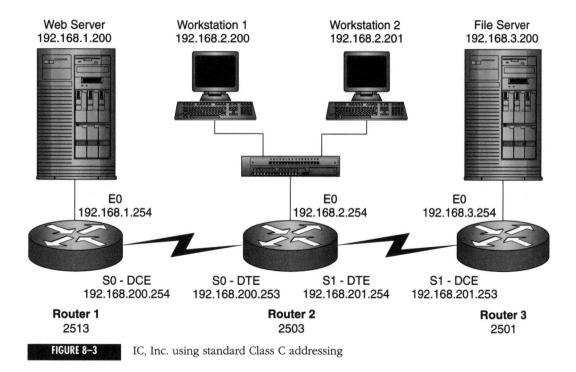

FIGURE 8–3   IC, Inc. using standard Class C addressing

The following is the output listing of our ping attempts. Notice that the first attempt may fail. This is because ARP has not yet responded with the MAC address for ping to send the data to.

```
Router1#ping 192.168.1.200

Type escape sequence to abort.
Sending 5, 100-byte ICMP Echos to 192.168.1.200, timeout is 2 seconds:
.!!!!
Success rate is 80 percent (4/5), round-trip min/avg/max = 1/2/4 ms
```

```
Router1#ping 192.168.200.253

Type escape sequence to abort.
Sending 5, 100-byte ICMP Echos to 192.168.200.253, timeout is 2

seconds:
!!!!!
Success rate is 100 percent (5/5), round-trip min/avg/max = 32/34/36 ms

Router2#ping 192.168.2.200

Type escape sequence to abort.
Sending 5, 100-byte ICMP Echos to 192.168.2.200, timeout is 2 seconds:
.!!!!
Success rate is 80 percent (4/5), round-trip min/avg/max = 1/2/4 ms
Router2#ping 192.168.2.201

Type escape sequence to abort.
Sending 5, 100-byte ICMP Echos to 192.168.2.201, timeout is 2 seconds:
.!!!!
Success rate is 80 percent (4/5), round-trip min/avg/max = 1/2/4 ms
Router2#ping 192.168.200.254

Type escape sequence to abort.
Sending 5, 100-byte ICMP Echos to 192.168.200.254, timeout is 2 seconds:
!!!!!
Success rate is 100 percent (5/5), round-trip min/avg/max = 32/40/68 ms
Router2#ping 192.168.201.253

Type escape sequence to abort.
Sending 5, 100-byte ICMP Echos to 192.168.201.253, timeout is 2 seconds:
!!!!!
Success rate is 100 percent (5/5), round-trip min/avg/max = 32/35/36 ms

Router3#ping 192.168.3.200

Type escape sequence to abort.
Sending 5, 100-byte ICMP Echos to 192.168.3.200, timeout is 2 seconds:
.!!!!
Success rate is 80 percent (4/5), round-trip min/avg/max = 1/2/4 ms
Router3#ping 192.168.201.254

Type escape sequence to abort.
Sending 5, 100-byte ICMP Echos to 192.168.201.254, timeout is 2 seconds:
!!!!!
Success rate is 100 percent (5/5), round-trip min/avg/max = 32/35/36 ms
```

Now that we have connectivity to all the local hosts, we can continue and build our routing table. We will configure one router at a time.

Router 1

In order to view our routing table, we can issue the command **show ip route**.

```
Router1#show ip route
Codes: C - connected, S - static, I - IGRP, R - RIP, M - mobile, B - BGP
       D - EIGRP, EX - EIGRP external, O - OSPF, IA - OSPF inter area
       N1 - OSPF NSSA external type 1, N2 - OSPF NSSA external type 2
       E1 - OSPF external type 1, E2 - OSPF external type 2, E - EGP
       i - IS-IS, L1 - IS-IS level-1, L2 - IS-IS level-2, * - candidate default
       U - per-user static route, o - ODR

Gateway of last resort is not set

C    192.168.200.0/24 is directly connected, Serial0
C    192.168.1.0/24 is directly connected, Ethernet0
Router1#
```

Here we see that there are two routes currently in the table. The first is for 192.168.200.0/24, and the second is for 192.168.1.0/24. Looking closer at the table, we can see that these two networks are directly connected to the router. Router 1 builds this limited information every time it reboots. Notice the letter "C" before the line. Using the codes found above the table, we can see that the "C" stands for connected. The next code is "S" for static. Let's create a static entry.

In order for this router to forward data to the network of 192.168.2.0, it has to send it to the next router, Router 2. But what address, and more specifically, what MAC address can Router 1 talk to? The only interface that is connected to Router 1 is 192.168.200.253. This is the next Pony Express station.

```
Router1#config term
Enter configuration commands, one per line.  End with CNTL/Z.
Router1(config)#ip route 192.168.2.0 255.255.255.0 192.168.200.253
Router1(config)#^Z
Router1#
%SYS-5-CONFIG_I: Configured from console by console
Router1#show ip route
Codes: C - connected, S - static, I - IGRP, R - RIP, M - mobile, B - BGP
       D - EIGRP, EX - EIGRP external, O - OSPF, IA - OSPF inter area
       N1 - OSPF NSSA external type 1, N2 - OSPF NSSA external type 2
       E1 - OSPF external type 1, E2 - OSPF external type 2, E - EGP
       i - IS-IS, L1 - IS-IS level-1, L2 - IS-IS level-2, * - candidate default
       U - per-user static route, o - ODR

Gateway of last resort is not set

C    192.168.200.0/24 is directly connected, Serial0
C    192.168.1.0/24 is directly connected, Ethernet0
S    192.168.2.0/24 [1/0] via 192.168.200.253
Router1#
```

The format of the command to create a static route entry is **ip route** *destination.network.address subnet.mask interface*. The parameter *interface* is the address of the router (Pony Express station) that can deliver the data.

Looking again at our routing table, we can see that there is a new entry that has shown up. It is prefixed with the letter "S" to indicate it is a static entry. To reach the network 192.168.2.0/24, the data will be sent to the router at 192.168.200.253.

The numbers in the brackets are important numbers. The first number is called the *administrative distance*. The lower the number, the more trusted the path is. This number will be different depending on the routing protocols that we use. Some routing protocols are more trustworthy than others. We will see more of this in the next chapter. The administrative distance of 1 means that this route is the best of all that it has received (next to directly connected routes). If, for some reason, we would like to make the static route a bit more unreliable, we could use the **ip route** *destination.network.address subnet.mask interface administrative.distance* command.

The second number is the cost of using that path. In the event that there are multiple paths to a destination network, the path with the lowest metric cost will be used. This cost varies depending on the protocol, and we will see more of this in the next chapter.

We have two more networks we need to reach: 192.168.201.0 and 192.168.3.0. Let's add them to our routing table.

```
Router1(config)#ip route 192.168.201.0 255.255.255.0 192.168.200.253
Router1(config)#ip route 192.168.3.0 255.255.255.0 192.168.200.253 80
Router1(config)#^Z
Router1#
%SYS-5-CONFIG_I: Configured from console by console
Router1#copy run start
Building configuration...
[OK]
```

When we use the **ip route** command, remember that the router does not care about the destination host itself. We specify the entire network. If we wanted to allow data to get to one host on a network, and none of the others, we could specify the exact host address instead of the network address. This will allow data to flow to that host, but to no other hosts on the same segment.

Notice that in the last command we changed the administrative distance to 80.

Let's examine the routing table now.

```
Router1#sho ip route
Codes: C - connected, S - static, I - IGRP, R - RIP, M - mobile, B - BGP
       D - EIGRP, EX - EIGRP external, O - OSPF, IA - OSPF inter area
       N1 - OSPF NSSA external type 1, N2 - OSPF NSSA external type 2
       E1 - OSPF external type 1, E2 - OSPF external type 2, E - EGP
       i - IS-IS, L1 - IS-IS level-1, L2 - IS-IS level-2, * - candidate default
       U - per-user static route, o - ODR
```

```
Gateway of last resort is not set

C    192.168.200.0/24 is directly connected, Serial0
S    192.168.201.0/24 [1/0] via 192.168.200.253
C    192.168.1.0/24 is directly connected, Ethernet0
S    192.168.2.0/24 [1/0] via 192.168.200.253
S    192.168.3.0/24 [80/0] via 192.168.200.253
Router1#
```

We have identified five total networks that we are connected to. Counting the entries in the routing table we have five, and therefore we listed all of them.

What happens when we try pinging now? Let's ping from the Web Server to the S0 interface of Router 2.

```
C:\>ping 192.168.200.253

Pinging 192.168.200.253 with 32 bytes of data:

Request timed out.
Request timed out.
Request timed out.
Request timed out.
```

We timed out because Router 2 does not yet know about the network 192.168.1.0. The data reached Router 2, but it could not find a way back; therefore, Router 2 dropped the data.

Router 2

We will now configure Router 2. Remember that there are a total of five networks, and this time the path to reach the destination network is split between two different routers. Let's view the routing table first.

```
Router2#show ip route
Codes: C - connected, S - static, I - IGRP, R - RIP, M - mobile, B - BGP
       D - EIGRP, EX - EIGRP external, O - OSPF, IA - OSPF inter area
       N1 - OSPF NSSA external type 1, N2 - OSPF NSSA external type 2
       E1 - OSPF external type 1, E2 - OSPF external type 2, E - EGP
       i - IS-IS, L1 - IS-IS level-1, L2 - IS-IS level-2, * - candidate default
       U - per-user static route, o - ODR

Gateway of last resort is not set

C    192.168.200.0/24 is directly connected, Serial0
C    192.168.201.0/24 is directly connected, Serial1
C    192.168.2.0/24 is directly connected, Ethernet0
Router2#
```

Here we can see that Router 2 already knows about three of the five networks. We only have to enter two networks, so this should be quick.

```
Router2#config term
Enter configuration commands, one per line.  End with CNTL/Z.
Router2(config)#ip route 192.168.1.0 255.255.255.0
192.168.200.254
Router2(config)#ip route 192.168.3.0 255.255.255.0
192.168.201.253
Router2(config)#^Z
Router2#
%SYS-5-CONFIG_I: Configured from console by console
Router2#copy run start
Building configuration...
[OK]
```

Again, we can view the results by looking at our routing table. Actually, let's just look at the two static entries.

```
Router2#show ip route static
S    192.168.1.0/24 [1/0] via 192.168.200.254
S    192.168.3.0/24 [1/0] via 192.168.201.253
Router2#
```

Here we added the parameter **static** to the command to display just the static entries. Notice that in order to reach the network of 192.168.1.0, the router will forward the data to Router 1. Also, if the data is destined for 192.168.3.0, the router will forward it to the other router—Router 3—instead. Since we are making the routing entries, it is up to us to do it intelligently.

In fact, if we do it wrong, we could end up with a routing loop. For instance, we could have said that to reach 192.168.3.0, we could send it to Router 1. Router 1 would receive the packet, see that it was destined for the 192.168.3.0 network, and after examining the routing table would forward the data back to Router 2. Thus, we created a loop, and nobody would be able to communicate with the File Server.

Router 3

At this point, everything looks good. Now we can finish up with Router 3.

```
Router3#config term
Enter configuration commands, one per line.  End with CNTL/Z.
Router3(config)#ip route 192.168.2.0 255.255.255.0 192.168.201.254
Router3(config)#ip route 192.168.1.0 255.255.255.0 192.168.201.254
Router3(config)#ip route 192.168.200.0 255.255.255.0 192.168.201.254
Router3(config)#^Z
Router3#
%SYS-5-CONFIG_I: Configured from console by console
Router3#copy run start
Building configuration...
[OK]
Router3#show ip route
```

```
Codes: C - connected, S - static, I - IGRP, R - RIP, M - mobile, B - BGP
       D - EIGRP, EX - EIGRP external, O - OSPF, IA - OSPF inter area
       N1 - OSPF NSSA external type 1, N2 - OSPF NSSA external type 2
       E1 - OSPF external type 1, E2 - OSPF external type 2, E - EGP
       i - IS-IS, L1 - IS-IS level-1, L2 - IS-IS level-2, * - candidate default
       U - per-user static route, o - ODR

Gateway of last resort is not set

S    192.168.1.0/24 [1/0] via 192.168.201.254
S    192.168.2.0/24 [1/0] via 192.168.201.254
C    192.168.3.0/24 is directly connected, Ethernet0
S    192.168.200.0/24 [1/0] via 192.168.201.254
C    192.168.201.0/24 is directly connected, Serial1
Router3#
```

If everything is correct, all nodes should be able to ping all other nodes. Time to test that out.

First, we try pinging from the Web Server to the File Server and to the workstations.

```
C:\>ping 192.168.3.200

Pinging 192.168.3.200 with 32 bytes of data:

Reply from 192.168.3.200: bytes=32 time<10ms TTL=128
Reply from 192.168.3.200: bytes=32 time<10ms TTL=128
Reply from 192.168.3.200: bytes=32 time<10ms TTL=128
Reply from 192.168.3.200: bytes=32 time<10ms TTL=128

C:\>ping 192.168.2.200

Pinging 192.168.2.200 with 32 bytes of data:

Reply from 192.168.2.200: bytes=32 time=20ms TTL=126
Reply from 192.168.2.200: bytes=32 time=20ms TTL=126
Reply from 192.168.2.200: bytes=32 time=20ms TTL=126
Reply from 192.168.2.200: bytes=32 time=20ms TTL=126

C:\>ping 192.168.2.201

Pinging 192.168.2.201 with 32 bytes of data:

Reply from 192.168.2.201: bytes=32 time=20ms TTL=126
Reply from 192.168.2.201: bytes=32 time=20ms TTL=126
Reply from 192.168.2.201: bytes=32 time=20ms TTL=126
Reply from 192.168.2.201: bytes=32 time=21ms TTL=126
```

At this point, we would want to verify connectivity from every node to every other node. We will assume at this point that everything is working.

Troubleshooting

But what if something is *not* working? There is a nice command that can be used to help us out. That command is **trace**, and will show us the path that a packet takes to reach its destination. Note that trace will try to talk to a DNS Server to resolve the IP addresses to hostnames. If there is no DNS Server, you can speed up the **trace** command by disabling the lookup. To do this, use the command **no ip domain-lookup**.

We will use **trace** to verify that the packet is going from Router 1 to the Web Server.

```
Router1>trace ?
  WORD       Trace route to destination address or hostname
  appletalk  AppleTalk Trace
  clns       ISO CLNS Trace
  ip         IP Trace
  oldvines   Vines Trace (Cisco)
  vines      Vines Trace (Banyan)

Router1>trace 192.168.3.200 ?
  <cr>

Router1>trace 192.168.3.200

Type escape sequence to abort.
Tracing the route to 192.168.3.200

  1 192.168.200.253 16 msec 16 msec 16 msec
  2 192.168.201.253 32 msec 32 msec 36 msec
  3 192.168.3.200 32 msec 32 msec 32 msec
Router1>
```

Here we can see that the packet went from Router 1 to Router 2, where Router 2 processed it, and to Router 3 where it was finally delivered to the destination host. This command can be very useful in tracking down a problem with a routing table. For instance, let's examine the next set of commands and see if we can find the problem.

```
Router2#ping 192.168.3.200

Type escape sequence to abort.
Sending 5, 100-byte ICMP Echos to 192.168.3.200, timeout is 2 seconds:
.....
Success rate is 0 percent (0/5)
Router2#trace 192.168.3.200

Type escape sequence to abort.
Tracing the route to 192.168.3.200
```

```
 1 192.168.200.254 16 msec 16 msec 20 msec
 2 192.168.200.253 32 msec 32 msec 32 msec
 3 192.168.200.254 28 msec 28 msec 28 msec
 4 192.168.200.253 44 msec 40 msec 44 msec
 5 192.168.200.254 40 msec 36 msec 40 msec
 6 192.168.200.253 56 msec 52 msec 56 msec
 7 192.168.200.254 48 msec 52 msec 48 msec
 8 192.168.200.253 64 msec 64 msec 68 msec
 9 192.168.200.254 64 msec 60 msec 64 msec
10 192.168.200.253 76 msec 88 msec 76 msec
11 192.168.200.254 72 msec 72 msec 72 msec
12 192.168.200.253 84 msec 84 msec 88 msec
13 192.168.200.254 84 msec 80 msec 80 msec
14 192.168.200.253 96 msec 96 msec 96 msec
15 192.168.200.254 92 msec 92 msec 96 msec
16 192.168.200.253 108 msec 108 msec 112 msec
17 192.168.200.254 104 msec 104 msec 108 msec
18 192.168.200.253 120 msec 116 msec 120 msec
19 192.168.200.254 116 msec 112 msec 116 msec
20 192.168.200.253 132 msec 128 msec 128 msec
21 192.168.200.254 128 msec 124 msec 128 msec
22 192.168.200.253 140 msec 140 msec 140 msec
23 192.168.200.254 140 msec 144 msec 136 msec
24 192.168.200.253 156 msec 152 msec 152 msec
25 192.168.200.254 144 msec 148 msec 148 msec
26 192.168.200.253 164 msec 160 msec 160 msec
27 192.168.200.254 160 msec 156 msec 156 msec
28 192.168.200.253 172 msec 172 msec 176 msec
29 192.168.200.254 172 msec 168 msec 168 msec
30 192.168.200.253 188 msec 184 msec 184 msec
Router2#
```

The **trace** command has a maximum hop of 30, which means it won't trace any packets past 30 routers. We reached that maximum here and the trace program ended. If we examine the trace output, we can see that the packet bounced between Routers 1 and 2. We have an example of a routing loop.

If we examine the routing table for Router 2, we should find the problem.

```
Router2#show ip route
Codes: C - connected, S - static, I - IGRP, R - RIP, M - mobile, B - BGP
       D - EIGRP, EX - EIGRP external, O - OSPF, IA - OSPF inter area
       N1 - OSPF NSSA external type 1, N2 - OSPF NSSA external type 2
       E1 - OSPF external type 1, E2 - OSPF external type 2, E - EGP
       i - IS-IS, L1 - IS-IS level-1, L2 - IS-IS level-2, * - candidate default
       U - per-user static route, o - ODR

Gateway of last resort is not set

C    192.168.200.0/24 is directly connected, Serial0
C    192.168.201.0/24 is directly connected, Serial1
```

```
S    192.168.1.0/24 [1/0] via 192.168.200.254
C    192.168.2.0/24 is directly connected, Ethernet0
S    192.168.3.0/24 [1/0] via 192.168.200.254
Router2#
```

Sure enough, the router is sending data destined for 192.168.3.0 to the wrong router. Router 1, in turn, is receiving the data and sending it back to us. To fix it, we issue the following commands:

```
Router2#conf term
Enter configuration commands, one per line.  End with CNTL/Z.
Router2(config)#no ip route 192.168.3.0 255.255.255.0
Router2(config)#ip route 192.168.3.0 255.255.255.0
192.168.201.253
Router2(config)#^Z
Router2#
%SYS-5-CONFIG_I: Configured from console by console
Router2#copy run start
Building configuration...
[OK]
```

Why did we erase the command with the **no** keyword first? If we had not done so, we would have simply added another route to get to the 192.168.3.0. The router would then have two routes, and it might use the wrong one. This eliminates any confusion, both by the router and by us trying to read the routing table.

Now we can test our connectivity again.

```
Router2#ping 192.168.3.200

Type escape sequence to abort.
Sending 5, 100-byte ICMP Echos to 192.168.3.200, timeout is 2 seconds:
!!!!!
Success rate is 100 percent (5/5), round-trip min/avg/max = 32/35/40 ms
Router2#
```

Another command that might be helpful is the **show arp** command. This command will display the MAC address of the devices that the router can communicate with. This can help troubleshoot a problem when **trace** determines that the packet is reaching the final network, but not to the correct host.

The two commands of **ping** and **trace** are great troubleshooting tools and should be remembered. Additionally, **show arp** can help aid in troubleshooting specific host problems.

Default Routing

Creating a routing table on each and every router for every routing table can be a tedious chore. It is also prone to mistakes. To help eliminate those problems, we could instead define each router with a default route.

In order to do this, we will define a default route of 0.0.0.0 with a subnet mask of 0.0.0.0. This allows the router to match any address not received with the default route. We then define the next hop a router should take.

```
Router1#conf t
Enter configuration commands, one per line.  End with CNTL/Z.
Router1(config)#ip route 0.0.0.0 0.0.0.0 192.168.200.253
Router1(config)#^Z
Router1#
%SYS-5-CONFIG_I: Configured from console by console
Router1#sho ip route
Codes: C - connected, S - static, I - IGRP, R - RIP, M - mobile, B - BGP
       D - EIGRP, EX - EIGRP external, O - OSPF, IA - OSPF inter area
       N1 - OSPF NSSA external type 1, N2 - OSPF NSSA external type 2
       E1 - OSPF external type 1, E2 - OSPF external type 2, E - EGP
       i - IS-IS, L1 - IS-IS level-1, L2 - IS-IS level-2, * - candidate default
       U - per-user static route, o - ODR

Gateway of last resort is 192.168.200.253 to network 0.0.0.0

C    192.168.200.0/24 is directly connected, Serial0
C    192.168.1.0/24 is directly connected, Ethernet0
S*   0.0.0.0/0 [1/0] via 192.168.200.253
Router1#
```

The default route is also known as the gateway of last resort. We can see this by reading the line that starts with "Gateway of last resort is. . .".

Let's add the default route to the other two routers as well.

```
Router2#conf t
Enter configuration commands, one per line.  End with CNTL/Z.
Router2(config)#ip route 0.0.0.0 0.0.0.0 192.168.200.254
Router2(config)#ip route 0.0.0.0 0.0.0.0 192.168.201.253
Router2(config)#^Z
Router2#
%SYS-5-CONFIG_I: Configured from console by console
Router2#sho ip route
Codes: C - connected, S - static, I - IGRP, R - RIP, M - mobile, B - BGP
       D - EIGRP, EX - EIGRP external, O - OSPF, IA - OSPF inter area
       N1 - OSPF NSSA external type 1, N2 - OSPF NSSA external type 2
       E1 - OSPF external type 1, E2 - OSPF external type 2, E - EGP
       i - IS-IS, L1 - IS-IS level-1, L2 - IS-IS level-2, * - candidate default
       U - per-user static route, o - ODR
```

```
Gateway of last resort is 192.168.200.254 to network 0.0.0.0

C    192.168.200.0/24 is directly connected, Serial0
C    192.168.201.0/24 is directly connected, Serial1
C    192.168.2.0/24 is directly connected, Ethernet0
S*   0.0.0.0/0 [1/0] via 192.168.200.254
                [1/0] via 192.168.201.253

Router3#conf term
Enter configuration commands, one per line.  End with CNTL/Z.
Router3(config)#ip route 0.0.0.0 0.0.0.0 192.168.201.254
Router3(config)#^Z
Router3#
%SYS-5-CONFIG_I: Configured from console by console
Router3#sho ip route
Codes: C - connected, S - static, I - IGRP, R - RIP, M - mobile, B - BGP
       D - EIGRP, EX - EIGRP external, O - OSPF, IA - OSPF inter area
       N1 - OSPF NSSA external type 1, N2 - OSPF NSSA external type 2
       E1 - OSPF external type 1, E2 - OSPF external type 2, E - EGP
       i - IS-IS, L1 - IS-IS level-1, L2 - IS-IS level-2, * - candidate default
       U - per-user static route, o - ODR

Gateway of last resort is 192.168.201.254 to network 0.0.0.0

C    192.168.3.0/24 is directly connected, Ethernet0
C    192.168.201.0/24 is directly connected, Serial1
S*   0.0.0.0/0 [1/0] via 192.168.201.254
```

Now that the default routes have been set, let's try pinging a couple of hosts.

```
Router2#ping 192.168.2.200

Type escape sequence to abort.
Sending 5, 100-byte ICMP Echos to 192.168.2.200, timeout is 2 seconds:
!!!!!
Success rate is 100 percent (5/5), round-trip min/avg/max = 1/2/4 ms
Router2#ping 192.168.2.201

Type escape sequence to abort.
Sending 5, 100-byte ICMP Echos to 192.168.2.201, timeout is 2 seconds:
!!!!!
Success rate is 100 percent (5/5), round-trip min/avg/max = 1/2/4 ms
Router2#ping 192.168.1.200

Type escape sequence to abort.
Sending 5, 100-byte ICMP Echos to 192.168.1.200, timeout is 2 seconds:
!!!!!
Success rate is 100 percent (5/5), round-trip min/avg/max = 32/52/68 ms
Router2#ping 192.168.3.200
```

```
Type escape sequence to abort.
Sending 5, 100-byte ICMP Echos to 192.168.3.200, timeout is 2 seconds:
!!!!!
Success rate is 100 percent (5/5), round-trip min/avg/max = 32/53/68 ms
Router2#
```

As we can see, we were pretty successful. However, there is a small technicality that we need to discuss. This network is a straightforward Class C address, but if we were to have a subnetted network, the default network address would not be enough. If the router does not know if a network even exists, it will drop the packet. To prevent this, we would issue the **ip classless** command on each of the routers. This will tell the router to forward any packets to the default router, even ones it does not know about.

Using the default route and the **ip classless** command, we can set up our routers fairly quickly. If a router were to fail, though, we would be in trouble. Even with backup routes, the routers need to be configured correctly. To help with this and other problems, we will examine dynamic routing in the next chapter.

Summary

In this chapter, we examine the ways we can set up routing tables on our routers to route network traffic. Without routing tables, or if the tables have been configured incorrectly, data will not get to its final destination. The first way to set up the routing tables consists of using static routes. The second way uses default gateways or routes with the **ip classless** command.

Scenario Lab 8.1

The addressing scheme has been decided and the routers are in place (see Figure 8–4). The CIO personally thanks you for the great job you have been doing, and decides to give you a pay raise. Now, however, the CIO would like to know how the routers will be able to get the data to the correct segments. Can you explain the principles of routing, including the actual data flow and what a routing table looks like?

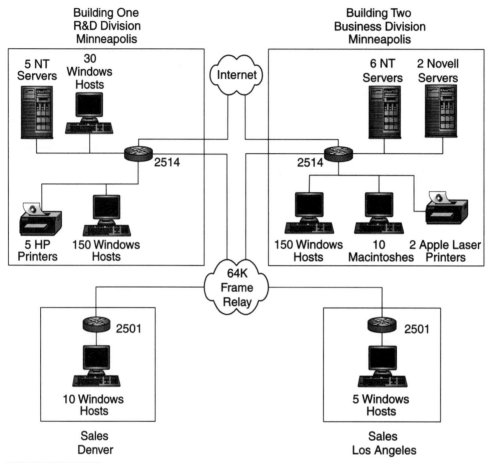

FIGURE 8–4   Creating static route tables for Network Solutions, Inc.

Practice Lab 8.1

In this lab, you will configure each of the routers in Figure 8–5 with the given IP addresses. Next, you will create the routing tables and test the routing using ping and trace.

- Configure Router 1 with the given IP addresses.
- Configure Router 2 with the given IP addresses.
- Configure each of the workstations with the given IP address.
- Test connectivity by trying to ping each of the nodes from Workstation 1.
- Set up a routing table in Router 1. Use the following command:

    ip route 192.168.30.0 255.255.255.0 192.168.20.253
- Set up the routing table in Router 2. Use a format similar to the previous step.
- Test connectivity by using **ping**. You should be able to ping all nodes from all other nodes.
- Test packet flow by using **trace** on the routers or **tracert** on the workstations (if they are Windows 95/98/NT).

    BONUS: Reconfigure the routers using a subnetted addressing scheme. Create the routing entries and test.

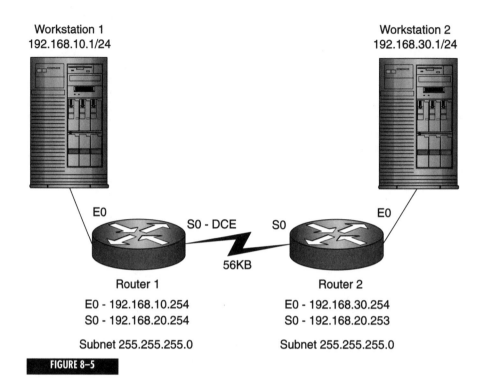

Workstation 1
192.168.10.1/24

Workstation 2
192.168.30.1/24

E0

S0 - DCE   S0

E0

56KB

Router 1

E0 - 192.168.10.254
S0 - 192.168.20.254

Subnet 255.255.255.0

Router 2

E0 - 192.168.30.254
S0 - 192.168.20.253

Subnet 255.255.255.0

FIGURE 8–5

Practice Lab 8.2

In this lab, you will configure each of the routers and the work-stations in Figure 8–6 with the given IP addresses and set up static routes.

- Configure the workstations with the given IP addresses.
- Configure the routers with the given IP addresses. Don't forget to set up the clock rate for the DCE interfaces.
- Verify that all interfaces are up by using the **show int** command.
- Verify connectivity using **ping**.
- Set up the routing tables for each of the routers.
- Verify connectivity to all nodes using **ping** and **trace**.

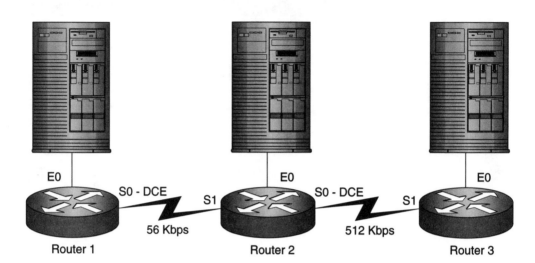

Router 1

Workstation IP: 172.16.0.1
E0 IP: 172.16.255.254
S0 IP: 172.17.255.254

Subnet Mask: 255.255.0.0

Router 2

Workstation IP: 172.18.0.1
E0 IP: 172.18.255.254
S1 IP: 172.17.255.253
S0 IP: 172.19.255.254

Subnet Mask: 255.255.0.0

Router 3

Workstation IP: 172.20.0.1
E0 IP: 172.20.255.254
S1 IP: 172.19.255.253

Subnet Mask: 255.255.0.0

FIGURE 8–6

Practice Lab 8.3

In this lab, you will set up default routes in a subnetted environment. After testing connectivity using **ping**, you will add the **ip classless** command and verify the results.

- Configure each of the workstations in Figure 8–7 with the given IP addresses.
- Configure each of the routers with the given IP addresses.
- Verify connectivity to each workstation from the local router.
- Type the command **no ip classless** at each router in global configuration mode.
- Create a default route for each of the routers. Router 2 will have two default routes. Use the format of **ip route 0.0.0.0 0.0.0.0 interface**.
- Use the command **sho ip route** to ensure that the gateway of last resort has been set.
- Try pinging the various workstations from each of the routers. You should find that only some workstations are replying. The reason is, that by turning off ip classless, routers that do not know of a network will automatically drop packets.
- At each of the routers. type the command **ip classless**.
- Ping each of the workstations from each of the routers. You should have full connectivity at this point.
- Use the command **show arp** on each of the routers to determine the MAC addresses of the locally connected devices.

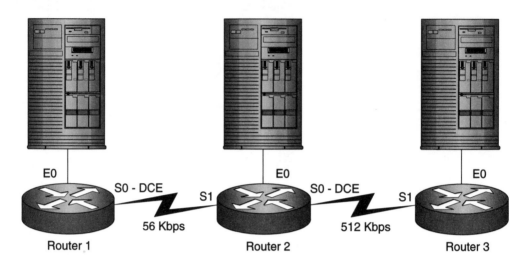

E0

S0 - DCE   S1

56 Kbps

Router 1

E0

S0 - DCE   S1

512 Kbps

Router 2

E0

Router 3

Workstation IP: 10.1.0.1
E0 IP: 10.1.255.254
S0 IP: 10.2.255.254

Subnet Mask: 255.255.0.0

Workstation IP: 10.3.0.1
E0 IP: 10.3.255.254
S1 IP: 10.2.255.253
S0 IP: 10.4.255.254

Subnet Mask: 255.255.0.0

Workstation IP: 10.5.0.1
E0 IP: 10.5.255.254
S1 IP: 10.4.255.253

Subnet Mask: 255.255.0.0

FIGURE 8–7

Exam Objective Checklist

By working through this chapter. you should have sufficient knowledge to answer these exam objectives:

- Describe the different classes of IP addresses (and subnetting).
- Prepare the initial configuration of your router and enable IP.
- Configure IP addresses.
- Verify IP addresses.

Practice Questions

Use Figure 8–8 to answer these questions.

1. Node A wants to communicate with Node B. Which MAC address will it send to?

    a. 11
    b. 22
    c. 66
    d. 77

2. Node A wants to communicate with Node C. Which MAC address will it send to?

    a. 88
    b. 33
    c. 77
    d. 66

3. What command will show the current routing table?

    a. show arp
    b. show route ip
    c. show ip route
    d. show route table

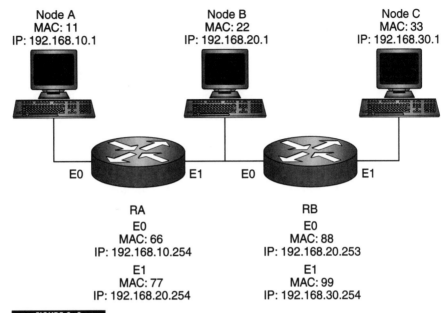

FIGURE 8–8

4. Which is the correct route entry for router RA?

   a. ip route 192.168.30.0 mask 255.255.255.0 192.168.20.253
   b. ip route 192.168.30.0 255.255.255.0 192.168.20.253
   c. ip route add 192.168.30.0 255.255.255.0 192.168.30.254
   d. ip route add 192.168.30.0 255.255.255.0 192.168.20.253

5. Which is the correct route entry for router RB?

   a. ip route 192.168.10.0 255.255.255.0 192.168.20.254
   b. ip route 192.168.10.0 255.255.255.0 192.168.10.254
   c. ip route 192.168.10.0 255.255.255.0 192.168.20.253
   d. ip route 192.168.10.0 255.255.255.0 192.168.30.254

6. Which is the correct output of the trace program when tracing from Node A to Node C?

   a. 1   192.168.20.253
      2   192.168.20.254
      3   192.168.10.1
   b. 1   192.168.10.254
      2   192.168.20.254
      3   192.168.20.253
      4   192.168.30.254
      5   192.168.30.1

c. 1   192.168.10.254
         2   192.168.20.253
         3   192.168.30.1
    d. 1   192.168.10.254
         2   192.168.20.1

7. Which is the correct command to add a default route?

    a. ip route 0.0.0.0 0.0.0.0 192.168.20.253
    b. ip route 0.0.0.0 192.168.20.253
    c. ip route default 0.0.0.0 192.168.20.253
    d. ip route default 0.0.0.0 0.0.0.0 192.168.20.253

8. Which command changes the administrative distance to 100?

    a. ip route 192.168.17.0 mask 255.255.255.0 distance 100
    b. ip route 192.168.17.0 255.255.255.255 100
    c. ip route 192.168.17.0 mask 255.255.255.0 100
    d. ip route 192.168.17.0 255.255.255.0 192.168.17.254 100

Dynamic Routing

In This Chapter

In the preceding chapter, we examined the use of static routes for allowing traffic flow through our routers. There are certain practical uses of static routes, including using them in small businesses and to hide parts of our network from the outside world. However, in a large routed environment, static routes are impractical. If a router needs to be removed, if the network environment changed, or we added to our network, static routes would be extremely clumsy. The solution to these problems is the use of a dynamic routing protocol. With dynamic routing protocols, each router will dynamically create a routing table by exchanging information with another router. As the network expands, these changes will propagate automatically throughout the network. This eliminates the need for us to update each router manually.

Routed versus Routing Protocols

A routed protocol is a protocol that can be used in a network with routers. The design of the protocol includes a Network layer, and therefore has a network address as well as a host address. Examples of a routed protocol include TCP/IP, IPX/SPX, and AppleTalk. An example of a nonrouted protocol is NetBEUI.

A routing protocol is a protocol that exchanges routing information between routers only, so that other routers can build a routing table and intelligently deliver data to its final destination. A network can consist of one or more routed protocols with one or more routing protocols. Examples of routing protocols include RIP (Routing Information Protocol), OSPF (Open Shortest Path First), NLSP (NetWare Link State Protocol), IGRP (Interior Gateway Routing Protocol), and EIGRP (Enhanced Interior Gateway Routing Protocol).

Interior versus Exterior Routing Protocols

Interior Gateway Protocols (IGP) are routing protocols that are used to share network information within the same administrative domain. This network information would include all subnets within the network. This means that if our organization is administered as one unit, and traffic normally flows across the entire network, we would use an IGP. Examples of IGP include RIP and IGRP.

An Exterior Gateway Protocol (EGP) is a protocol that is used to exchange information between two or more administrative domains. These administrative domains are sometimes referred to as Autonomous Systems (AS). This type of protocol is predominantly used for networks connecting to the Internet. If the entire Internet used an IGP, every router would have thousands of entries in the routing table. Besides being inefficient, routers would have to be a lot larger in size. Instead, the routers on the borders of the networks would exchange information about the higher-level network only, and not the internal networks. CIDR, or a classless routing, is a prime example of using EGP with the Internet. Instead of advertising a network's internal subnets, CIDR can be used to group the entire network into a single route table. Data is then forwarded to the router in the internal network, and from there it is further divided out into the subnets. For example, in Figure 9–1 there are three ASs, or three different networks. Each of the routers in the AS are administered by the same unit. The internal routing protocol is an IGP, and this advertises all subnets within that network. The routers on the border to the Internet are also running an EGP protocol. This allows each of the networks to know that the others exist, but only as an AS. If Node A in AS 1 sends data to Node C in AS 3, the border router in AS 1 knows that Node C exists somewhere in AS 3. Once the data reaches the border router in AS 3, it can further forward the data through the internal network to the final node.

The most common EGP protocol used is Border Gateway Protocol (BGP).

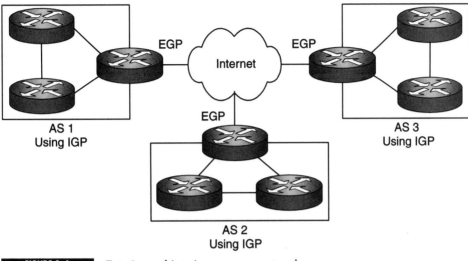

FIGURE 9–1 Exterior and interior gateway protocols

Differences Among Interior Gateway Protocols

There are a number of differences that distinguish one IGP from another. While certain protocols are more enhanced than others, we will focus only on RIP and IGRP. There are many books that discuss the design considerations, including the benefits and disadvantages of each routing protocol. At this point in our career, RIP and IGRP are a good starting point for learning about routing protocols. Since they are tested on the CCNA test, it adds to the benefit of discussing them here.

Distance Vector

Routers that use Distance Vector routing protocols send their entire routing tables to any adjacent routers. Not only do they send the entire routing table, but they continue to send them every 30 to 90 seconds. This time is configurable and is different for every protocol. This advertisement of routing tables is performed through broadcasts. In fact, if we have a large number of routing table entries, the broadcasts will include only partial tables. This requires more than one broadcast to send the entire table.

Distance Vector protocols work on the principle of hop counts. A hop count is the number of routers that a packet has to traverse in order to reach its final destination. The problem with this solution, though, is that it does not take bandwidth and/or load into account. For example, in Figure 9–2 we can see a typical network using three routers. The 56K link is for redundancy in case the link between A and C (or B and C) goes down. For traffic to flow

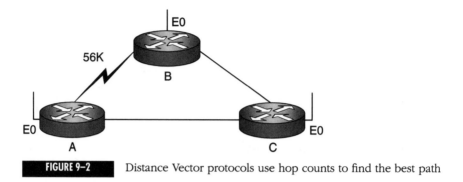

FIGURE 9–2   Distance Vector protocols use hop counts to find the best path

from A to B, it would ideally go through C, because the LAN is much faster than the WAN link. However, since Distance Vector protocols see that as two hops, the best path from A to B is one hop across the WAN link.

There are other issues involved with Distance Vector protocols, and we will examine these later in the chapter. Examples of Distance Vector protocols include RIP and IGRP

Link State

Link State protocols maintain three separate tables for determining routing paths. Because of this, memory requirements are typically higher than with Distance Vector protocols. With this type of protocol, each router sends out link state packets (LSPs) to all other routers in the network. These packets are like "Hello" packets in that they introduce the routers to each other. The routers then place the neighbors in a neighbor's table, and all the routers in a topology table. This allows the router to get a better, overall view of the network. When the topology table is finished, the router then uses a "shortest path first" (SPF) algorithm to determine the best path to a given network, and places this information into the routing table. This algorithm will typically take into account the bandwidth and the load on the links, and therefore a better path than just the hop count will be used. In Figure 9–2 for instance, a Link State protocol will know that the better path from A to B is through C.

Link State protocols will flood a network upon initialization because of all of the LSPs that are being sent. However, once this initial phase is completed, these protocols do not routinely pass their entire routing tables. In fact, when a topology change is detected, they only send out the changes that have occurred through LSPs. This allows each router to recalculate the SPF algorithm and choose the optimum path.

OSPF and NLSP are examples of Link State protocols.

Although Link State protocols are typically better at routing, they are more complex to set up and maintain. They also require more memory and processing power due to the SPA calculations. For a small network, Distance Vector protocols work great. However, we should think about implementing Link State protocols with larger networks to increase performance and reliability.

Classful versus Classless

Some routing protocols are *classful*, meaning they do not pass subnet mask information with the network advertisements. This means that these protocols require a single subnet mask throughout the network. Examples of classful routing protocols include RIP and IGRP.

Classless routing protocols carry the subnet mask with the network being advertised. This allows for Variable Length Subnet Masking (VLSM), which is like subnetting a subnet. VLSM allows us to subnet a network to the exact requirements needed. For instance, if we needed one segment to have only two hosts and another segment to have 150 hosts, we could use VLSM to achieve these results without wasting any addresses. Examples of Classless routing protocols include RIP version 2, OSPF, and EIGRP.

Routing Information Protocol

RIP is a Classful, Distance Vector, Interior Gateway protocol that has been around for many years. In fact, RIP was one of the protocols used when ARPANET was still in existence. RIP was documented in RFC 1058 in 1988, and has subsequently been revised.

The best way to discuss RIP is to implement it and then review the settings. We will use our network diagram of IC, Inc. shown in Figure 9-3.

First, let's make sure our routers are set up and that the routing tables are clear.

```
Router1#show ip route
Codes: C - connected, S - static, I - IGRP, R - RIP, M - mobile, B - BGP
       D - EIGRP, EX - EIGRP external, O - OSPF, IA - OSPF inter area
       N1 - OSPF NSSA external type 1, N2 - OSPF NSSA external type 2
       E1 - OSPF external type 1, E2 - OSPF external type 2, E - EGP
       i - IS-IS, L1 - IS-IS level-1, L2 - IS-IS level-2, * - candidate default
       U - per-user static route, o - ODR

Gateway of last resort is not set

C    192.168.200.0/24 is directly connected, Serial0
C    192.168.1.0/24 is directly connected, Ethernet0
Router1#

Router2#show ip route
Codes: C - connected, S - static, I - IGRP, R - RIP, M - mobile, B - BGP
       D - EIGRP, EX - EIGRP external, O - OSPF, IA - OSPF inter area
```

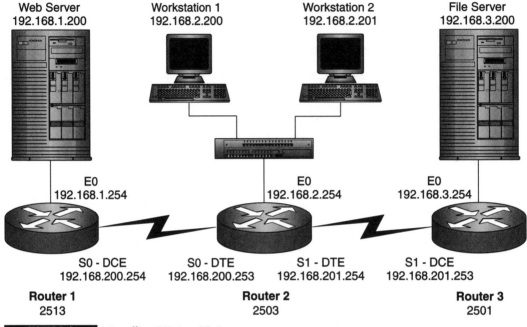

Web Server
192.168.1.200

Workstation 1
192.168.2.200

Workstation 2
192.168.2.201

File Server
192.168.3.200

E0
192.168.1.254

E0
192.168.2.254

E0
192.168.3.254

S0 - DCE
192.168.200.254

S0 - DTE
192.168.200.253

S1 - DTE
192.168.201.254

S1 - DCE
192.168.201.253

Router 1
2513

Router 2
2503

Router 3
2501

FIGURE 9–3   Installing RIP into IC, Inc.

```
      N1 - OSPF NSSA external type 1, N2 - OSPF NSSA external type 2
      E1 - OSPF external type 1, E2 - OSPF external type 2, E - EGP
      i - IS-IS, L1 - IS-IS level-1, L2 - IS-IS level-2, * - candidate default
      U - per-user static route, o - ODR

Gateway of last resort is not set

C    192.168.200.0/24 is directly connected, Serial0
C    192.168.2.0/24 is directly connected, Ethernet0
Router2#


Router3#show ip route
Codes: C - connected, S - static, I - IGRP, R - RIP, M - mobile, B - BGP
       D - EIGRP, EX - EIGRP external, O - OSPF, IA - OSPF inter area
       N1 - OSPF NSSA external type 1, N2 - OSPF NSSA external type 2
       E1 - OSPF external type 1, E2 - OSPF external type 2, E - EGP
       i - IS-IS, L1 - IS-IS level-1, L2 - IS-IS level-2, * - candidate default
       U - per-user static route, o - ODR

Gateway of last resort is not set

C    192.168.3.0/24 is directly connected, Ethernet0
C    192.168.201.0/24 is directly connected, Serial1
Router3#
```

We can see that the routing tables are clean except for the automatically detected direct connect routes. The interfaces are all configured. We could test connectivity by using **ping**, but we will assume that everything is working correctly at this point. However, we should never make assumptions like that in the field.

It's time to turn on RIP. By default, there are no dynamic routing protocols enabled on the Cisco routers. We have to turn the correct one on.

```
Router1(config)#router ?
  bgp        Border Gateway Protocol (BGP)
  egp        Exterior Gateway Protocol (EGP)
  eigrp      Enhanced Interior Gateway Routing Protocol (EIGRP)
  igrp       Interior Gateway Routing Protocol (IGRP)
  isis       ISO IS-IS
  iso-igrp   IGRP for OSI networks
  mobile     Mobile routes
  odr        On Demand stub Routes
  ospf       Open Shortest Path First (OSPF)
  rip        Routing Information Protocol (RIP)
  static     Static routes

Router1(config)#router rip
Router1(config-router)#^Z
```

Notice the prompt change. This indicates that we were in router configuration mode.

At this point, RIP is now enabled. However, it is not actually doing anything. RIP needs to be told what to advertise. Before we do that, let's enable some debugging so that we can see when things start happening. We can enable debugging by using the **debug ip** command. In this case, we want to see just the RIP packets.

```
Router1#debug ip rip
RIP protocol debugging is on
```

This method will turn on detailed debugging information, but if we just wanted the summary information, we would issue the command **debug ip rip events** instead.

RIP will broadcast its routing table every 30 seconds. However, after waiting for 30 seconds, there is no response because we need to tell RIP to advertise its network. To do this, we issue the **network** command in router configuration mode and specify the network it should advertise. Also, for any networks that are advertised, the broadcasts will be sent out the same interface as the network. For example, we will tell RIP to advertise the network of 192.168.200.0, and therefore, broadcasts will subsequently only be sent out the 192.168.200.254 interface.

Remember that RIP is classful. If our network is subnetted, we would not be able to specify a single subnet to advertise. Instead, RIP will automatically change the subnet parameter to a standard class of address and advertise all subnets on that router. For example, if we had a subnetted environment using 172.16.30.0/24, RIP would only advertise 172.16.0.0/16 because this is the standard Class B address. Additionally, all interfaces that make up this network will be used to broadcast.

Let's get RIP going by advertising our network.

```
Router1(config-router)#network 192.168.200.0
Router1(config-router)#^Z

RIP: sending v1 update to 255.255.255.255 via Serial0 (192.168.200.254) -
suppressing null update
```

As soon as we enabled a network address, RIP started sending out broadcasts. Every 30 seconds we will see that same debug statement. Notice that the advertisement is only going out the serial interface. We did not specify to advertise the 192.168.1.0 network, and therefore it will not send any broadcasts out that port. Let's enable that network as well.

```
Router1#conf t
Enter configuration commands, one per line.  End with CNTL/Z.
Router1(config)#router rip
Router1(config-router)#network 192.168.1.0
Router1(config-router)#^Z

RIP: sending v1 update to 255.255.255.255 via Ethernet0 (192.168.1.254)
     network 192.168.200.0, metric 1
RIP: sending v1 update to 255.255.255.255 via Serial0 (192.168.200.254)
     network 192.168.1.0, metric 1[OK]
```

As soon as we told RIP to advertise the Ethernet segment, the broadcasts started going out that interface as well as the serial interface. Now that RIP is running, let's examine our routing table.

```
Router1#show ip route
Codes: C - connected, S - static, I - IGRP, R - RIP, M - mobile, B - BGP
       D - EIGRP, EX - EIGRP external, O - OSPF, IA - OSPF inter area
       N1 - OSPF NSSA external type 1, N2 - OSPF NSSA external type 2
       E1 - OSPF external type 1, E2 - OSPF external type 2, E - EGP
       i - IS-IS, L1 - IS-IS level-1, L2 - IS-IS level-2, * - candidate default
       U - per-user static route, o - ODR

Gateway of last resort is not set

C    192.168.200.0/24 is directly connected, Serial0
C    192.168.1.0/24 is directly connected, Ethernet0
Router1#
```

There is no new information in our routing table because we are not talking with anyone else. No other routers are configured to use RIP. We are shouting, but no one is listening. To do this, we need to enable RIP on the next router.

```
Router2#conf t
Enter configuration commands, one per line.  End with CNTL/Z.
Router2(config)#router rip
Router2(config-router)#network 192.168.2.0
Router2(config-router)#^Z
Router2#debug ip rip
RIP protocol debugging is on
RIP: sending v1 update to 255.255.255.255 via Ethernet0 (192.168.2.254) -
suppressing null update
RIP: ignored v1 packet from 192.168.200.254 (not enabled on Serial0)[OK]
Router2#
```

Now that we have enabled the network of 192.168.2.0, the broadcasts are being sent out that interface. However, since we did not tell RIP to advertise the 192.168.200.0 network, when the broadcast from Router 1 was heard, RIP ignored it. Since RIP does not broadcast its routing table to interfaces that have not been configured, it also ignores any broadcasts that are heard on that same interface.

What happens when we start advertising the network of 192.168.200.0?

```
Router2(config)#router rip
Router2(config-router)#network 192.168.200.0
Router2(config-router)#^Z
Router2#

RIP: sending v1 update to 255.255.255.255 via Ethernet0 (192.168.2.254)
     network 192.168.200.0, metric 1
RIP: sending v1 update to 255.255.255.255 via Serial0 (192.168.200.253)
     network 192.168.2.0, metric 1
RIP: received v1 update from 192.168.200.254 on Serial0
     192.168.1.0 in 1 hops
RIP: sending v1 update to 255.255.255.255 via Ethernet0 (192.168.2.254)
     network 192.168.200.0, metric 1
     network 192.168.1.0, metric 2
RIP: sending v1 update to 255.255.255.255 via Serial0 (192.168.200.253)
     network 192.168.2.0, metric 1
Router2#
```

Although it may not occur immediately (remember that RIP broadcasts are sent every 30 seconds), the routing table will be broadcasted on both the Ethernet and Serial 0 interfaces. We are now receiving as well as transmitting routing tables.

If we examine our routing tables now, we should see that both routers have dynamically learned some routes.

```
Router1#sho ip route
Codes: C - connected, S - static, I - IGRP, R - RIP, M - mobile, B - BGP
       D - EIGRP, EX - EIGRP external, O - OSPF, IA - OSPF inter area
       N1 - OSPF NSSA external type 1, N2 - OSPF NSSA external type 2
       E1 - OSPF external type 1, E2 - OSPF external type 2, E - EGP
       i - IS-IS, L1 - IS-IS level-1, L2 - IS-IS level-2, * - candidate default
       U - per-user static route, o - ODR

Gateway of last resort is not set

C    192.168.200.0/24 is directly connected, Serial0
C    192.168.1.0/24 is directly connected, Ethernet0
R    192.168.2.0/24 [120/1] via 192.168.200.253, 00:00:07, Serial0
Router1#

Router2#sho ip route
Codes: C - connected, S - static, I - IGRP, R - RIP, M - mobile, B - BGP
       D - EIGRP, EX - EIGRP external, O - OSPF, IA - OSPF inter area
       N1 - OSPF NSSA external type 1, N2 - OSPF NSSA external type 2
       E1 - OSPF external type 1, E2 - OSPF external type 2, E - EGP
       i - IS-IS, L1 - IS-IS level-1, L2 - IS-IS level-2, * - candidate default
       U - per-user static route, o - ODR

Gateway of last resort is not set

C    192.168.200.0/24 is directly connected, Serial0
C    192.168.201.0/24 is directly connected, Serial1
R    192.168.1.0/24 [120/1] via 192.168.200.254, 00:00:23, Serial0
C    192.168.2.0/24 is directly connected, Ethernet0
Router2#
```

Both tables have a new entry that is prefaced with the letter "R." If we examine the code table, we can see that the "R" stands for RIP. Router 1 has learned of the network 192.168.2.0 from RIP. Router 2 has also learned of a network, 192.168.1.0, from RIP.

If we continue to examine the routing table, we will learn even more information. For example, not only do we see the network address, we also see those two numbers in brackets again. Remember that the first number is the administrative distance, or how trustworthy this network information is, and the second number is the metric. In this case, because RIP is a Distance Vector protocol, the metric is a hop count. We can see that in order to get our data to the network of 192.168.2.0, it will have to pass through one router. If we examine our network diagram in Figure 9–3, we can see that this is a true statement. The data must flow from Router 1 to Router 2 (hop count of 1), to the final network and to the destination host.

The administrative distance will change with different routing protocols, but why is it important at all? There are times when we may run more than one routing protocol in the same network, or at least part of it. If the router hears a network advertisement from more than one routing protocol, it will choose the one with the lowest administrative distance and ignore the rest.

Additional information in the routing table includes the address of the interface on which the advertisement was heard and how old the route is. Since RIP broadcasts every 30 seconds, this age value will never be more than that.

Now that the routing table is populating, we can test this by pinging from Workstation 2 to the Web Server.

```
C:\>ping 192.168.1.200

Pinging 192.168.1.200 with 32 bytes of data:

Reply from 192.168.1.200: bytes=32 time=30ms TTL=126
Reply from 192.168.1.200: bytes=32 time=20ms TTL=126
Reply from 192.168.1.200: bytes=32 time=20ms TTL=126
Reply from 192.168.1.200: bytes=32 time=20ms TTL=126
```

Everything seems to be working great! Let's finish setting up RIP on Router 2 and install it completely on Router 3.

```
Enter configuration commands, one per line.  End with CNTL/Z.
Router2(config)#router rip
Router2(config-router)#network 192.168.201.0
Router2(config-router)#^Z
Router2#copy run start
Building configuration...
[OK]
Router2#

Router3(config)#router rip
Router3(config-router)#network 192.168.3.0
Router3(config-router)#network 192.168.201.0
Router3(config-router)#^Z
Router3#copy run start
Building configuration...
[OK]
Router3#
```

Since RIP has been turned on and configured correctly, we should see complete *convergence* within 60 seconds. Convergence is the time it takes for all the routers to achieve a stable state of information. Our network is small and should take no more than 60 seconds (Router 1 to Router 2 is 30 seconds, and then an additional 30 seconds from Router 2 to Router 3) to achieve this state, but larger networks may take much longer. Distance Vector protocols have a slower convergence than Link State protocols.

Now that 60 seconds have passed, let's look at our routing tables.

```
Router1#undebug all
All possible debugging has been turned off
```

```
Router1#sho ip route
Codes: C - connected, S - static, I - IGRP, R - RIP, M - mobile, B - BGP
       D - EIGRP, EX - EIGRP external, O - OSPF, IA - OSPF inter area
       N1 - OSPF NSSA external type 1, N2 - OSPF NSSA external type 2
       E1 - OSPF external type 1, E2 - OSPF external type 2, E - EGP
       i - IS-IS, L1 - IS-IS level-1, L2 - IS-IS level-2, * - candidate default
       U - per-user static route, o - ODR

Gateway of last resort is not set

C    192.168.200.0/24 is directly connected, Serial0
R    192.168.201.0/24 [120/1] via 192.168.200.253, 00:00:20, Serial0
C    192.168.1.0/24 is directly connected, Ethernet0
R    192.168.2.0/24 [120/1] via 192.168.200.253, 00:00:20, Serial0
R    192.168.3.0/24 [120/2] via 192.168.200.253, 00:00:20, Serial0
Router1#
```

We turned off debugging so that we would not continuously be presented with the RIP updates. In the first router, we can see that all of our networks have been entered into the routing table.

```
Router2#undebug all
All possible debugging has been turned off
Router2#sho ip route
Codes: C - connected, S - static, I - IGRP, R - RIP, M - mobile, B - BGP
       D - EIGRP, EX - EIGRP external, O - OSPF, IA - OSPF inter area
       N1 - OSPF NSSA external type 1, N2 - OSPF NSSA external type 2
       E1 - OSPF external type 1, E2 - OSPF external type 2, E - EGP
       i - IS-IS, L1 - IS-IS level-1, L2 - IS-IS level-2, * - candidate default
       U - per-user static route, o - ODR

Gateway of last resort is not set

C    192.168.200.0/24 is directly connected, Serial0
C    192.168.201.0/24 is directly connected, Serial1
R    192.168.1.0/24 [120/1] via 192.168.200.254, 00:00:08, Serial0
C    192.168.2.0/24 is directly connected, Ethernet0
R    192.168.3.0/24 [120/1] via 192.168.201.253, 00:00:12, Serial1
Router2#

Router3#sho ip route
Codes: C - connected, S - static, I - IGRP, R - RIP, M - mobile, B - BGP
       D - EIGRP, EX - EIGRP external, O - OSPF, IA - OSPF inter area
       N1 - OSPF NSSA external type 1, N2 - OSPF NSSA external type 2
       E1 - OSPF external type 1, E2 - OSPF external type 2, E - EGP
       i - IS-IS, L1 - IS-IS level-1, L2 - IS-IS level-2, * - candidate default
       U - per-user static route, o - ODR

Gateway of last resort is not set
```

```
R    192.168.1.0/24 [120/2] via 192.168.201.254, 00:00:01, Serial1
R    192.168.2.0/24 [120/1] via 192.168.201.254, 00:00:02, Serial1
C    192.168.3.0/24 is directly connected, Ethernet0
R    192.168.200.0/24 [120/1] via 192.168.201.254, 00:00:02, Serial1
C    192.168.201.0/24 is directly connected, Serial1
```

As we can see, all of our routers have the routing tables completely filled out. Convergence has been reached and our network is happy. This is much easier than having to enter each routing table by hand. This is so easy, there must be a catch, right?

It turns out the Distance Vector protocols suffer from routing loops. This is due to the fact that convergence takes so long. It is possible that a network could fail and yet the network entry would still exist in all the routing tables.

In Figure 9–4 there are three routers all running RIP. Everything is in a nice state and then all of a sudden, Network A crashes. Router A sends an update to Router B and Router C when the next update occurs. Now Router B and Router C know that Network A is unreachable. However, before Router C can tell Router D, Router D broadcasts to Router C that it can reach Network A. It tells it this because Network A is in its routing table and can be reached through Router C. Router C updates its table stating that data can get to Network A through Router D. Thus, a routing loop has developed.

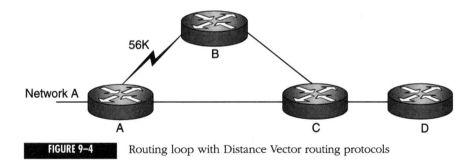

FIGURE 9–4 Routing loop with Distance Vector routing protocols

When the routing loop develops, the packets will flow between C and D until the TTL of the packet expires. Additionally, when Router C next updates Router D, it will add a hop count, or metric, to the path to reach Network A. This is because Router C now thinks it has a path through Router D and will logically increment the hop count. Next, Router D broadcasts back to Router C and increments the hop count, and so on. This will occur until infinity is reached, or perhaps a little sooner. This routing loop is called the "Count To Infinity" problem. With RIP, a hop count of 16 is considered infinity. When a hop count of 16 is reached, the network is considered unreachable. This also means that RIP will not work with paths that are longer than 15 hops away.

There are many ways to prevent routing loops. The routing loop occurred because each router advertised its known routes back to the source it came from. If this could be eliminated, this type of routing loop could be prevented. This is called *Split Horizon*. Split Horizon guarantees that a route will not be advertised out the same interface that it heard the route from in the first place. In the preceding example, Router D would never advertise a path to Network A back to Router C.

We can actually see Split Horizon in action. Let's examine the debug information on Router 2.

```
Router2#debug ip rip
RIP protocol debugging is on
Router2#
RIP: received v1 update from 192.168.201.253 on Serial1
     192.168.3.0 in 1 hops
RIP: received v1 update from 192.168.200.254 on Serial0
     192.168.1.0 in 1 hops
RIP: sending v1 update to 255.255.255.255 via Ethernet0 (192.168.2.254)
     network 192.168.200.0, metric 1
     network 192.168.201.0, metric 1
     network 192.168.1.0, metric 2
     network 192.168.3.0, metric 2
RIP: sending v1 update to 255.255.255.255 via Serial0 (192.168.200.253)
     network 192.168.201.0, metric 1
     network 192.168.2.0, metric 1
     network 192.168.3.0, metric 2
RIP: sending v1 update to 255.255.255.255 via Serial1 (192.168.201.254)
     network 192.168.200.0, metric 1
     network 192.168.1.0, metric 2
     network 192.168.2.0, metric 1
Router2#undebug all
All possible debugging has been turned off
Router2#
```

The last RIP update is going out the 192.168.201.254 interface (S1) and is being broadcast to Router 3. Notice that the networks being broadcast do not include the 192.168.3.0 network. Split Horizon is in effect, thereby not sending the update it heard from Router C back to Router C.

Another method of stopping router loops includes something called *Poison Reverse*. When a network is detected as having gone down, the detecting router will update its route table. The update will change the network route to having a metric hop of 16. This makes the network unreachable. In addition to Poison Reverse, another method called *Triggered Updates* causes the update of the unreachable network to be announced immediately to neighbor routers instead of waiting for the regular update interval. This will cause a flood of broadcasts ("bad news travels fast") as the downed network information is propagated throughout the network.

There is still one problem with Poison Reverse and Triggered Updates. In Figure 9–5, if Network A were to go down, Router A would poison its update table by listing Network A with a metric hop of 16. Triggered Update would then allow Router A to broadcast the changes to Router B and Router D immediately. However, before Router B or Router D could propagate the update to Router C, Router C makes a normal 30-second broadcast update. Router B or Router D (whichever did not originally broadcast the route information to Router C) would receive an update stating incorrect information about Network A.

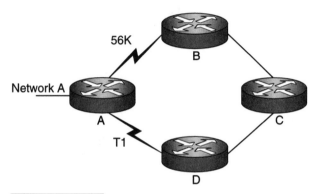

FIGURE 9–5   Poison Reverse and Triggered Updates may not be enough

There is one last method that can be used in conjunction with all the previous methods. This is called *hold-down*. This interval is used to keep the previous example from happening. When a network is declared unreachable, a hold-down timer is started. During this time, updated information about the network will be ignored. It also has the benefit of reducing *flapping*, a condition that exists when a link continually goes offline and then back online.

This, and other interval time periods, can be examined with the **show ip protocols** command.

```
Router2>sho ip proto
Routing Protocol is "rip"
  Sending updates every 30 seconds, next due in 24 seconds
  Invalid after 180 seconds, hold down 180, flushed after 240
  Outgoing update filter list for all interfaces is
  Incoming update filter list for all interfaces is
  Redistributing: rip
  Default version control: send version 1, receive any version
    Interface       Send   Recv   Key-chain
    Ethernet0        1      1 2
    Serial0          1      1 2
    Serial1          1      1 2
```

```
Routing for Networks:
  192.168.2.0
  192.168.200.0
  192.168.201.0
Routing Information Sources:
  Gateway          Distance       Last Update
  192.168.201.253     120         00:00:15
  192.168.200.254     120         00:00:07
Distance: (default is 120)

Router2>
```

This information shows that the hold-down period is 180 seconds. Additionally, there is an invalid time-out that is used to determine when a route has disappeared. This could occur if a router failed. Since no more RIP broadcasts are coming from the router, the neighbor routers will define the routes that were broadcast from the router as invalid. This period is 180 seconds. After a route is declared unreachable or invalid, the route will be cleared from the routing table after the flush interval of 240 seconds.

We can simulate these types of network failures and determine the effects throughout the routing tables. We will remove the Ethernet connection from Router 3 to simulate a bad patch cable.

```
Router3#sho ip route
Codes: C - connected, S - static, I - IGRP, R - RIP, M - mobile, B - BGP
       D - EIGRP, EX - EIGRP external, O - OSPF, IA - OSPF inter area
       N1 - OSPF NSSA external type 1, N2 - OSPF NSSA external type 2
       E1 - OSPF external type 1, E2 - OSPF external type 2, E - EGP
       i - IS-IS, L1 - IS-IS level-1, L2 - IS-IS level-2, * - candidate default
       U - per-user static route, o - ODR

Gateway of last resort is not set

R    192.168.1.0/24 [120/2] via 192.168.201.254, 00:00:06, Serial1
R    192.168.2.0/24 [120/1] via 192.168.201.254, 00:00:06, Serial1
R    192.168.200.0/24 [120/1] via 192.168.201.254, 00:00:06, Serial1
C    192.168.201.0/24 is directly connected, Serial1
Router3#
```

Router 3 immediately removes the bad network from the route table. It knows that this network is offline. By pulling the patch cable, the interface immediately went down. With debugging enabled, we can see the triggered update occur with a metric count of 16.

```
%LINEPROTO-5-UPDOWN: Line protocol on Interface Ethernet0, changed state to down

RIP: sending v1 update to 255.255.255.255 via Serial1 (192.168.201.253)
     network 192.168.3.0, metric 16
```

```
Router2#sho ip route
Codes: C - connected, S - static, I - IGRP, R - RIP, M - mobile, B - BGP
       D - EIGRP, EX - EIGRP external, O - OSPF, IA - OSPF inter area
       N1 - OSPF NSSA external type 1, N2 - OSPF NSSA external type 2
       E1 - OSPF external type 1, E2 - OSPF external type 2, E - EGP
       i - IS-IS, L1 - IS-IS level-1, L2 - IS-IS level-2, * - candidate default
       U - per-user static route, o - ODR

Gateway of last resort is not set

C    192.168.200.0/24 is directly connected, Serial0
C    192.168.201.0/24 is directly connected, Serial1
R    192.168.1.0/24 [120/1] via 192.168.200.254, 00:00:10, Serial0
C    192.168.2.0/24 is directly connected, Ethernet0
R    192.168.3.0/24 is possibly down, routing via 192.168.201.253, Serial1
Router2#
```

On Router 2 we can see that the hold-down is in effect. Router 3 sent an update immediately through the triggered update method and now the route is listed as being "possibly down."

```
Router1#sho ip route
Codes: C - connected, S - static, I - IGRP, R - RIP, M - mobile, B - BGP
       D - EIGRP, EX - EIGRP external, O - OSPF, IA - OSPF inter area
       N1 - OSPF NSSA external type 1, N2 - OSPF NSSA external type 2
       E1 - OSPF external type 1, E2 - OSPF external type 2, E - EGP
       i - IS-IS, L1 - IS-IS level-1, L2 - IS-IS level-2, * - candidate default
       U - per-user static route, o - ODR

Gateway of last resort is not set

C    192.168.200.0/24 is directly connected, Serial0
R    192.168.201.0/24 [120/1] via 192.168.200.253, 00:00:13, Serial0
C    192.168.1.0/24 is directly connected, Ethernet0
R    192.168.2.0/24 [120/1] via 192.168.200.253, 00:00:13, Serial0
R    192.168.3.0/24 is possibly down, routing via 192.168.200.253, Serial0
Router1#
```

Again, triggered update occurred immediately and Router 1 also knows that the route is possibly down. We can see the hold-down timer by using the **sho ip route** command and specifying an exact network.

```
Router2#sho ip route 192.168.3.0
Routing entry for 192.168.3.0/24
  Known via "rip", distance 120, metric 4294967295 (inaccessible)
  Redistributing via rip
  Advertised by rip (self originated)
  Last update from 192.168.201.253 on Serial1, 00:02:54 ago
  Hold down timer expires in 32 secs
Router2#
```

When examining the route directly on Router 2, we can see that the hold-down timer will expire in 32 seconds. When this happens, the flush timer will get set to remove the route from the routing table.

```
Router1#sho ip route 192.168.3.0
Routing entry for 192.168.3.0/24
  Known via "rip", distance 120, metric 4294967295 (inaccessible)
  Redistributing via rip
  Advertised by rip (self originated)
  Last update from 192.168.200.253 on Serial0, 00:04:22 ago
```

The hold-down time is expired and the flush interval is about to expire. The route will be removed from the routing table now. We can verify this by examining the route table.

```
Router1#sho ip route 192.168.3.0
% Network not in table
Router1#sho ip route
Codes: C - connected, S - static, I - IGRP, R - RIP, M - mobile, B - BGP
       D - EIGRP, EX - EIGRP external, O - OSPF, IA - OSPF inter area
       N1 - OSPF NSSA external type 1, N2 - OSPF NSSA external type 2
       E1 - OSPF external type 1, E2 - OSPF external type 2, E - EGP
       i - IS-IS, L1 - IS-IS level-1, L2 - IS-IS level-2, * - candidate default
       U - per-user static route, o - ODR

Gateway of last resort is not set

C    192.168.200.0/24 is directly connected, Serial0
R    192.168.201.0/24 [120/1] via 192.168.200.253, 00:00:15, Serial0
C    192.168.1.0/24 is directly connected, Ethernet0
R    192.168.2.0/24 [120/1] via 192.168.200.253, 00:00:15, Serial0
Router1#
```

At this point, we will get our network back up and running again. To help speed up the hold-down timers, if any exist, we can issue the command **clear ip route ***, and it will clear the table. The next update that occurs will repopulate the table.

Let's verify the route tables for each of the routers. By examining Router 1, we can be sure that everything is back to normal.

```
Router1#sho ip route
Codes: C - connected, S - static, I - IGRP, R - RIP, M - mobile, B - BGP
       D - EIGRP, EX - EIGRP external, O - OSPF, IA - OSPF inter area
       N1 - OSPF NSSA external type 1, N2 - OSPF NSSA external type 2
       E1 - OSPF external type 1, E2 - OSPF external type 2, E - EGP
       i - IS-IS, L1 - IS-IS level-1, L2 - IS-IS level-2, * - candidate default
       U - per-user static route, o - ODR

Gateway of last resort is not set
```

```
C    192.168.200.0/24 is directly connected, Serial0
R    192.168.201.0/24 [120/1] via 192.168.200.253, 00:00:19, Serial0
C    192.168.1.0/24 is directly connected, Ethernet0
R    192.168.2.0/24 [120/1] via 192.168.200.253, 00:00:19, Serial0
R    192.168.3.0/24 [120/2] via 192.168.200.253, 00:00:19, Serial0
Router1#
```

The network address of 192.168.3.0 is listed, so our convergence is finished.

What happens if the link should come back up during the hold-down period? To simulate this we will again unplug the Ethernet port from Router 3. Next, we will view the routing table on Router 2 to ensure that we are in a hold-down period.

```
Router2#sho ip route
Codes: C - connected, S - static, I - IGRP, R - RIP, M - mobile, B - BGP
       D - EIGRP, EX - EIGRP external, O - OSPF, IA - OSPF inter area
       N1 - OSPF NSSA external type 1, N2 - OSPF NSSA external type 2
       E1 - OSPF external type 1, E2 - OSPF external type 2, E - EGP
       i - IS-IS, L1 - IS-IS level-1, L2 - IS-IS level-2, * - candidate default
       U - per-user static route, o - ODR

Gateway of last resort is not set

C    192.168.200.0/24 is directly connected, Serial0
C    192.168.201.0/24 is directly connected, Serial1
R    192.168.1.0/24 [120/1] via 192.168.200.254, 00:00:01, Serial0
C    192.168.2.0/24 is directly connected, Ethernet0
R    192.168.3.0/24 is possibly down, routing via 192.168.201.253, Serial1
Router2#
```

We can see that the network of 192.168.3.0 is possibly down. Next, let's turn on debugging on Router 2. We should keep in mind that debugging causes extra processing overhead on the router, and that it will affect the latency through the router. When finished debugging, it would be very beneficial to our network to turn debugging off.

Finally, we will plug the Ethernet cable back in on Router 3.

```
RIP: received v1 update from 192.168.201.253 on Serial1
     192.168.3.0 in 1 hops
Router2#sho ip route 192.168.3.0
Routing entry for 192.168.3.0/24
  Known via "rip", distance 120, metric 4294967295 (inaccessible)
  Redistributing via rip
  Advertised by rip (self originated)
  Last update from 192.168.201.253 on Serial1, 00:01:58 ago
  Hold down timer expires in 74 secs

Router2#sho ip route
```

```
Codes: C - connected, S - static, I - IGRP, R - RIP, M - mobile, B - BGP
       D - EIGRP, EX - EIGRP external, O - OSPF, IA - OSPF inter area
       N1 - OSPF NSSA external type 1, N2 - OSPF NSSA external type 2
       E1 - OSPF external type 1, E2 - OSPF external type 2, E - EGP
       i - IS-IS, L1 - IS-IS level-1, L2 - IS-IS level-2, * - candidate default
       U - per-user static route, o - ODR

Gateway of last resort is not set

C    192.168.200.0/24 is directly connected, Serial0
C    192.168.201.0/24 is directly connected, Serial1
R    192.168.1.0/24 [120/1] via 192.168.200.254, 00:00:06, Serial0
C    192.168.2.0/24 is directly connected, Ethernet0
R    192.168.3.0/24 is possibly down, routing via 192.168.201.253, Serial1
Router2#undebug all
All possible debugging has been turned off
Router2#
```

Even though Router 3 is advertising that the network is back online and running, Router 2 ignores the message until the hold-down timer expires. Additionally, it will keep advertising 192.168.3.0 as unreachable to all routers. When the hold-down timer expires and before the flush timer expires, the broadcast from Router 3 will be heard and the route will be reestablished.

By stepping through each of the different problems that can occur in a network, we can see the different results that may occur, and learning this can aid us in future troubleshooting.

Additional RIP Knowledge

Occasionally, we may have a need to listen to RIP broadcasts, but not to advertise any networks. This can be used to isolate some of the interfaces on a router, while still allowing other interfaces full use of the network. This can be accomplished through something called *Passive RIP*. Passive RIP is especially useful in subnetted environments since we can keep one interface from broadcasting information that would normally be included in the classful advertisements. This is shown in Figure 9–6.

In this diagram, the network is subnetted to 24 bits, and RIP has been turned on with the network address of 172.31.0.0. We can examine our routing tables to make sure everything is running smoothly.

```
Router1#sho ip route
<lines deleted>

Gateway of last resort is not set

     172.31.0.0/24 is subnetted, 5 subnets
R       172.31.20.0 [120/1] via 172.31.10.253, 00:00:09, Serial0
R       172.31.3.0 [120/2] via 172.31.10.253, 00:00:09, Serial0
```

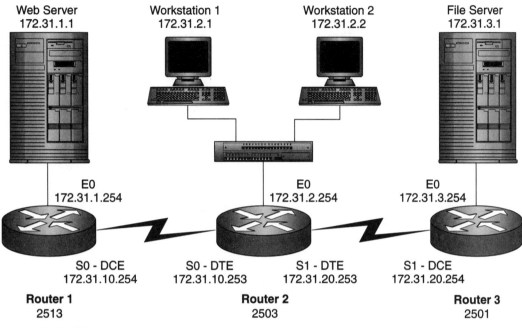

Web Server
172.31.1.1

Workstation 1
172.31.2.1

Workstation 2
172.31.2.2

File Server
172.31.3.1

E0
172.31.1.254

E0
172.31.2.254

E0
172.31.3.254

S0 - DCE
172.31.10.254

S0 - DTE
172.31.10.253

S1 - DTE
172.31.20.253

S1 - DCE
172.31.20.254

Router 1
2513

Router 2
2503

Router 3
2501

FIGURE 9–6   Subnetted class b using the Passive RIP interface

```
R       172.31.2.0 [120/1] via 172.31.10.253, 00:00:09, Serial0
C       172.31.1.0 is directly connected, Ethernet0
C       172.31.10.0 is directly connected, Serial0
Router1#

Router2#sho ip route
<lines deleted>

Gateway of last resort is not set

     172.31.0.0/24 is subnetted, 5 subnets
C       172.31.20.0 is directly connected, Serial1
R       172.31.3.0 [120/1] via 172.31.20.254, 00:00:09, Serial1
C       172.31.2.0 is directly connected, Ethernet0
R       172.31.1.0 [120/1] via 172.31.10.254, 00:00:22, Serial0
C       172.31.10.0 is directly connected, Serial0
Router2#

Router3#sho ip route
<lines deleted>

Gateway of last resort is not set

     172.31.0.0/24 is subnetted, 5 subnets
```

```
C       172.31.20.0 is directly connected, Serial1
C       172.31.3.0 is directly connected, Ethernet0
R       172.31.2.0 [120/1] via 172.31.20.253, 00:00:22, Serial1
R       172.31.1.0 [120/2] via 172.31.20.253, 00:00:22, Serial1
R       172.31.10.0 [120/1] via 172.31.20.253, 00:00:22, Serial1
Router3#
```

We can see that all of our routes have been established, meaning the convergence is complete.

Now suppose that we don't want to advertise any of the interfaces on Router 3, but we do want to hear all the advertisements from the other routers in our network. To do this, we will specify that Serial 1 is a passive interface.

```
Router3(config)#router rip
Router3(config-router)#passive-interface ?
  Ethernet  IEEE 802.3
  Null      Null interface
  Serial    Serial

Router3(config-router)#passive-interface serial 1
Router3(config-router)#^Z
Router3#copy run start
Building configuration...
[OK]
Router3#
```

If we now clear the route tables with the command **clear ip route *** to speed up the process, we can see that the route table on Router 2 does not have a route listed for 172.31.3.0.

```
Router2>sho ip route
Codes: C - connected, S - static, I - IGRP, R - RIP, M - mobile, B - BGP
       D - EIGRP, EX - EIGRP external, O - OSPF, IA - OSPF inter area
       N1 - OSPF NSSA external type 1, N2 - OSPF NSSA external type 2
       E1 - OSPF external type 1, E2 - OSPF external type 2, E - EGP
       i - IS-IS, L1 - IS-IS level-1, L2 - IS-IS level-2, * - candidate default
       U - per-user static route, o - ODR

Gateway of last resort is not set

     172.31.0.0/24 is subnetted, 4 subnets
C       172.31.20.0 is directly connected, Serial1
C       172.31.2.0 is directly connected, Ethernet0
R       172.31.1.0 [120/1] via 172.31.10.254, 00:00:07, Serial0
C       172.31.10.0 is directly connected, Serial0
Router2>
```

Just as we expected! There is no route for the network. One last step we can perform to verify this is to debug Router 3 and examine the outgoing RIP broadcasts.

```
RIP: sending v1 update to 255.255.255.255 via Ethernet0 (172.31.3.254)
     subnet  172.31.20.0, metric 1
     subnet  172.31.2.0, metric 2
     subnet  172.31.1.0, metric 3
     subnet  172.31.10.0, metric 2
RIP: received v1 update from 172.31.20.253 on Serial1
     172.31.2.0 in 1 hops
     172.31.1.0 in 2 hops
     172.31.10.0 in 1 hops
```

In the debug mode, we can see that RIP is being received on Serial 1 and is being broadcast on Ethernet 0 only. Thus, passive RIP is working.

Now that we understand the process of how RIP works, we can move on to IGRP. In order to do this, we need to turn off RIP on each of the routers. This can be accomplished by the following set of commands on each router:

```
Router3(config)#no router rip
Router3(config)#^Z
Router3#sho ip protocols
Router3#copy run start
Building configuration...
[OK]
Router3#
```

Since there is no protocol information, we can assume that RIP is turned off.

Broadcasting across WAN links is not something that is normally done. However, if we would like RIP to work across Frame Relay or other types of WAN links, we can tell RIP to broadcast its routing tables to neighbor routers. In RIP configuration mode, we can issue the **neighbor** command and specify the remote router. For example, if Router 2 and Router 3 were separated by a Frame Relay link, we could issue the command **neighbor 192.168.201.253** on Router 2, and **neighbor 192.168.201.254** on Router 3. The RIP updates would then be sent across the Frame Relay and received by the other routers.

Interior Gateway Routing Protocol

IGRP is a Distance Vector protocol that has been enhanced. It is a Cisco proprietary protocol that is only used between Cisco routers. It is similar in function to RIP in that it contains features such as Poison Reverse, Hold-Down, and Split Horizon. It also uses the **neighbor** command to send updates across Frame Relay.

IGRP does have some additional features, though. The metric hop count increases to 255 for larger networks, although 100 hops is the default. It performs a calculation based on user-configurable settings, including bandwidth, reliability, delay, and load. By default, most of these settings are not configured,

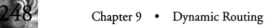

and so the metric that is used is the configured bandwidth plus the delay in microseconds. The bandwidth parameter is automatically determined on LAN links, but must be manually configured on WAN links using the **bandwidth** command.

Let's configure our routers to use IGRP and examine the parameters in more detail. We will continue to use the diagram in Figure 9-6 with the network address of 172.31.0.0 further subnetted.

```
Router1(config)#router igrp ?
  <1-65535>  Autonomous system number

Router1(config)#router igrp 100
Router1(config-router)#network 172.31.0.0
Router1(config-router)#^Z
Router1#
```

The first thing to notice is that IGRP requires a parameter when turning it on. IGRP uses Autonomous Systems (AS) to communicate routing information. This means that we could set up multiple AS areas for finer administrative control. Only routers that participate in the same AS number will update their routing tables. All other updates will be ignored. Now we can configure Router 2 with the same AS and watch the routing tables update.

```
Router2(config)#router igrp 100
Router2(config-router)#network 172.31.0.0
Router2(config-router)#^Z
Router2#
```

Again, notice that the AS numbers are the same. We can examine the interval periods by issuing the command **show ip protocols**. This will tell us the update interval as well as the invalid, hold-down, and flush intervals.

```
Router2#sho ip protocols
Routing Protocol is "igrp 100"
  Sending updates every 90 seconds, next due in 17 seconds
  Invalid after 270 seconds, hold down 280, flushed after 630
  Outgoing update filter list for all interfaces is
  Incoming update filter list for all interfaces is
  Default networks flagged in outgoing updates
  Default networks accepted from incoming updates
  IGRP metric weight K1=1, K2=0, K3=1, K4=0, K5=0
  IGRP maximum hopcount 100
  IGRP maximum metric variance 1
  Redistributing: igrp 100
  Routing for Networks:
    172.31.0.0
  Routing Information Sources:
    Gateway         Distance      Last Update
    172.31.10.254        100      00:00:58
```

```
        Distance: (default is 100)

    Router2#
```

We can see that IGRP does in fact have a 90-second update interval. Also, about half-way down the information list, we can see the metric weight that is used to calculate the metric value. These are the values listed in the "K=" line.

Examining our routing table, we can see if any updates are occurring.

```
Router2#sho ip route
Codes: C - connected, S - static, I - IGRP, R - RIP, M - mobile, B - BGP
       D - EIGRP, EX - EIGRP external, O - OSPF, IA - OSPF inter area
       N1 - OSPF NSSA external type 1, N2 - OSPF NSSA external type 2
       E1 - OSPF external type 1, E2 - OSPF external type 2, E - EGP
       i - IS-IS, L1 - IS-IS level-1, L2 - IS-IS level-2, * - candidate default
       U - per-user static route, o - ODR

Gateway of last resort is not set

     172.31.0.0/24 is subnetted, 4 subnets
C       172.31.20.0 is directly connected, Serial1
C       172.31.2.0 is directly connected, Ethernet0
I       172.31.1.0 [100/8576] via 172.31.10.254, 00:00:55, Serial0
C       172.31.10.0 is directly connected, Serial0
Router2#
```

Notice that there is a new entry that lists the network 172.31.1.0 that was received on the Serial 0 interface of 172.31.10.254. The I in the first column represents the value as being an IGRP route.

If we examine the numbers in brackets, we can see the administrative distance and the metric count. For IGRP, the administrative distance is 100. This means that IGRP is more reliable than RIP, and if the same route was received by both IGRP and RIP announcements, the one received by IGRP would be used and the other would be discarded. Table 9.1 shows the default administrative distances for other protocols as well.

TABLE 9.1 Default administrative distances

Routing Source	Default Administrative Distance
Directly Connected	0
Static Route	1
EIGRP Summary	5
External BGP	20
EIGRP	90
IGRP	100

TABLE 9.1	Default administrative distances *(Continued)*

Routing Source	Default Administrative Distance
OSPF	110
IS-IS	115
RIP	120
EGP	140
Internal BGP	200
Unknown	255

The second value in the column represents the metric count for the network path. This value is larger than the single metric hop count of RIP, because it does take into account bandwidth and other information as listed earlier.

In fact, the metric count that is being used is wrong. If we examine the serial interface in detail, we will see something interesting.

```
Router2#sho int s0
Serial0 is up, line protocol is up
  Hardware is HD64570
  Internet address is 172.31.10.253/24
  MTU 1500 bytes, BW 1544 Kbit, DLY 20000 usec, rely 255/255, load 1/255
  Encapsulation HDLC, loopback not set, keepalive set (10 sec)
  <lines deleted>
Router2#
```

On the fourth line, the values that are used to determine the metric are listed. Notice that the default bandwidth for WAN links is 1.544 Mbps, or a T1 connection. We should change that value to accurately represent the bandwidth of the link.

```
Router2(config-if)#band 56
Router2(config-if)#^Z
Router2#
Router2#clear ip route *
Router2#sho ip route
Codes: C - connected, S - static, I - IGRP, R - RIP, M - mobile, B - BGP
       D - EIGRP, EX - EIGRP external, O - OSPF, IA - OSPF inter area
       N1 - OSPF NSSA external type 1, N2 - OSPF NSSA external type 2
       E1 - OSPF external type 1, E2 - OSPF external type 2, E - EGP
       i - IS-IS, L1 - IS-IS level-1, L2 - IS-IS level-2, * - candidate default
       U - per-user static route, o - ODR

Gateway of last resort is not set
```

```
       172.31.0.0/24 is subnetted, 4 subnets
C        172.31.20.0 is directly connected, Serial1
C        172.31.2.0 is directly connected, Ethernet0
I        172.31.1.0 [100/180671] via 172.31.10.254, 00:00:02, Serial0
C        172.31.10.0 is directly connected, Serial0
Router2#
```

Once we changed the bandwidth parameter and cleared out our routing table, we can see that the new metric is 180671, which is much higher than the original 8576. This means that the 56K link is much less desirable, which is true when compared to a T1 line. If we examine Router 1, we will see similar results.

```
Router1#sho ip route
Codes: C - connected, S - static, I - IGRP, R - RIP, M - mobile, B - BGP
       D - EIGRP, EX - EIGRP external, O - OSPF, IA - OSPF inter area
       N1 - OSPF NSSA external type 1, N2 - OSPF NSSA external type 2
       E1 - OSPF external type 1, E2 - OSPF external type 2, E - EGP
       i - IS-IS, L1 - IS-IS level-1, L2 - IS-IS level-2, * - candidate default
       U - per-user static route, o - ODR

Gateway of last resort is not set

       172.31.0.0/24 is subnetted, 4 subnets
I        172.31.20.0 [100/10476] via 172.31.10.253, 00:00:57, Serial0
I        172.31.2.0 [100/8576] via 172.31.10.253, 00:00:57, Serial0
C        172.31.1.0 is directly connected, Ethernet0
C        172.31.10.0 is directly connected, Serial0
Router1#conf t
Enter configuration commands, one per line.  End with CNTL/Z.
Router1(config)#int s0
Router1(config-if)#band 56
Router1(config-if)#^Z
Router1#
```

Router 1 shows that the 172.31.20.0 and the 172.31.2.0 networks are fairly decent in metric count. However, after we update the bandwidth on the serial interface, our metric count changes drastically.

```
Router1#sho ip route
Codes: C - connected, S - static, I - IGRP, R - RIP, M - mobile, B - BGP
       D - EIGRP, EX - EIGRP external, O - OSPF, IA - OSPF inter area
       N1 - OSPF NSSA external type 1, N2 - OSPF NSSA external type 2
       E1 - OSPF external type 1, E2 - OSPF external type 2, E - EGP
       i - IS-IS, L1 - IS-IS level-1, L2 - IS-IS level-2, * - candidate default
       U - per-user static route, o - ODR

Gateway of last resort is not set

       172.31.0.0/24 is subnetted, 4 subnets
```

```
I       172.31.20.0 [100/182571] via 172.31.10.253, 00:00:27, Serial0
I       172.31.2.0 [100/180671] via 172.31.10.253, 00:00:27, Serial0
C       172.31.1.0 is directly connected, Ethernet0
C       172.31.10.0 is directly connected, Serial0
Router1#
```

Next, we configure Router 3 and examine its routing table. Again, we need to set the bandwidth on both ends of the WAN link.

```
Router2(config)#int s1
Router2(config-if)#band 128
Router2(config-if)#^Z
Router2#
%SYS-5-CONFIG_I: Configured from console by console
Router2#copy run start
Building configuration...
[OK]
Router2#

Router3(config)#int s1
Router3(config-if)#band 128
Router3(config-if)#exit
Router3(config)#router igrp 101
Router3(config-router)#network 172.31.0.0
Router3(config-router)#^Z
Router3#

Router3#sho ip route
Codes: C - connected, S - static, I - IGRP, R - RIP, M - mobile, B - BGP
       D - EIGRP, EX - EIGRP external, O - OSPF, IA - OSPF inter area
       N1 - OSPF NSSA external type 1, N2 - OSPF NSSA external type 2
       E1 - OSPF external type 1, E2 - OSPF external type 2, E - EGP
       i - IS-IS, L1 - IS-IS level-1, L2 - IS-IS level-2, * - candidate default
       U - per-user static route, o - ODR

Gateway of last resort is not set

     172.31.0.0/24 is subnetted, 2 subnets
C       172.31.20.0 is directly connected, Serial1
C       172.31.3.0 is directly connected, Ethernet0
Router3#
```

There must be some problem here. There should be updates arriving from Router 2, and yet the routing table is empty. To determine what is causing the problem, we can use the **debug** command. It is similar to RIP, but it requires a parameter of either **events** or **transactions**. The latter is for a more detailed debugging of IGRP. Once it is turned on, we may have to wait for 90 seconds before the update interval expires and a new update is sent out.

```
Router3#debug ip igrp ?
  events         IGRP protocol events
  transactions   IGRP protocol transactions

Router3#debug ip igrp transactions
IGRP protocol debugging is on
Router3#
IGRP: sending update to 255.255.255.255 via Ethernet0 (172.31.3.254)
      subnet 172.31.20.0, metric=80125
IGRP: sending update to 255.255.255.255 via Serial1 (172.31.20.254)
      subnet 172.31.3.0, metric=1100
```

The updates are occurring, but nothing is coming in from the serial link. Next, we need to debug Router 2 and see if the updates are being received.

```
Router2#debug ip igrp trans
IGRP protocol debugging is on
Router2#
IGRP: sending update to 255.255.255.255 via Ethernet0 (172.31.2.254)
      subnet 172.31.20.0, metric=80125
      subnet 172.31.1.0, metric=180671
      subnet 172.31.10.0, metric=180571
IGRP: sending update to 255.255.255.255 via Serial0 (172.31.10.253)
      subnet 172.31.20.0, metric=80125
      subnet 172.31.2.0, metric=1100
IGRP: sending update to 255.255.255.255 via Serial1 (172.31.20.253)
      subnet 172.31.2.0, metric=1100
      subnet 172.31.1.0, metric=180671
      subnet 172.31.10.0, metric=180571
IGRP: received update from 172.31.10.254 on Serial0
      subnet 172.31.1.0, metric 180671 (neighbor 1100)
Router2#undebug all
All possible debugging has been turned off
```

Updates are being sent out the Serial 1 interface, but are not being heard. This tells us that something is probably wrong with our IGRP configuration.

```
Router2#sho ip protocol
Routing Protocol is "igrp 100"
  Sending updates every 90 seconds, next due in 78 seconds
  Invalid after 270 seconds, hold down 280, flushed after 630
  Outgoing update filter list for all interfaces is
  Incoming update filter list for all interfaces is
  Default networks flagged in outgoing updates
  Default networks accepted from incoming updates
  IGRP metric weight K1=1, K2=0, K3=1, K4=0, K5=0
  IGRP maximum hopcount 100
  IGRP maximum metric variance 1
  Redistributing: igrp 100
  Routing for Networks:
    172.31.0.0
```

```
       Routing Information Sources:
         Gateway         Distance      Last Update
         172.31.10.254       100       00:00:03
       Distance: (default is 100)

     Router3#sho ip proto
     Routing Protocol is "igrp 101"
       Sending updates every 90 seconds, next due in 35 seconds
       Invalid after 270 seconds, hold down 280, flushed after 630
       Outgoing update filter list for all interfaces is not set
       Incoming update filter list for all interfaces is not set
       Default networks flagged in outgoing updates
       Default networks accepted from incoming updates
       IGRP metric weight K1=1, K2=0, K3=1, K4=0, K5=0
       IGRP maximum hopcount 100
       IGRP maximum metric variance 1
       Redistributing: igrp 101
       Routing for Networks:
         172.31.0.0
       Routing Information Sources:
         Gateway         Distance      Last Update
       Distance: (default is 100)
```

There's the problem! Router 3 has been configured to be a part of AS
101, while Routers 1 and 2 are part of 100. Once we fix this problem, our
routing tables should populate correctly.

```
Router3(config)#no router igrp 101
Router3(config)#router igrp 100
Router3(config-router)#network 172.31.0.0
Router3(config-router)#^Z
Router3#

Router3#sho ip route
Codes: C - connected, S - static, I - IGRP, R - RIP, M - mobile, B - BGP
       D - EIGRP, EX - EIGRP external, O - OSPF, IA - OSPF inter area
       N1 - OSPF NSSA external type 1, N2 - OSPF NSSA external type 2
       E1 - OSPF external type 1, E2 - OSPF external type 2, E - EGP
       i - IS-IS, L1 - IS-IS level-1, L2 - IS-IS level-2, * - candidate default
       U - per-user static route, o - ODR

Gateway of last resort is not set

     172.31.0.0/24 is subnetted, 5 subnets
C       172.31.20.0 is directly connected, Serial1
C       172.31.3.0 is directly connected, Ethernet0
I       172.31.2.0 [100/80225] via 172.31.20.253, 00:00:34, Serial1
I       172.31.1.0 [100/182671] via 172.31.20.253, 00:00:34, Serial1
I       172.31.10.0 [100/182571] via 172.31.20.253, 00:00:34, Serial1
Router3#
```

That's much better. Our network is running, thanks to our well-developed debugging skills. Time for another raise!

Multiprotocol Routing (MPR)

What happens if we enable both RIP and IGRP on the network? Both protocols will operate independently of each other exchanging route tables. However, when the router receives network information from two different protocols, it will use the route with the lowest administrative distance. Additionally, the protocols will not exchange information. This means that if Router 1 used RIP, Router 3 used IGRP, and Router 2 used both RIP and IGRP, Router 1 will never know about the networks connected to Router 3.

This process is known as *separated multiprotocol routing*. The concept means that there are multiple routing tables for each routing protocol, and that each protocol will advertise its routing information regardless of the other routing protocols.

A better method is called *integrated multiprotocol routing*. This method still maintains multiple routing tables for each routing protocol, but when the routing tables are redistributed, they are done through a single routing protocol. EIGRP is a protocol that can act as an integrated multiprotocol.

Summary

Routing protocols are protocols that transmit network information to routers. Routers can then use these updates to build routing tables dynamically. Routing protocols can be classified as either Interior or Exterior. Interior protocols can be further classified as Distance Vector or Link State, and Classful or Classless. Distance Vector protocols transmit entire routing tables every 30 to 90 seconds. These tables reflect information from other routers and are subject to incorrect information. Link State protocols have a topological view of the entire network and can make instant routing table changes when a network change is detected. Examples of Link State protocols include OSPF and NLSP. Examples of Distance Vector protocols include RIP and IGRP. Distance Vector protocols can suffer from routing loops, and therefore implement some type of routing control. These types are known as Split Horizon, Poison Reverse, and Hold-Down. RIP is a good routing protocol for small networks, but starts to decline in performance in large networks. RIP suffers from a low metric of 15 possible hops. IGRP is a Cisco proprietary protocol that was designed to prevent some of the shortcomings of RIP. IGRP can reach routers up to 255 hops away, although the default is 100 hops. Additionally, IGRP can be configured to take more into account than just hop counts. These additional parameters include bandwidth, reliability, and load. This makes IGRP a better protocol in small to medium-sized networks.

Scenario Lab 9.1

Now that you have explained the details of a static routing table to the CIO, he is beginning to see why he is paying you so much money (see Figure 9–7). Now, to impress the CIO even more, can you describe how you would implement dynamic routing in this network? Which routing protocol will you use? Don't forget about the Frame Relay requirements.

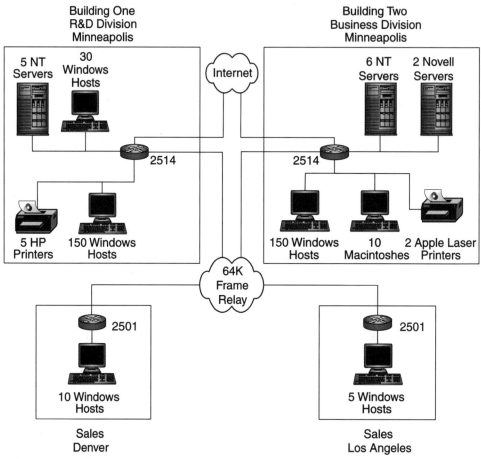

Practice Lab 9.1

In this lab, you will configure each of the routers in Figure 9–8 with the given IP addresses. Next, you will install RIP and verify the routing tables have been updated. Finally, you will monitor RIP updates.

- Set up the network using the given IP addresses. Verify connectivity to each of the workstations.
- Enable RIP on each of the routers. Specify each of the networks to advertise on each router. Verify the routing tables have been updated by using the command **show ip route**.
- Test connectivity by using **ping** on Workstation 1 to ping Workstation 2.
- Turn on debugging for Router 1 and examine the updates. How often are the updates being received and sent?
- Remove the cable from E0 on Workstation 2. Continue monitoring the RIP updates on Router 1. How long did it take to hear about the network being down?
- Plug the cable back in and continue monitoring RIP. How long before the convergence is complete and Router 1 again knows about the Ethernet network on Router 2?

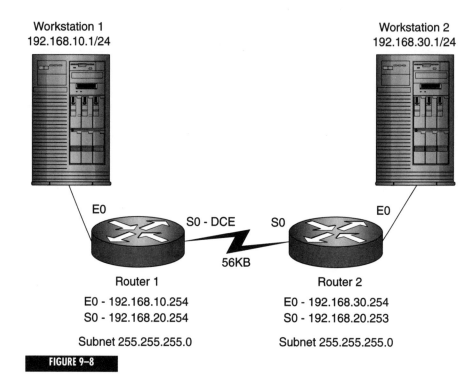

Workstation 1
192.168.10.1/24

Workstation 2
192.168.30.1/24

E0

S0 - DCE   S0

E0

56KB

Router 1
E0 - 192.168.10.254
S0 - 192.168.20.254

Subnet 255.255.255.0

Router 2
E0 - 192.168.30.254
S0 - 192.168.20.253

Subnet 255.255.255.0

FIGURE 9-8

Practice Lab 9.2

In this lab, you will turn RIP on and examine the routing updates in Figure 9–9. You will simulate a network failure and then examine the delays associated with such a failure.

- Set up the network as shown using the given IP addresses. Verify connectivity to each of the workstations.
- Enable RIP on each of the routers and monitor the routing tables. Specify each network to advertise. How long should convergence take after the last router is enabled?
- From each of the workstations, **ping** the other workstations to verify connectivity.
- Use **trace** (tracert on Windows) to watch the path of the packet flow. Turn off the domain name lookups in order to speed up **trace**.
- Examine the timer intervals using the **show ip protocols** command. How long is the hold-down period?
- Turn on debugging on Router 3. Use the version with the most detail.
- Remove the Ethernet cable from Router 1 and continue monitoring the RIP updates on Router 3. How long before Router 3 is aware of the downed network?
- Plug the Ethernet cable back into Router 1. Examine the routing table on Router 1. Was the network immediately put back into service?

- Watching the debugging statements on Router 3, is Router 2 advertising the downed network as being back up?
- Examine the time left for the hold-down period on Router 2. Examine the routing table on Router 2. Keep watching between the two lists. Is there a correlation when Router 2 adds the network back into the Routing table?

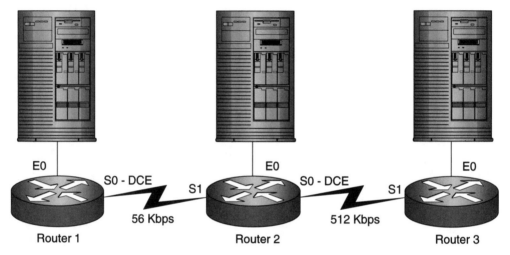

Router 1	Router 2	Router 3
Workstation IP: 172.16.0.1	Workstation IP: 172.18.0.1	Workstation IP: 172.20.0.1
E0 IP: 172.16.255.254	E0 IP: 172.18.255.254	E0 IP: 172.20.255.254
S0 IP: 172.17.255.254	S1 IP: 172.17.255.253	S1 IP: 172.19.255.253
	S0 IP: 172.19.255.254	
Subnet Mask: 255.255.0.0	Subnet Mask: 255.255.0.0	Subnet Mask: 255.255.0.0

FIGURE 9–9

Practice Lab 9.3

In this lab, you will enable IGRP on the routers and examine the routing tables in Figure 9–10. You will experiment with having multiple Autonomous Systems defined. Finally, you will examine the network in the event of a network failure.

- Set up the network as shown using the given IP addresses. Verify connectivity to each of the workstations.
- Enable IGRP on Routers 1 and 2 using the AS number 100. Specify each of the networks to advertise.
- View the route table on the last router you configure. How long should it take for convergence to complete?
- Enable IGRP on Router 3 with the AS number of 110. Watch the routing tables on all routers. Are there any changes?
- Try pinging 172.20.0.1 from Router 1. Were you successful? Why, or why not?
- Remove the IGRP from Router 3 and enable IGRP with the AS number of 100. Watch the routing tables. How long does it take for convergence to take place?
- Examine the timer intervals for IGRP. How long is the hold-down interval?
- Enable debugging for IGRP on Router 3. Use the method with the most detailed debugging.
- Remove the Ethernet cable from Router 1. Examine the debug updates on Router 3. How long before Router 3 knows that something is wrong with the network? Can you explain this?

- Plug the Ethernet cable back into Router 1. Watch the debug messages on Router 3. Examine the route table on Router 3. Has the route been updated yet?
- Enable debugging on Router 2 and examine the information received from Router 1. Is Router 1 announcing the availability of the Ethernet network? Has Router 2 updated the routing table?
- After the hold-down timers expire on Router 2 and Router 3, is the network convergence finished?

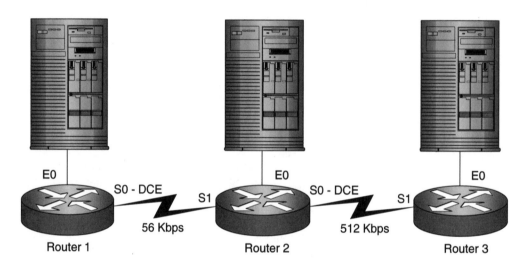

Workstation IP: 172.16.0.1
E0 IP: 172.16.255.254
S0 IP: 172.17.255.254

Subnet Mask: 255.255.0.0

Workstation IP: 172.18.0.1
E0 IP: 172.18.255.254
S1 IP: 172.17.255.253
S0 IP: 172.19.255.254

Subnet Mask: 255.255.0.0

Workstation IP: 172.20.0.1
E0 IP: 172.20.255.254
S1 IP: 172.19.255.253

Subnet Mask: 255.255.0.0

FIGURE 9–10

Exam Objective Checklist

By working through this chapter, you should have sufficient knowledge to answer these exam objectives:

- List problems that each routing type encounters when dealing with topology changes, and describe techniques to reduce the number of these problems.
- Add the RIP routing protocol to your configuration.
- Add the IGRP routing protocol to your configuration.
- Explain the services of separate and integrated multi-protocol routing.

Practice Questions

1. Which of the following are routing protocols? (Choose all that apply)

    a. RIP
    b. TCP/IP
    c. IGRP
    d. IPX/SPX
    e. AppleTalk
    f. BGP
    g. EIGRP
    h. NSLP
    i. OSPF

2. Which type of protocol updates its routing tables every update interval?

    a. Link State
    b. Distance Vector
    c. Classful
    d. Classless

3. RIP and IGRP can be classified as what?

    a. Exterior protocols
    b. Routed protocols
    c. Classful protocols
    d. Link State protocols

4. Which command will list the interval for the hold-down?

    a. show ip route

    b. show protocols

    c. show ip protocols

    d. show hold-down

    e. show ip hold-down interval

5. Which of the following is the term used for a router to identify a network as unreachable immediately upon loss of the path?

    a. Split Horizon

    b. Poison Reverse

    c. Triggered Update

    d. Hold-Down

6. Which of the following prevents routers from advertising routes on the same interface they heard the route from?

    a. Split Horizon

    b. Poison Reverse

    c. Triggered Update

    d. Hold Down

7. Which of the following prevents routers from "flapping?"

    a. Split Horizon

    b. Poison Reverse

    c. Triggered Update

    d. Hold Down

8. You have enabled RIP by using the **router rip** command. When you examine the routing tables, however, there is no route information. What other command do you need?

    a. int s0 rip

    b. network 172.16.0.0 rip

    c. network 172.16.0.0

    d. neighbor 172.16.0.0

9. Which two commands are used to debug RIP?

    a. debug rip

    b. debug ip rip

    c. debug ip rip events

    d. debug ip rip transactions

10. Which two commands are used to debug IGRP?

    a. debug igrp

    b. debug ip igrp

    c. debug ip igrp events

    d. debug ip igrp transactions

11. Which command will turn off IGRP with the Autonomous System number 101?

    a. no igrp as 101

    b. no router igrp 101

    c. no router igrp

    d. no router 101 igrp

12. IGRP can be used to calculate the bandwidth of a network for better route decisions. Which command must be used to configure a serial link correctly?

    a. bandwidth

    b. band width

    c. clock rate

    d. clockrate

13. What command will refresh the routing table?

    a. refresh ip route

    b. clear ip route *

    c. no ip route

    d. no ip route *

Managing the Cisco Router

In This Chapter

- ◆ Load the Router with New IOS Images

- ◆ Use Different Methods to Configure a Router

- ◆ Recover Lost Passwords

As the router performs its work in our environment, there may come a time when disaster strikes. We need a method of saving our configuration files and our IOS image files for just such an event. Additionally, configuring our routers may not be as easy as setting them up in the network and making them work. Sometimes, we have to ship our router to a remote site and have it get configured there. We will examine these methods in this chapter.

Disasters Can Occur

Imagine that we came into work today and our boss said something along the lines like, "Did you hear the storm that came through last night? The lightning strikes were phenomenal!" Our first instinct should be to worry about the network and, specifically, the routers. Perhaps the lightning strikes hit our building and our routers were damaged. This would not be a happy day, and it could get worse. Did we remember to save our IOS images and our configuration files so that we can just reload them in the event of an emergency such as this?

These are common concerns that a network administrator should keep in mind. In order to alleviate some of the potential problems from a disaster, we should be keeping copies of our files. Let's examine how this can be done.

The Boot Process

When a router is powered on, it performs a process known as POST, or Power-On Self-Test. This process tests the hardware in the router to make sure everything is working correctly. As the process runs, it starts various diagnostic routines in each of the ROM chips on the router. When all have passed the check, the router can then proceed with the boot process.

After the POST, the router then will try to load and run a version of the IOS image file. This file will be searched for in a certain order that includes looking for it in ROM, in FLASH memory, or a TFTP server. Remember that TFTP is the Trivial File Transfer Protocol that uses UDP. It is a process that can send and receive files, but there is no security implemented. The initial order is to search for the IOS in FLASH, then a TFTP server, and finally ROM. The ROM version is a scaled-down version of the IOS and has just enough functionality for us to load a full version of the IOS from some other location. If we should decide to change the order, we can configure the router to do this by using the following commands:

```
Router2#conf t
Enter configuration commands, one per line.  End with CNTL/Z.
Router2(config)#boot ?
  bootstrap   Bootstrap image file
  buffersize  Specify the buffer size for netbooting a config file
  host        Router-specific config file
  network     Network-wide config file
  system      System image file

Router2(config)#boot system ?
  WORD   System image filename
  flash  Boot from flash memory
  mop    Boot from a Decnet MOP server
  rcp    Boot from a server via rcp
  tftp   Boot from a tftp server

Router2(config)#boot system flash ios.filename
Router2(config)#boot system tftp ios.filename tftp.address
Router2(config)#boot system rom
```

This will cause the router to try to load the IOS image from FLASH, then a TFTP server, and finally, the boot ROM. Notice that you must specify the IOS image name for booting from TFTP, but that it is optional when using the FLASH boot method. This IOS image name will be discussed further in the next section. These commands are then stored in NVRAM for retrieval during a reboot.

To determine the default method that the router will use, examine the version information.

```
Router2#show version
Cisco Internetwork Operating System Software
<text deleted>

Configuration register is 0x2102
```

The last line in the statement tells us our method of boot; specifically, the last digit in the hex value. This value determines the method of booting. In this instance, we can see the value 2, which tells the router to boot using the boot commands found in NVRAM.

If we want to change the method of rebooting, we can issue the command **config-register** and specify a new value as shown in the following example:

```
Router2#conf t
Enter configuration commands, one per line.   End with CNTL/Z.
Router2(config)#config-register 0x2101
```

This causes the router to reboot directly to ROM mode.

Once the router has booted the IOS, it displays the hardware and software information that has been detected and loaded. This is the screen that displays during the initial boot. You can also review this information by using the **show version** command.

Finally, the router then tries to load the configuration file to configure the router for normal operation. This file resides in the NVRAM if the router has been configured before. If it is not there, or it has been corrupted, then the router will enter an initial configuration screen. We have already seen this screen back in Chapter 5, "Introduction to Cisco Routers." At this point, we can continue the wizard, or we can abort it and manually enter the configuration commands.

Figure 10–1 shows the basic architecture of the router. Note that some routers will load the IOS into memory and run it from there. Other models run the IOS straight from the FLASH memory. The 2500 series routers are the latter.

Working with the IOS Image

When we initially receive the router, it may or may not have an IOS image already loaded. If one has been loaded, it may not be the one that we want. We may even want to upgrade the IOS to a new version with newer features. In order to do this, we will need a TFTP server that we can access. Let's use Figure 10–2 to review our network diagram of IC, Inc.

Random Access Memory (RAM)	Non-Volatile RAM (NVRAM)	FLASH
Running Internetwork Operating System (IOS)	Startup Configuration	Internetwork Operating System (IOS)
Buffers and Routing Tables		
Running Configuration		

FIGURE 10-1   Basic architecture of the Cisco router

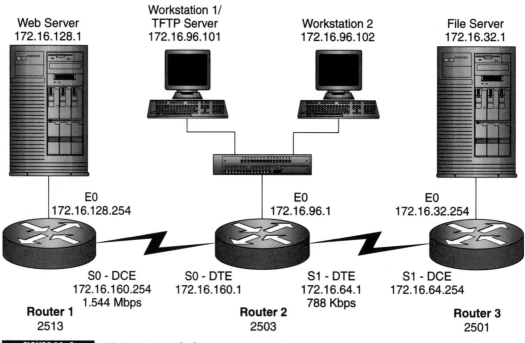

FIGURE 10-2   IC, Inc. network diagram

As we can see, we have a TFTP server located on Workstation 1. We have our three routers, all with an IOS image that we should probably be saving. Let's do just that. We should probably **ping** the workstation just to be sure we have good connectivity.

```
Router2#ping 172.16.96.101

Type escape sequence to abort.
Sending 5, 100-byte ICMP Echos to 172.16.96.101, timeout is 2 seconds:
!!!!!
Success rate is 100 percent (5/5), round-trip min/avg/max = 1/2/4 ms
```

We received a response, so our connectivity is good. We should also probably make sure the TFTP application is running. This may require us to physically visit the machine, or we can just continue, and if everything works, then we know the TFTP server was running. Additionally, it might be a good idea to ensure that we have enough storage space to save our IOS and configuration files. Keep in mind that the TFTP server is an unsecured service. Basically, anyone can get access to our server and could potentially erase our configuration and IOS image files. Or worse, a hacker could modify one of the configuration files, waiting for it to be reinstalled on a router by us, giving the hacker complete access to our network.

At this point, we can now start the copy process.

```
Router2#copy flash tftp

System flash directory:
File   Length    Name/status
  1    6239492   c2500-d-1.113-3.t.bin
[6239556 bytes used, 2149052 available, 8388608 total]
Address or name of remote host [172.16.96.101]? <enter>
Source file name? c2500-d-1.113-3.t.bin
Destination file name [c2500-d-1.113-3.t.bin]? router2-113-3.bin
Verifying checksum for 'c2500-d-1.113-3.t.bin' (file # 1)...  OK
Copy 'c2500-d-1.113-3.t.bin' from Flash to server
  as 'router2-113-3.bin'? [yes/no]y
!!!!!!!!!!!!!!!!!!!!!!!!!!!!!!!!!!!!!!!!!!!!!!!!!!!!!!!!!!!!!!!!!!!!!!!
!!!!!!!!!!!!!!!!!!!!!!!!!!!!!!!!!!!!!!!!!!!!!!!!!!!!!!!!!!!!!!!!!!!!!!!
!!!!!!!!!!!!!!!!!!!!!!!!!!!!!!!!!!!!!!!!!!!!!!!!!!!!!!!!!!!!!!!!!!!!!!!
!!!!!!!!!!!!!!!!!!!!!!!!!!!!!!!!!!!!!!!!!!!!!!!!!!!!!!!!!!!!!!!!!!!!!!!
!!!!!!!!!!!!!!!!!!!!!!!!!!!!!!!!!!!!!!!!!!!!!!!!!!!!!!!!!!!!!!!!!!!!!!!
!!!!!!!!!!!!!!!!!!!!!!!!!!!!!!!!!!!!!!!!!!!!!!!!!!!!!!!!!!!!!!!!!!!!!!!
!!!!!!!!!!!!!!!!!!!!!!!!!!!!!!!!!!!!!!!!!!!!!!!!!!!!!!!!!!!!!!!!!!!!!!!
!!!!!!!!!!!!!!!!!!!!!!!!!!!!!!!!!!!!!!!!!!!!!!!!!!!!!!!!!!!!!!!!!!!!!!!
!!!!!!!!!!!!!!!!!!!!!!!!!!!!!!!!!!!!!!!!!!!!!!!!!!!!!!!!!!!!!!!!!!!!!!!
!!!!!!!!!!!!!!!!!!!!!!!!!!!!!!!!!!!!!!!!!!!!!!!!!!!!!!!!!!!!!!!!!!!!!!!
!!!!!!!!!!!!!!!!!!!!!!!!!!!!!!!!!!!!!!!!!!!!!!!!!!!!!!!!!!!!!!!!!!!!!!!
!!!!!!!!!!!!!!!!!!!!!!!!!!!!!!!!!!!!!!!!!!!!!!!!!!!!!!!!!!!!!!!!!!!!!!!
!!!!!!!!!!!!!!!!!!!!!!!!!!!!!!!!!!!!!!!!!!!!!!!!!!!!!!!!!!!!!!!!!!!!!!!
!!!!!!!!!!!!!!!!!!!!!!!!!!!!!!!!!!!!!!!!!!!!!!!!!!!!!!!!!!!!!!!!!!!!!!!
!!!!!!!!!!!!!!!!!!!!!!!!!!!!!!!!!!!!!!!!!!!!!!!!!!!!!!!!!!!!!!!!!!!!!!!
```

```
!!!!!!!!!!!!!!!!!!!!!!!!!!!!!!!!!!!!!!!!!!!!!!!!!!!!!!!!!!!!!!!!!!!!!
!!!!!!!!!!!!!!!!!!!!!!!!!!!!!!!!!!!!!!!!!!!!!!!!!!!!!!!!!!!!!!!!!!!!!
!!!!!!!!!!!!!!!!!!!!!!!!!!!!!!!!!!!!!!!!!!!!!!!!!!!!
Upload to server done
Flash device copy took 00:01:17 [hh:mm:ss]
```

Notice that we started the process by typing the command **copy flash tftp**. Remember that the copy command takes the argument *source* and *destination*, in that order. So we are copying the FLASH to the TFTP server. After this, the router responds with the contents of the FLASH. In this case, the FLASH contains one file called c2500-d-l.113-3.t.bin. If the FLASH is large enough, it could contain other images. Notice the size is roughly 6MB!

Next, we enter the name of the FLASH file that we want to copy to the TFTP server. We then enter a name to store it on the server. Normally, we would keep the names the same since we can reference this name in the IOS documentation. However, we renamed the file to remind us that it came from Router 2 and that the version is 11.3(3). We also have to keep in mind naming conventions. If this TFTP server were stored on a computer that could only reference the 8.3 naming convention, we would have to modify our name to fit. After the router verifies that the IOS is not corrupted, it contacts the TFTP server and then gives us one more chance to abort the copy.

The next few lines are exclamation points that tell us that 512 bytes have been copied for each one displayed. If there were a lost datagram, we would see the period symbol. Finally, the copy finishes in just 1 minute and 17 seconds.

At this point, we would want to go to each of the other routers and perform similar commands. Note, though, that if all three routers are running the same version of IOS, we really only need one copy. The same copy will work for all the routers.

Imagine that sometime in the future, Cisco releases a new version of their IOS and it has some desperately needed new features to keep our company competitive in the market. After downloading the new IOS from their Web site (because we have a maintenance contract with them), we need to implement it onto our routers.

```
Router2#copy tftp flash
                      ****  NOTICE  ****
Flash load helper v1.0
This process will accept the copy options and then terminate
the current system image to use the ROM based image for the copy.
Routing functionality will not be available during that time.
If you are logged in via telnet, this connection will terminate.
Users with console access can see the results of the copy operation.
                  ---- ******** ----
Proceed? [confirm] <enter>

System flash directory:
```

```
File  Length    Name/status
  1   6239492   c2500-d-1.113-3.t.bin
[6239556 bytes used, 2149052 available, 8388608 total]
```

At this point, we again see the name of the file that resides in FLASH memory. Once again, if we actually had enough storage, we could store more than one version of the IOS. This would allow us to choose one of several versions to boot by using the boot commands to point to the correct image to load.

```
Address or name of remote host [172.16.96.101]? <enter>
Source file name? router2-113-3.bin
Destination file name [router2-113-3.bin]? c2500-d-1.113-3.t.bin
Accessing file 'router2-113-3.bin' on 172.16.96.101...
Loading router2-113-3.bin from 172.16.96.101 (via Ethernet0): ! [OK]
```

After entering the name of the file to retrieve from the TFTP server, we can choose the name to store it in FLASH. Here we set the name back to the original name of the image before we saved it. Notice that the router will check to make sure it can communicate with the TFTP server before continuing.

```
Erase flash device before writing? [confirm] <enter>
Flash contains files. Are you sure you want to
erase? [confirm] <enter>
```

After finding the TFTP server, we are prompted if we want to erase the FLASH. We would not erase the FLASH if we wanted to store more than one version of the IOS. Here we continue, and again it asks us to be sure that we want to erase the FLASH.

```
Copy 'router2-113-3.bin' from server
  as 'c2500-d-1.113-3.t.bin' into Flash WITH erase? [yes/no]yes

%SYS-5-RELOAD: Reload requested
%FLH: router2-113-3.bin from 172.16.96.101 to flash ...

System flash directory:
File  Length    Name/status
  1   6239492   c2500-d-1.113-3.t.bin
[6239556 bytes used, 2149052 available, 8388608 total]
Accessing file 'router2-113-3.bin' on 172.16.96.101...
Loading router2-113-3.bin .from 172.16.96.101 (via Ethernet0): ! [OK]

Erasing device... eeeeeeeeeeeeeeeeeeeeeeeeeeeeeeeeee ...erased
Loading router2-113-3.bin from 172.16.96.101 (via Ethernet0):
!!!!!!!!!!!!!!!!!!!!!!!!!!!!!!!!!!!!!!!!!!!!!!!!!!!!!!!!!!!!!!!!!!!
!!!!!!!!!!!!!!!!!!!!!!!!!!!!!!!!!!!!!!!!!!!!!!!!!!!!!!!!!!!!!!!!!!!
<many characters deleted>
!
[OK - 6239492/8388608 bytes]
```

```
Verifying checksum... OK (0x44AF)
Flash copy took 0:03:40 [hh:mm:ss]
%FLH: Re-booting system after download
```

Finally, the FLASH is erased and reloaded with the new image from the TFTP server. After the new version is installed, the router is rebooted.

We can view the FLASH by using the command **show flash**. If there was enough memory, we could store multiple FLASH files. Again, to choose the FLASH file to load, we would issue the command **boot system flash** *image.filename*.

```
Router2#sho flash

System flash directory:
File   Length    Name/status
  1    6239492   c2500-d-1.113-3.t.bin
[6239556 bytes used, 2149052 available, 8388608 total]
8192K bytes of processor board System flash (Read ONLY)
```

A question may arise at this point: What happened to the configuration of the router? If we review the architecture diagram again (see Figure 10–1), we can see that NVRAM and FLASH are two separate entities. This means that one has no affect on the other. It would be a lot of work if we wanted to upgrade the IOS and then had to redo the configuration of the router. Thanks to Cisco for this insight, an upgrade will only take us offline for the short period of rebooting the router during the copy of the IOS. To make things even nicer for us, if the router supports running the IOS from main memory instead of FLASH, the router will not be unavailable at all; or at least not until we manually reboot to finish the process.

Working with the Configuration Files

Up until this point, we have been working with the configuration files held in NVRAM and memory. We have been doing this with the **copy run start** and the **copy start run** commands. These configuration files are just as important, if not more so, than the IOS images, and therefore we should be backing them up as well.

In order to back up our configuration files, we will still use the **copy** command, but this time our destination will be the TFTP server.

```
Router2>enable
Router2#copy start tftp
Remote host []? 172.16.96.101
Name of configuration file to write[router2-confg]? router2-confg
Write file router2-confg on host 172.16.96.101? [confirm] <enter>
Writing router2-confg .!! [OK]
```

Once again, we need to specify the IP address of the TFTP server in order to save our files. We are then asked for the name of the destination file that we are copying to. We could name this anything we want, and here we kept the name *router2-confg*. Actually, this name has some deeper meaning that we will be examining later in this chapter. After confirming the information we entered, the file is then saved on the TFTP server.

To retrieve the file is almost as easy. Here we have two options, though. We can retrieve the file and have it stored in NVRAM, or we can actually retrieve the file and drop it into our running configuration and have it implemented immediately. We will perform the latter.

```
Router2#copy tftp run
Host or network configuration file [host]? <enter>
Address of remote host [255.255.255.255]? 172.16.96.101
Name of configuration file [router2-confg]? <enter>
Configure using router2-confg from 172.16.96.101? [confirm] <enter>
Loading router2-confg from 172.16.96.101 (via Ethernet0): !
[OK - 656/32723 bytes]

%SYS-5-CONFIG: Configured from router2-confg by console tftp from 172.16.96.101
```

Because we specified that this was a host configuration file, the default name of the file to retrieve was our hostname-confg, or *router2-confg*. After verifying connectivity to the TFTP server, the file was retrieved and placed into the running configuration and overrode the current settings.

If we were to examine the router configuration file that was stored on the TFTP server, we would potentially notice three things:

- The file is stored as text and can be modified.
- If we use Notepad to open the file, it is one really long line.
- The passwords are stored in clear text (except for the secret password).

Since the file is stored as a text file, we have the ability to go in and modify it at our leisure. However, before we do that, let's get it into a format we can read. In order to do this, we need to open the file in the old DOS edit program. However, DOS edit doesn't like names greater than eight characters in length. After renaming the file, save it as the same name. Once the file has been renamed, we can then use Notepad or continue to use edit to modify the configuration script file. Any commands that we would normally type at the configuration prompt can be entered here. Additionally, we can add comment lines in the code by using the exclamation point at the beginning of a line.

The last issue is the biggest. Our passwords for our console, terminal, and enable passwords are sitting out in clear text for the world to view. There is a way to stop this. We need to issue the command **service password-encryption**. Once this is performed, our passwords will be stored in an encrypted format within the text file.

```
Router2#conf t
Enter configuration commands, one per line.  End with CNTL/Z.
Router2(config)#service password-encryption
Router2(config)#^Z

Router2#show run
Building configuration...

Current configuration:
!
version 11.3
service password-encryption
service tcp-small-servers
!
hostname Router2
!
enable password 7 030752180500
```

The last line displayed shows us the password has been encrypted.

Besides using a TFTP server, there are three additional methods of configuring our routers. The first method is to use the **setup** command to start the setup script. However, there are certain limitations to using this. For instance, we have the option to configure RIP and IGRP, but we cannot configure OSPF. However, it is still a quick way to get a base configuration created.

The second method is only available with IOS 11.1(2) or later. This method allows us to use a Web browser to configure a router. In order to do this, the command **ip http server** must be issued on the router. After that, we can use the Web browser to monitor and issue IOS commands to the router as shown in Figure 10–3.

The final method is known as the AutoInstall. The previous configuration methods assume that we will have access to the router to configure it into the network. However, there are times when we may not be onsite to set up a router. The one catch to this is that there must be a router that is already configured directly attached to one of the new router's interfaces. This method only works with IOS 9.1 or greater.

To examine AutoInstall, we will step through the process. Refer to Figure 10–4 during the steps.

1. First, the router that is preconfigured must have a host address of 1 or 2 (this is only necessary with HDLC encapsulation across a WAN link). We will use Router2 with Serial 1 interface of 172.16.64.1.

2. Configure the preconfigured router with the command **ip helper-address** *address*. The *address* parameter is the TCP/IP address of the TFTP server. This must be performed on the serial interface that will be connecting to the new router. Additionally, we may need to specify the DCE parameters. The DCE cable cannot be used on the new router interface.

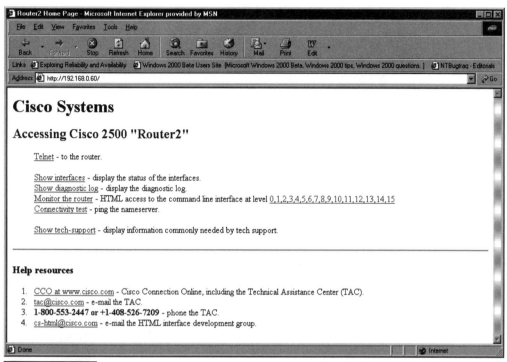

FIGURE 10-3 Using a Web browser to configure a router

```
Router2#conf t
    Router2(config)#int s1
    Router2(config-if)#ip helper-address 172.16.96.101
    Router2(config-if)#clockrate 800000
    Router2(config-if)#bandwidth 768
    Router2(config-if)#dce-terminal-timing-enabled
    Router2(config-if)#^Z
```

3. Create a file on the TFTP server called network-confg. This file will be used to assign the name of the new router to its IP address. The serial interface will either have a host of 1 or 2, depending on the preconfigured router. In our example, Router2 has been configured with 172.16.64.1, so the new router (Router3) will automatically use 172.16.64.2 on its serial interface 1 (S1). This process is called SLARP, or Serial Line Address Resolution Protocol. The file should have the line **ip host Router3 172.16.64.2** placed inside and then saved.

4. Configure a text file with the name used in the network-confg file, and store the configuration information for the new router. As was pointed

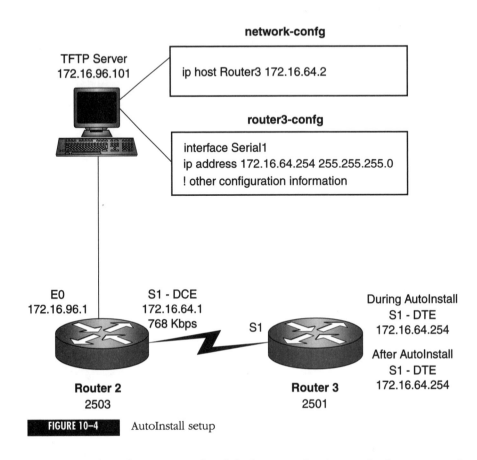

FIGURE 10–4   AutoInstall setup

out earlier, this name is the default name that is saved when we used the command **copy start tftp**. For our example the configuration file is named router3-confg. This file is then placed on the TFTP server. The configuration information can be as much or as little as we wish. The only thing it should have in this configuration file is the IP address for the interface on the serial link, and possibly a password for the Telnet session. This allows us to telnet in and finish the configuration after the router has been installed. Note also, this minimal configuration would only be good for one hop. If more hops were needed to reach the new router, some type of routing would need to be implemented.

After this is finished, we can ship the router to the new location. Once it arrives, someone (with perhaps less technical skill than ourselves) can attach the serial cable and turn on the router. When the router is turned on without a configuration file in NVRAM, it will detect a valid connection on the serial interface. It will then send out the SLARP announcement. The configured router on the other end of the serial link will send back its own IP address and subnet mask. If the received IP address is 1, then the new router will use 2, and vice versa.

After the new router chooses an IP address, it will then send out a request to the TFTP server for the file called network-confg. This file, configured by us, has the name of the router with the given IP address.

Finally, the new router will then ask the TFTP server for *name*-confg or *name.cfg*, where name is the name determined from the network-confg file. This file is then sent to the new router, where it will configure itself with the given parameters. The result looks like this:

```
Notice: NVRAM invalid, possibly due to write erase.

SLARP: interface Serial1 resolved.  This interface has been automatically
resolved thru the SLARP process.  The router will now attempt to retrieve its
name and configuration file.

Loading network-confg from 172.16.96.101 (via Serial1): !
[OK - 29/32723 bytes]
Configuration mapped ip address 172.16.64.2 to Router3
Loading router3-confg from 172.16.96.101 (via Serial1): !
[OK - 471/32723 bytes]

Press RETURN to get started!

%LINK-5-SLARP: Serial1 address 172.16.64.2, resolved by 172.16.64.1
%LINK-3-UPDOWN: Interface Ethernet0, changed state to up
%LINK-3-UPDOWN: Interface Serial0, changed state to down
%LINK-3-UPDOWN: Interface Serial1, changed state to up
%LINEPROTO-5-UPDOWN: Line protocol on Interface Ethernet0, changed state to up
%LINEPROTO-5-UPDOWN: Line protocol on Interface Serial0, changed state to down
%LINEPROTO-5-UPDOWN: Line protocol on Interface Serial1, changed state to up
%PARSER-4-BADCFG: Unexpected end of configuration file.

%SYS-5-CONFIG: Configured from network-confg by console tftp from 172.16.96.101
%SYS-5-CONFIG: Configured from network-confg by console tftp from 172.16.96.101
%SYS-5-RESTART: System restarted --
Cisco Internetwork Operating System Software
IOS (tm) 2500 Software (C2500-I-L), Version 11.2(3)P, SHARED PLATFORM, RELEASE S
OFTWARE (fc1)
Copyright (c) 1986-1996 by cisco Systems, Inc.
Compiled Tue 31-Dec-96 16:18 by tamb
Router3>sho ip route
Codes: C - connected, S - static, I - IGRP, R - RIP, M - mobile, B - BGP
       D - EIGRP, EX - EIGRP external, O - OSPF, IA - OSPF inter area
       N1 - OSPF NSSA external type 1, N2 - OSPF NSSA external type 2
       E1 - OSPF external type 1, E2 - OSPF external type 2, E - EGP
       i - IS-IS, L1 - IS-IS level-1, L2 - IS-IS level-2, * - candidate default
       U - per-user static route, o - ODR
```

```
Gateway of last resort is not set

     172.16.0.0/24 is subnetted, 5 subnets
I       172.16.160.0 [100/17020] via 172.16.64.1, 00:00:35, Serial1
I       172.16.128.0 [100/17120] via 172.16.64.1, 00:00:35, Serial1
C       172.16.32.0 is directly connected, Ethernet0
I       172.16.96.0 [100/15120] via 172.16.64.1, 00:00:35, Serial1
C       172.16.64.0 is directly connected, Serial1

Router3> copy run start
```

Lost Passwords

There are times when passwords to the router may be lost or forgotten. For example, we could be hired to upgrade and maintain a network consisting of Cisco routers. This network may have been set up by a previous employee or contractor, and now there is no one around who knows the password. Some people refer to this as "job security." In any event, it may be necessary to break into the router and restore the passwords.

In order to do this, we need to be running a terminal program connected to the console port. This, of course, means we must have physical access to the router. An example terminal program would be HyperTerminal that comes with Windows products. Note, however, that the HyperTerminal with Windows NT does not work correctly for this procedure. A new private edition version can be downloaded from www.hilgraeve.com, the maker of HyperTerminal.

The first step is to determine the normal configuration register value. We saw this value earlier when we examined the boot methods. Type **show version** at the router prompt and read the last line. Write down the value of the register. In our example previously, the value was 0x2102.

Next, physically power off the router and wait 10 seconds. When we reboot the router, we should see the following:

```
System Bootstrap, Version 5.2(8a), RELEASE SOFTWARE
Copyright (c) 1986-1995 by cisco Systems
2500 processor with 2048 Kbytes of main memory
```

At this point, we need to enter the break character to enter the ROM monitoring mode. To do this with HyperTerminal, press the Ctrl-break keys together. We are now taken to the ROM prompt.

```
Abort at 0x10EA882 (PC)
>
```

At the prompt, enter the command **o/r 0x42**.

```
>o/r 0x42
>i

System Bootstrap, Version 5.2(8a), RELEASE SOFTWARE
Copyright (c) 1986-1995 by cisco Systems
2500 processor with 2048 Kbytes of main memory
```

The **o/r** command replaces the boot register so that we will boot without the contents of NVRAM. The **i** command reloads the router. At this point, we are asked to enter the setup script. We won't enter the script, but instead we will reload the contents of NVRAM into the running configuration.

```
Would you like to enter the initial configuration dialog? [yes]: n

Press RETURN to get started!

<enter>

%LINK-5-CHANGED: Interface Ethernet0, changed state to administratively down
%LINK-5-CHANGED: Interface Serial0, changed state to administratively down
%LINK-5-CHANGED: Interface Serial1, changed state to administratively down

Router>enable
Router#copy star run

Router3#
```

Notice that we were not asked for our password. Now that we are in configuration mode, we can reset our passwords.

```
Router3#conf t
Enter configuration commands, one per line.  End with CNTL/Z.
Router3(config)#enable secret cisco
Router3(config)#config-register 0x2102
Router3(config)#^Z
%SYS-5-CONFIG_I: Configured from console by cons
Router3#copy run star
Building configuration...
```

We used the command **config-register 0x2102** to reset the boot method back to looking for the contents of NVRAM. The value 0x2102 was retrieved from our first step in this process. After a reload, we are back in business.

There is one small problem, though. If you examine the prompts when we restarted the router, when we bypassed the NVRAM configuration mode, all the interfaces were administratively shut down. We would actually need to give the command **no shutdown** for each of the interfaces to get us back into full operation.

```
Router3#conf t
Enter configuration commands, one per line.  End with CNTL/Z.
Router3(config)#int s1
Router3(config-if)#no shut
Router3(config-if)#int e0
%LINK-3-UPDOWN: Interface Serial1, changed state to up shut
Router3(config-if)#no shut
%LINK-3-UPDOWN: Interface Ethernet0, changed state to up
Router3(config-if)#^Z
Router3# copy run star
```

This is a fairly straightforward process, but one with some serious concern. Anyone who has physical access to our routers can break in. For this reason, it is often essential that routers be locked away in a secure room.

Summary

Properly managing a Cisco router involves maintaining backup copies of both the IOS image and the configuration file. Before being able to successfully accomplish this, it is important to understand the architecture of the Cisco router and the differences between FLASH memory, NVRAM, and ROM. Once these are understood and utilized correctly, we can use a TFTP server to save the files using the command **copy** *source* **tftp**, where source is running-config, startup-config, or flash. Configuring the router can be accomplished in many ways, including using the **setup** command, modifying a text file and importing it from a TFTP server, manually using the IOS commands in configuration mode, using a Web browser with the router configured properly, and Auto-Install. Finally, by modifying the contents of the configuration registry in ROM monitor mode, we can bypass the NVRAM contents and restore any lost passwords.

Scenario Lab 10.1

Network Solutions has been growing at a rapid pace. A new remote sales site has been set up in New York (see Figure 10–5). Unfortunately, you do not have the time to fly out there just to set up a single router. Define a method of installing this router remotely. Additionally, concerns of router failure are becoming the focus of many meetings. Devise a method of storing the appropriate files in the event that a router needs to be upgraded or replaced.

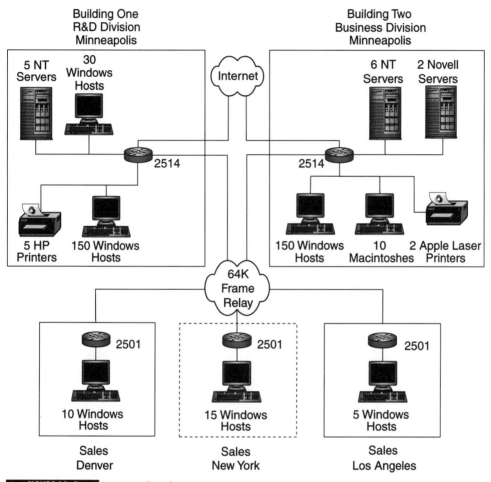

FIGURE 10-5 Network Solutions, Inc.—new remote site

Practice Lab 10.1

In this lab, you will set up a TFTP server and save the current configurations on each of the routers in Figure 10–6. Additionally, you will save one of the IOS images to the FTP server. Finally, you will reload a configuration back to the router.

- Set up the network as shown. Install RIP for the routing protocol. Test connectivity by using **ping**.
- Start the TFTP server and verify connection to Workstation 1.
- Copy the configuration file from Router 1 to the TFTP server. Note the time it took to perform this step. Be sure to name the file something identifying it as coming from Router 1.
- Copy the configuration file from Router 2 to the TFTP server. Again, note the time it took to perform this step. Can you explain the difference?
- Copy the IOS image from Router 1 to the TFTP server.
- Examine the configuration files on the TFTP server. Can you see the passwords in clear text?
- Encrypt the passwords on Router 1 using the service password-encryption command. Save the new configuration to the TFTP and examine it. Can you see the passwords now?
- Restore the configuration from the TFTP server to Router 1.
- Bonus: Try setting up Router 2 to use the AutoInstall method. Refer to the chapter for the exact steps.

Workstation 1 - 192.168.10.1/24
TFTP Server

Workstation 2 - 192.168.30.1/24

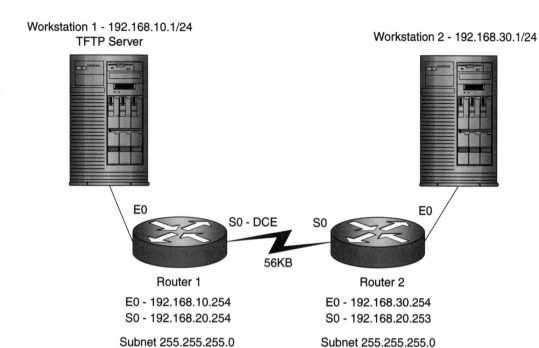

E0   S0 - DCE   S0   E0

56KB

Router 1

E0 - 192.168.10.254
S0 - 192.168.20.254

Subnet 255.255.255.0

Router 2

E0 - 192.168.30.254
S0 - 192.168.20.253

Subnet 255.255.255.0

FIGURE 10–6

Practice Lab 10.2

In this lab, you will practice setting up a router for access using a Web browser. Also, you will recover a lost password.

- Set up the network as shown in Figure 10–7. Install RIP for the routing protocol. Test connectivity by pinging each workstation.
- Enable Router 1 to be accessed via a Web browser. Use a Web browser on one of the workstations to examine the router settings.
- Set the enable password on Router 2 to cisco.
- Conveniently forget the password.
- Use the new version of HyperTerm, or some other terminal software, to recover the password. You must be able to send a break character to Router 2 in order to perform the steps.

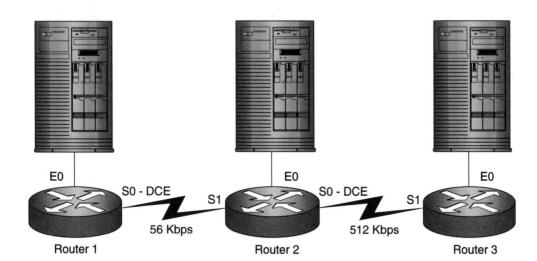

EO | SO - DCE | S1 | EO | SO - DCE | S1 | EO

56 Kbps | 512 Kbps

Router 1 | Router 2 | Router 3

Workstation IP: 172.16.0.1
EO IP: 172.16.255.254
SO IP: 172.17.255.254

Subnet Mask: 255.255.0.0

Workstation IP: 172.18.0.1
EO IP: 172.18.255.254
S1 IP: 172.17.255.253
SO IP: 172.19.255.254

Subnet Mask: 255.255.0.0

Workstation IP: 172.20.0.1
EO IP: 172.20.255.254
S1 IP: 172.19.255.253

Subnet Mask: 255.255.0.0

FIGURE 10-7

Exam Objective Checklist

By working through this chapter, you should have sufficient knowledge to answer these exam objectives:

- Manage configuration files from the privileged exec mode.
- Copy and manipulate configuration files.
- List the commands to load Cisco IOS software from: FLASH memory, a TFTP server, or ROM.
- Prepare to back up, upgrade, and load a backup Cisco IOS software image.

Practice Questions

1. What command will show the configuration register used during boot?

   a. Config-register
   b. Show version
   c. Show config
   d. Config show

2. Name two of the pieces of the router architecture.

   a. CMOS
   b. NVRAM
   c. Flash
   d. OS

3. What is a disadvantage to using a TFTP server?

   a. It can only run on a Unix platform.
   b. It cannot save IOS images.
   c. It is an unsecured application.
   d. It does not work with Cisco routers.

4. Which is the correct command to save the IOS to a TFTP server?

   a. copy tftp flash
   b. copy flash tftp
   c. copy start tftp
   d. copy tftp start

5. Which is the correct command to restore the IOS image from a TFTP server?

    a. copy tftp flash
    b. copy flash tftp
    c. copy start tftp
    d. copy tftp start

6. Which is the correct command to save the configuration file to a TFTP server?

    a. copy tftp flash
    b. copy flash tftp
    c. copy start tftp
    d. copy tftp start

7. What is the correct command to encrypt passwords when stored in a configuration file?

    a. Password encryption
    b. Service encryption
    c. Password service-encryption
    d. Service password-encryption

8. What are three methods of configuring a Cisco router?

    a. AutoInstall
    b. Web browser
    c. Autodiscovery
    d. Setup

9. Which command must be used to setup AutoInstall on a preconfigured router?

    a. Autoinstall address
    b. ip autoinstall address
    c. ip helper-address
    d. tftp helper-address

10. Which statement is true about lost or forgotten passwords?

    a. The password can never be recovered.
    b. The password can be recovered from a remote site.
    c. The password can be recovered with physical access to the router.
    d. Passwords are reset when the router is powered off.

11. Which command can be used to tell the Cisco router to boot from the ROM first?

   a. Boot system rom
   b. System boot rom
   c. Boot system
   d. Boot rom

12. Which command can be used to tell the Cisco router which IOS image to boot from?

   a. Boot system flash
   b. Boot system flash *ios.filename*
   c. Boot flash
   d. Boot flash *ios.filename*

IPX/SPX

In This Chapter

◆ IPX Addressing

◆ Encapsulation Types

◆ IPX Routing

Xerox created a protocol known as XNS (Xerox Network Systems) for internetworking with LANs, and it was widely used by different vendors. Novell, a company that created a Network Operating System (NOS), incorporated XNS into their software. As Novell software began to evolve, Novell made modifications to XNS and changed the name to IPX/SPX (Internet Packet Exchange/Sequenced Packet Exchange). Like TCP/IP, IPX/SPX is a protocol suite that encompasses many protocols all working together. As Novell NetWare became more popular, IPX became a major protocol running on LANs. IPX/SPX is a Client-Server and Server-Server protocol. There is no peer-to-peer capability. This means there must be a server in order to offer any resources. Today there are many installations of IPX running with Novell and Cisco routers. It is important for everyone working with Cisco routers to gain an understanding of IPX.

IPX/SPX Model

IPX/SPX has a model that is not unlike the OSI model, but the functionality of some of the OSI layers are rolled into one or more layers of the IPX/SPX. Figure 11–1 is a rough representation of the IPX/SPX model when compared to the OSI model.

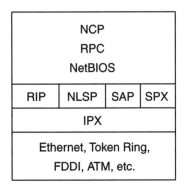

Application	NCP
Presentation	RPC
Session	NetBIOS
Transport	RIP NLSP SAP SPX
Network	IPX
Data Link	Ethernet, Token Ring,
Physical	FDDI, ATM, etc.

FIGURE 11–1   IPX/SPX compared to the OSI

IPX is a connectionless protocol that is similar in function to IP. It is responsible for the underlying structure of the protocol, including network addressing and routing. Whereas IP uses ports to communicate with the correct protocol in the upper layers, IPX uses sockets that perform similar functions.

SPX is the connection-oriented protocol that is used for guaranteeing delivery of packets. Applications can use SPX through one of the upper-layer protocols.

RIP and NLSP are the routing protocols that can be used with IPX/SPX. NLSP is the Link State protocol, while RIP is the Distance Vector protocol.

SAP (Service Advertisement Protocol) is used for servers to advertise the different services, such as file sharing, print sharing, and logon services that are offered by the different servers on the network.

The upper-layer protocols are used by applications to communicate over the network. For the remaining chapter, we will focus only on the middle layers.

Network Addressing

IPX addresses consist of a network portion and a host portion. Unlike TCP/IP, the host portion cannot be further subgrouped for finer network control. However, the network portion is 32 bits long, which allows for many more networks than TCP/IP. The host portion of the address is 48 bits long, and is usually the MAC address of the network interface. The address is usually written in hexadecimal, and the format is *network.host*.

The network portion of the address is similar to the TCP/IP network address. Each segment must be assigned a network address, and it must be unique throughout the network. In addition, all hosts on the same segment must have the same network address in order to communicate. An example of a network address would be 00007F00. To make things even easier for us, we can remove the leading 0s when specifying network addresses. For example, we can simply use the network address of 7F00.

When TCP/IP and IPX/SPX are running together in the same network, it is common practice to take the TCP/IP network address and convert it to hexadecimal, and use that value for the IPX network address. This makes troubleshooting much easier because we can always convert the hex back to decimal and determine where in our network the problem lies.

NetWare servers also have an internal network address that is assigned by the administrator. This address is used to identify the services that the server is offering. The network address must also be unique, not only among all internal networks, but with all network addresses in our physical network.

The host portion of the address uniquely identifies a host on a network. The address is usually the MAC address, but it does not have to be. We should not assume that the Data Link layer MAC address and the IPX host address are the same thing. They perform different functions.

Since the MAC address is used for the host address, it makes life a lot easier for assigning addresses. We do not need to manually configure each host, or set up a DHCP server to dynamically assign addresses to these hosts.

The format of the MAC address is 48 bits long and is written in hexadecimal notation. For example, Workstation 2 has a MAC address of 0050.0470.A2DC. Notice how we represent the address in three equal parts separated by a period. Using the previous example of a network address, the full network address for this node is then 7F00.0050.0470.A2DC.

Serial interfaces on routers do not have MAC addresses. To compensate for this, Cisco uses the first LAN interface's MAC address for all serial addresses. This is usually not a problem, since each interface is on its own network. However, if we do not have any LAN interfaces, we can assign a unique host number to the interfaces.

Encapsulation

While assigning IPX addresses is much easier than using TCP/IP to accomplish the same feat, IPX does have a significant drawback. IPX defines nine different encapsulation types. These encapsulation types are used to format the data into frames for transmitting on the network. Two machines that are configured with different frame types will not talk! If we were asked to consult at a location that had a large installed Novell base, it would require some effort to find out which of the encapsulation types were being used. Many networks, for whatever reasons, have multiple types running. The quickest way is to have physical access to each of the Novell servers, and use the **config** command to display each of the interfaces and encapsulation types.

Table 11.1 shows the different encapsulation types for LANs. Notice that Ethernet itself has four different types from which to choose.

TABLE 11.1	IPX encapsulation types	
Novell IPX Type	**Cisco IOS Equivalent**	**Cisco Default?**
Ethernet_802.3	Novell-ether	Yes
Ethernet_802.2	Sap	No
Ethernet_II	Arpa	No
Ethernet_SNAP	Snap	No
Token Ring	Sap	Yes
Token Ring_SNAP	Snap	No
FDDI_SNAP	Snap	Yes
FDDI_802.2	Sap	No
FDDI_Raw	Novell-fddi	No

While Cisco defaults to all Ethernet interfaces using Novell-ether, NetWare 3.12 and later versions default to Ethernet_802.2, which is Cisco Sap. Keeping this in mind can prevent some annoying hours of troubleshooting while clients can't see servers. Also, when configuring the routers, we have to use the Cisco keywords and not the Novell words for the encapsulation type.

If we examine Figure 11–2, we can see that multiple encapsulation types are being used. Workstation A and Workstation B can communicate (but since Novell does not have peer-peer capabilities, there is no actual communication taking place), but neither can communicate with the server. Only Workstation C can access the server.

To work around this, we can either change all the nodes to the same encapsulation type, or we can have the router route between the two types. In order to route, we need to specify a second encapsulation type on the interface. To do this, we can use a concept called *subinterfaces*. Subinterfaces are virtual connections on a single interface. Using this method, we can have multiple encapsulation types used for routing, but it must have its own unique network address. We will examine how to do this in the next section.

Now that we understand the basics of addressing and encapsulation, it's time to configure our routers.

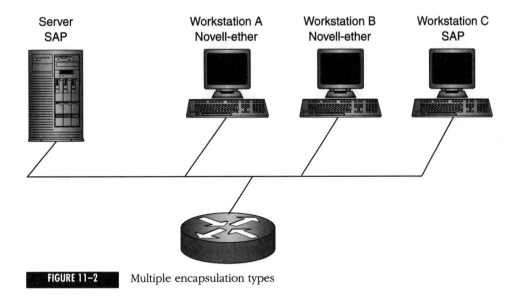

Server	Workstation A	Workstation B	Workstation C
SAP	Novell-ether	Novell-ether	SAP

FIGURE 11–2 Multiple encapsulation types

Configuring Cisco Routers

Before we start configuring our routers, we need a plan. Figure 11–3 represents IC, Inc., with Novell clients and a Novell server. We have identified both the external and the internal network addresses. Using a map in this fashion can definitely make our life easier when installing even a small network. We should also remember to keep thorough documentation. Even though there are 48 bits for the network address, it is quite possible for us to want to reuse the same network number at a later date.

Now that we have our diagram, we can start configuring the routers. We will start with Router 1.

```
Router1(config)#ipx ?
  access-list                       Named access-list
  accounting-list                   Select nets for which IPX accounting
                                    information is kept
  accounting-threshold              Sets the maximum number of accounting
                                    entries
  accounting-transits               Sets the maximum number of transit
                                    entries
  backup-server-query-interval      Set minimum interval between successive
                                    backup server table queries
  broadcast-fastswitching           Fastswitch directed broadcast packets
  default-output-rip-delay          Interpacket delay for RIP updates
  default-output-sap-delay          Interpacket delay for SAP updates
  default-route                     Enable default route recognition
```

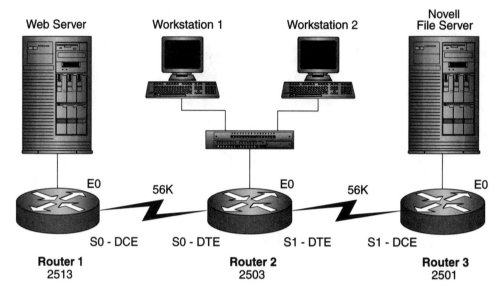

FIGURE 11-3   IC, Inc. using Novell with multiple encapsulations

default-triggered-rip-delay	Interpacket delay for triggered RIP updates
default-triggered-sap-delay	Interpacket delay for triggered SAP updates
eigrp-sap-split-horizon	EIGRP SAP obeys split horizon
flooding-unthrottled	NLSP flooding should be unthrottled
gns-response-delay	Set msec delay in replying to a GNS Request
gns-round-robin	Round-robin responses to get nearest server
internal-network	Specify internal IPX network for router
maximum-hops	Sets the maximum number of hops
maximum-paths	Forward IPX packets over multiple paths
netbios-socket-input-checks	Limit input of non-type 20 netbios bc packets
per-host-load-share	Load share per end host (use one path only)
ping-default	Set default to cisco or Novell Standard Pings
potential-pseudonode	Keep backup route and service data for NLSP potential pseudonode

route	Set an IPX static routing table entry
route-cache	IPX fastswitch cache configuration
router	Control IPX routing
routing	Enable IPX routing
sap	Set an IPX static SAP table entry
sap-queue-maximum	Set maximum SAP processing queue depth
server-split-horizon-on-server-paths	Split horizon SAP on server, not route, paths
spx-spoof	SPX spoof options
type-20-helpered	Forward Type-20 using helper lists, ignore trace
type-20-input-checks	Do additional input checks on type 20 propagation packets
type-20-output-checks	Do additional output checks on type 20 propagation packets

```
Router1(config)#ipx routing
Router1(config)#int e0
Router1(config-if)#ipx network ?
  <1-FFFFFFFD>  IPX network number (default route enabled)
Router1(config-if)#ipx network 100 encapsulation ?
  arpa          IPX Ethernet_II
  hdlc          HDLC on serial links
  novell-ether  IPX Ethernet_802.3
  novell-fddi   IPX FDDI RAW
  sap           IEEE 802.2 on Ethernet, FDDI, Token Ring
  snap          IEEE 802.2 SNAP on Ethernet, Token Ring, and FDDI

Router1(config-if)#ipx network 100 encapsulation sap
Router1(config-if)#int s0
Router1(config-if)#ipx network 150
Router1(config-if)#^Z
Router1#
%SYS-5-CONFIG_I: Configured from console by console
Router1#copy run start
Building configuration...
[OK]
Router1#
```

The first thing to notice is that there are many IPX commands. We will only touch the surface of those, but if we were working with Cisco routers in a large Novell network, many of these commands could aid us in increasing the performance.

When we issued the command **ipx routing**, we turned on IPX, but we also enabled RIP for IPX by default. Now is a good time to mention that RIP for IPX and RIP for TCP/IP are two different protocols. They do not work together, and they each have their own nuances.

Once IPX is enabled, we configure the interfaces with the network and encapsulation types (if different from the defaults). Since Novell-ether is the default for Cisco routers, and we are using SAP on the Ethernet interface, we need to change that. Also notice that we did not specify the type of HDLC on the serial interface. HDLC will be covered in more detail in Chapter 14, "WAN Technologies," but this is the only encapsulation type option allowed on serial interfaces.

Once we have configured our network numbers, we can view the IPX information on each interface.

```
Router1#sho ipx inter e0
Ethernet0 is up, line protocol is up
  IPX address is 100.0000.0c47.b113, SAP [up]
  Delay of this IPX network, in ticks is 1 throughput 0 link delay 0
  IPXWAN processing not enabled on this interface.
  IPX SAP update interval is 60 seconds
  IPX type 20 propagation packet forwarding is disabled
  Incoming access list is not set
  Outgoing access list is not set
  IPX helper access list is not set
  SAP GNS processing enabled, delay 0 ms, output filter list is not set
  SAP Input filter list is not set
  SAP Output filter list is not set
  SAP Router filter list is not set
  Input filter list is not set
  Output filter list is not set
  Router filter list is not set
  Netbios Input host access list is not set
  Netbios Input bytes access list is not set
  Netbios Output host access list is not set
  Netbios Output bytes access list is not set
  Updates each 60 seconds aging multiples RIP: 3 SAP: 3
  SAP interpacket delay is 55 ms, maximum size is 480 bytes
  RIP interpacket delay is 55 ms, maximum size is 432 bytes
  IPX accounting is disabled
  IPX fast switching is configured (enabled)
  RIP packets received 0, RIP packets sent 2
  SAP packets received 0, SAP packets sent 1
Router1#
```

Using this command, we can see that the full network address (listed on line 2 of the output) is 100.0000.0c47.b113. The 100 specifies the network address, which is indeed what we entered. The remaining portion is our MAC address on the Ethernet interface. Also, right after this it tells us that we are using SAP for the encapsulation type.

Examining Serial 0, we receive the following output:

```
Router1#sho ipx int s0
Serial0 is up, line protocol is down
  IPX address is 150.0000.0c47.b113 [up]
  Delay of this IPX network, in ticks is 6 throughput 0 link delay 0
  IPXWAN processing not enabled on this interface.
  IPX SAP update interval is 60 seconds
```

```
IPX type 20 propagation packet forwarding is disabled
Incoming access list is not set
Outgoing access list is not set
IPX helper access list is not set
SAP GNS processing enabled, delay 0 ms, output filter list is not set
SAP Input filter list is not set
SAP Output filter list is not set
SAP Router filter list is not set
Input filter list is not set
Output filter list is not set
Router filter list is not set
Netbios Input host access list is not set
Netbios Input bytes access list is not set
Netbios Output host access list is not set
Netbios Output bytes access list is not set
Updates each 60 seconds aging multiples RIP: 3 SAP: 3
SAP interpacket delay is 55 ms, maximum size is 480 bytes
RIP interpacket delay is 55 ms, maximum size is 432 bytes
Watchdog processing is disabled, SPX spoofing is disabled, idle time 60
IPX accounting is disabled
IPX fast switching is configured (enabled)
RIP packets received 0, RIP packets sent 2
SAP packets received 0, SAP packets sent 1
Router1#
```

Here we can see that our network address is 150.0000.0c47.b113. Again, the first part identifies the network as 150. The second part defines our MAC address. If we compare this MAC address to the Ethernet port's MAC address, we can see they are identical. Remember that serial interfaces do not have MAC addresses, so they use the first LAN's MAC address.

Next, we can configure Router 2. Here we are going to specify a sub-interface so that we can have multiple encapsulation types on the segment.

```
Router2(config)#ipx routing
Router2(config)#int e0
Router2(config-if)#ipx network 200
Router2(config-if)#int e0.1
Router2(config-subif)#ipx network 200 encap sap
%IPX network 200 already exists on interface Ethernet0
Router2(config-subif)#ipx network 201 encap sap
Router2(config-subif)#int s0
Router2(config-if)#ipx network 150
Router2(config-if)#int s1
Router2(config-if)#ipx network 250
Router2(config-if)#^Z
Router2#
%SYS-5-CONFIG_I: Configured from console by console
Router2#copy run start
```

Using the e0.1 format created the subinterface, the e0 specified the
Ethernet interface and then the .1 specified the virtual connection. This number can be from 0 to 4292967295, which allows for quite a few virtual connections! When we tried to specify the same network number as the primary
interface, we received an error message. This is proof that each interface must
have its own unique network number.

We can examine our interfaces again, but this time we will use a summary report.

```
Router2#sho ipx interface brief
Interface           IPX Network Encapsulation Status               IPX State
BRI0                unassigned  not config'd administratively down n/a
BRI0:1              unassigned  not config'd administratively down n/a
BRI0:2              unassigned  not config'd administratively down n/a
Ethernet0           200         NOVELL-ETHER up                    [up]
Ethernet0.1         201         SAP          up                    [up]
Serial0             150         HDLC         up                    [up]
Serial1             250         HDLC         up                    [up]
```

This list is a bit cleaner to read when all we are interested in are the IPX
network numbers and the encapsulation types. Notice that the serial ports are
using HDLC.

We have one last router to configure. The output is listed next.

```
Router3#conf t
Enter configuration commands, one per line.  End with CNTL/Z.
Router3(config)#ipx routing
Router3(config)#int e0
Router3(config-if)#ipx network 300
Router3(config-if)#int s1
Router3(config-if)#ipx network 250
Router3(config-if)#^Z
Router3#copy run start
Building configuration...
[OK]
Router3#sho ipx int brief
Interface           IPX Network Encapsulation Status               IPX State
Ethernet0           300         NOVELL-ETHER up                    [up]
Serial0             unassigned  not config'd administratively down n/a
Serial1             250         HDLC         up                    [up]
Router3#
```

Remember that by enabling IPX, we automatically enabled RIP for IPX.
We can verify this by checking our protocols and our routing table.

```
Router3#sho proto
Global values:
  Internet Protocol routing is enabled
  IPX routing is enabled
```

```
Ethernet0 is up, line protocol is up
  IPX address is 300.0000.0c91.a1ed
Serial0 is administratively down, line protocol is down
Serial1 is up, line protocol is up
  IPX address is 250.0000.0c91.a1ed

Router3#sho ipx route
Codes: C - Connected primary network,    c - Connected secondary network
       S - Static, F - Floating static, L - Local (internal), W - IPXWAN
       R - RIP, E - EIGRP, N - NLSP, X - External, A - Aggregate
       s - seconds, u - uses, U - Per-user static

6 Total IPX routes. Up to 1 parallel paths and 16 hops allowed.

No default route known.

C         250 (HDLC),          Se1
C         300 (NOVELL-ETHER),  Et0
R         100 [13/02] via      250.0000.0c8e.46a0,   57s, Se1
R         150 [07/01] via      250.0000.0c8e.46a0,   58s, Se1
R         200 [07/01] via      250.0000.0c8e.46a0,   58s, Se1
R         201 [07/01] via      250.0000.0c8e.46a0,   58s, Se1
Router3#
```

The routes are being advertised correctly using RIP. IPX RIP is a Distance Vector protocol that uses two measurements for the metric. The first metric is based on a unit called a *tick*, which is equivalent to one-eighteenth of a second, or approximately 55 milliseconds. This is the primary measurement used to decide on a path to a network. If two equal paths exist, the hop count itself is the tie-breaker. In our listing of the networks we can see the two numbers in brackets. The first number is the ticks, and the second is the hop. Router 3 takes two hops to forward packets to the 100 network. This makes sense because the data has to flow through Router 2 and then through Router 1 before reaching the final destination.

If there are two or more equal-cost paths to a network, only the first path learned is kept. Any additional path information to the same network is discarded. However, IPX RIP can be configured to perform load balancing by enabling multiple paths. This is accomplished through the command **ipx maximum-paths**. This command requires a parameter that lists how many paths will be used. For example, **ipx maximum-paths 3** will allow three different paths to be used for load balancing. We have to be careful when implementing this because some IPX software does not work when packets are received out of order, which can happen with the load-balancing algorithm.

IPX RIP broadcasts are sent out at 60-second intervals and include the entire routing table if possible. Actually, up to 50 routes can be advertised in a single broadcast, so larger networks may require more broadcasts each interval. Additionally, IPX RIP does include Split Horizon to help prevent routing loops.

Once convergence is completed, how do we actually test connectivity? The answer lies in ping. While ping itself was created for the use of TCP/IP, the IOS implements an extended ping that can be used to test IPX networks. To run it, simply issue the command **ping** followed by the Enter key.

```
Router3#ping
Protocol [ip]: ipx
Target IPX address: 100.0000.0c47.b113
Repeat count [5]:
Datagram size [100]:
Timeout in seconds [2]:
Verbose [n]:
Novell Standard Echo [n]:
Type escape sequence to abort.
Sending 5, 100-byte IPX cisco Echoes to 100.0000.0c47.b113, timeout is 2 seconds
:
!!!!!
Success rate is 100 percent (5/5), round-trip min/avg/max = 68/68/72 ms
```

We received all five replies, so we know that the connectivity is good. We used the IPX address of the Ethernet address of Router 1. We can get the IPX address from Router 1 using either the **show int e0** or **show ipx int e0** command.

We can debug IPX RIP using the **debug** command. There are two levels of debugging, **events** and **activity**. The events parameter is a brief listing of the RIP updates, while activity is the detailed listing.

```
Router3#debug ipx ?
  all            IPX activity (all)
  compression    IPX compression
  eigrp          IPX EIGRP packets
  ipxwan         Novell IPXWAN events
  nlsp           IPX NLSP activity
  packet         IPX activity
  redistribution IPX route redistribution
  routing        IPX RIP routing information
  sap            IPX Service Advertisement information
  spoof          IPX and SPX Spoofing activity

Router3#debug ipx routing ?
  activity  IPX RIP routing activity
  events    IPX RIP routing events

Router3#debug ipx routing act
IPX routing debugging is on
Router3#
IPXRIP: positing full update to 250.ffff.ffff.ffff via Serial1 (broadcast)
IPXRIP: Update len 40 src=250.0000.0c91.a1ed, dst=250.ffff.ffff.ffff(453)
    network 300, hops 1,  delay 7
```

```
IPXRIP: update from 250.0000.0c8e.46a0
    100 in 2 hops, delay 13
    150 in 1 hops, delay 7
    201 in 1 hops, delay 7
    200 in 1 hops, delay 7
IPXRIP: positing full update to 300.ffff.ffff.ffff via Ethernet0 (broadcast)
IPXRIP: Update len 72 src=300.0000.0c91.a1ed, dst=300.ffff.ffff.ffff(453)
    network 200, hops 2,   delay 8
    network 201, hops 2,   delay 8
    network 150, hops 2,   delay 8
     network 100, hops 3,   delay 14
     network 250, hops 1,   delay 2
```

We can see the tables being sent and received to a network address of 250.ffff.ffff.ffff. This is similar to the TCP/IP broadcast address of 10.255.255.255. The host address is all 1s, which indicates the broadcast. Every 60 seconds, Router 3 posts its routing table out the 300 (Ethernet) and 250 (Serial 1) network. Additionally, information is being received from Router 2.

To turn off debugging (and we should remember to do this!), we use the **no** command. We could also use the **undebug all** command to turn off all debugging.

Service Advertisement Protocol

Novell servers advertise the services they offer through SAP. SAP is a proprietary protocol created by Novell and is broadcast based. The services that a server offers are part of the broadcast and are listed as the SAP type. This number may be specific to a client/sever application, or general in nature such as file sharing and print sharing. In order for clients to locate servers with the service needed, SAPs must be identified throughout the network. All NetWare servers will process SAPs and include their own information into the SAP list. When the update interval arrives (60 seconds by default), the server will broadcast out the new SAP list for all other servers. Using this method, all servers know about all other servers.

The problem lies in the fact that the list is advertised through broadcasts, and since broadcasts are not forwarded across routers, clients will only learn about other servers on their segment. To help solve this problem, Cisco routers are configured to be SAP servers when IPX is enabled. This allows Cisco routers to act as servers by forwarding SAP lists to other segments and to answer queries from clients. Note, however, that Cisco routers do not actually have any services for clients. They simply help pass the SAP list through the network.

Returning to Figure 11–3, we can see there is a Novell server on the 300 IPX network. Without the aid of Cisco routers, only clients on the 300 network would be able to find the server.

When the server is configured correctly and the SAP broadcast occurs, we will see the internal network number for any servers listed, as well as the servers and the services they each offer.

```
Router3#sho ipx route
Codes: C - Connected primary network,    c - Connected secondary network
       S - Static, F - Floating static, L - Local (internal), W - IPXWAN
       R - RIP, E - EIGRP, N - NLSP, X - External, A - Aggregate
       s - seconds, u - uses, U - Per-user static

7 Total IPX routes. Up to 1 parallel paths and 16 hops allowed.

No default route known.


C          250 (HDLC),         Se1
C          300 (NOVELL-ETHER), Et0
R            1 [02/01] via      300.0050.0470.a1cc,   58s, Et0
R          100 [13/02] via      250.0000.0c8e.46a0,   42s, Se1
R          150 [07/01] via      250.0000.0c8e.46a0,   42s, Se1
R          200 [07/01] via      250.0000.0c8e.46a0,   42s, Se1
R          201 [07/01] via      250.0000.0c8e.46a0,   42s, Se1
Router3#
```

Router 3 now sees a new path in the list. The network address of 1 is the internal address of the Novell server. The path was learned from 300.0050.0470.a1cc, which is the Novell server itself.

```
Router3#sho ipx servers
Codes: S - Static, P - Periodic, E - EIGRP, N - NLSP, H - Holddown, + = detail
U - Per-user static
2 Total IPX Servers

Table ordering is based on routing and server info

   Type Name                   Net      Address      Port    Route Hops Itf
P     4 NOVELL                 1.0000.0000.0001:0451         2/01   1  Et0
P   640 FILESERVER             1.0000.0000.0001:E885         2/01   1  Et0
Router3#
```

The next command lists the SAP table that Router 3 is currently maintaining. We can see that the Novell server is offering two services. The first column shows this table as being periodic, which means we are receiving the information every 60 seconds. The first line lists Type as 4, which identifies this server as offering standard file services. Notice the network address. Normally, the Novell server will offer its own MAC address as the host address for the internal network. In this case, the Novell server has been reconfigured. The metric, hops, and interface rounds out the information received from the SAP list.

We can debug SAP just like RIP.

```
Router3#debug ipx sap ?
  activity  IPX Service Advertisement packets
  events    IPX Service Advertisement events

Router3#debug ipx sap activity
IPX service debugging is on
Router3#
```

```
IPXSAP: Response (in) type 0x2 len 96 src:300.0050.0470.a1cc dest:300.ffff.ffff.
ffff(452)
 type 0x4, "NOVELL", 1.0000.0000.0001(451), 1 hops
IPXSAP: positing update to 250.ffff.ffff.ffff via Serial1 (broadcast) (full)
IPXSAP: Update type 0x2 len 160 src:250.0000.0c91.a1ed dest:250.ffff.ffff.ffff(4
52)
 type 0x640, "FILESERVER", 1.0000.0000.0001(E885), 2 hops
 type 0x4, "NOVELL", 1.0000.0000.0001(451), 2 hops
IPXSAP: positing update to 300.ffff.ffff.ffff via Ethernet0 (broadcast) (full)
IPXSAP: suppressing null update to 300.ffff.ffff.ffff
IPXSAP: Response (in) type 0x2 len 96 src:300.0050.0470.a1cc dest:0.ffff.ffff.ff
ff(452)
```

We can see the list of SAPs being received on the interfaces, as well as those that are being broadcast by the router. In this case, the broadcast is being sent from the router to 250.ffff.ffff.ffff. Router 2 will hear the SAP, incorporate it into the table it is maintaining, and send the new table to Router 1. Eventually, all routers will have a complete SAP table to answer client's requests.

Get Nearest Server

Once the routers and servers have a complete list of all services being offered on the network, clients can request a specific service through a broadcast. This broadcast is known as Get Nearest Server (GNS). When the request is made, the nearest Novell server will respond with a server address for the client. This address is located in the SAP table. If there is no server on the local segment, the Cisco router will respond to the GNS query. If the SAP table does not list a service that is being requested by the client, no server or router will return a response. The client will time-out and will not have access to that service.

This method of using SAP tables to advertise services works well in a WAN environment. The SAP broadcasts ensure that unnecessary traffic from the client will not traverse WAN links. Instead, the client will query the router, which has been getting SAP updates from the router on the other side of the WAN link.

If we would like the router to delay before answering any requests, we can use the command **ipx gns-response-delay**. This will allow Novell servers to respond to requests if they can, and leave the router to do its real job, routing.

When a server or router receives a request from a client, it will look in its SAP table for the nearest server. This is important because "nearest" could be on a remote segment or even across a WAN link. If we want to eliminate the possibility of a client talking to remote servers, we can issue the command **ipx gns-reply-disable**.

Finally, the server or router will respond with the address of the nearest server. However, if there are multiple servers with equal costs, the server that was heard from most recently will be the one whose address is returned. This can lead to poor performance if a large number of client requests are all made within the same time period, and all are sent to the same server. We can solve this problem by allowing the Cisco router to use a round-robin approach to returning server addresses. By issuing the command **ipx gns-round-robin**, the Cisco router will alternate when returning the server address to the client. This allows for a load-balancing mechanism to be implemented.

Summary

In this chapter, we learned how to enable IPX/SPX, a Novell proprietary protocol, on Cisco routers. IPX addresses are divided into network and host parts. The format of the address is network.host, where each is displayed in hexadecimal format. Typically, the host address is the MAC address of the LAN interface. Serial interfaces do not have MAC addresses, and therefore will use the MAC address of the first LAN interface. IPX network addresses consist of external and internal addresses, and must be unique throughout the network. Internal addresses are used by Novell servers to advertise the services they offer. These advertisements are provided through SAP, a broadcast protocol that is used to exchange service offering among all servers. Additionally, Cisco routers are configured by default to propagate SAP tables across network segments. IPX includes RIP for IPX for dynamic routing. Once the routing tables have converged and the SAP tables are fully populated, clients can issue GNS queries to find specific services. Novell servers and Cisco routers can respond to the GNS queries by examining the SAP table for the nearest server that offers the requested service. Debugging IPX and SAP consists of using the **debug ipx** command and the parameters associated with it.

Scenario Lab 11.1

Although originally designed to be phased out, the Novell servers have been upgraded and integrated into the existing network (see Figure 11–4). The CIO has stated that each NOS has its strengths, and he would like to utilize Novell's. You have been asked to write a description of work to be performed to allow all clients access to the Novell servers, and to any other servers that may be added. Include a description of what SAP and RIP are, and how to monitor them.

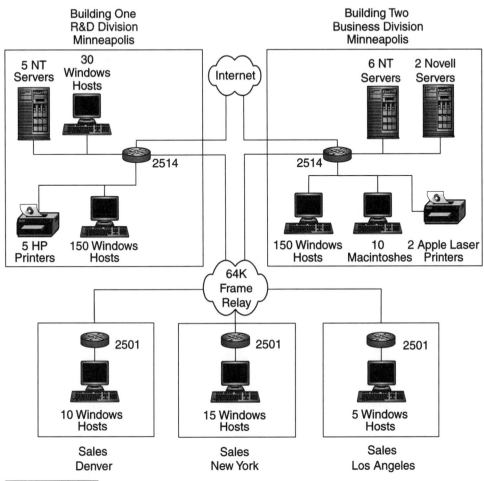

FIGURE 11-4 Network Solutions incorporating Novell IPX/SPX

Practice Lab 11.1

In this lab, you will enable IPX on the routers in Figure 11–5. You will examine the routing table and test connectivity using extended ping. Finally, you will examine the SAP table and identify any Novell servers.

- Set up the Novell server to use the 802.3_Ethernet encapsulation. The Cisco IOS equivalent is Novell-ether. Use the internal address of 100.
- Set up the Novell client to also use 802.3_Ethernet frame type.
- Enable IPX routing on each of the routers.
- Configure the interfaces to use the given IPX network addresses.
- Examine the routing table using the command **sho ipx route**. You should see the networks 1000, 1500, 2000, and 100 listed in the route table. Examine the table on both routers.
- Monitor the RIP events on Router 1. How often are the updates occurring?
- Use the command **sho ipx servers**. Is the Novell server listed with at least one service?
- Monitor the SAP events on Router 2. How often are the updates occurring?

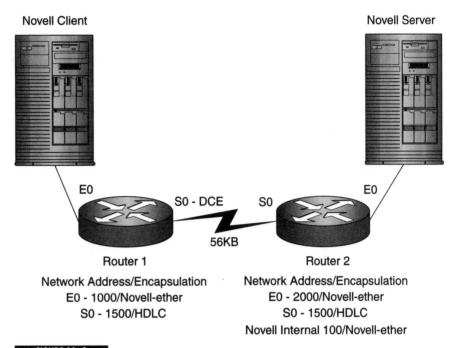

Novell Client

Novell Server

E0

S0 - DCE   S0

E0

56KB

Router 1

Router 2

Network Address/Encapsulation
E0 - 1000/Novell-ether
S0 - 1500/HDLC

Network Address/Encapsulation
E0 - 2000/Novell-ether
S0 - 1500/HDLC
Novell Internal 100/Novell-ether

FIGURE 11–5

Exam Objective Checklist

By working through this chapter, you should have sufficient knowledge to answer these exam objectives:

- Describe the two parts of network addressing, and then identify the parts in specific protocol address examples.
- List the required IPX address and encapsulation type.
- Enable the Novell IPX protocol and configure interfaces.
- Monitor Novell IPX operation on the router.

Practice Questions

1. Which command will show the MAC address of the Ethernet interface?

    a. Show ipx interface ethernet
    b. Show ipx interface ethernet 0
    c. Sho interface ethernet
    d. Show ethernet ipx

2. Which Cisco IOS encapsulation is equivalent to Ethernet_802.3?

    a. Novell-ether
    b. sap
    c. snap
    d. arpa

3. Which Cisco IOS encapsulation is equivalent to Ethernet_802.2?

    a. Novell-ether
    b. sap
    c. snap
    d. arpa

4. Which Cisco IOS encapsulation is equivalent to FDDI_SNAP?

    a. Novell-ether
    b. sap
    c. snap
    d. arpa

5. Which of the following is a valid IPX address?

    a. 7F00.00.50.04.70.a2.dc
    b. 00007F00.0050.0470.a2dc
    c. 7F0000.500470.a2dc
    d. 0000&f0000500470a2dc

6. Which command enables IPX?

    a. enable ipx
    b. enable ipx routing
    c. ipx routing
    d. router ipx

7. Which set of commands assigns the network address of 2FF to Ethernet 0?

    a. int e0
        ipx network 2FF
    b. ipx routing 2FF
        ipx network e0
    c. ipx routing e0
        network ipx 2FF
    d. ipx network e0 2FF

8. Which set of commands assigns the network address of 2FF to Ethernet 0, subinterface 1?

    a. int e0
        subinterface 1
        ipx network 2FF
    b. int e0.1
        ipx network 2FF
    c. ipx routing e0.1
        ipx network 2FF
    d. ipx network e0 2FF

9. Which command will tell you which routing protocols have been enabled?

    a. sho routing protocols
    b. sho route
    c. sho protocols
    d. sho all

10. Which command will enable Cisco routers to perform load balancing?

    a. ipx load balance 3
    b. ipx maximum path 3
    c. ipx load balance
    d. ipx maximum-paths 3

11. Which command will display the detailed information of IPX RIP?

    a. ipx routing activity
    b. debug ipx routing activity
    c. ipx routing events
    d. debug ipx routing events

12. Which command will display the detailed information of SAP?

    a. ipx sap activity
    b. debug ipx sap activity
    c. ipx sap events
    d. debug ipx sap events

AppleTalk

In This Chapter

- ◆ AppleTalk Addressing
- ◆ Configuring AppleTalk

AppleTalk is a proprietary protocol created by Apple Computer to allow Macintosh users the ability to access files and printers in a network. While not as common a protocol as TCP/IP or IPX/SPX, there is still a large install base of AppleTalk. AppleTalk has a lot of similarities to TCP/IP and also to IPX/SPX. Having a working knowledge of the two latter protocols allows quicker understanding of AppleTalk.

AppleTalk Model

As with the other protocols we have examined throughout this book, the AppleTalk protocol is also a suite of protocols that has its own model. Figure 12–1 is a rough comparison of the AppleTalk model with the OSI model.

The hardware protocols include Ethernet, Token Ring, FDDI, and LocalTalk. LocalTalk is an older protocol that runs over telephone wires and is not supported on Cisco equipment. The hardware protocols are referred to as EtherTalk, TokenTalk, and FDDITalk, respectively, by Apple network engineers.

323

Application	Application Protocols	
Presentation		
Session	ZIP	
Transport	RTMP	NBP
Network	DDP	AARP
Data Link	Link Access protocols	
Physical	Hardware protocols	

FIGURE 12–1   AppleTalk model

The Link Access Protocols (LAP) include FDDI (FLAP), Ethernet (ELAP), Token Ring (TLAP), and LocalTalk (LLAP). These protocols are responsible for acting as the middle layer between the hardware and software protocols.

AppleTalk Address Resolution Protocol (AARP) is the equivalent of TCP/IP's ARP. AARP is used to help dynamically assign an address to the node. This process is accomplished through broadcasts sent out onto the local segment. AARP will randomly choose a node address and then ask if any other node on the segment has the same address. If not, that becomes the address of the node. If someone does complain, then AARP will randomly choose a new node address and try the broadcast again. AARP is also responsible for mapping to the MAC address, which can then directly communicate with nodes on the segment.

Datagram Delivery Protocol (DDP) is AppleTalk's main protocol. It is the equivalent to IP and IPX. DDP is a connectionless protocol that is concerned with routing packets to the correct networks.

Routing Table Maintenance Protocol (RTMP) is a Distance Vector protocol similar to RIP. DDP uses Split Horizon for preventing routing loops, and it uses hop counts for the metric. DDP advertises its entire routing table every 10 seconds on the segment, which can lead to poor performance in a large AppleTalk network. A better protocol in this instance is EIGRP.

Name Binding Protocol is the protocol that is used to map node names to node addresses. AppleTalk was designed to be very user friendly. This allowed a user to request information from a server by a name, instead of an address. In fact, most of the networking functions are hidden from the user. When a user wants to connect to a server, the user chooses a name from the Chooser menu. This, in turn, sends a request through NBP to find the node address. Once the node address is found, DDP can get the packets to the correct network.

Zone Information Protocol (ZIP) is a protocol that allows the use of multiple logical networks within the same segment. This concept is similar to VLANs in that it decreases the size of the broadcast domain. ZIP uses NBP

to maintain a complete listing of all the zones that make up the network. ZIP entries are maintained in the Zone Information Table (ZIT).

Network Addressing

AppleTalk addresses are 24 bits in length and compose both a network and a host address. The first 16 bits are for the network address and uniquely identify the LAN or WAN. The last 8 bits are used to uniquely identify a node on the LAN or WAN. Addresses are represented in decimal notation such as 20.10. Like IPX, AppleTalk addresses cannot be further subdivided.

There are two methods, or phases, of configuring network addresses in AppleTalk. The first phase, AppleTalk Phase 1, uses a single network number to identify each segment. This means there is no way to have multiple networks share the same physical segment. Phase 1 also has a limitation of 127 workstations and 127 servers on the network. These limitations were addressed with the next phase.

AppleTalk Phase 2 has two classifications associated with it. The first, called nonextended Phase 2, allows a single network segment to have 253 hosts, but these hosts are not restricted in the numbers of workstations versus servers. This means that we can have a network segment with 253 workstations, or 253 servers, or any combination thereof. We are still limited to one network number per segment, however.

The second classification builds upon the first and is called extended Phase 2. Besides allowing the mix of 253 nodes on a single network, it also increases the usability of the network by allowing multiple network addresses on the same physical segment. Instead of a network address, Phase 2 uses the term *cable range*. Thus, a segment could have the cable range of 1–20, which would mean there are 20 different network (1–20) addresses on the segment. Each of these segments can then have 253 nodes. If we wanted to have no more than 253 nodes possible on a segment, the cable range would be a single network number. For example, to have a maximum of 253 nodes, we can use the cable range of 21–21. This indicates the network address is 21. Using these cable ranges allows a network administrator the flexibility of configuring the network to best suit the needs of the organization. If the network administrator really wanted to, a cable range of 1–65,000 could exist on the same physical segment. This would mean there could be 65,000 × 253 nodes total, or roughly 16.5 million hosts on a segment. That would be a serious broadcast problem!

One additional resource Phase 2 gives us is the use of *multiple zones*. A zone is a logical grouping of nodes that is created by the administrator. We could create zones based on business roles, such as Accounting, Sales, and Marketing. We could also create zones based on geography, such as zones for Minneapolis, Los Angeles, and Washington, D.C.

Putting It All Together

In Figure 12–2, we have a small AppleTalk network that has two zones logically configured based on business cost centers. When Node C comes online, it will grab a temporary network number in the range of 65280–65504. Next, it randomly chooses a node number and then AARPs to see if any other node has that given network and node address. For example, assume that Node C takes the temporary network address of 65280 and randomly chooses the node address of 10. The current address then for the node is 65280.78. Next, AARP is used to determine if anyone else has this node address. Since no one does, the node retains the address. Next, a ZIP request is made to find the cable range on the node's segment. The router responds with 150–152. The node then randomly chooses one of these networks and again AARPs to determine if anyone has the same node address. Suppose that Node C chooses the cable range of 152. The node address is now 152.78. When the

Engineering Zone

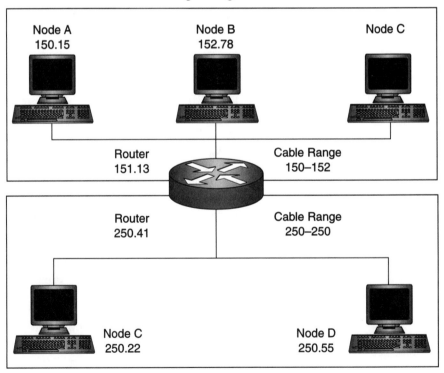

Marketing Zone

FIGURE 12–2   Automatic node assignment with AARP

AARP is sent out, Node B will respond, saying that the node address belongs to it. Node C will then choose a new node address such as 152.87. AARP requests are again sent out, and this time no node has the same address. Node C is now online and ready to communicate. Node C will also store the node address so that the next time Node C boots, it will immediately try to use the same node address.

When a user wants to access a resource such as a file server, the user opens the Chooser menu and chooses the requested service. Meanwhile, the Chooser has sent a request to the router for a list of the zones that make up the network. The router returns the information found in the Zone Information Table (ZIT). The ZIT maintains a complete listing of network addresses to zone names. At this time, the user then chooses the zone where the file server is located. An NBP request is forwarded to the cable range in the selected zone. Each file server hears the request and responds with the name of the file server. This list is returned to the client, and the Chooser menu is populated. The user then selects one of the file servers and a connection is made transparently.

Configuring Cisco Routers

It's time to configure our routers. We are going to take a break from IC, Inc. and look at a specialized network of Apple computers. Figure 12–3 is a diagram of the test network.

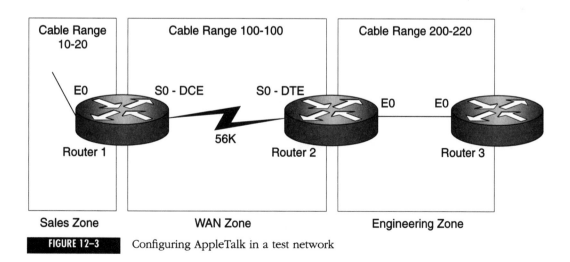

FIGURE 12-3 Configuring AppleTalk in a test network

We can now start configuring our routers. Let's start with Router 1. First, we need to enable AppleTalk. Remember that we need to have the correct

IOS in order to have the protocol available to us. To turn on AppleTalk, we issue the command **appletalk routing**. This is similar to enabling IPX. Also, like IPX, routing is automatically started. In this case, RTMP is enabled.

```
Router1(config)#appletalk routing ?
  eigrp  Enable AT/EIGRP routing
  <cr> Router1(config)#appletalk routing
```

Next, we configure the cable ranges and the Zone names for each of the interfaces.

```
Router1(config)#int e0
Router1(config-if)#appletalk ?
  access-group          Apply an access list to inbound or outbound packets
  address               Set appletalk Phase 1 address
  arp-timeout           arp-timeout
  cable-range           Set appletalk Phase 2 address
  discovery             Reset discovery mode for new cable range discovery
  distribute-list       Filter networks from routing updates
  domain-group          Specify appletalk domain
  eigrp-bandwidth-percent  Set EIGRP bandwidth limit
  eigrp-splithorizon    Enable Split Horizon processing generating AT/EIGRP
                        updates
  eigrp-timers          AT/EIGRP hello and holdtime timers
  free-trade-zone       Enhanced security for one-way shared networks
  getzonelist-filter    Filter zone-list replies
  glean-packets         Glean AARP information from packets
  protocol              Select AppleTalk routing protocol
  route-cache           Enable appletalk route cache
  rtmp-splithorizon     Enable Split Horizon processing generating AT/RTMP
                        updates
  rtmp-stub             Send only RTMP stubs, no routes in updates
  send-rtmps            Send Appletalk routing updates
  zip-reply-filter      Filter ZIP replies
  zone                  Assign an appletalk zone name
Router1(config-if)#appletalk cable-range 10-20
Router1(config-if)#appletalk zone Sales
Router1(config-if)#int s0
Router1(config-if)#clockrate 56000
Router1(config-if)#band 56
Router1(config-if)#dce
Router1(config-if)#dce-terminal-timing-enable
Router1(config-if)#appletalk cable 100-100
Router1(config-if)#appletalk zone WAN
Router1(config-if)#^Z
%SYS-5-CONFIG_I: Configured from console by cons
Router1#copy run start
Building configuration...
[OK]
Router1#
```

At this point, we can start doing some monitoring to determine if everything is configured correctly. We can examine the interfaces themselves as shown next.

```
Router1#sho appletalk int
Ethernet0 is up, line protocol is up
  AppleTalk cable range is 10-20
  AppleTalk address is 19.60, Valid
  AppleTalk zone is "Sales"
  AppleTalk address gleaning is disabled
  AppleTalk route cache is enabled
Serial0 is up, line protocol is up
  AppleTalk port disabled, Acquiring port net information
  AppleTalk cable range is 100-100
  AppleTalk address is 100.129, Valid
  AppleTalk zone is "WAN"
  AppleTalk address gleaning is not supported by hardware
  AppleTalk route cache is disabled, port down
Router1#
```

We can see that the address for Ethernet 0 is 19.60, and Serial 0 is 100.129, and both addresses are listed as valid. If the interfaces were in the process of finding a valid address, the status would indicate "Not Valid." Notice also that we can see the zones that are addressed for each interface.

At this point, we can configure Router 2 using the same commands.

```
Router2(config)#apple routing
Router2(config)#int e0
Router2(config-if)#apple cable 200-220
Router2(config-if)#apple zone Engineering
Router2(config-if)#int s0
Router2(config-if)#apple cable 100-100
Router2(config-if)#apple zone WAN
Router2(config-if)#^Z
Router2#copy run start
Building configuration...
[OK]
Router2#
```

Now that the second router is configured, let's check the interface addresses and status.

```
Router2#sho apple int
BRI0 is administratively down, line protocol is down
  AppleTalk protocol processing disabled
BRI0:1 is administratively down, line protocol is down
  AppleTalk protocol processing disabled
BRI0:2 is administratively down, line protocol is down
  AppleTalk protocol processing disabled
Ethernet0 is up, line protocol is up
```

```
     AppleTalk cable range is 200-220
     AppleTalk address is 215.210, Valid
     AppleTalk zone is "Engineering"
     AppleTalk address gleaning is disabled
     AppleTalk route cache is enabled
  Serial0 is up, line protocol is up
     AppleTalk cable range is 100-100
     AppleTalk address is 100.213, Valid
     AppleTalk zone is "WAN"
     AppleTalk port configuration verified by 100.129
     AppleTalk address gleaning is not supported by hardware
     AppleTalk route cache is enabled
  Serial1 is administratively down, line protocol is down
     AppleTalk protocol processing disabled
  Router2#
```

Here we can see that the ISDN interface has not been configured, but that Ethernet 0 has an address of 215.210, and Serial 0 has an address of 100.213.

At this point, we should have some routing information set up. Remember that just by enabling the AppleTalk protocol, RTMP is also enabled.

```
Router2#sho apple route
Codes: R - RTMP derived, E - EIGRP derived, C - connected, A - AURP
       S - static  P - proxy
3 routes in internet

The first zone listed for each entry is its default (primary) zone.

R Net 10-20 [1/G] via 100.129, 8 sec, Serial0, zone Sales
C Net 100-100 directly connected, Serial0, zone WAN
C Net 200-220 directly connected, Ethernet0, zone Engineering
Router2#
```

Router 2 has two directly connected interfaces, and the cable range of 10–20 has been dynamically learned through Serial 0. The metric includes the hop count and a letter. The letter "G" stands for "Good," and tells us the route has been verified within the last 20 seconds. Other indicators are "S" and "B," which stand for "Suspect" and "Bad," respectively. Note that each route also shows the zone associated with it.

We can examine the zones that are known to a router through the **show appletalk zone** command. This is the Zone Information Table (ZIT).

```
Router2#sho app zone
Name                            Network(s)
Engineering                     200-220
WAN                             100-100
Sales                           10-20
Total of 3 zones
Router2#
```

So far, everything looks good. We are going to configure Router 3 slightly different, however. When two or more routers are directly connected through a LAN link, the router can be configured to do an Auto Discovery to get the cable range and dynamically choose a network address. To do this, we can either specify a cable range of 0–0, or give a temporary cable range and then use the command **appletalk discovery**. We will do the latter.

```
Router3(config)#apple routing
Router3(config)#int e0
Router3(config-if)#apple cable 1-1
Router3(config-if)#apple discovery
Router3(config-if)#^Z
Router3#
%SYS-5-CONFIG_I: Configured from console by console
Router3#copy run start
Router3#sho apple int
Ethernet0 is up, line protocol is up
  AppleTalk cable range is 200-220
  AppleTalk address is 200.8, Valid
  AppleTalk zone is "Engineering"
  AppleTalk port configuration provided by 215.210
  AppleTalk discovery mode is enabled
  AppleTalk address gleaning is disabled
  AppleTalk route cache is enabled
Serial0 is administratively down, line protocol is down
  AppleTalk protocol processing disabled
Serial1 is administratively down, line protocol is down
  AppleTalk protocol processing disabled
Router3#
```

Here we can see that Router 3 did indeed get dynamically assigned the zone and the proper cable range and node address. This allows us to create a "seed" router that we manually configure. After that, any routers with an interface on the same segment will automatically be configured. We still need to manually set the other interfaces on WAN segments, however.

Let's check our routing table to be sure everything has updated correctly.

```
Router3#sho apple route
Codes: R - RTMP derived, E - EIGRP derived, C - connected, A - AURP
       S - static  P - proxy
3 routes in internet

The first zone listed for each entry is its default (primary) zone.

R Net 10-20 [2/G] via 215.210, 9 sec, Ethernet0, zone Sales
R Net 100-100 [1/G] via 215.210, 9 sec, Ethernet0, zone WAN
C Net 200-220 directly connected, Ethernet0, zone Engineering
Router3#
```

We can see each of the routes in our routing table. We used **ping** to test connectivity with IPX and IP, and we can do the same with AppleTalk. First, let's update our diagram see Figure 12–4. We can see each of the AppleTalk addresses assigned to the nodes. Now, we can use **ping** to verify that data does indeed flow from Router 1 to Router 3.

```
Router1#ping apple 200.8

Type escape sequence to abort.
Sending 5, 100-byte AppleTalk Echos to 200.8, timeout is 2 seconds:
!!!!!
Success rate is 100 percent (5/5), round-trip min/avg/max = 40/42/44 ms
```

Here we used a quicker version of the extended ping. Instead of answering all the questions, we can just specify the protocol and the node address. In this case, we receive 100-percent response, so our network is up and running.

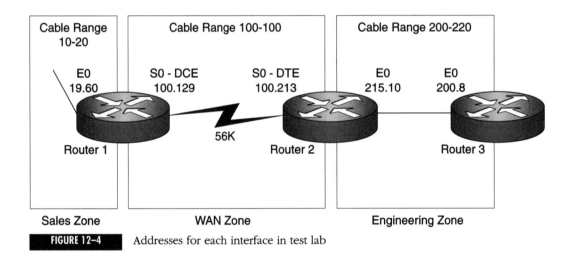

FIGURE 12–4   Addresses for each interface in test lab

As with the other protocols, we can debug the AppleTalk protocol through various commands. For instance, we can view the settings of the AppleTalk protocol through the command **show appletalk globals**.

```
Router3#sho apple globals
AppleTalk global information:
  Internet is incompatible with older, AT Phase1, routers.
  There are 3 routes in the internet.
  There are 3 zones defined.
  Logging of significant AppleTalk events is disabled.
  ZIP resends queries every 10 seconds.
```

```
RTMP updates are sent every 10 seconds.
RTMP entries are considered BAD after 20 seconds.
RTMP entries are discarded after 60 seconds.
AARP probe retransmit count: 10, interval: 200 msec.
AARP request retransmit count: 5, interval: 1000 msec.
DDP datagrams will be checksummed.
RTMP datagrams will be strictly checked.
RTMP routes may not be propagated without zones.
Routes will not be distributed between routing protocols.
Routing between local devices on an interface will not be performed.
IPTalk uses the udp base port of 768 (Default).
AppleTalk EIGRP is not enabled.
Alternate node address format will not be displayed.
Access control of any networks of a zone hides the zone.
Router3#
```

This information tells us how often RTMP updates, when an entry is considered bad, and other information relevant to the protocol.

We can also use the **debug** command itself to debug AppleTalk. However, as we can see in the following list, there is a large selection of items we can debug.

```
Router1#debug apple ?
    arp                   Appletalk address resolution protocol
    aurp-connection       AURP connection
    aurp-packet           AURP packets
    aurp-update           AURP routing updates
    domain                AppleTalk Domain function
    eigrp-all             All AT/EIGRP functions
    eigrp-external        AT/EIGRP external functions
    eigrp-hello           AT/EIGRP hello functions
    eigrp-packet          AT/EIGRP packet debugging
    eigrp-query           AT/EIGRP query functions
    eigrp-redistribution  AT/EIGRP route redistribution
    eigrp-request         AT/EIGRP external functions
    eigrp-target          Appletalk/EIGRP for targeting address
    eigrp-update          AT/EIGRP update functions
    errors                Information about errors
    events                Appletalk special events
    fs                    Appletalk fast-switching
    iptalk                IPTalk encapsulation and functionality
    load-balancing        AppleTalk load-balancing
    macip                 MacIP functions
    nbp                   Name Binding Protocol (NBP) functions
    packet                Per-packet debugging
    redistribution        Route Redistribution
    remap                 AppleTalk Remap function
    responder             AppleTalk responder debugging
    routing               (RTMP&EIGRP) functions
    rtmp                  (RTMP) functions
    zip                   Zone Information Protocol functions
```

We will examine the output from the routing protocol itself. To do this, we need the parameter **rtmp**.

```
Router1#debug apple rtmp
AT: src=Ethernet0:19.60, dst=10-20, size=22, 2 rtes, RTMP pkt sent
AT: src=Serial0:100.129, dst=100-100, size=16, 1 rte, RTMP pkt sent
AT: Route ager starting on Main AT RoutingTable (3 active nodes)
AT: Route ager finished on Main AT RoutingTable (3 active nodes)
AT: RTMP from 100.213 (new 0,old 1,bad 0,ign 0, dwn 0)
```

As we are debugging RTMP, we should see updates occur every 10 seconds. We can view the ports that the update is being sent out on, as well as the incoming port, and which router sent the packet. Notice the difference between the packets going out Ethernet 0 versus the packets going out Serial 0. Here is another example of Split Horizon in effect. We do not send the route learned from 100.213 back to it.

One last monitoring tool allows us to see the neighbor routers that will be sending updates.

```
Router2#sho apple neighbors
AppleTalk neighbors:
  200.8          Ethernet0, uptime 00:01:17, 7 secs
       Neighbor is reachable as a RTMP peer
  100.129        Serial0, uptime 00:00:30, 0 secs
       Neighbor is reachable as a RTMP peer
Router2#
```

Summary

AppleTalk is a proprietary protocol created by Apple Computer for allowing Macintosh users access to network file shares and network printers. AppleTalk runs on any of the standard LAN architectures and is a routable protocol. The full node address is composed of a 16-bit network address with an 8-bit node address. There are two phases of network addressing that can be used. The first has a maximum of 127 workstations and 127 servers on a single segment. Further, there is only one zone for the entire network. Phase 2 comes in two versions, nonextended and extended. Nonextended is similar to Phase 1, but allows 253 nodes of varying workstations and servers. Extended mode allows for multiple network addresses on a single physical segment, and also allows for the creation of zones for logical separation. Configuring Cisco routers includes enabling the protocol, which also enables RTMP, configuring the cable range and zones.

Scenario Lab 12.1

The marketing department was the only department to use Macintoshes for the graphics capabilities. Now, there will be additional Macintosh computers installed in a couple of the remote sites (see Figure 12–5). The CIO has asked you to create a report on the steps necessary to implement these additional computers. The AppleTalk protocol will continue to be used in the internetwork. What recommendations do you have for establishing routing, addressing, and logical network division?

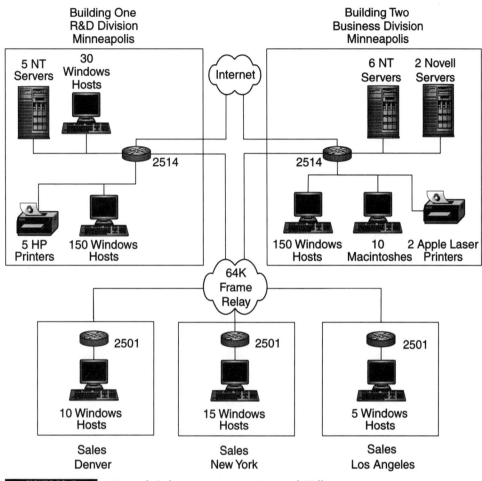

FIGURE 12-5   Network Solutions incorporating AppleTalk

Practice Lab 12.1

In this lab, you will set up AppleTalk routing and specify the cable ranges in Figure 12–6. Next, you will examine the routing table to verify that routing is taking place. Finally, you will use extended ping to verify connectivity to the different nodes.

- Enable AppleTalk routing on Router 1.
- Configure the E0 interface to use the cable range of 100–199. Configure the S0 interface to use the cable range 1–1. Don't forget to set up the clock rate on S0.
- Configure E0 to be a part of the Sales Zone. Add the WAN zone to the S0 interface.
- What is the address of each of the interfaces on Router 1? (Hint: Use **show appletalk interface**.)
- Configure Router 2 using the information in the diagram.
- View the routing table on each of the routers. You should see a dynamic entry for the remote Ethernet segment.
- View the ZIT by using the command **show appletalk zone**.
- Use extended ping to verify connectivity to each of the router interfaces.
- Turn on debugging and view the RTMP updates. How often do the updates occur?

Bonus: Install a third router onto the Ethernet segment of Router 2 and enable Auto Discovery. Test by viewing the route table, ZIT, and by pinging all router interfaces.

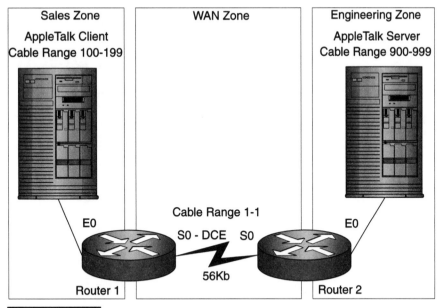

FIGURE 12–6

Exam Objective Checklist

By working through this chapter, you should have sufficient knowledge to answer this exam objective:

- Describe the two parts of network addressing, then identify the parts in specific protocol address examples.

Practice Questions

1. What is the correct format for an AppleTalk address?

   a. 200.200.145.31
   b. 45.34.24.23.23
   c. 101.56
   d. 12.3.44.3.3

2. Which phase of AppleTalk has a limitation of 127 workstations per node?

   a. Phase 1
   b. Phase 2
   c. Phase 3
   d. Phase 127

3. Which phase of AppleTalk has a limitation of 253 workstations per node?

   a. Phase 1
   b. Phase 2
   c. Phase 3
   d. Phase 127

4. Which phase of AppleTalk allows one zone for the network?

    a. Phase 1
    b. Phase 2
    c. Phase 3
    d. Phase 127

5. Which phase of AppleTalk allows up to 255 zones in a segment?

    a. Phase 1
    b. Phase 2
    c. Phase 3
    d. Phase 127

6. Which protocol is used to dynamically assign an address to a node?

    a. ARP
    b. NBP
    c. AARP
    d. ZIP

7. What command enables AppleTalk routing?

    a. route appletalk
    b. routing appletalk
    c. appletalk
    d. appletalk routing

8. What command assigns the network address range of 100-110 to an interface?

    a. network 100-110
    b. appletalk network 100-110
    c. appletalk cable-range 100-110
    d. cable-range 100-110

9. Which command will show the AppleTalk addresses?

    a. show appletalk addresses
    b. show appletalk interface
    c. show interface appletalk
    d. show interface

10. Which command will show the ZIT?

    a. show zone-information-table
    b. show ZIT
    c. show appletalk zone
    d. show route zone

Security with Access Lists

In This Chapter

- AppleTalk Access Lists
- Standard IPX Access Lists
- Standard IP Access Lists
- Extended IP Access Lists

Access lists allow us to restrict or quiet our network by filtering unwanted traffic to or from a network. Cisco routers have the ability to perform filtering at the Data Link layer and higher. By restricting access, the network engineer can be sure that unwanted network traffic is limited, which leaves more bandwidth for the critical business applications. Further, a common problem with network security is user accident, and by preventing access to critical servers, those accidents can be reduced or eliminated.

Basics of Access Lists

In order to perform filtering, two steps must be accomplished. The first step involves creating an access list of one or more entries. The second step is then performed to apply the access list to a group for each interface.

The access list looks similar to a spreadsheet. The columns indicate the number of the access list. Groups of access lists within a range represent different protocols. For instance, the first 99 columns (1–99) are used for standard access lists for TCP/IP. The rows in each column indicate an entry into that list for that protocol. The following chart is a rough example.

98 (TCP/IP)	99 (TCP/IP)	800 (IPX)	801 (IPX)
Deny Host A	Deny Host B	Permit A	Deny B
	Permit Host A	Permit B	Permit All Hosts
		Deny All Hosts	

Using the "chart," Cisco routers will examine each row until a match is found. When a match is found, no further entries will be checked. For instance, if the packet being filtered is TCP/IP on an interface that is using access list 99, then the router will determine if the source is Host B. If it is, the packet will be dropped. If it is not B, then the next line will be examined.

There is a caveat to using access lists. The IOS places, at the end of every access list, an implicit deny all. In the case of access list 98, it is denying everyone! Forgetting about this implicit deny can cause us hours of frustration on troubleshooting an access list.

After the access list is created, it has to be implemented on one or more interfaces. Each interface has a group associated with it. The group is a group of protocols, and each protocol can have one, and only one, access list applied to it. Using the same example of a spreadsheet, the group looks something like the following.

Protocol	Serial 0 Group	Serial 1 Group	Ethernet 0 Group
TCP/IP	99	98	
IPX/SPX	800		801
AppleTalk			650

After this step has been performed, Serial 0 will filter traffic against TCP/IP and IPX/SPX protocols. If any other protocol is received, it is handled normally. The protocol (TCP/IP or IPX/SPX) will then be checked against the access list and dealt with appropriately.

We will be examining access lists as they pertain to AppleTalk, IPX/SPX, and TCP/IP. All of them work in a similar fashion, and learning how to use one will help us learn the other protocol access lists.

AppleTalk Access Lists

Basic access control with AppleTalk consists of denying network numbers or zones from entering or exiting an interface. The network numbers can consist of either a Phase 1 network number or a Phase 2 cable range.

AppleTalk access lists range from 600–699. To start creating access lists, we will refer to our diagram in Figure 13–1. This is our test network using AppleTalk that we used in Chapter 12, "AppleTalk."

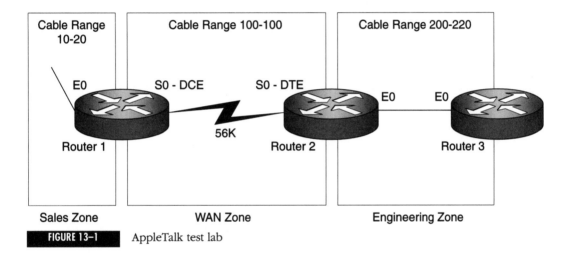

Cable Range 10-20	Cable Range 100-100	Cable Range 200-220
E0	S0 - DCE S0 - DTE E0 E0	
	56K	
Router 1	Router 2	Router 3
Sales Zone	WAN Zone	Engineering Zone

FIGURE 13–1   AppleTalk test lab

Suppose that we wanted to set up a limitation on the number of users accessing the WAN link. We could create an access list that would deny half of the cable range 10–20 from actually using the WAN link. Let's deny 14 and 15.

```
Router1(config)#access-list ?
  <1-99>       IP standard access list
  <100-199>    IP extended access list
  <1000-1099>  IPX SAP access list
  <1100-1199>  Extended 48-bit MAC address access list
  <1200-1299>  IPX summary address access list
  <200-299>    Protocol type-code access list
  <300-399>    DECnet access list
  <600-699>    Appletalk access list
  <700-799>    48-bit MAC address access list
  <800-899>    IPX standard access list
  <900-999>    IPX extended access list
```

We can see that the **access-list** command takes as the first argument a number that defines the protocol, including standard and extended, that will be used to filter the interface(s). Since we are working with AppleTalk, we will choose a number between 600–699.

```
Router1(config)#access-list 600 ?
  deny    Specify packets to reject
  permit  Specify packets to forward
```

Next, we need to decide if this is going to be a permit or deny line. We can have multiple permit and deny entries, but the access list is searched through sequentially. We have to be careful we don't exclude something early in the list that later we want to include. This can be tricky to do!

```
Router1(config)#access-list 600 deny ?
  <1-65279>         Appletalk network number
  additional-zones  Default filter action for unspecified zones
  cable-range       Filter on cable range
  includes          Filter on cable range inclusively
  nbp               Specify nbp filter
  network           Filter an appletalk network
  other-access      Default filter action
  other-nbps        Default filter action for nbp
  within            Filter on cable range exclusively
  zone              Filter on appletalk zone

Router1(config)#access-list 600 deny includes ?
  Start-End  Apple cable range

Router1(config)#access-list 600 deny includes 14-15 ?
  broadcast-deny    Specify denial of broadcasts
  broadcast-permit  Specify permission of broadcasts
  <cr>

Router1(config)#access-list 600 deny includes 14-15
Router1(config)#access-list 600 permit other-access
Router1(config)#
```

After we have chosen to apply a deny filter, we need to define what we are trying to filter. We chose the **includes** parameter for inclusively denying ports 14 and 15. We could also have written the same filter to read **access list 600 deny within 13-16**. The **within** statement is used for filtering cable ranges exclusively, or not including the endpoints.

When an access list is created, it automatically has an implicit *deny everything* at the end of the list. This is important to remember because if we were trying to deny just 14 and 15 networks, and we didn't include the **access-list 600 permit other-access**, the implicit deny would have filtered the entire cable range. Using the parameter of **other-access** defines the default filter for all other networks.

Once the filter is created, we can apply it to an interface. But which interface do we want to use? To answer that question, we have to decide what we are really trying to accomplish. If this router has other LAN connections that we want to allow the cable range full access 10–20, then we need to put it on the serial interface. The next question is, "Do we want to put it on Serial 0 of Router 1 or Router 2?" Remember that we are trying to limit the traffic across the WAN link. If the data has to flow across the link before being filtered, it would defeat the purpose. Therefore, the best place to put the access list is on Serial 0 of Router 1.

```
Router1(config)#int s0
Router1(config-if)#appletalk ?
  access-group              Apply an access list to inbound or outbound packets
  address                   Set appletalk Phase 1 address
  arp-timeout               arp-timeout
  cable-range               Set appletalk Phase 2 address
  client-mode               Allow PPP client connections.
  discovery                 Reset discovery mode for new cable range discovery
  distribute-list           Filter networks from routing updates
  domain-group              Specify appletalk domain
  eigrp-bandwidth-percent   Set EIGRP bandwidth limit
  eigrp-splithorizon        Enable Split Horizon processing generating AT/EIGRP
                            updates
  eigrp-timers              AT/EIGRP hello and holdtime timers
  free-trade-zone           Enhanced security for one-way shared networks
  getzonelist-filter        Filter zone-list replies
  glean-packets             Glean AARP information from packets
  protocol                  Select AppleTalk routing protocol
  route-cache               Enable appletalk route cache
  rtmp-splithorizon         Enable Split Horizon processing generating AT/RTMP
                            updates
  rtmp-stub                 Send only RTMP stubs, no routes in updates
  send-rtmps                Send Appletalk routing updates
  zip-reply-filter          Filter ZIP replies
  zone                      Assign an appletalk zone name

Router1(config-if)#appletalk access-group ?
  <600-699>  A valid AppleTalk access list number

Router1(config-if)#appletalk access-group 600 ?
  in   inbound packets
  out  outbound packets
  <cr>

Router1(config-if)#apple access 600 out
Router1(config-if)#^Z
Router1#copy run start
```

We use the command **appletalk access-group** to specify which filter we would like on this interface. Notice that we can choose the direction we want to filter. In this case, we want to filter any packets that are trying to leave the serial 0 interface, so we specify the **out** parameter.

To view the access lists, we can use the **show** command.

```
Router1#show apple access-lists
AppleTalk access list 600:
  deny includes 14-15
  permit other-access
Router1#
```

We can see that our access list has been created and is stored in the configuration file. We have to remember to save our changes to the running configuration, or this access list will be lost on a power cycle.

To verify the list is actually running on interface Serial 0, we can look at the interface information.

```
Router1#sho apple int s0
Serial0 is up, line protocol is up
  AppleTalk cable range is 100-100
  AppleTalk address is 100.129, Valid
  AppleTalk zone is "WAN"
  AppleTalk port configuration verified by 100.213
  AppleTalk address gleaning is not supported by hardware
  AppleTalk route cache is enabled
  AppleTalk outgoing access list is 600
Router1#
```

The last line tells us that the AppleTalk access list 600 is being filtered on outgoing data through Serial 0. We are now filtering out half the cable range from accessing the WAN site. The problem with using network numbers is that we do not have any control over which node gets which address. We are restricting half our cable range, but we cannot guarantee who is in that range.

A better method is to restrict access by zones. For example, suppose we did not want to allow the Engineering zone access to the Sales zone. First, let's verify connectivity by using the extended ping command.

```
Router3#ping appletalk 19.60

Type escape sequence to abort.
Sending 5, 100-byte AppleTalk Echos to 19.60, timeout is 2 seconds:
!!!!!
Success rate is 100 percent (5/5), round-trip min/avg/max = 36/40/44 ms
Router3#
```

We have verified connectivity between the Engineering and the Sales zone. Next we can set up the access list as shown here:

```
Router1#conf t
Enter configuration commands, one per line.  End with CNTL/Z.
Router1(config)#access-list 625 deny zone Engineering
```

```
Router1(config)#access-list 625 permit additional-zones
Router1(config)#access-list 625 permit other-access
Router1(config)#int e0
Router1(config-if)#appletalk access-group 625 out
Router1(config-if)#^Z
%SYS-5-CONFIG_I: Configured from console by console
Router1#copy run start
```

Notice that after explicitly denying access to Engineering, we permit all other zones. Remember that the IOS places an implicit deny all zones at the end of the access list.

We can test the filter using extended ping again.

```
Router2#ping 19.60

Type escape sequence to abort.
Sending 5, 100-byte AppleTalk Echos to 19.60, timeout is 2 seconds:
!!!!!
Success rate is 100 percent (5/5), round-trip min/avg/max = 40/42/44 ms
Router2#
```

We have connectivity between the WAN zone (Router 2) and the Sales zone. Note the originating zone is the zone of the interface that the router uses to initiate the ping. In this case, Serial 0 is the originating ping source and the zone is WAN. Next, let's try pinging from Router 3.

```
Router3#ping 19.60

Type escape sequence to abort.
Sending 5, 100-byte AppleTalk Echos to 19.60, timeout is 2 seconds:
.....
Success rate is 0 percent (0/5)
Router3#
```

It's just as we expected. Router 3, or more appropriately, the Engineering zone, cannot communicate with the Sales zone. The packets are arriving at Router 1, but the filter is being applied and the packets are dropped.

AppleTalk includes additional features for filtering, including filtering the Zone Information Table on each router and filtering the GETZONELIST request from users that open the Chooser. These options can be further used to manage the security of an AppleTalk network.

IPX Access Lists

Configuring IPX access lists is slightly more detailed than AppleTalk. With IPX access lists, we can configure filters based on both the source and the destination networks. Additionally, we can single out a single host in either the source or destination.

Standard IPX access lists are defined using the access numbers from 800 to 899. We can use any or all of these numbers to create our lists. As with AppleTalk, when we create an access list, the Cisco IOS places an implicit "deny all" at the end of the list. Again, we have to be very careful when creating access lists so that we don't inadvertently filter out all traffic when our intention was to filter out a single type of traffic. Extended access lists work in the same fashion, but we have the ability to filter on more detailed information. We will look at extended access lists later in this chapter.

Standard Access Lists

We will use the diagram shown in Figure 13–2 to create our access lists. This diagram is IC, Inc., and it is the same network diagram that we used when we implemented IPX in Chapter 11, "IPX/SPX." To verify this, we will examine our RIP routing table and the SAP table on Router 1. If Router 1 shows all routes and the file server, then we can be sure that everything is running correctly at this time.

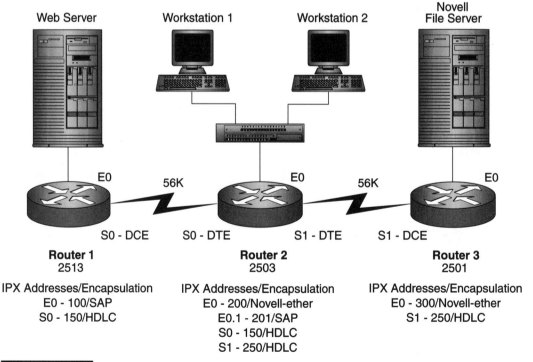

FIGURE 13-2   IC, Inc. using IPX

```
Router1#sho ipx route
Codes: C - Connected primary network,    c - Connected secondary network
       S - Static, F - Floating static, L - Local (internal), W - IPXWAN
       R - RIP, E - EIGRP, N - NLSP, X - External, A - Aggregate
       s - seconds, u - uses, U - Per-user static

7 Total IPX routes. Up to 1 parallel paths and 16 hops allowed.

No default route known.

C        100 (SAP),         Et0
C        150 (HDLC),        Se0
R          1 [14/03] via    150.0000.0c8e.46a0,    54s, Se0
R        200 [07/01] via    150.0000.0c8e.46a0,    54s, Se0
R        201 [07/01] via    150.0000.0c8e.46a0,    54s, Se0
R        250 [07/01] via    150.0000.0c8e.46a0,    54s, Se0
R        300 [13/02] via    150.0000.0c8e.46a0,    54s, Se0
Router1#
```

```
Router1#sho ipx servers
Codes: S - Static, P - Periodic, E - EIGRP, N - NLSP, H - Holddown, + = detail
U - Per-user static
2 Total IPX Servers

Table ordering is based on routing and server info

   Type Name                    Net      Address    Port     Route Hops Itf
P     4 NOVELL                   1.0000.0000.0001:0451     14/03   3  Se0
P   640 FILESERVER               1.0000.0000.0001:E885     14/03   3  Se0
Router1#
```

Router 1 has all of the networks listed in the routing table, including the internal address of the file server. Additionally, the SAP table includes the file server with the two services that it offers.

To create a standard IPX access list, we perform the same type of functions as with AppleTalk. In our diagram, we will prevent any traffic from the network 150 from reaching the 300 network. In order to do this, where is the best place to put the access list? Since we can check for source and destination, we can prevent the data from even crossing the WAN link between Router 2 and Router 3 by placing the access list on Router 2.

```
Router2#conf t
Enter configuration commands, one per line.  End with CNTL/Z.
Router2(config)#access-list ?
  <1-99>      IP standard access list
  <100-199>   IP extended access list
  <1000-1099> IPX SAP access list
  <1100-1199> Extended 48-bit MAC address access list
  <1200-1299> IPX summary address access list
```

```
<200-299>     Protocol type-code access list
<300-399>     DECnet access list
<600-699>     Appletalk access list
<700-799>     48-bit MAC address access list
<800-899>     IPX standard access list
<900-999>     IPX extended access list

Router2(config)#access-list 800 ?
  deny    Specify packets to reject
  permit  Specify packets to permit

Router2(config)#access-list 800 deny ?
  -1            Any IPX net
  <0-FFFFFFFF>  Source net
  N.H.H.H       Source net.host address


Router2(config)#access-list 800 deny 150 ?
  -1            Any IPX net
  <0-FFFFFFFF>  Destination net
  N.H.H.H       Destination net.host address
  <cr>

Router2(config)#access-list 800 deny 150 300 ?
  <cr>

Router2(config)#access-list 800 deny 150 300
Router2(config)#access-list 800 permit -1 -1
```

There are a couple of things to note here. First, the IPX access list range is shown from 800 to 899. Second, we can deny or permit a network address or a single host on a network. The same is true for the destination. The arguments include the source first, and then the destination. In our example, we are denying traffic from network 150 (source) that is trying to get to network 300 (destination).

The IOS includes an implicit "deny all" at the end of the access list. Therefore, our last entry in our access list is to allow everyone else that doesn't match any of the preceding lines. The −1 is a wildcard that matches all networks and hosts. The last line then reads "permit any source to reach any destination." Since the source network address of 150 matched the first line, it will never reach the second line. All other networks and hosts will not match the first line, and therefore will fall through to the next line.

Before we implement the access list, let's verify what it looks like. We can also verify connectivity by using extended ping before we actually implement the filter.

```
Router2#show ipx access
IPX standard access list 800
    deny 150 300
```

```
    permit FFFFFFFF FFFFFFFF
Router2#

Router1#ping 300.0000.0c91.a1ed

Type escape sequence to abort.
Sending 5, 100-byte IPX cisco Echoes to 300.0000.0c91.a1ed, timeout is 2
seconds
:
!!!!!
Success rate is 100 percent (5/5), round-trip min/avg/max = 64/67/68 ms
Router1#
```

Now that we have responses from Router 3 back to Router 1, we can implement the access list on Router 2.

```
Router2#conf t
Enter configuration commands, one per line.  End with CNTL/Z.
Router2(config)#int s0

Router2(config-if)#ipx access-group ?
  <800-999>  A valid IPX access list number
  WORD       Access-list name

Router2(config-if)#ipx access-group 800 ?
  in   inbound packets
  out  outbound packets
  <cr>

Router2(config-if)#ipx access-group 800 in ?
  <cr>

Router2(config-if)#ipx access-group 800 in
Router2(config-if)#
```

We can verify the access list is actually in use by using the **sho ipx int s0** command.

```
Router2#sho ipx int s0
Serial0 is up, line protocol is up
  IPX address is 150.0000.0c8e.46a0 [up]
  Delay of this IPX network, in ticks is 6 throughput 0 link delay 0
  IPXWAN processing not enabled on this interface.
  IPX SAP update interval is 60 seconds
  IPX type 20 propagation packet forwarding is disabled
  Incoming access list is 800
  Outgoing access list is not set
  IPX helper access list is not set
  SAP GNS processing enabled, delay 0 ms, output filter list is not set
  SAP Input filter list is not set
```

```
     SAP Output filter list is not set
     SAP Router filter list is not set
     Input filter list is not set
     Output filter list is not set
     Router filter list is not set
     Netbios Input host access list is not set
     Netbios Input bytes access list is not set
     Netbios Output host access list is not set
     Netbios Output bytes access list is not set
     Updates each 60 seconds aging multiples RIP: 3 SAP: 3
     SAP interpacket delay is 55 ms, maximum size is 480 bytes
     RIP interpacket delay is 55 ms, maximum size is 432 bytes
     Watchdog processing is disabled, SPX spoofing is disabled, idle time 60
     IPX accounting is disabled
     IPX fast switching is configured (enabled)
     RIP packets received 546, RIP packets sent 550
     SAP packets received 1, SAP packets sent 541
Router2#
```

The seventh line down shows us that access list 800 is set to filter incoming packets. It's time to test the filter now.

```
Router1#ping 300.0000.0c91.a1ed

Type escape sequence to abort.
Sending 5, 100-byte IPX cisco Echoes to 300.0000.0c91.a1ed, timeout is 2
seconds
:
.....
Success rate is 0 percent (0/5)
Router1#
```

Our access list works perfectly! Network traffic from 150 cannot reach network 300. Router 2 is dropping all packets at the incoming interface.

Creating access lists can be a tricky business because of the ordering. It is much easier for us to develop a plan on paper and then, after logically testing it out, implementing it on the router itself. With a plan and a diagram, it is easy to test "What if?" scenarios by choosing specific hosts on the various networks to attempt access to the network we are denying.

Extended Access Lists

We can also implement extended access lists with IPX/SPX that can filter traffic based on protocols and the various sockets within. A socket in IPX/SPX is similar to a port in TCP/IP. The format of the command is **access-list {900-999} {deny/ permit} {protocol} {source} {socket} {destination} {socket}**. Each parameter in the braces is an argument that is specifically defined. For instance, **access-list 900 deny any 250 cping 150 all** will deny any protocol from network 150 from reaching the network 250 and using the cisco ping socket (cping).

Sap Filters

SAP announcements allow all NetWare servers to know about all other NetWare servers. This, in turn, allows NetWare clients to access servers not on their own segment. However, there are times when we want to prevent hosts from reaching a certain server. Although we can set up an access list, it is easier to set up and maintain a SAP filter instead. By using a SAP filter, the SAP tables on the local segment will not show the server we are trying to deny access to.

To set up a SAP filter, we need to create an access list. We will keep the file server type 4 from being seen by Routers 1 and 2.

```
Router3(config)#access-list ?
  <1-99>      IP standard access list
  <100-199>   IP extended access list
  <1000-1099> IPX SAP access list
  <1100-1199> Extended 48-bit MAC address access list
  <1200-1299> IPX summary address access list
  <200-299>   Protocol type-code access list
  <300-399>   DECnet access list
  <600-699>   Appletalk access list
  <700-799>   48-bit MAC address access list
  <800-899>   IPX standard access list
  <900-999>   IPX extended access list

Router3(config)#access-list 1000 ?
  deny    Specify packets to reject
  permit  Specify packets to forward

Router3(config)#access-list 1000 deny ?
  -1            Any IPX net
  <0-FFFFFFFF>  Source net
  N.H.H.H       Source net.host address

Router3(config)#access-list 1000 deny 1.0000.0000.0001 ?
  <0-FFFF>  Service type-code (0 matches all services)
  N.H.H.H   Source net.host mask
  <cr>

Router3(config)#access-list 1000 deny 1.0000.0000.0001 4 ?
  WORD  A SAP server name
  <cr>

Router3(config)#access-list 1000 deny 1.0000.0000.0001 4
Router3(config)#access-list 1000 permit  -1 0
```

We have to remember that the IOS includes an implicit deny with every access list. Here we will permit all other services from all servers (including 1.0000.0000.0001) except type 4 from being propagated to the next router. Once the access list is created, we apply it to the **output-sap-filter**.

```
Router3(config)#int s1
Router3(config-if)#ipx output-sap-filter 1000
Router3(config-if)#^Z
Router3#
```

Now that the filter is in place, we should still be able to see the file services offered on Router 3 and all hosts on the Ethernet segment.

```
Router3#sho ipx server
Codes: S - Static, P - Periodic, E - EIGRP, N - NLSP, H - Holddown, + = detail
U - Per-user static
2 Total IPX Servers

Table ordering is based on routing and server info

     Type Name                      Net     Address    Port    Route Hops Itf
P      4 NOVELL                     1.0000.0000.0001:0451     2/01   1   Et0
P    640 FILESERVER                 1.0000.0000.0001:E885     2/01   1   Et0
Router3#
```

Routers 1 and 2 should not show the type 4 being serviced by the file server.

```
Router2#sho ipx server
Codes: S - Static, P - Periodic, E - EIGRP, N - NLSP, H - Holddown, + = detail
U - Per-user static
1 Total IPX Servers

Table ordering is based on routing and server info

     Type Name                      Net     Address    Port    Route Hops Itf
P    640 FILESERVER                 1.0000.0000.0001:E885     8/02   2   Se1
Router2#
```

```
Router1#sho ipx server
Codes: S - Static, P - Periodic, E - EIGRP, N - NLSP, H - Holddown, + = detail
U - Per-user static
1 Total IPX Servers

Table ordering is based on routing and server info

     Type Name                      Net     Address    Port    Route Hops Itf
P    640 FILESERVER                 1.0000.0000.0001:E885     14/03  3   Se0
Router1#
```

Everything is as it should be! We have hidden the file services and effectively granted the right to use that server only to the Ethernet segment of Router 3.

IP Access Lists

Now that we have examined the AppleTalk and the IPX/SPX access lists, we are ready to move on to the slightly more difficult TCP/IP access lists. IP access lists are by far more common than any of the other protocols, but if a network that we are working on is primarily IPX/SPX, then according to that organization, IPX/SPX access lists are more common.

The reason that IP access lists are more difficult is because they use a wild-card masking that can be considered an inverse subnet mask. Before we move on let's reexamine our IC, Inc. network diagram as shown in Figure 13–3.

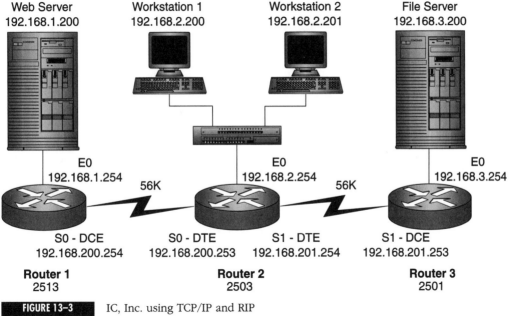

| Web Server 192.168.1.200 | Workstation 1 192.168.2.200 | Workstation 2 192.168.2.201 | File Server 192.168.3.200 |

E0 192.168.1.254   56K   E0 192.168.2.254   56K   E0 192.168.3.254

S0 - DCE 192.168.200.254   S0 - DTE 192.168.200.253   S1 - DTE 192.168.201.254   S1 - DCE 192.168.201.253

Router 1 2513   **Router 2** 2503   **Router 3** 2501

FIGURE 13–3   IC, Inc. using TCP/IP and RIP

Suppose that we wanted to prevent Workstation 1 from reaching beyond Router 2. We could apply an access list to Router 2 that would include the parameters **192.168.2.200 0.0.0.0**. The second set of octets is the wild-card mask. For every bit that is a 0 in the wildcard mask, the source being checked against must match the source listed in the access list. For example, if 192.168.2.201 is trying to reach the Web Server, Router 2 will examine the source of the actual packet (192.168.2.201) against the IP access list. The wild-card of the first octet is all 0s. This means that the first octet must match the source specified in the access list. Both the data being received is from 192 and the source in the access list has 192. Next, we do the same with the next two octets. Since the wildcard mask is all 0s, the octets must match exactly. The data is coming from 192.168.2, and the source in the access list matches the 192.168.2. However, the final octet is again matched against a wildcard mask of 0. This means the data coming in (201) must match exactly that in the access list (200). Since they don't, the data is allowed to pass through.

What if we wanted to prevent all hosts on the 2 segment from reaching beyond Router 2? We would apply an access list using the parameters of **192.168.2.0 0.0.0.255**. The first three octets again must match exactly with the data being examined. However, the fourth octet contains all 1s (255 in binary is 11111111), and a 1 means "We don't care what the bit is," or in other words, it is our wildcard. So if a host of 192.168.2.200 tries to get beyond the network, the wildcard will match up as follows:

Access List Source	192	168	2	0
Wildcard Mask	0	0	0	255
Match anything with:	192	168	2	*

The address of 192.168.2.200 matches 192.168.2.* (where * is the wildcard, or the "who cares" bits), so the data will not be allowed through.

To examine this in one more step, if we applied the access list with the parameters of **192.168.2.0 0.0.0.15**, what would be the result? Since 240 in binary is 00001111, we really want to match the fourth octet with the first 4 bits being 0. This means this mask will filter 0–15 and everything else will be allowed through. This can be seen in the following chart (looking at only the fourth octet):

Source Address	Binary	Wildcard	Match?
0	00000000	00001111	Yes
1	00000001	00001111	Yes
2	00000010	00001111	Yes
3	00000011	00001111	Yes
4	00000100	00001111	Yes
5	00000101	00001111	Yes
6	00000110	00001111	Yes
7	00000111	00001111	Yes
8	00001000	00001111	Yes
9	00001001	00001111	Yes
10	00001010	00001111	Yes
11	00001011	00001111	Yes
12	00001100	00001111	Yes
13	00001101	00001111	Yes

Continues

Source Address	Binary	Wildcard	Match?
14	00001110	00001111	Yes
15	00001111	00001111	Yes
16	00010000	00001111	No
17	00010001	00001111	No
> 17	Varies	00001111	No

So we can see that as long as the first 4 bits remain 0, a match occurs and the filter will be acted upon.

Now that we have a grasp on the wildcard matching, the rest of the access lists are almost identical to the other protocols.

Standard Access Lists

To implement a standard access list, we will stop traffic from Workstation 2 from reaching the file server. First, we will verify connectivity.

```
C:\>ping 192.168.3.200

Pinging 192.168.3.200 with 32 bytes of data:

Reply from 192.168.3.200: bytes=32 time=20ms TTL=126
Reply from 192.168.3.200: bytes=32 time=10ms TTL=126
Reply from 192.168.3.200: bytes=32 time=10ms TTL=126
Reply from 192.168.3.200: bytes=32 time=10ms TTL=126

C:\>
```

Next, we need to decide where to place the access list. Do we want to place the access list on Router 3? If we did, the data would travel across the WAN link before being filtered. The best place would be on Router 2. First, we create the access list.

```
Router2(config)#access-list ?
  <1-99>       IP standard access list
  <100-199>    IP extended access list
  <1000-1099>  IPX SAP access list
  <1100-1199>  Extended 48-bit MAC address access list
  <1200-1299>  IPX summary address access list
  <200-299>    Protocol type-code access list
  <300-399>    DECnet access list
  <600-699>    Appletalk access list
  <700-799>    48-bit MAC address access list
  <800-899>    IPX standard access list
  <900-999>    IPX extended access list
```

```
Router2(config)#access-list 1 ?
  deny     Specify packets to reject
  permit   Specify packets to forward

Router2(config)#access-list 1 deny ?
  Hostname or A.B.C.D  Address to match
  any                  Any source host
  host                 A single host address


Router2(config)#access-list 1 deny 192.168.2.201 ?
  A.B.C.D  Wildcard bits
  log      Log matches against this entry
  <cr>

Router2(config)#access-list 1 deny 192.168.2.201 0.0.0.0 ?
  log  Log matches against this entry
  <cr>

Router2(config)#access-list 1 deny 192.168.2.201 0.0.0.0
```

We can see that the standard access lists for IP run from 1 to 99. The format of the access list is very similar to what we have been working with. After specifying the source address, we specify the wildcard mask. Again, by making the mask all 0s we are requiring an exact match. There is a simpler form that we can use. If all we want to do is specify a single node, we do not need to include the wildcard mask. We could just as easily have typed **access-list 1 deny 192.168.2.201**.

Next, we apply the access list to the interface. Since we want to place the access list as close to the source as possible, we will place it on the E0 port.

```
Router2(config)#int e0
Router2(config-if)#ip access-group 1 in
Router2(config-if)#^Z
Router2#
```

Now that the access list is in place (we can verify this by using the command **sho ip int e0**), we can test the connectivity again.

```
C:\>ping 192.168.3.200

Pinging 192.168.3.200 with 32 bytes of data:

Reply from 192.168.2.254: Destination net unreachable.
Reply from 192.168.2.254: Destination net unreachable.
Reply from 192.168.2.254: Destination net unreachable.
Reply from 192.168.2.254: Destination net unreachable.

C:\>
```

We can see the access list is working perfectly. We can also ping from Workstation 2 to verify that those packets are getting through.

```
C:\>ping 192.168.3.200

Pinging 192.168.3.200 with 32 bytes of data:

Reply from 192.168.2.254: Destination net unreachable.
Reply from 192.168.2.254: Destination net unreachable.
Reply from 192.168.2.254: Destination net unreachable.
Reply from 192.168.2.254: Destination net unreachable.

C:\>
```

This was unexpected! We know that the list we set up identified just 192.168.2.200, yet the other Workstation is not getting through. Let's verify our access list.

```
Router2#sho access-l
Standard IP access list 1
    deny    192.168.2.200
Router2#
```

There is our problem. We forgot that the IOS places the implicit deny at the end of the access list. Everything is being denied! We can fix this quickly enough.

```
Router2#conf t
Enter configuration commands, one per line.  End with CNTL/Z.
Router2(config)#access-list 1 permit any
Router2(config)#^Z
Router2#
```

Now we can try pinging from Workstation 2 again.

```
C:\>ping 192.168.3.200

Pinging 192.168.3.200 with 32 bytes of data:

Reply from 192.168.3.200: bytes=32 time=20ms TTL=126
Reply from 192.168.3.200: bytes=32 time=10ms TTL=126
Reply from 192.168.3.200: bytes=32 time=10ms TTL=126
Reply from 192.168.3.200: bytes=32 time=10ms TTL=126

C:\>
```

Much better! Here is a perfect example of forgetting to include the final entry in the access list if we want to permit all other traffic.

Let's change our access list to deny all nodes on the network 192.168.2.0 from accessing servers outside the segment. How can we change our access list? Well, it turns out that we cannot modify, nor can we insert or delete lines. We could write the configuration to a TFTP server, modify the contents of the text file, and then read it back in. In fact, if we have a lot of logic in an access list, this is a preferred method. In our case, we will just create a new access list.

```
Router2#conf t
Enter configuration commands, one per line.  End with CNTL/Z.
Router2(config)#access-list 2 deny 192.168.2.0 0.0.0.255
Router2(config)#access-list 2 permit any
Router2(config)#^Z
Router2#
```

Why create a new access list? If we were working in a production environment and we had deleted the access list that was working and then recreated it incorrectly, we would be in trouble. This way, we can keep the previous access list and implement it immediately if trouble arises from the new list. Only when we are sure that the list is good should we delete the old list.

Next, we apply the list to the Ethernet interface.

```
Router2(config)#int e0
Router2(config-if)#ip access-group 2 in
Router2(config-if)#^Z
Router2#sho ip int e0
Ethernet0 is up, line protocol is up
  Internet address is 192.168.2.254/24
  Broadcast address is 255.255.255.255
  Address determined by setup command
  MTU is 1500 bytes
  Helper address is not set
  Directed broadcast forwarding is enabled
  Multicast reserved groups joined: 224.0.0.9
  Outgoing access list is not set
  Inbound  access list is 2
  Proxy ARP is enabled
  Security level is default
  Split horizon is enabled
  ICMP redirects are always sent
  ICMP unreachables are always sent
  ICMP mask replies are never sent
  IP fast switching is enabled
  IP fast switching on the same interface is disabled
  IP multicast fast switching is enabled
  Router Discovery is disabled
  IP output packet accounting is disabled
  IP access violation accounting is disabled
  TCP/IP header compression is disabled
  Probe proxy name replies are disabled
  Gateway Discovery is disabled
  Policy routing is disabled
  Network address translation is disabled
Router2#
```

We can see that the new access group is 2, and that it completely replaced the first list. To test out our new access list, we will try pinging from Workstation 2.

```
C:\>ping 192.168.3.200

Pinging 192.168.3.200 with 32 bytes of data:

Reply from 192.168.2.254: Destination net unreachable.
Reply from 192.168.2.254: Destination net unreachable.
Reply from 192.168.2.254: Destination net unreachable.
Reply from 192.168.2.254: Destination net unreachable.
```

Standard access lists are easy to implement and monitor, but if we need more control, such as denying specific hosts from reaching other hosts and denying certain protocols, we will have to use the extended access lists.

Extended Access Lists

An extended access list has the format of **access-list {100–199} {deny/permit} {protocol} {source} {source wildcard} {destination} {destination wildcard} {equivalence} {port number}**. Within this format if we specify the parameter "any" with the source and/or destination, then we do not specify a wildcard. The parameter "any" allows us to permit or deny all hosts in the entire network and even beyond into internets.

To test this, we will create an access list that denies Workstation 2 from accessing the Web server using port 80. This will still allow file access (if available) and utilities such as ping to reach the Web Server. First, let's verify that we can reach the Web server. To do this, we will use Internet Explorer and verify that a Web page comes up. This can be seen in Figure 13–4.

Next, we will implement the access list.

```
Router2#conf t
Enter configuration commands, one per line.  End with CNTL/Z.
Router2(config)#access-list ?
  <1-99>       IP standard access list
  <100-199>    IP extended access list
  <1000-1099>  IPX SAP access list
  <1100-1199>  Extended 48-bit MAC address access list
  <1200-1299>  IPX summary address access list
  <200-299>    Protocol type-code access list
  <300-399>    DECnet access list
  <600-699>    Appletalk access list
  <700-799>    48-bit MAC address access list
  <800-899>    IPX standard access list
<900-999>    IPX extended access list
```

Note that the IP extended access lists range from 100 to 199.

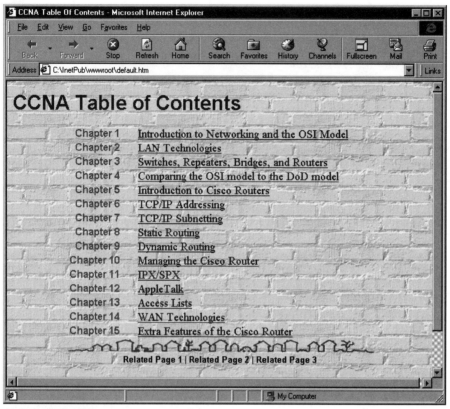

FIGURE 13–4   Web page access

```
Router2(config)#access-list 100 deny ?
  <0-255>  An IP protocol number
  ahp      Authentication Header Protocol
  eigrp    Cisco's EIGRP routing protocol
  esp      Encapsulation Security Payload
  gre      Cisco's GRE tunneling
  icmp     Internet Control Message Protocol
  igmp     Internet Gateway Message Protocol
  igrp     Cisco's IGRP routing protocol
  ip       Any Internet Protocol
  ipinip   IP in IP tunneling
  nos      KA9Q NOS compatible IP over IP tunneling
  ospf     OSPF routing protocol
  pcp      Payload Compression Protocol
  tcp      Transmission Control Protocol
  udp      User Datagram Protocol
```

At this point, it might be a good time for us to review the TCP/IP model. IP as a protocol is a connectionless protocol that passes data back up to the next layer to TCP or UDP. It is important to remember this because if we want to block a specific port of 80, we have to identify the correct protocol to filter. If we had chosen IP as the protocol and then we specify port 80, no access would be blocked. Additionally, some protocols such as DNS can use either UDP or TCP. so we have to make sure we are filtering exactly what we want.

```
Router2(config)#access-list 100 deny tcp ?
  A.B.C.D  Source address
  any      Any source host
  host     A single source host

Router2(config)#access-list 100 deny tcp 192.168.2.200 0.0.0.255 ?
  A.B.C.D  Destination address
  any      Any destination host
  eq       Match only packets on a given port number
  gt       Match only packets with a greater port number
  host     A single destination host
  lt       Match only packets with a lower port number
  neq      Match only packets not on a given port number
  range    Match only packets in the range of port numbers

Router2(config)#$ 100 deny tcp 192.168.2.201 0.0.0.0 192.168.1.200 ?
  A.B.C.D  Destination wildcard bits

Router2(config)#$tcp 192.168.2.201 0.0.0.0 192.168.1.200 0.0.0.0 ?
  eq           Match only packets on a given port number
  established  Match established connections
  gt           Match only packets with a greater port number
  log          Log matches against this entry
  log-input    Log matches against this entry, including input interface
  lt           Match only packets with a lower port number
  neq          Match only packets not on a given port number
  precedence   Match packets with given precedence value
  range        Match only packets in the range of port numbers
  tos          Match packets with given TOS value
  <cr>

Router2(config)#$tcp 192.168.2.201 0.0.0.0 192.168.1.200 0.0.0.0 eq www
Router2(config)#
```

First, notice how we reached the end of the line (78 characters), and so the IOS started shifting the characters to the left 10 at a time. The dollar sign indicates this to us. Also, we then chose to filter on the TCP protocol port 80. We could have used a greater than (gt), or less than (lt), or even a range of protocols.

There are many other ports that we can filter on. The following is the default list that is displayed with the ? parameter.

```
Router2(config)#$tcp 192.168.2.201 0.0.0.0 192.168.1.200 0.0.0.0 eq ?
  <0-65535>   Port number
  bgp         Border Gateway Protocol (179)
```

```
chargen       Character generator (19)
cmd           Remote commands (rcmd, 514)
daytime       Daytime (13)
discard       Discard (9)
domain        Domain Name Service (53)
echo          Echo (7)
exec          Exec (rsh, 512)
finger        Finger (79)
ftp           File Transfer Protocol (21)
ftp-data      FTP data connections (used infrequently, 20)
gopher        Gopher (70)
hostname      NIC hostname server (101)
ident         Ident Protocol (113)
irc           Internet Relay Chat (194)
klogin        Kerberos login (543)
kshell        Kerberos shell (544)
login         Login (rlogin, 513)
lpd           Printer service (515)
nntp          Network News Transport Protocol (119)
pim-auto-rp   PIM Auto-RP (496)
pop2          Post Office Protocol v2 (109)
pop3          Post Office Protocol v3 (110)
smtp          Simple Mail Transport Protocol (25)
sunrpc        Sun Remote Procedure Call (111)
syslog        Syslog (514)
tacacs        TAC Access Control System (49)
talk          Talk (517)
telnet        Telnet (23)
time          Time (37)
uucp          Unix-to-Unix Copy Program (540)
whois         Nicname (43)
www           World Wide Web (HTTP, 80)
Router2(config)#
```

This list is very useful if we cannot remember that DNS works at port 53, or that SMTP works at port 25, or any of the other common port numbers. Notice that after the keywords, the default port is listed. If we needed a different port, such as if our Web server had a hidden address of 8080, we could just specify that port number directly.

Next, we need to ensure that everyone else can get past the implicit deny at the end of this access list.

```
Router2(config)#access-list 100 permit tcp any any
Router2(config)#
```

Finally, we need to apply the filter to the incoming packets on the Ethernet port.

```
Router2(config-if)#ip access-group 100 in
Router2(config-if)#^Z

Router2#sho ip access-list
Extended IP access list 100
    deny tcp host 192.168.2.200 host 192.168.1.200 eq www
    permit tcp any any
Router2#
```

Now that the access list is being applied to Ethernet 0 we can test it. Hitting the Refresh button on the browser causes the display shown in Figure 13–5.

FIGURE 13–5   Screen shot with error message

Although difficult to read in the screen shot, the error message does tell us that the server cannot be reached.

To truly appreciate the access list, we will examine it once again.

```
Router2#sho ip access-list
Extended IP access list 100
    deny tcp host 192.168.2.201 host 192.168.1.200 eq www (8 matches)
    permit tcp any any
Router2#
```

We can see that there were eight matches to the first filter list. This logging is automatically occurring and can be used to ensure that the filter is working correctly. If we try to access the Web server from Workstation 1 and then view the access list again, we can see that the matches are being filtered on the second line.

```
Router2#sho ip access-list
Extended IP access list 100
    deny tcp host 192.168.2.201 host 192.168.1.200 eq www (8 matches)
    permit tcp any any (37 matches)
Router2#
```

If we would like to clear our counters, we can issue the **clear access-list counters** command.

```
Router2#clear access-list counters 100
Router2#sho ip access-list
Extended IP access list 100
    deny tcp host 192.168.2.201 host 192.168.1.200 eq www
    permit tcp any any
Router2#
```

Just so that we have a chance to practice, let's try stopping both Workstations 1 and 2 from accessing the Web server. We know we can do this with the wildcard mask. First, let's convert 200 and 201 (host addresses) to binary:

200 – 11001000   201 – 11001001

Notice that the first 7 bits are identical. Therefore, we want the last bit to be the wildcard. Our wildcard should be 1 (00000001) and the source should be 200. This will filter for either 200 or 201.

Next, let's create the access list.

```
Router2(config)#access-list 101 deny tcp 192.168.2.200 0.0.0.1
192.168.1.200 0.0.0.0 eq www
Router2(config)#access-list 101 permit tcp any any
Router2(config)#int e0
Router2(config-if)#ip access-group 101 in
Router2(config-if)#^Z
Router2#sho ip access
Extended IP access list 100
    deny tcp host 192.168.2.201 host 192.168.1.200 eq www
    permit tcp any any
```

```
Extended IP access list 101
     deny tcp 192.168.2.200 0.0.0.1 host 192.168.1.200 eq www
Router2#
```

If we calculated correctly, we should see the filter counter go up when trying to reach the Web server from Workstation 1.

```
Router2#sho ip access
Extended IP access list 100
    deny tcp host 192.168.2.201 host 192.168.1.200 eq www
    permit tcp any any
Extended IP access list 101
    deny tcp 192.168.2.200 0.0.0.1 host 192.168.1.200 eq www (8 matches)
    permit tcp any any
Router2#
```

The counters should also go up when Workstation 2 tries to access the Web server.

```
Router2#sho ip access
Extended IP access list 100
    deny tcp host 192.168.2.201 host 192.168.1.200 eq www
    permit tcp any any
Extended IP access list 101
    deny tcp 192.168.2.200 0.0.0.1 host 192.168.1.200 eq www (16 matches)
    permit tcp any any
Router2#
```

And finally, when another workstation from the same segment tries, it should be able to get through.

```
Router2#sho ip access
Extended IP access list 100
    deny tcp host 192.168.2.201 host 192.168.1.200 eq www
    permit tcp any any
Extended IP access list 101
    deny tcp 192.168.2.200 0.0.0.1 host 192.168.1.200 eq www (16 matches)
    permit tcp any any (9 matches)
Router2#
```

Summary

Access lists are used to prevent unwanted traffic from entering or leaving a router's interface. Access lists are implemented in two steps. The first step requires the list to be created with all the entries. Each entry is examined during the filtering process until a match is made. When a match is found, the router will perform the requested step, which will be either to forward or to discard the packet. At the end of every access list, the IOS places an implicit "deny all." The second step requires the access list to be added to the access group on one or more interfaces. This allows the router to filter the traffic appropriately. AppleTalk access lists can work with hosts, networks, and zones. IPX/SPX access lists can work with source and destination nodes or networks. Additionally, extended IPX/SPX access lists can filter on specific sockets to fine-tune the filtering. Standard TCP/IP access lists filter on source node or network addresses. Extended TCP/IP access lists can filter on both source and destination, as well as protocols. Additionally, the extended access list can also filter on specific ports within the protocol.

Scenario Lab 13.1

The CIO has decided that the remote sales offices should not be using the Internet access for anything other than straight Web access (see Figure 13–6). Additionally, there is a group of five machines in New York that are used for local consultants. The CIO would like to make sure they cannot access the Novell and NT servers in Minneapolis. Can you describe a method of implementing an access policy to arrive at the CIO's requests?

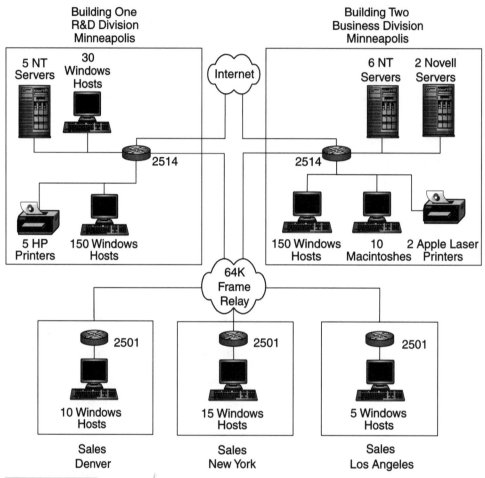

FIGURE 13–6   Network Solutions requiring access lists

Practice Lab 13.1

In this lab, you will implement a standard TCP/IP access to prevent Workstation 2 from accessing the Web Server on Workstation 1.

- Set up the lab as shown in Figure 13–7. Test the connectivity by using ping.
- Create a standard TCP/IP access list to prevent Workstation 2 from reaching the Web server. Which router do you want to place the list on?
- Enable the filter by adding it to the group for the interface on the chosen router.
- Test connectivity by using ping. If you cannot get a response, continue to the next step.
- Change the IP address on Workstation 2 and try pinging Workstation 1. You should be successful.
- Create a new access list and prevent all hosts on 192.168.30.0 network.
- Implement the access list on the interface you used for the last interface.
- Examine the counters using the **sho ip access-list** command.
- Try pinging Workstation 1 again. You should not be able to.
- Examine the counters again.
- Try changing Workstation 2's IP address to other addresses, and verify that you cannot reach Workstation 1.

Workstation 1 - 192.168.10.1/24
Web Server

Workstation 2 - 192.168.30.1/24

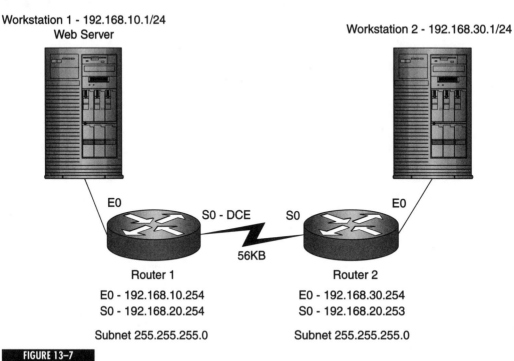

E0

S0 - DCE   S0

E0

56KB

Router 1   Router 2

E0 - 192.168.10.254   E0 - 192.168.30.254
S0 - 192.168.20.254   S0 - 192.168.20.253

Subnet 255.255.255.0   Subnet 255.255.255.0

FIGURE 13–7

Practice Lab 13.2

In this lab, you will filter IPX traffic by preventing the Novell client from reaching the Novell server. Next, you will filter the SAP traffic so that Router 1 does not even know about the Novell server.

- Set up the network as shown in Figure 13–8. Verify connectivity by using the extended ping command. You will have to find the node addresses on the client and the server yourself. The router's node address can be found by using the **show ipx interface** command.
- Set up an access list to prevent the client from connecting to the server. Verify by using ping.
- Set up an access list and use the SAP filter method to prevent Router 2 from sending the SAP type 4 to Router 1.
- Verify the filter is working by using the **show ipx servers** command.

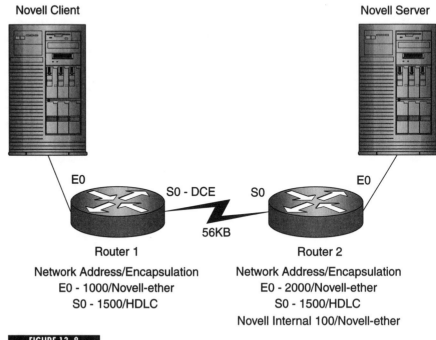

Novell Client

Novell Server

E0

S0 - DCE   S0

56KB

E0

Router 1

Network Address/Encapsulation
E0 - 1000/Novell-ether
S0 - 1500/HDLC

Router 2

Network Address/Encapsulation
E0 - 2000/Novell-ether
S0 - 1500/HDLC
Novell Internal 100/Novell-ether

FIGURE 13–8

Practice Lab 13.3

In this lab, you will create an extended access list and deny
Workstation 2 from accessing port 80 on the Web server. You
will monitor the counters of both access entries in the filter.

- Set up the lab as shown in Figure 13–9. Use RIP or IGRP
  for the dynamic routing. Verify connectivity using ping.
- Set up a Web server and use a Web browser on Workstation 1 and Workstation 2 to access a Web page.
- Create an access list to keep Workstation 2 from
  accessing the Web server. For this lab, place the filter
  on the incoming port S0 of Router 1.
- View the counters of the access list using the command **sho ip access-list**.
- Try to access the Web server from Workstation 2. You
  should not be successful.
- View the counters of the access list again. Can you see
  the difference from the first time?
- Try to access the Web server from Workstation 1. You
  should be able to.
- View the counters a third time and note the difference.
- BONUS: Try to create an extended access list on
  Router 1 that stops traffic from as few machines as
  possible, but including both Workstation 1 and Work-
  station 2. What wildcard mask would you use?

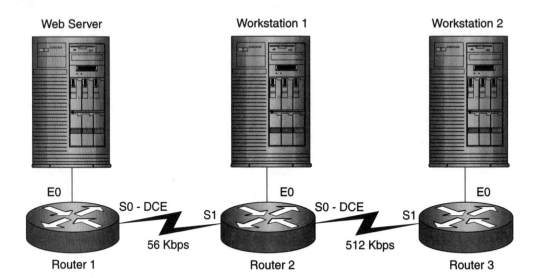

Web Server   Workstation 1   Workstation 2

E0   E0   E0

S0 - DCE   S0 - DCE
                S1   S1
      56 Kbps   512 Kbps

Router 1   Router 2   Router 3

Workstation IP: 172.16.0.1   Workstation IP: 172.18.0.1   Workstation IP: 172.20.0.1
E0 IP: 172.16.255.254   E0 IP: 172.18.255.254   E0 IP: 172.20.255.254
S0 IP: 172.17.255.254   S1 IP: 172.17.255.253   S1 IP: 172.19.255.253
                               S0 IP: 172.19.255.254

Subnet Mask: 255.255.0.0   Subnet Mask: 255.255.0.0   Subnet Mask: 255.255.0.0

FIGURE 13–9

Exam Objective Checklist

By working through this chapter, you should have sufficient knowledge to answer these exam objectives:

- Configure standard access lists to configure IP traffic.
- Monitor and verify selected access list operations on the router.
- Configure extended access lists to filter IP traffic.
- Configure IPX access lists and SAP filters to control basic Novell traffic.

Practice Questions

1. Which statement about access lists is correct?

   a. All entries in the access list are used.
   b. Only the first entry in the access list is used.
   c. Only the first entry in an access list is used when a match is found.
   d. Cisco IOS places an implicit grant all at the end of the access list.

2. What is the correct range for a standard AppleTalk access list?

   a. 100–199
   b. 200–299
   c. 500–599
   d. 600–699

3. Which of the following access lists will filter traffic from network 192.168.1.0 from reaching 192.168.2.0?

   a. access-list 1 deny 192.168.2.0 0.0.0.0
   b. access-list 1 deny 192.168.2.0 0.0.0.255
   c. access-list 1 deny 192.168.1.0 0.0.0.0
   d. access-list 1 deny 192.168.1.0 0.0.0.255

4. Which of the following access lists will filter the entire cable range 20–25?

    a. access-list 601 permit cable within 20-25
    b. access-list 601 deny cable includes 20-25
    c. access-list 601 permit network within 20-25
    d. access-list 601 deny network includes 20-25

5. What is the correct range for a standard IPX/SPX access list?

    a. 1000–1099
    b. 1200–1299
    c. 800–899
    d. 900–999

6. Which access list will deny all nodes on all networks from accessing the Novell server on network 500?

    a. access-list 800 deny –1 –1
    b. access-list 800 deny 500 any
    c. access-list 800 deny any 500
    d. access-list 800 deny –1 500

7. Which of the following is the complete access list to allow only host 192.168.17.5 to reach the DNS Server?

    a. access-list 100 deny ip any any
        access-list 100 permit tcp 192.168.17.5 0.0.0.0 any eq domain
    b. access-list 100 permit tcp 192.168.17.5 0.0.0.0 any eq 53
        access-list 100 deny ip any any
    c. access-list 100 allow tcp any 192.168.17.5 eq DNS
        access-list 100 deny –1 –1
    d. access-list 100 permit tcp 192.168.17.5 any eq 53
        access-list 100 permit any any

8. What is the correct range for a standard TCP/IP access list?

    a. 1–99
    b. 100–199
    c. 1000–1099
    d. 1100–1199

9. What is the correct range for an extended TCP/IP access list?

    a. 1–99
    b. 100–199
    c. 1000–1099
    d. 1100–1199

10. Which access list is valid?

    a. access-list 1000 deny 10.0000.0000.0001 0

    b. access-list 1000 deny –1 –1

    c. access-list 800 deny 10.0000.0000.0001

    d. access-list 800 deny –1 –1 0

11. Which access list is valid?

    a. access-list 99 deny ip any any

    b. access-list 99 permit udp any any eq ftp

    c. access-list 100 deny ip any any eq ftp

    d. access-list 100 deny tcp any any eq ftp

12. Which of the following can be used with the command **ipx output-sap-filter 1000**?

    a. access-list 1000 deny 10.0000.0000.0001 4

    b. access-list 1000 deny –1 –1

    c. access-list 1000 permit 4 10.0000.0000.0001 –1

    d. access-list 1000 permit sap 10.0000.0000.0001 4

13. What command can be used to view the access lists of any protocols?

    a. show any access-list

    b. show access-list

    c. show access list

    d. show any access lit

WAN Technologies

In This Chapter

WAN technologies are the most important technologies to understand for a CCIE. Most network administrators can deal effectively with LAN technologies, but when it comes to connecting those LANs to the Internet or to company-to-company WANs, the skills decline rapidly. Although the CCNA is the first step to attaining the CCIE and, as such, focuses mostly on the Cisco router and LAN technologies, it is still a beginning point for building the skills necessary to incorporate WANs. In this chapter, we will examine two of the more common WANs, ISDN and Frame Relay, and how they can be used with the Cisco routers. We will also examine two encapsulation types that can be used with the serial interfaces: PPP and HDLC.

How Serial Links Work

Serial links are used to connect the customer's equipment (Customer Premises Equipment, or CPE) to the WAN carrier's equipment. Typically, the CPE consists of a DTE (Data Terminal Equipment) device that connects to the

383

carrier's DCE (Date Circuit-terminating Equipment) device. Figure 14–1 shows this relationship.

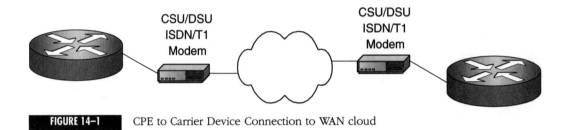

FIGURE 14–1   CPE to Carrier Device Connection to WAN cloud

The DCE equipment identifies the beginning of the responsibility of the WAN carrier and continues through to the DCE equipment on the other side. This area does become gray when integrating the CSU/DSU or T1 into the router itself.

HDLC

HDLC, or High-Level Data-Link Control, is a Link Layer protocol that has been standardized by the ISO. It has been tweaked and prodded, and now there is an IEEE 802.2 specification for it. HDLC is a protocol that is used across synchronous serial links and provides for timing communications across the link. The problem with it is that it does not inherently support multiple protocols on the same link. Cisco and most other vendors have implemented their own versions of HDLC to support multiprotocols. Because of this, we can only use the PPP encapsulation type when communicating with other vendor's routers. HDLC is the default.

To change the encapsulation type, we issue the **encapsulation** command for the appropriate interface. It is important to note that we cannot turn off an encapsulation mode using the **no** keyword. We must issue the **encaps** command with a different encapsulation type. It is also important to note that BOTH ends of the serial link must be running the same encapsulation type, or the line will not come up.

The following shows the different encapsulation types.

```
Router1#conf t
Enter configuration commands, one per line.   End with CNTL/Z.
Router1(config)#int s0
Router1(config-if)#encap ?
  atm-dxi       ATM-DXI encapsulation
  frame-relay   Frame Relay networks
  hdlc          Serial HDLC synchronous
```

```
lapb         LAPB (X.25 Level 2)
ppp          Point-to-Point protocol
smds         Switched Megabit Data Service (SMDS)
x25          X.25

Router1(config-if)#encap hdlc
Router1(config-if)#
```

We can verify the encapsulation being used by examining the interface information as shown next.

```
Router1#sho int s0
Serial0 is up, line protocol is up
  Hardware is HD64570
  Internet address is 192.168.200.254/24
  MTU 1500 bytes, BW 1544 Kbit, DLY 20000 usec, rely 255/255, load 1/255
  Encapsulation HDLC, loopback not set, keepalive set (10 sec)
  Last input 00:00:07, output 00:00:03, output hang never
  Last clearing of "show interface" counters never
  Queueing strategy: fifo
  Output queue 0/40, 295 drops; input queue 0/75, 0 drops
  5 minute input rate 0 bits/sec, 0 packets/sec
  5 minute output rate 0 bits/sec, 0 packets/sec
     8220 packets input, 684418 bytes, 0 no buffer
     Received 6798 broadcasts, 0 runts, 0 giants, 0 throttles
     0 input errors, 0 CRC, 0 frame, 0 overrun, 0 ignored, 0 abort
     6953 packets output, 517443 bytes, 0 underruns
     0 output errors, 0 collisions, 22 interface resets
     0 output buffer failures, 0 output buffers swapped out
     40 carrier transitions
     DCD=up  DSR=up  DTR=up  RTS=up  CTS=up
Router1#
```

The fifth line indicates the encapsulation type as being HDLC.

PPP

PPP, or Point-To-Point Protocol, is a Data Link protocol that is supported on many types of physical links, including asynchronous (modems), ISDN, synchronous serial, and High-Speed Serial Interface (HSSI). PPP includes support for multiprotocols and, therefore, is one of the more common encapsulation types. It is defined in RFC 1631, which has since been updated in RFC 2153. This means that most vendors implement the same protocol; therefore, this is the primary protocol used over serial link devices when communicating between multiple vendors.

PPP is the descendant of SLIP, Serial Line Interface Protocol. The features that were missing in SLIP were integrated into PPP, including authentication and encryption.

There are two types of authentication included in PPP: PAP and CHAP. PAP, or Password Authentication Protocol, is the weaker of the password encryptions because the password is sent in clear text across the link. This makes it susceptible to playback attacks where a hacker intercepts the password and then plays it back from the hacker's location.

CHAP, Challenge Handshake Authentication Protocol, is a stronger authentication protocol because the password is not sent across the wire. Instead, a challenge is sent from the first node defining a specific algorithm to use. This algorithm is performed on the password and the result is sent back. The first node then performs the same algorithm on its password and checks the result against that which was returned. If they match, the password is the same.

To initiate PPP as the encapsulation type, we need to use the **encapsulation** command. We will perform this on our network shown in Figure 14–2.

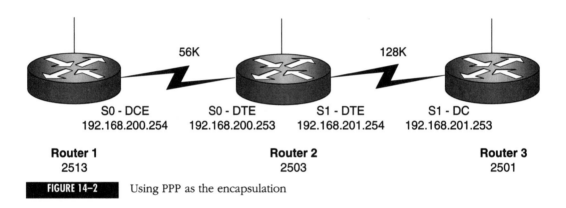

| **FIGURE 14–2** | Using PPP as the encapsulation |

We will use the PPP encapsulation between Routers 1 and 2.

```
Router1(config)#int s0
Router1(config-if)#encaps ?
  atm-dxi      ATM-DXI encapsulation
  frame-relay  Frame Relay networks
  hdlc         Serial HDLC synchronous
  lapb         LAPB (X.25 Level 2)
  ppp          Point-to-Point protocol
  smds         Switched Megabit Data Service (SMDS)
  x25          X.25

Router1(config-if)#encaps ppp
Router1(config-if)#
%LINEPROTO-5-UPDOWN: Line protocol on Interface Serial0, changed state to down
```

Notice that as soon as we changed the encapsulation type, the interface went down. This occurred because Router 2 has not been changed. We will do that now.

```
Router2(config)#int s0
Router2(config-if)#encaps ppp
Router2(config-if)#
%LINEPROTO-5-UPDOWN: Line protocol on Interface Serial0, changed state to up
```

The link came back up, and now we can use ping to verify connectivity. Remember that the encapsulation type must be the same only for directly connected devices. Router 2 and Router 3 are communicating through HDLC. Router 2 will strip off the encapsulation and pass it to the Network layer. Once the path is determined through Router 2 to Router 3, Router 2 will encapsulate it with the HDLC encapsulation type for transmission.

```
Router1#ping 192.168.201.253

Type escape sequence to abort.
Sending 5, 100-byte ICMP Echos to 192.168.201.253, timeout is 2 seconds:
!!!!!
Success rate is 100 percent (5/5), round-trip min/avg/max = 48/49/52 ms
Router1#
```

We proved that the encapsulation type only needs to be the same between two devices. We can verify the encapsulation type by using the **sho int s0** command.

```
Router1#sho int s0
Serial0 is up, line protocol is up
  Hardware is HD64570
  Internet address is 192.168.200.254/24
  MTU 1500 bytes, BW 1544 Kbit, DLY 20000 usec, rely 255/255, load 1/255
  Encapsulation PPP, loopback not set, keepalive set (10 sec)
  LCP Open
  Open: IPCP, CDPCP
  Last input 00:00:00, output 00:00:03, output hang never
  Last clearing of "show interface" counters never
  Queueing strategy: fifo
  Output queue 0/40, 295 drops; input queue 0/75, 0 drops
  5 minute input rate 0 bits/sec, 0 packets/sec
  5 minute output rate 0 bits/sec, 0 packets/sec
     8633 packets input, 710560 bytes, 0 no buffer
     Received 7211 broadcasts, 0 runts, 0 giants, 0 throttles
     0 input errors, 0 CRC, 0 frame, 0 overrun, 0 ignored, 0 abort
     7376 packets output, 539801 bytes, 0 underruns
     0 output errors, 0 collisions, 28 interface resets
     0 output buffer failures, 0 output buffers swapped out
     50 carrier transitions
     DCD=up  DSR=up  DTR=up  RTS=up  CTS=up
Router1#
```

If we wanted to set up authentication between the two routers, we would need to specify a name and password on each router. Once that is done we could then specify the type and order of authentication to use. For example, we will set up authentication between Router 1 and Router 2.

```
Router1(config)#username Router2 password secret
Router1(config)#int s0
Router1(config-if)#ppp ?
  authentication  Set PPP link authentication method
  bridge          Enable PPP bridge translation
  chap            Set CHAP authentication parameters
  compression     Enable PPP Compression control negotiation
  max-bad-auth    Allow multiple authentication failures
  multilink       Make interface multilink capable
  pap             Set PAP authentication parameters
  quality         Set minimum Link Quality before link is down
  reliable-link   Use LAPB with PPP to provide a reliable link
  timeout         Set PPP timeout parameters
  use-tacacs      Use TACACS to verify PPP authentications

Router1(config-if)#ppp authentication ?
  chap     Challenge Handshake Authentication Protocol (CHAP)
  ms-chap  Microsoft Challenge Handshake Authentication Protocol (MS-CHAP)

  pap      Password Authentication Protocol (PAP)

Router1(config-if)#ppp authentication chap ?
  callin   Authenticate remote on incoming call only
  ms-chap  Microsoft Challenge Handshake Authentication Protocol (MS-CHAP)

  pap      Password Authentication Protocol (PAP)
  <cr>

Router1(config-if)#ppp authentication chap pap ?
  callin   Authenticate remote on incoming call only
  ms-chap  Microsoft Challenge Handshake Authentication Protocol (MS-CHAP)

  <cr>

Router1(config-if)#ppp authentication chap pap
Router1(config-if)#
%LINEPROTO-5-UPDOWN: Line protocol on Interface Serial0, changed state to down
```

First, we specified the name of the remote router, Router 2, and that we expect Router 2 to use the password secret. In fact, on Cisco routers, both have to use the same password.

Next, we specified that Serial 0 should use **ppp authentication**, and we specified **chap** and then **pap**, in that order. If Router 2 did not support **chap**, then it would be able to authenticate using **pap**. If we did not want to accept the weaker encryption type, we would just specify **chap**.

Notice the line went down immediately. The authentication immediately failed, and thus the link went down. We can actually monitor this through the use of the **debug ppp authentication** command.

```
Router1#debug ppp authe
PPP authentication debugging is on
Router1#
Se0 PPP: Phase is AUTHENTICATING, by this end
Se0 CHAP: O CHALLENGE id 78 len 28 from "Router1"
Se0 PPP: Phase is AUTHENTICATING, by this end
Se0 CHAP: O CHALLENGE id 79 len 28 from "Router1"
Se0 PPP: Phase is AUTHENTICATING, by this end
Se0 CHAP: O CHALLENGE id 80 len 28 from "Router1"
```

To finish the authentication, we need to modify Router 2.

```
Router2(config)#username Router1 password secret
Router2(config)#
%LINEPROTO-5-UPDOWN: Line protocol on Interface Serial0, changed state to up
```

Note how the serial link came up immediately. We configured Router 2 to supply the correct password to Router 1. Also, since we did not configure authentication on Router 2, the authentication is occurring in only one direction.

```
Router2(config)#int s0
Router2(config-if)#ppp auth chap
```

Now authentication is occurring in both directions. If we were to try to switch one of the routers the link would go down and stay down until we reconfigured the new router.

ISDN

ISDN is a digital service that is designed to run over standard copper telephone cables. ISDN stands for Integrated Services Digital Network, and can support both voice and data over the same line at the same time. With ISDN, we can provide better quality telephone service, faster data transfer, videoconferencing, and faster initial connections.

ISDN is actually a group of protocols that have been updated many times since the initial birth in the late 1960s. The International Telecommunication Union Telecommunication Standardization Sector (ITU-U) has defined the protocols into three groups, or series.

- **E Series.** This series defines the protocol specifications that deal with the existing telephone standards. All protocols begin with an "E" in this series, and E.164 is an example.

- **I Series.** The "I" series defines the protocol concepts, terminology, and services that ISDN uses. Protocols begin with "I," and I.100 is an example.
- **Q Series.** This series defines the switching and signaling aspects of ISDN. Protocols begin with "Q," and an example protocol is Q.921.

ISDN can use several different encapsulation types, including HDLC, which is the default, PPP, and LAPD (Link Access Procedure D channel). Again, both ends of the connection must be running the same encapsulation type.

There are some acronyms that are associated with ISDN that should be covered before going any further.

- **TE1—Terminal Endpoint 1.** This is a device that has an ISDN interface built in to the device. An example would be the Cisco 2503 router.
- **TE2—Terminal Endpoint 2.** This is a device that does not directly connect to ISDN. Instead, the device requires a TA to connect to ISDN.
- **TA—Terminal Adapter.** A device that connects a TE2 device to ISDN and converts the signals to BRI.
- **NT1—Network Termination 1.** Converts the BRI signal into the actual signal used on the service provider's line.
- **NT2—Network Termination 2.** A device or junction in which all TE1 and TA devices are combined and multiplexed to the ISDN line. Such a device could be an ISDN switch for multiple business phones.
- **R Reference Point.** This references the point between the TE2 and TA devices.
- **S Reference Point.** This references the point between the TE1 and an NT2 device.
- **T Reference Point.** This references the point between the NT2 and the NT1 devices.
- **U Reference Point.** This references the point between the NT1 and the service provider's line.

ISDN is delivered in two different service types: BRI and PRI.

BRI

BRI, Basic Rate Interface, provides two channels (B or bearer channels) that provide 64 Kbps of bandwidth. Additionally, there is a single channel (D or delta channel) that is used for control and signaling. The bandwidth for this channel is 16 Kbps. BRI is sometimes referred to as 2B+D.

To connect to ISDN using BRI, we either need a router with a BRI interface (such as the 2503 and the 2520), or we need to buy an ISDN modem to connect to our serial interface. Additionally, we need to find out if the service provider provides the NT1. The NT1 is a device that converts the BRI into a form the ISDN line uses. In the United States, the customer is typically responsible for the NT1. If this is the case, we need to ensure that we have a U interface (refer back to the U Reference Point), which includes the NT1.

Let's walk through the configuration steps for a BRI interface using a 2503 router.

```
Router2(config)#isdn ?
  leased-line       Sets a BRI interface to support leased lines on B & D
                    channels
  switch-type       Select the ISDN switch type
  tei-negotiation   Set when ISDN TEI negotiation should occur (global)

Router2(config)#isdn switch-type ?
  basic-1tr6     1TR6 switch type for Germany
  basic-5ess     AT&T 5ESS switch type for the U.S.
  basic-dms100   Northern DMS-100 switch type
  basic-net3     NET3 switch type for UK and Europe
  basic-ni       National ISDN switch type
  basic-ts013    TS013 switch type for Australia
  ntt            NTT switch type for Japan
  vn3            VN3 and VN4 switch types for France
  <cr>

Router2(config)#isdn switch-type basic-dms100

Router2(config)#int bri0
Router2(config-if)#ip addr 192.168.3.254 255.255.255.0
Router2(config-if)#isdn spid1 1234567
Router2(config-if)#isdn spid2 7654321
Router2(config-if)#encaps ppp
Router2(config-if)#dialer load-threshold 128
```

The first thing that needs to be done is to specify the type of ISDN switch the service provider is using. If this is incorrectly set, the ISDN interface will not be able to negotiate a connection.

Next, we modify the BRI interface and give it an IP address (if we are using TCP/IP). We also need to specify the SPID (Service Profile Identifiers). This could be considered the phone number, and it is made up of seven digits. By having the SPID, the Central Office (CO) will allow us to make ISDN calls. We have a SPID for each B channel.

The last line allows us to bring up the second B channel when the load reaches 50%. The load threshold is based on 255 units. 128/255 is roughly 50%.

We could also use the command **dialer-list** to specify *interesting traffic*. Interesting traffic is traffic that is permitted through an access list. By doing this, we are essentially creating a filter that traffic must get through before the ISDN line is brought up. This allows us to keep costs down on the ISDN line.

We can view the information about the BRI interface by using the **show int bri0** and the **show isdn** commands.

```
Router2#show isdn ?
  active    ISDN active calls
  history   ISDN call history
  memory    ISDN memory information
  status    ISDN Line Status
  timers    ISDN Timer values

Router2#show isdn status
Global ISDN Switchtype = basic-dms100
ISDN BRI0 interface
        dsl 0, interface ISDN Switchtype = basic-dms100
    Layer 1 Status:
        DEACTIVATED
    Layer 2 Status:
        Layer 2 NOT Activated
    Spid Status:
        TEI Not Assigned, ces = 1, state = 1(terminal down)
            spid1 configured, no LDN, spid1 NOT sent, spid1 NOT valid
        TEI Not Assigned, ces = 2, state = 1(terminal down)
            spid2 configured, no LDN, spid2 NOT sent, spid2 NOT valid
    Layer 3 Status:
        0 Active Layer 3 Call(s)
    Activated dsl 0 CCBs = 0
    Total Allocated ISDN CCBs = 0
Router2#show isdn history
-----------------------------------------------------------------------------
                             ISDN CALL HISTORY
-----------------------------------------------------------------------------
History Table MaxLength = 100 entries
History Retain Timer = 15 Minutes
-----------------------------------------------------------------------------
Call Calling     Called       Duration   Remote   Time until    Recorded Charges
Type Number      Number       Seconds    Name     Disconnect    Units/Currency
-----------------------------------------------------------------------------
-----------------------------------------------------------------------------

Router2#
```

PRI

Primary Rate Interface (PRI) is an ISDN service that is composed of 23 B channels and a single D channel. PRI is also referred to as 23B+1D. The D channel is 64 Kbps in bandwidth, and the total bandwidth is 1.544 Mbps. This is also referred to as a T1 or DS1. This type of PRI is found in the United States and Japan.

In most of the world, the PRI is 30B+1D for a total of 2.048 Mbps, and is referred to as an E1.

PRI does not connect to an NT1 device. Instead, it connects to a CSU/DSU. Configuring a PRI includes specifying the **framing**, **linecode**, and **pri-group timeslots**.

Frame Relay

Frame Relay is probably the most popular WAN protocol. It is a Data Link layer protocol that can be used to connect multiple routers anywhere in the world.

Perhaps the biggest feature of Frame Relay is the ability to share bandwidth with other users without having to pay the cost of a full T1 or leased line. Instead, an office that may be located in Minneapolis requests a specific Local Access Rate from a service provider. This rate is the speed of the connection between the office and the provider. Suppose that Minneapolis requested a 56 Kbps link. The service provider would give the office a DLCI (Data Link Connection Identifier) that maps the router at the office to the Frame Relay switch at the service provider. More importantly, it maps the router's network address to the DLCI. Now imagine that the remote office in Denver also orders a connection of 56 Kbps to their local provider. They would also be given a DLCI.

Once both offices are set up, the network engineers would set up a Frame Relay map that is similar to a static route. The DLCI for each router would be used to create a Permanent Virtual Circuit (PVC), which is similar to having a leased line. Data between the two offices will be switched through the Frame Relay cloud to arrive at the opposite site. Denver and Minneapolis would then be able to communicate through their own virtual private channel.

When each of the offices subscribed to a 56 Kbps, the speed is considered the Committed Information Rate (CIR). This means that at any time, the office will be guaranteed 56 Kbps bandwidth. This also means the offices pay for the full 56 Kbps. However, if the T1 that is being shared between multiple offices is not being fully utilized, it is possible for a single office to use more than the 56 Kbps. This is known as Excess Burst. Although the burst cannot be relied upon, this is the reason that the 56 Kbps link seems faster at night when everyone has gone home. It probably is running faster than 56 Kbps!

Configuring Frame Relay on Cisco Routers

To configure a Frame Relay, we will need a new network diagram. In Figure 14–3, we have three routers connected through different speeds, or local access rates, to a Frame Relay cloud. The routers belong to the same network of 192.168.200.0. The subset picture is the logical look at how the routers are configured. This is called the "hub and spoke" configuration, where Router 1 is the hub.

To continue our understanding of Frame Relay, we will start configuring with Router 1.

```
Router1(config)#int s0
Router1(config-if)#ip addr 192.168.200.254 255.255.255.0
Router1(config-if)#encaps frame-relay ?
  ietf  Use RFC1490 encapsulation
```

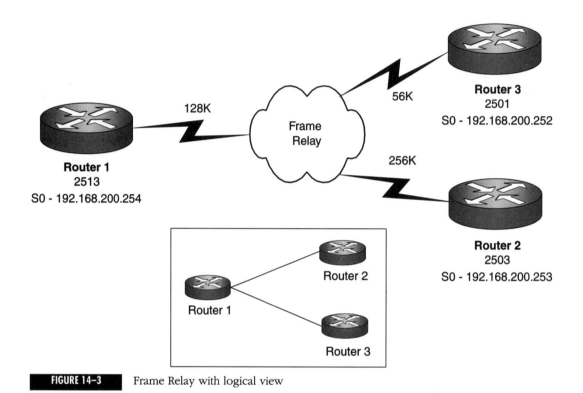

FIGURE 14–3   Frame Relay with logical view

```
<cr>
Router1(config-if)#encaps frame-relay
Router1(config-if)#no shut
Router1(config-if)#
%LINEPROTO-5-UPDOWN: Line protocol on Interface Serial0, changed state to up
%LINK-3-UPDOWN: Interface Serial0, changed state to up
%FR-5-DLCICHANGE: Interface Serial0 - DLCI 102 state changed to ACTIVE
%FR-5-DLCICHANGE: Interface Serial0 - DLCI 103 state changed to ACTIVE
```

When we changed the encapsulation type to Frame Relay, we had a single choice offered to us. The **ietf** type is used when connecting a Cisco router to a non-Cisco router. The default, however, is cisco encapsulation. We chose to stay with the cisco type because we are only connecting to Cisco routers.

Notice that we have some new status messages appearing. The DLCIs have been assigned automatically to our interface. The PVC has automatically been created through a process called "inverse arp." When we configured the interface to be part of a Frame Relay cloud, the router contacted the Frame Relay switch and asked to be identified. The switch sent back the DLCI number for the interface. Next, the router sent a request asking for other routers that it knows about. There aren't any at this time, so no response is returned.

We can examine the PVC at this time by issuing the command **show frame-relay pvc**.

```
Router1#sho frame pvc

PVC Statistics for interface Serial0 (Frame Relay DTE)

DLCI = 102, DLCI USAGE = UNUSED, PVC STATUS = ACTIVE, INTERFACE = Serial0

   input pkts 251          output pkts 19          in bytes 77594
   out bytes 570           dropped pkts 0          in FECN pkts 0
   in BECN pkts 0          out FECN pkts 0         out BECN pkts 0
   in DE pkts 0            out DE pkts 0
   out bcast pkts 19        out bcast bytes 570           Num Pkts Switched 0

   pvc create time 00:18:01, last time pvc status changed 00:18:01

DLCI = 103, DLCI USAGE = UNUSED, PVC STATUS = ACTIVE, INTERFACE = Serial0

   input pkts 251          output pkts 19          in bytes 77594
   out bytes 570           dropped pkts 0          in FECN pkts 0
   in BECN pkts 0          out FECN pkts 0         out BECN pkts 0
   in DE pkts 0            out DE pkts 0
   out bcast pkts 19        out bcast bytes 570           Num Pkts Switched 0

   pvc create time 00:18:01, last time pvc status changed 00:18:02
Router1#
```

Router 1 has dynamically configured itself with two DLCIs.
Let's continue on to Router 2.

```
Router2(config)#int s0
Router2(config-if)#ip addr 192.168.200.253 255.255.255.0
Router2(config-if)#encap frame
Router2(config-if)#no shut
Router2(config-if)#
%LINEPROTO-5-UPDOWN: Line protocol on Interface Serial0, changed state to up
%LINK-3-UPDOWN: Interface Serial0, changed state to up
%FR-5-DLCICHANGE: Interface Serial0 - DLCI 201 state changed to ACTIVE
```

Again we were assigned a DLCI dynamically through inverse ARP. This time, however, the router did receive a response from the Frame Relay switch telling it the DLCI number of Router 1. Next, Router 2 sent out a request asking for Router 1 to identify itself by returning its network address. This response was received and placed into a map. We can examine this map with the command **show frame-relay map**.

```
Router2#sho frame map
Serial0 (up): ip 192.168.200.254 dlci 201(0xC9,0x3090), dynamic,
             broadcast,, status defined, active
Router2#
```

The map shows that the router 192.168.200.254 can be reached through the local DLCI of 201. If we ping, the packet would be sent through the serial interface to the Frame Relay switch, where it will be switched to Router 1.

```
Router2#ping 192.168.200.254

Type escape sequence to abort.
Sending 5, 100-byte ICMP Echos to 192.168.200.254, timeout is 2 seconds:
!!!!!
Success rate is 100 percent (5/5), round-trip min/avg/max = 24/26/28 ms
Router2#
```

The same is true with Router 1. It has been told that there is a new router attached to the cloud, and that Router 1 asked for the network address of Router 2. In fact, they will continue asking each other through Inverse ARP messages every 60 seconds for the network addresses of each other.

There is a downside to using the Inverse ARP. This method will only work when all routers are connected to the same Frame Relay switch. If the routers span multiple switches, we must enter the map table manually. Inverse ARP will not be able to fill it in for us.

Let's finish by configuring Router 3.

```
Router3(config)#int s0
Router3(config-if)#ip addr 192.168.200.252 255.255.255.0
Router3(config-if)#encap fram
Router3(config-if)#no shut
Router3(config-if)#

%LINEPROTO-5-UPDOWN: Line protocol on Interface Serial0, changed state to up
%LINK-3-UPDOWN: Interface Serial0, changed state to up
%FR-5-DLCICHANGE: Interface Serial0 - DLCI 301 state changed to ACTIVE
```

We can verify our DLCI and the mappings using the show commands as described previously. Instead, let's test connectivity by pinging the hub router, Router1.

```
Router3#ping 192.168.200.254

Type escape sequence to abort.
Sending 5, 100-byte ICMP Echos to 192.168.200.254, timeout is 2 seconds:
!!!!!
Success rate is 100 percent (5/5), round-trip min/avg/max = 48/50/52 ms
Router3#
```

As expected, we did receive a reply. But what happens if we want to access the other spoke router?

```
Router3#ping 192.168.200.253

Type escape sequence to abort.
```

```
Sending 5, 100-byte ICMP Echos to 192.168.200.253, timeout is 2 seconds:
.....
Success rate is 0 percent (0/5)
Router3#
```

We are unable to reach Router 2! The problem stems from the fact that Router 2 and Router 3 do not know about each other, and therefore the Frame Relay map does not have the route included.

To get around this, we will create static Frame Relay maps on Routers 2 and 3. This could also occur, as noted earlier, if the routers span multiple Frame Relay switches.

```
Router3(config)#int s0
Router3(config-if)#frame map ?
  appletalk  AppleTalk
  bridge     Bridging
  decnet     DECnet
  ip         IP
  ipx        Novell IPX
  llc2       llc2


Router3(config-if)#frame map ip ?
  A.B.C.D  Protocol specific address

Router3(config-if)#frame map ip 192.168.200.253 ?
  <16-1007>  DLCI

Router3(config-if)#frame map ip 192.168.200.253 301 ?
  broadcast            Broadcasts should be forwarded to this address
  cisco                Use CISCO Encapsulation
  compress             Enable TCP/IP and RTP/IP header compression
  ietf                 Use RFC1490 Encapsulation
  nocompress           Do not compress TCP/IP headers
  payload-compression  Use payload compression
  rtp                  RTP header compression parameters
  tcp                  TCP header compression parameters
  <cr>

Router3(config-if)#frame map ip 192.168.200.253 301 broadcast ?
  broadcast            Broadcasts should be forwarded to this address
  cisco                Use CISCO Encapsulation
  compress             Enable TCP/IP and RTP/IP header compression
  ietf                 Use RFC1490 Encapsulation
  nocompress           Do not compress TCP/IP headers
  payload-compression  Use payload compression
  rtp                  RTP header compression parameters
  tcp                  TCP header compression parameters
  <cr>

Router3(config-if)#frame map ip 192.168.200.253 301 broadcast
Router3(config-if)#^Z
```

```
Router3#
%SYS-5-CONFIG_I: Configured from console by console
Router3#sho frame map
Serial0 (up): ip 192.168.200.253 dlci 301(0x12D,0x48D0), static,
              broadcast,
              CISCO, status defined, active
Serial0 (up): ip 192.168.200.254 dlci 301(0x12D,0x48D0), dynamic,
              broadcast,, status defined, active
Router3#
```

To add to the Frame Relay map, we have to specify the interface that we are modifying. The command is similar to the static route command. We are specifying that any IP packets that are destined for 192.168.200.253 should go out the interface with the source DLCI as 301. The broadcast parameter at the end of the line forwards broadcasts to this address. This is useful if we want to forward routing updates such as RIP.

Finally, we looked at the Frame Relay map and saw the new entry. Once we do the same steps to Router 2, we will be able to ping Router 2 from Router 3, and vice versa.

```
Router2(config)#int s0
Router2(config-if)#frame map ip 192.168.200.252 201
Router2(config-if)#^Z

Router2#sho frame map
Serial0 (up): ip 192.168.200.252 dlci 201(0xC9,0x3090), static,
              CISCO, status defined, active
Serial0 (up): ip 192.168.200.254 dlci 201(0xC9,0x3090), dynamic,
              broadcast,, status defined, active

Router2#ping 192.168.200.252

Type escape sequence to abort.
Sending 5, 100-byte ICMP Echos to 192.168.200.252, timeout is 2 seconds:
!!!!!
Success rate is 100 percent (5/5), round-trip min/avg/max = 72/74/84 ms
Router2#
```

We now have a fully functional network spanning a Frame Relay cloud.

There is one other parameter we may be interested in. There is a communication mechanism that is used between DTE devices (routers) and the Frame Relay switch. This is known as Local Management Interface, or simply LMI. This mechanism is used to maintain flow of data between the devices, update the status of DLCIs, and use multicast addressing for global DLCIs. The LMI defaults to the type cisco, but can be configured to any of the following:

```
Router2(config)#int s0
Router2(config-if)#frame-relay lmi-type ?
  cisco
```

```
ansi
q933a
```

The service provider of the Frame Relay cloud determines which type to use. However, it should be pointed out that beginning with IOS 11.2, the LMI type uses an autosense method to set it dynamically.

Subinterfaces

There are times when we might not want to have multiple DLCI numbers assigned to the same physical port. For instance, we may want to connect multiple subnets to the hub router. Also, when Frame Relay is enabled, by default Split Horizon is disabled.

Remember that Split Horizon helps prevent routing loops by not broadcasting the announcements it heard from an interface back through the same interface. Distance Vector routing protocols such as RIP do not know about PVCs, and therefore will not broadcast back out the same interface. The default solution is to turn off Split Horizon. This can be a bad thing, though, because routing loops can be created. To combat this, we will use a different network diagram as shown in Figure 14–4.

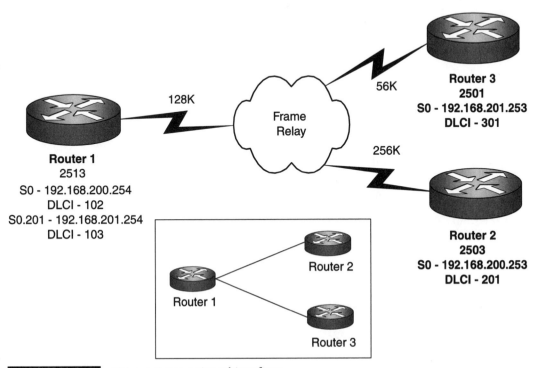

FIGURE 14–4   Using point-to-point subinterfaces

We can see that there are now two subnets, and although they are sharing the same physical interface, it will appear to Distance Vector protocols
that there are two separate interfaces. This allows us to use Split Horizon in
our network.

The first thing to do is change the IP addresses on Routers 2 and 3.

```
Router2(config)#int s0
Router2(config-if)#ip addr 192.168.200.253 255.255.255.0
Router2(config-if)#no frame map ip 192.168.200.252

Router3(config)#int s0
Router3(config-if)#ip addr 192.168.201.253 255.255.255.0
Router3(config-if)#no frame map ip 192.168.200.253
Router3(config-if)#exit
Router3(config)#router rip
Router3(config-router)#no network 192.168.200.0
Router3(config-router)#network 192.168.201.0
Router3(config-router)#^Z
```

We have cleared our mapping because we will be using routing through
Router 1 to reach the other spoke router. Therefore, all traffic will flow
through Router 1.

Next, we need to change a couple of things on Router 1.

```
Router1(config-if)#no ip addr 192.168.200.254 255.255.255.0
Router1(config)#int s0.200 ?
  multipoint       Treat as a multipoint link
  point-to-point   Treat as a point-to-point link
Router1(config)#int s0.200 point
```

First, we removed the IP address from the physical interface. Instead, we
will be using addresses on the subinterfaces. Next, we specified that the interface S0.200 will be a point-to-point link. If we wanted to have a single subnet
address and have it connected to multiple routers, we could use multilink. This
is essentially what we did with the physical interface. However, multilink does
NOT turn off Split Horizon, so routing tables will not propagate properly.

```
Router1(config-subif)#ip addr 192.168.200.254 255.255.255.0
Router1(config-subif)#frame ?
  class                Define a map class on the interface
  de-group             Associate a DE group with a DLCI
  interface-dlci       Define a DLCI as part of a subinterface
  inverse-arp          Enable/disable inverse ARP on a DLCI
  ip                   Frame Relay Internet Protocol config commands
  map                  Map a protocol address to a DLCI address
  payload-compression  Use payload compression
  priority-dlci-group  Define a priority group of DLCIs
```

```
Router1(config-subif)#frame interface ?
  <16-1007>  Define a DLCI as part of the current subinterface

Router1(config-subif)#frame interface 102
```

By issuing the interface command, we are specifying that DLCI 102 belongs to this subinterface. If we did not do that, then the DLCIs would be assigned to the physical address instead.

```
Router1(config-fr-dlci)#exit
Router1(config)#int s0.201 point
Router1(config-subif)#ip addr 192.168.201.254 255.255.255.0
Router1(config-subif)#frame int 103
Router1(config-subif)#exit
Router1(config)#router rip
Router1(config-router)#network 192.168.201.0
```

We also started advertising the new network.

Now it's time to check our PVCs and make sure they are configured correctly.

```
Router1#sho frame pvc

PVC Statistics for interface Serial0 (Frame Relay DTE)

DLCI = 102, DLCI USAGE = LOCAL, PVC STATUS = ACTIVE, INTERFACE = Serial0.200

  input pkts 17            output pkts 8           in bytes 1022
  out bytes 1129           dropped pkts 0          in FECN pkts 0
  in BECN pkts 0           out FECN pkts 0         out BECN pkts 0
  in DE pkts 0             out DE pkts 0
  out bcast pkts 8           out bcast bytes 1129
  pvc create time 00:05:08, last time pvc status changed 00:05:08

DLCI = 103, DLCI USAGE = LOCAL, PVC STATUS = ACTIVE, INTERFACE = Serial0.201

  input pkts 17            output pkts 1           in bytes 1062
  out bytes 283            dropped pkts 0          in FECN pkts 0
  in BECN pkts 0           out FECN pkts 0         out BECN pkts 0
  in DE pkts 0             out DE pkts 0
  out bcast pkts 1           out bcast bytes 283
  pvc create time 00:05:09, last time pvc status changed 00:05:09
Router1#
```

We can see that the DLCIs have been mapped to the correct subinterfaces. This was automatically done for us through Inverse ARP. Next, we can check our frame map table.

```
Router1#sho frame map
Serial0.200 (up): point-to-point dlci, dlci 102(0x66,0x1860), broadcast
           status defined, active
```

```
Serial0.201 (up): point-to-point dlci, dlci 103(0x67,0x1870), broadcast
        status defined, active
Router1#
```

Notice that the mapping is identified as a point-to-point for each sub-interface.

Once we turn Split Horizon back on, all the interfaces will have RIP running as it should be used.

```
Router1(config)#int s0.200
Router1(config-subif)#ip split
Router1(config-subif)#exit
Router1(config)#int s0.201
Router1(config-subif)#ip split

Router2(config)#int s0
Router2(config-if)#ip split

Router3(config)#int s0
Router3(config-if)#ip split
```

We can debug RIP at this point to ensure that it is working correctly. Using point-to-point PVCs allows us the flexibility to use multiple network addresses through the same interface.

Summary

WAN protocols are used throughout the world to connect LANs together for the purpose of exchanging information. HDLC is a standard protocol, but vendors implement their own version to overcome the lack of multiprotocol support. PPP is a protocol that is defined in the RFCs and is compatible between different vendors. PPP can be used between Cisco and non-Cisco routers. PPP supports encryption and authentication, including PAP and CHAP. ISDN is a digital service that is used to provide both voice and data over existing telephone cables. ISDN consists of PRI (23B+1D), that has a maximum bandwidth of 1.544 Mbps, and BRI (2B+1D), which can have a bandwidth of 192 Kbps. Each B channel is 64 Kbps, and the D channel, used for control and session establishment and teardown, is 16 Kbps. The D channel for a PRI is 64 Kbps. Frame Relay gives a business the ability to share bandwidth with other businesses over a T1 line. By subscribing to a specific bandwidth (the Committed Information Rate, or CIR), the business is guaranteed that amount of bandwidth. Frame Relay uses PVC identifiers called DLCIs to set up the permanent connection between two or more routers. Frame Relay encapsulation types include cisco and ietf. Additionally, Frame Relay uses LMIs to manage the connection between the DTE and the provider's switch. LMI encapsulation types include ansi, cisco, and q933I, but starting with IOS 11.2, the router will autosense the type. Subinterfaces can be used with Frame Relay to provide multiple logical interfaces within the same physical interface.

Scenario Lab 14.1

After learning about Frame Relay in more detail, you are shocked to discover that all along, you have been running RIP with Split Horizon disabled for the Frame Relay interfaces (see Figure 14–5). Luckily, no router loops developed, so now would be a good time to create documentation establishing a way to use Split Horizon across each of the interfaces. When you have finished, giving it to the CIO in the proper manner will make it appear as if you are truly managing the network at all times. Another raise is in order!

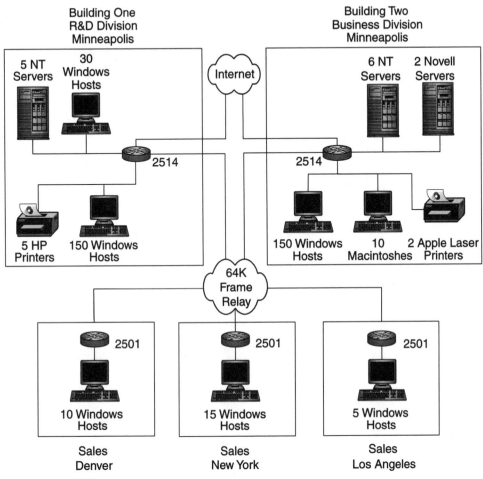

FIGURE 14–5 Network Solutions requiring access lists

Exam Objective Checklist

By working through this chapter, you should have sufficient knowledge to answer these exam objectives:

- Differentiate between the following WAN services: Frame Relay, ISDN/LAPD, HDLC, and PPP.
- Recognize key Frame Relay terms and features.
- List commands to configure Frame Relay LMIs, maps, and subinterfaces.
- List commands to monitor Frame Relay operation in the router.
- Identify PPP operations to encapsulate WAN data on Cisco routers.
- State a relevant use and context for ISDN networking.
- Identify ISDN protocols, function groups, reference points, and channels.
- Describe Cisco's implementation of ISDN BRI.

Practice Questions

1. Which of the following are valid serial line encapsulation types? (Select all that apply)

    a. frame-relay
    b. ppp
    c. hdlc
    d. slip

2. BRI is sometimes referred to as what?

    a. 23B+1D
    b. 30B+1D
    c. 3B+1D
    d. 2B+1D

3. What are the correct speeds for the B and D channels?

    a. 64 Kbps/64 Kbps
    b. 64 Kbps/16 Kbps
    c. 16 Kbps/64 Kbps
    d. 16 Kbps/56 Kbps

4. Which set of ISDN protocols is responsible for defining existing telephone networks?

    a. I Series
    b. Q Series
    c. E Series
    d. M Series

5. Which set of ISDN protocols is responsible for defining switching and signaling?

    a. I Series

    b. Q Series

    c. E Series

    d. M Series

6. Which set of ISDN protocols is responsible for defining concepts and terminology?

    a. I Series

    b. Q Series

    c. E Series

    d. M Series

7. What command will show if the ISDN interface and the protocol is up?

    a. show bri 0

    b. show int bri 0

    c. show int isdn

    d. show int isdn 0

8. Which command will set the ISDN switch type to DMS100?

    a. isdn switch basic-dms100

    b. isdn encaps basic-dms100

    c. encaps isdn basic-dms100

    d. switch isdn basic-dms100

9. Which is the default LMI type?

    a. ansi

    b. q933a

    c. cisco

    d. hdlc

10. Which frame relay encapsulation type is required if the two connecting devices are not both Cisco?

    a. cisco

    b. ppp

    c. hdlc

    d. ietf

11. Which command would show the DLCIs as they have been assigned through Inverse ARP?

    a. show frame pvc
    b. show frame dlci
    c. show dlci
    d. show pvc

12. Which command will establish a static frame mapping from Router 1 (192.168.17.1) with DLCI 120 to Router 2 (192.168.17.2) with DLCI 130?

    a. frame map ip 192.168.17.1 130
    b. frame map ip 192.168.17.2 130
    c. frame map ip 192.168.17.1 120
    d. frame map ip 192.168.17.2 120

Extra Features of the Cisco Router

In This Chapter

There are many features of the Cisco router that have not been covered in this book. While many of those features are specific in nature, there are a few items that can help while troubleshooting networks. In this chapter, we examine the Cisco Discovery Protocol and some of the more common **show** and **debug** commands. We also examine how we can use Telnet to connect to multiple routers for configuration from remote sites. Finally, we look at how we can do some basic logging of status messages and have some user accountability for any changes.

Cisco Discovery Protocol

CDP is a Cisco proprietary protocol that runs at the Data Link layer. This protocol, when a Cisco device boots up, sends out broadcasts looking for any neighboring Cisco devices that are also running CDP. This protocol became available with IOS 10.3. Since this runs at the Data Link layer, the devices can be running any upper-layer protocol and still show in the CDP list.

CDP is sent to the multicast address of 0100.0ccc.cccc through all interfaces. Since it is a multicast, it will only propagate to directly connected devices, and no further. This multicast is sent every 60 seconds by default.

To examine the details of CDP, refer to the network diagram in Figure 15–1. We have set up the routers in a Hub and Spoke formation. There is also a 10/100 Mbps switch running off of the hub router, which we have named HubRouter.

To view the current CDP entries, use the command **show cdp neighbors**.

```
HubRouter#sho cdp neigh
Capability Codes: R - Router, T - Trans Bridge, B - Source Route Bridge
                  S - Switch, H - Host, I - IGMP, r - Repeater

Device ID          Local Intrfce     Holdtme    Capability  Platform   Port ID
Switch              Eth 0            146           S        WS-C2916M-Fas 0/2
Spoke2              Ser 1            162           R        2500          Ser 0
Spoke3              Ser 2            162           R        2500          Ser 0
Spoke1              Ser 0            174           R        2500          Ser 0
```

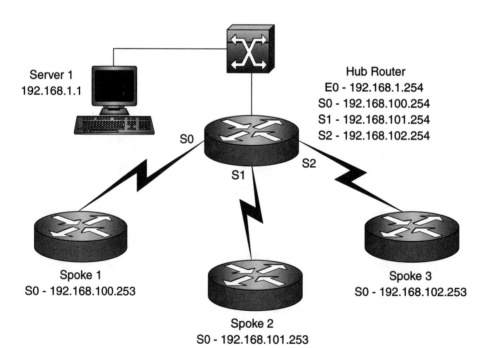

FIGURE 15–1   Hub and spoke layout

Here is a list of all neighbor routers and the switch. The table shows the interface it was detected on, as well as the platform of the device. Each of the routers is listed as a 2500 series model (2501, 2503, and 2513 actually), and the switch is listed as a 2916M. If we want more information on a specific device, we can issue the command **show cdp entry** *hostname*. Let's look at Spoke 3 in detail.

```
HubRouter#sho cdp entry Spoke3
-------------------------
Device ID: Spoke3
Entry address(es):
  IP address: 192.168.102.253
Platform: cisco 2500,  Capabilities: Router
Interface: Serial2,  Port ID (outgoing port): Serial0
Holdtime : 154 sec

Version :
Cisco Internetwork Operating System Software
IOS (tm) 2500 Software (C2500-D-L), Version 11.3(3)T, RELEASE SOFTWARE (fc1)
Copyright (c) 1986-1998 by cisco Systems, Inc.
Compiled Mon 20-Apr-98 17:49 by ccai
```

As we can see, it shows us the IOS version number, the IP address, and any other network addresses such as IPX and AppleTalk, if also configured. If we wanted to look at all of the devices in detail, we could issue the command **sho cdp neighbor detail** or **show cdp entry**.

If we examine the output a little closer, we can see that there is a holdtime. This timer is used to determine if an entry should be removed. The default timer is 180 seconds. This means that if a device has not been heard from in 180 seconds it will be removed from the table. Since all devices announce themselves every 60 seconds, this value should never get below 120 (or close to it at least). This allows for two packets to disappear before being removed from the list.

We can change the interval of the holdtimer by issuing the command **cdp holdtime** *seconds*. This interval is used to tell the neighbor devices how long to hold this device's updates. We will configure Spoke 3 with a holdtime of 45 seconds.

```
Spoke3#conf t
Enter configuration commands, one per line.  End with CNTL/Z.
Spoke3(config)#cdp holdtime 45
Spoke3(config)#^Z
```

To verify our interval, we can use the command **show cdp**. We will also view the new timer on the hub router.

```
Spoke3#sho cdp
Global CDP information:
        Sending CDP packets every 60 seconds
        Sending a holdtime value of 45 seconds
```

```
HubRouter#sho cdp neigh
Capability Codes: R - Router, T - Trans Bridge, B - Source Route Bridge
                  S - Switch, H - Host, I - IGMP, r - Repeater

Device ID      Local Intrfce    Holdtme    Capability  Platform    Port ID
Switch             Eth 0        164            S        WS-C2916M-Fas 0/2
Spoke2             Ser 1        179            R        2500        Ser 0
Spoke3             Ser 2        44             R        2500        Ser 0
Spoke1             Ser 0        131            R        2500        Ser 0
```

Notice that the holdtime is now 44 seconds remaining. What happens when the holdtime expires? Remember that we did not change the interval of the CDP itself, only the holdtime. This means that the entry will expire after 45 seconds, only to be renewed 15 seconds after that. To find out, we will turn on debugging.

```
HubRouter#debug cdp ?
  adjacency   CDP neighbor info
  events      CDP events
  ip          CDP ip info
  packets     CDP packet-related information

HubRouter#debug cdp adj
CDP neighbor info debugging is on
```

By watching the adjacency debugging, we will see the following output occur every 60 seconds.

```
CDP-AD: Aging entry for Spoke3, on interface Serial2
```

To fix this, we need to readjust the CDP announcement timer on Spoke 3. We can do that with the command **cdp timer** *seconds*.

```
Spoke3(config)#cdp timer 30
```

Spoke 3 will now send CDP packets every 30 seconds. This will cause more network traffic, but will also show any problems in our network faster.

If we would like to turn off CDP, we have two options. We can either disable CDP on a specific interface by issuing the command **no cdp enable** in the interface configuration mode, or we can use the command **no cdp run**, which will turn off CDP entirely on that device.

Show Commands

There are hundreds of **show** commands that can be used to help monitor and troubleshoot Cisco routers. While it is beyond the scope of this book and the

CCNA test to cover them all, we will examine some of the more common and/or beneficial commands.

1. **Show access-lists** Used to display the contents of the access lists.
2. **Show buffers** The show buffers command can be used to display the different buffers, the size of each buffer, and the hits and misses of each.

```
HubRouter#show buffers
Buffer elements:
     500 in free list (500 max allowed)
     5994 hits, 0 misses, 0 created

Public buffer pools:
Small buffers, 104 bytes (total 50, permanent 50):
     49 in free list (20 min, 150 max allowed)
     1881 hits, 0 misses, 0 trims, 0 created
     0 failures (0 no memory)
Middle buffers, 600 bytes (total 25, permanent 25):
     25 in free list (10 min, 150 max allowed)
     1497 hits, 0 misses, 0 trims, 0 created
     0 failures (0 no memory)
Big buffers, 1524 bytes (total 50, permanent 50):
     50 in free list (5 min, 150 max allowed)
     334 hits, 0 misses, 0 trims, 0 created
     0 failures (0 no memory)
VeryBig buffers, 4520 bytes (total 10, permanent 10):
     10 in free list (0 min, 100 max allowed)
     0 hits, 0 misses, 0 trims, 0 created
     0 failures (0 no memory)
Large buffers, 5024 bytes (total 0, permanent 0):
     0 in free list (0 min, 10 max allowed)
     0 hits, 0 misses, 0 trims, 0 created
     0 failures (0 no memory)
Huge buffers, 18024 bytes (total 0, permanent 0):
     0 in free list (0 min, 4 max allowed)
     0 hits, 0 misses, 0 trims, 0 created
     0 failures (0 no memory)
```

The buffers range in size from Small to Huge to handle the different size of data packets that are being routed in the router. For example, the Big buffers are usually used for Ethernet packets.

3. **Show CDP [neighbor | interface | entry]** Used to view the CDP information for timers, neighbor protocols, addresses, and platforms.
4. **Show controllers** Used to verify the status and accounting of the various interfaces.
5. **Show debug** Used to show the types of debugging that are currently active.
6. **Show flash [<cr> | all | chips |detailed]** Used to view information about the FLASH and the contents being held in it.

```
HubRouter#show flash all

System flash directory:
File  Length    Name/status
          addr      fcksum  ccksum
  1    6239492   c2500-d-1.113-3.t.bin
          0x40      0x44AF  0x44AF
[6239556 bytes used, 10537660 available, 16777216 total]
16384K bytes of processor board System flash (Read ONLY)

        Chip    Bank    Code      Size      Name
         1       1      01AD     2048KB     AMD    29F016
         2       1      01AD     2048KB     AMD    29F016
         3       1      01AD     2048KB     AMD    29F016
         4       1      01AD     2048KB     AMD    29F016
         1       2      01AD     2048KB     AMD    29F016
         2       2      01AD     2048KB     AMD    29F016
         3       2      01AD     2048KB     AMD    29F016
         4       2      01AD     2048KB     AMD    29F016
Executing current image from System flash
```

7. **Show frame-relay [lmi | route | traffic]** Used to view the various information, including the LMI type and the DLCI to network address mapping for Frame Relay interfaces.

8. **Show interface statistics** Used to view the packets in and out on each of the interfaces.

```
HubRouter#show int stat
Interface BRI0 is disabled

Interface BRI0:1 is disabled

Interface BRI0:2 is disabled

Ethernet0
        Switching path   Pkts In   Chars In   Pkts Out   Chars Out
              Processor       689     149292        950       94104
            Route cache         0          0          0           0
                  Total       689     149292        950       94104
Serial0
        Switching path   Pkts In   Chars In   Pkts Out   Chars Out
              Processor       737      48435        939       63641
            Route cache         0          0          0           0
                  Total       737      48435        939       63641
Serial1
        Switching path   Pkts In   Chars In   Pkts Out   Chars Out
              Processor       715      43107        927       62872
            Route cache         0          0          0           0
                  Total       715      43107        927       62872
```

```
Serial2
            Switching path    Pkts In    Chars In    Pkts Out    Chars Out
                  Processor       766       60543         942        65801
              Route cache          0           0           0            0
                     Total        766       60543         942        65801
Interface Serial3 is disabled
```

9. **Show [ipx/ipx/appletalk] route**   Used to view the routing tables for the various protocols.

10. **Show ip protocols**   Used to view the specific information about the routing protocols, including networks being advertised, and the neighbor routers that are also advertising.

```
HubRouter#sho ip proto
Routing Protocol is "rip"
  Sending updates every 30 seconds, next due in 23 seconds
  Invalid after 180 seconds, hold down 180, flushed after 240
  Outgoing update filter list for all interfaces is
  Incoming update filter list for all interfaces is
  Redistributing: rip
  Default version control: send version 1, receive any version
     Interface        Send  Recv    Key-chain
     Ethernet0          1    1 2
     Serial0            1    1 2
     Serial1            1    1 2
     Serial2            1    1 2
  Routing for Networks:
     192.168.1.0
     192.168.100.0
     192.168.101.0
     192.168.102.0

  Routing Information Sources:
     Gateway            Distance      Last Update
     192.168.101.253        120       01:20:56
  Distance: (default is 120)
```

11. **Show ip traffic**   Used to view the statistics of the various protocols that have been processed by the router, including packets received and sent, broadcasts received and sent, and any detected errors.

```
HubRouter#sho ip traffic
IP statistics:
  Rcvd:  591 total, 321 local destination
         0 format errors, 0 checksum errors, 0 bad hop count
         0 unknown protocol, 0 not a gateway
         0 security failures, 0 bad options, 0 with options
  Opts:  0 end, 0 nop, 0 basic security, 0 loose source route
         0 timestamp, 0 extended security, 0 record route
         0 stream ID, 0 strict source route, 0 alert, 0 cipso
```

```
         0 other
  Frags: 0 reassembled, 0 timeouts, 0 couldn't reassemble
         0 fragmented, 0 couldn't fragment
  Bcast: 259 received, 881 sent
  Mcast: 3 received, 15 sent
  Sent:  922 generated, 0 forwarded
         5 encapsulation failed, 0 no route

ICMP statistics:
  Rcvd: 0 format errors, 0 checksum errors, 0 redirects, 0 unreachable
        15 echo, 10 echo reply, 0 mask requests, 0 mask replies, 0 quench
        0 parameter, 0 timestamp, 0 info request, 0 other
        0 irdp solicitations, 0 irdp advertisements
  Sent: 0 redirects, 0 unreachable, 15 echo, 15 echo reply
        0 mask requests, 0 mask replies, 0 quench, 0 timestamp
        0 info reply, 0 time exceeded, 0 parameter problem
        0 irdp solicitations, 0 irdp advertisements

UDP statistics:
  Rcvd: 296 total, 0 checksum errors, 31 no port
  Sent: 897 total, 0 forwarded broadcasts

TCP statistics:
  Rcvd: 0 total, 0 checksum errors, 0 no port
  Sent: 0 total

Probe statistics:
  Rcvd: 0 address requests, 0 address replies
        0 proxy name requests, 0 where-is requests, 0 other
  Sent: 0 address requests, 0 address replies (0 proxy)
        0 proxy name replies, 0 where-is replies

EGP statistics:
  Rcvd: 0 total, 0 format errors, 0 checksum errors, 0 no listener
  Sent: 0 total

IGRP statistics:
  Rcvd: 0 total, 0 checksum errors
  Sent: 0 total

OSPF statistics:
  Rcvd: 0 total, 0 checksum errors
        0 hello, 0 database desc, 0 link state req
        0 link state updates, 0 link state acks

  Sent: 0 total

IP-IGRP2 statistics:
  Rcvd: 0 total
  Sent: 0 total
```

```
PIMv2 statistics: Sent/Received
  Total: 0/0, 0 checksum errors, 0 format errors
  Registers: 0/0, Register Stops: 0/0,  Hellos: 0/0
  Join/Prunes: 0/0, Asserts: 0/0, grafts: 0/0
  Bootstraps: 0/0, Candidate_RP_Advertisements: 0/0

IGMP statistics: Sent/Received
  Total: 0/0, Format errors: 0/0, Checksum errors: 0/0
  Host Queries: 0/0, Host Reports: 0/0, Host Leaves: 00
  DVMRP: 0/0, PIM: 0/0

ARP statistics:
  Rcvd: 0 requests, 0 replies, 34 reverse, 0 other
  Sent: 5 requests, 0 replies (0 proxy), 7 reverse
```

12. **Show logging**   Used to display the settings for logging, and the current contents of the logging buffer.

```
HubRouter#sho log history
Syslog History Table:1 maximum table entries,
saving level warnings or higher
 49 messages ignored, 0 dropped, 0 recursion drops
 22 table entries flushed
 SNMP notifications not enabled
   entry number 23 : LINK-3-UPDOWN
    Interface Serial0, changed state to up
    timestamp: 120165


HubRouter#sho log
Syslog logging: enabled (0 messages dropped, 0 flushes, 0 overruns)
    Console logging: level debugging, 98 messages logged
    Monitor logging: level debugging, 0 messages logged
    Trap logging: level informational, 76 message lines logged
    Buffer logging: level debugging, 98 messages logged

Log Buffer (4096 bytes):
ED: Interface Serial0, changed state to administratively down
%LINK-5-CHANGED: Interface Ethernet0, changed state to administratively down
%LINK-5-CHANGED: Interface Serial1, changed state to administratively down
%LINK-5-CHANGED: Interface Serial2, changed state to administratively down
%LINK-5-CHANGED: Interface Serial3, changed state to administratively down
%IP-5-WEBINST_KILL: Terminating DNS process
%SYS-5-RESTART: System restarted ñ
```

13. **Show memory [free | summary | io]**   Used to show the contents of the memory, including the free areas and the processes running in each memory location.

```
HubRouter#show mem sum
            Head    Total(b)   Used(b)   Free(b)   Lowest(b) Largest(b)
Processor   76B8C   1606772    943616    663156    645524    651716
     I/O    200000  2097152    460972    1636180   1636180   1636012

        Processor memory

Alloc PC        Size      Blocks     Bytes     What

0x30367C2       276       1          276       Lance Instance
0x303A7E8       112       2          224       HD64570 Instance
0x306DEE8       24        2          48        Init
0x306EB8E       24        2          48        Init
0x306EBB6       24        2          48        Init
0x306EBDC       24        2          48        Init
--More--
```

14. **Show processes [cpu | memory | <cr>]** Used to view the current CPU utilization, previous load in 5 seconds, 1 minute, and 5 minute intervals, number of times invoked, and the total runtime of the various processes.

```
HubRouter#show proc
CPU utilization for five seconds: 13%/13%; one minute: 17%; five minutes: 17%
 PID QTy      PC Runtime (ms)   Invoked   uSecs     Stacks TTY Process
   1 Csp  31A1948       220      1425      154   740/1000    0 Load Meter

   2 M*         0      8876      1319     6729  2532/4000    0 Exec

   3 Lst  31928A8     12884       356    36191  1768/2000    0 Check heaps

   4 Cwe  3198722         0         1        0  1732/2000    0 Pool Manager

   5 Mst  3131D82         0         2        0  1704/2000    0 Timers
```

15. **Show protocols** Used to view the current protocols that are being routed, and the status and network address of each of the interfaces.

```
HubRouter#show proto
Global values:
  Internet Protocol routing is enabled
BRI0 is administratively down, line protocol is down
BRI0:1 is administratively down, line protocol is down
BRI0:2 is administratively down, line protocol is down
Ethernet0 is up, line protocol is up
  Internet address is 192.168.1.254/24
Serial0 is up, line protocol is up
  Internet address is 192.168.100.254/24
Serial1 is up, line protocol is up
  Internet address is 192.168.101.254/24
```

```
Serial2 is up, line protocol is up
  Internet address is 192.168.102.254/24
Serial3 is administratively down, line protocol is down
HubRouter#
```

16. **Show running-config** Used to view the configuration as it is currently running on the router.
17. **Show startup-config** Used to view the configuration that will be loaded upon a reboot.
18. **Show tech-support** Used to report a problem to Cisco technical support. Includes the outputs from **show version**, **show running-config**, **show controllers**, **show stack**, **show interfaces**, **show buffers**, **show processes memory**, and **show processes cpu**.

Debugging

There are many different aspects of debugging a Cisco router. Debugging itself can take an entire set of books, and is therefore out of the scope of this book. However, learning what some of the commands are and reemphasizing the ones we have used is a good way to get a quick handle on troubleshooting networks.

In order to turn on debugging, we use the command **debug** followed by one or more parameters. Once debugging is on, processor utilization can greatly increase, causing slower performance through the router. Debugging routers should be used with caution, and should always be shut off when finished.

To turn off debugging, issue the command **no debug all** or **undebug all**. We can also turn off specific debugging instead of the all parameter. For instance, to turn on rip debugging, we would issue the command **debug ip rip** and then to turn it off, we would issue the command **no debug ip rip**.

1. **Debug arp** Used to monitor ARP packets as they are sent and received on the router.

```
HubRouter#debug arp
ARP packet debugging is on

IP ARP: sent rep src 192.168.1.254 00e0.1e68.275b,
                dst 192.168.1.254 ffff.ffff.ffff Ethernet0
IP ARP: sent rep src 192.168.1.254 00e0.1e68.275b,
                dst 192.168.1.254 ffff.ffff.ffff Ethernet0
```

2. **Debug bri** Used to monitor ISDN BRI interfaces and communications.
3. **Debug cdp [adjacency | events | ip | packets]** Used to debug the CDP announcements between the router and all neighbors.

```
HubRouter#debug cdp pa
CDP packet info debugging is on
CDP-PA: Packet sent out on Ethernet0
CDP-PA: Packet sent out on Serial0
CDP-PA: Packet sent out on Serial1
CDP-PA: Packet sent out on Serial2
CDP-PA: Packet received from Switch on interface Ethernet0
**Entry NOT found in cache**
CDP-PA: Packet received from Spoke2 on interface Serial1
**Entry NOT found in cache**
CDP-PA: Packet received from Spoke3 on interface Serial2
**Entry  found in cache**
CDP-PA: Packet received from Spoke1 on interface Serial0
**Entry NOT found in cache**
```

4. **Debug ethernet-interface**   Used to debug problems with the Ethernet interface.

```
HubRouter#debug ether
Ethernet network interface debugging is on
HubRouter#
%LANCE-5-LOSTCARR: Unit 0, lost carrier. Transceiver problem?
```

5. **Debug frame-relay**   Used to monitor various types of information with Frame Relay interfaces. For instance, **debug frame lmi** can be used to monitor the LMI packets that are exchanged between the router and the Frame Relay switch.

6. **Debug [ip | ipx | appletalk]**   Many debug options exist when trying to debug the protocol itself. Careful planning and a lot of experience will tell us which debugging option to use. Examples include **debug ip rip**, **debug ip routing**, **debug ip tcp**, **debug ipx routing activity**, **debug ipx sap**, **debug apple nbp**, **debug apple routing**, and **debug apple zip**.

7. **Debug isdn**   More options exist for debugging ISDN, including events, q921, and q931.

8. **Debug packet**   Used to monitor packets that the router cannot identify.

9. **Debug serial interface**   This can be used to troubleshoot timing issues when a serial interface will not come up. When viewing this output, the values for myseq, mineseen, and yourseen should continue to increment. If they do not, there is a problem at one or both ends of the connection.

```
HubRouter#debug serial inter
Serial network interface debugging is on
Serial1: HDLC myseq 908, mineseen 908*, yourseen 911, line up
Serial2: HDLC myseq 0, mineseen 0, yourseen 0, line up
Serial0: HDLC myseq 895, mineseen 895*, yourseen 898, line up
Serial1: HDLC myseq 909, mineseen 909*, yourseen 912, line up
Serial2: HDLC myseq 1, mineseen 1*, yourseen 1, line up
Serial0: HDLC myseq 896, mineseen 896*, yourseen 899, line up
```

```
Serial1: HDLC myseq 910, mineseen 910*, yourseen 913, line up
Serial2: HDLC myseq 2, mineseen 2*, yourseen 2, line up
```

10. Debug tftp Used to troubleshoot problems with a TFTP server when using the **copy** command.

Telnet

Throughout this book we have been configuring the routers through the console port. This can be very impractical to have to run to every router or switch and plug in a console cable. Worse, we have to keep changing ports on the routers to access a different one.

Telnet is an application that can be used to remotely access nodes that run a terminal session. Telnet is performed through the TCP/IP protocol suite, and as such, at least one interface on the router or switch must have an IP address.

In our network diagram, the IP addresses have each been assigned to the serial ports. In addition, the routing tables maintain a complete listing of the routes necessary to get to and from the initial host supporting the Telnet session.

To Telnet to another router, we must have a vty password set. Without a password set, the connection will be refused.

```
HubRouter#telnet 192.168.100.253
Trying 192.168.100.253 ... Open


Password required, but none set

[Connection to 192.168.100.253 closed by foreign host]
HubRouter#
```

To enable the password, we need to use the **line** command. Also, since we do not know which vty we will be accessing when we connect, we must specify a password for all the ports. There are five ports created: 0–4.

```
Spoke1(config)#line vty 0 4
Spoke1(config-line)#login
Spoke1(config-line)#password virtual
Spoke1(config-line)#^Z
Spoke1#

Spoke2(config)#line vty 0 4
Spoke2(config-line)#login
Spoke2(config-line)#password virtual
Spoke2(config-line)#^Z
Spoke2#
```

```
Spoke3(config)#line vty 0 4
Spoke3(config-line)#login
Spoke3(config-line)#password virtual
Spoke3(config-line)#^Z
Spoke3#
```

Now that we have the vty ports set with passwords, we can Telnet to them.

```
HubRouter#telnet 192.168.100.253
Trying 192.168.100.253 ... Open

User Access Verification

Password:<virtual>
Spoke1>
```

Once we are in the virtual terminal session, we can do anything that we would normally be able to do through the console port. However, there is one more password we have to be concerned with. If there is no enable password to get to privileged mode, the router will deny a Telnet connection.

```
Spoke1>enable
% No password set
Spoke1>
```

There are some nice security features built into the IOS, and these are two of them. We are required to have passwords before anyone can access the router remotely. Once the password is set, we can enter privileged mode.

```
Spoke1(config)#enable secret secret

Spoke2(config)#enable secret secret

Spoke3(config)#enable secret secret

Spoke1>enable
Password: <secret>
Spoke1#
```

Using this method, we can connect to multiple routers and configure them. It would be better if we could connect to multiple routers and work on each of them at the same time—it turns out that we can. In order to return to the initial router, we need to enter the escape sequence followed by the letter x. In HyperTerm, we can generate the Escape key by pressing Ctrl-Shift-6 (Ctrl-^).

```
Spoke1#<Ctrl-Shift-6 x>
HubRouter#
```

Now that we are back to the initial router, we can initiate a new connection. Let's connect to Spoke 2 and Spoke 3.

```
HubRouter#telnet 192.168.101.253
Trying 192.168.101.253 ... Open

User Access Verification

Password:<virtual>
Spoke2>enable
Password:<secret>
Spoke2#<Ctrl-Shift-6 x>

HubRouter#telnet 192.168.102.253
Trying 192.168.102.253 ... Open

User Access Verification

Password:<virtual>
Spoke3>ena
Password:<secret>
Spoke3#<Ctrl-Shift-6 x>
HubRouter#
```

Now that we have three connections open, how do we resume a session? The key word is "resume." We will use the **resume** command to return to a Telnet session. But which session do we want to return to? For this, we will use the command **where**, which lists our current Telnet sessions.

```
HubRouter#where
Conn Host              Address          Byte  Idle Conn Name
    1 192.168.100.253   192.168.100.253     0     4 192.168.100.253
    2 192.168.101.253   192.168.101.253     0     3 192.168.101.253
*   3 192.168.102.253   192.168.102.253     0     2 192.168.102.253

HubRouter#
```

Suppose we wanted to resume with the second connection. Notice the Conn column (the first column). This is the number we will use to resume a connection.

```
HubRouter#resume 2
[Resuming connection 2 to 192.168.101.253 ... ]

Spoke2#
```

To end a Telnet session, we can use the keyword **exit** or **logout**.

```
Spoke2#exit

[Connection to 192.168.101.253 closed by foreign host]
HubRouter#
```

We can also disconnect a session directly from the initiating router by using the **disconnect** *session* command, where session is the Conn number.

```
HubRouter#disc 1
Closing connection to 192.168.100.253 [confirm]y
HubRouter#
```

The default settings are to send any debug output to the console. If we want to initiate debugging from within a Telnet session, we have to use the command **terminal monitor**. This command will copy the debug information to the Telnet connection. For example, we want to view the RIP debug information on Spoke 3. This is how we would do it.

```
HubRouter#telnet 192.168.102.253
Trying 192.168.102.253 ... Open


User Access Verification

Password:<virtual>
Spoke3>ena
Password:<secret>
Spoke3#term mon
Spoke3#debug ip rip
RIP protocol debugging is on
Spoke3#
RIP: received v1 update from 192.168.102.254 on Serial0
     192.168.1.0 in 1 hops
     192.168.100.0 in 1 hops
     192.168.101.0 in 1 hops
Spoke3#term no mon
Spoke3#term mon
Spoke3#
RIP: sending v1 update to 255.255.255.255 via Serial0 (192.168.102.253) -
     suppressing null update
Spoke3#undebug ip rip
RIP protocol debugging is off
Spoke3#
```

Remember that debugging causes overhead on the CPU of the router, so use it wisely. Also, even though we issued the command **term no mon** to turn off the monitoring, the debugging is still on and being sent to the console port.

Logging

There are times when we would like a copy of all the log messages that can occur. For instance, we would like to know when the router configuration was last changed. If we set up username and passwords (see the next section), we would like to know who made the last change.

To enable logging, we use the command **logging on**. This is already turned on by default. To turn off logging so that the status messages only get sent to the console port, use the **no logging on** command.

By default, the messages will also be logged to an internal buffer. To view the buffer, we use the command **show logging**.

```
HubRouter#show log
Syslog logging: enabled (0 messages dropped, 0 flushes, 0 overruns)
    Console logging: level debugging, 583 messages logged
    Monitor logging: level debugging, 0 messages logged
    Trap logging: disabled
    Buffer logging: level debugging, 583 messages logged

Log Buffer (4096 bytes):

%SYS-5-CONFIG_I: Configured from console by console
%SYS-5-CONFIG_I: Configured from console by console
RIP: sending v1 update to 255.255.255.255 via Ethernet0 (192.168.1.254)
    network 192.168.102.0, metric 1
    network 192.168.100.0, metric 1
    network 192.168.101.0, metric 1
RIP: sending v1 update to 255.255.255.255 via Serial0 (192.168.100.254)
    network 192.168.102.0, metric 1
    network 192.168.1.0, metric 1
    network 192.168.101.0, metric 1
RIP: sending v1 update to 255.255.255.255 via Serial1 (192.168.101.254)
    network 192.168.102.0, metric 1
    network 192.168.1.0, metric 1
    network 192.168.100.0, metric 1
RIP: sending v1 update to 255.255.255.255 via Serial2 (192.168.102.254)
    network 192.168.1.0, metric 1
    network 192.168.100.0, metric 1
    network 192.168.101.0, metric 1
CDP-PA: Packet received from Spoke2 on interface Serial1
**Entry  found in cache**
CDP-PA: Packet received from Spoke3 on interface Serial2
**Entry  found in cache**
HubRouter#
```

The preceding is an example of the buffer contents. Notice that the size of the buffer is 4096. Although this value can be increased, it is recommended not to change this size unless absolutely warranted. To change the value, use the command **logging buffered size**, where size is in bytes.

We can also log messages to a syslog server. This server is running a service or *daemon* (a term used to describe processes that run in the background) that will read messages sent to a specific port. We can set logging to be sent to a syslog server, and then the server itself can be set to archive our logs. This allows us a measure of auditing.

To enable logging to a syslog server, we issue the command **logging**.

```
HubRouter(config)#logging ?
  Hostname or A.B.C.D  IP address of the logging host
  buffered             Set buffered logging parameters
  console              Set console logging level
  facility             Facility parameter for syslog messages
  history              Configure syslog history table
  monitor              Set terminal line (monitor) logging level
  on                   Enable logging to all supported destinations
  source-interface     Specify interface for source address in logging
                       transactions
  trap                 Set syslog server logging level

HubRouter(config)#logging 192.168.1.1 ?
  <cr>

HubRouter(config)#logging 192.168.1.1
```

At this point, all messages will be sent to 192.168.1.1. If we have a syslog server running, we will be able to view the messages as they occurred, and potentially any archived messages as well. We can also specify the types of messages that should be logged to the syslog server. There are eight levels of logging.

Level	Keyword	Description
0	Emergencies	The router has become unusable
1	Alerts	Something requires immediate attention
2	Critical	Critical conditions that are affecting operations
3	Errors	Errors are occurring that are affecting operations
4	Warnings	Warning conditions
5	Notification	Standard notifications that are more important than level
6	Informational	Standard informational messages
7	Debugging	All debugging output

In order to change the status messages being sent to the syslog server, we need to use the command **logging trap** *level*. The level is the keyword as shown previously.

```
HubRouter(config)#logging trap debug
```

All debugging will now be sent to the syslog server over the network. Once debugging is turned on, we can view the information at the syslog console. An example is shown in Figure 15–2. This is a Windows NT version of a syslog daemon.

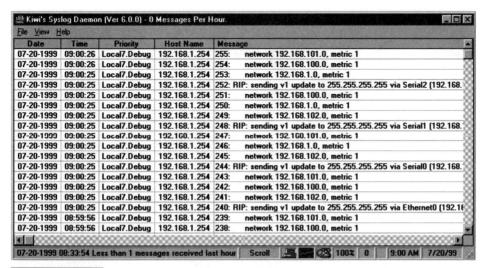

FIGURE 15–2 Syslog console capture of status messages

Usernames

There are times when we need the ability to audit different users when accessing our router. Although it would be preferable to set up a RADIUS or TACACS+ server for the authentication, we can do basic authentication with the IOS. To do this, we need to create the username. We use the command **username** to set this up.

```
Spoke3(config)#username ?
  WORD  User name

Spoke3(config)#username Robert ?
  access-class          Restrict access by access-class
  autocommand           Automatically issue a command after the user logs in
  callback-dialstring   Callback dialstring
  callback-line         Associate a specific line with this callback
  callback-rotary       Associate a rotary group with this callback
  dnis                  Do not require password when obtained via DNIS
  nocallback-verify     Do not require authentication after callback
```

```
noescape        Prevent the user from using an escape character
nohangup        Do not disconnect after an automatic command
nopassword      No password is required for the user to log in
password        Specify the password for the user
privilege       Set user privilege level
<cr>
```

```
Spoke3(config)#username Robert privilege ?
  <0-15>  User privilege level
```

```
Spoke3(config)#username Robert privilege 15 ?
  access-class        Restrict access by access-class
  autocommand         Automatically issue a command after the user logs in
  callback-dialstring Callback dialstring
  callback-line       Associate a specific line with this callback
  callback-rotary     Associate a rotary group with this callback
  dnis                Do not require password when obtained via DNIS
  nocallback-verify   Do not require authentication after callback
  noescape            Prevent the user from using an escape character
  nohangup            Do not disconnect after an automatic command
  nopassword          No password is required for the user to log in
  password            Specify the password for the user
  privilege           Set user privilege level
  <cr>
```

```
Spoke3(config)#username Robert privilege 15 password ?
  0     Specifies an UNENCRYPTED password will follow
  7     Specifies a HIDDEN password will follow
  LINE  The UNENCRYPTED (cleartext) user password
```

```
Spoke3(config)#username Robert privilege 15 password 0 Robert
Spoke3(config)#^Z
```

We gave Robert the privilege level of 15, which is the same privilege level as using the **enable** password. We could actually restrict his usage to a lower level, but it gets tricky setting up all the commands that he can use. Basically, the configuration commands are all running at level 15 and would have to be modified using the **privilege config** command.

If we were to set up all the users like this, what would happen if they logged in and looked at the running-config or startup-config?

```
Spoke3#sho run
Building configuration...

Current configuration:
!
version 11.3
no service password-encryption
!
hostname Spoke3
```

```
!
enable secret 5 $1$S2mC$udbUMqQL4Yb5K0jsJrVx81
!
username Robert privilege 15 password 0 Robert
!
```

The users would see each other's passwords. We can change this by issuing the command **service password-encryption**. This will cause all passwords to be encrypted before being written to the configuration file.

```
Spoke3(config)#service password-encryption
Spoke3(config)#^Z
Spoke3#sho run
Building configuration...

Current configuration:
!
version 11.3
service password-encryption
!
hostname Spoke3
!
enable secret 5 $1$S2mC$udbUMqQL4Yb5K0jsJrVx81
!
username Robert privilege 15 password 7 1520040E01383F
!
```

Any of the configuration that is done by Robert will be logged as being done by Robert.

```
HubRouter>login
Username: Robert
Password: <Robert>
HubRouter#conf t
Enter configuration commands, one per line.  End with CNTL/Z.
HubRouter(config)#^Z
HubRouter#
%SYS-5-CONFIG_I: Configured from console by Robert on console
```

If we were using our syslog server, we would be able to see the exact date and time that Robert made modifications. In this fashion, we have some limited user accountability.

Summary

In this chapter, we looked at some of the extra features that can be utilized with the Cisco router. CDP is a Cisco proprietary protocol that is used to track Cisco products at the Data Link layer. There are many **show** and **debug** commands that can be used to monitor and troubleshoot Cisco routers. We also looked at methods of logging status messages, including logging to the buffer and logging to a syslog daemon or service. The status messages can be filtered before sending to the syslog server by using the **logging trap** command. Telnet is an application that allows us to monitor and configure routers from remote locations. It is also possible to use multiple sessions to configure multiple routers at the same time. Finally, we looked at a limited way of having user accountability when changes are made to the router configurations.

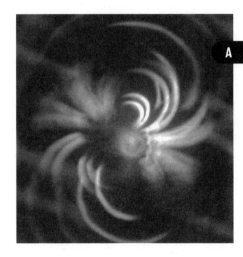

Chapter 1 Practice Questions

1. The technology used to connect multiple computers together in a single office is called:

    a. LAN
    b. WAN
    c. MAN
    d. InterNet

    A. LAN

2. Connecting multiple networks together using an outside carrier's signal, such as the telephone service, is known as:

    a. LAN
    b. WAN
    c. Protocol
    d. InterNet

    B. WAN

3. Why should we use layered models in a network architecture? (Select all that apply)

    a. It tells us exactly how to perform a specific function.
    b. It allows us to take a complex method and break it into smaller, more manageable methods.

c. A change to one layer has no effect on any other layer.

    d. A change to one layer affects all other layers.

    e. Restricts us to using only one network vendor.

    f. It makes troubleshooting networks easier by being able to locate the exact layer causing the problem.

    B, C, F

4. Which layer is responsible for finding a communication partner on the network?

    a. Transport

    b. Data Link

    c. Application

    d. Physical

    C. Application

5. What is the correct order for the shown layers (bottom to top)?

    a. Presentation

    b. Transport

    c. Application

    d. Network

    e. Data Link

    f. Physical

    g. Session

    F, E, D, B, G, A, C

6. True or False: The Transport layer can communicate directly with the Network and Presentation layers?

    FALSE (Session and Network)

7. Which of the following is performed at the Presentation layer? (Choose two)

    a. Presents data to the Application layer

    b. Sets checkpoints in the data stream for reliability

    c. Provides character conversion between dissimilar operating systems (such as PC to mainframe)

    d. Adds the network addresses to the header

    A, C

8. The Presentation layer protocols include: (Choose two)

    a. PICT

    b. SQL

    c. TCP

d. IPX

    e. JPEG

    A, E

9. The function of the Session layer is: (Choose two)

    a. Determine if half-duplex or full-duplex is being used

    b. Present data to the Network layer

    c. Place checkpoints into the data stream for reliability

    d. Provides flow control

    A, C

10. The Session layer protocols include: (Choose three)

    a. PICT

    b. SQL

    c. TCP

    d. X Windows

    e. NFS

    B, D, E

11. Which layer is responsible for multiplexing data from upper layers and placing the data into a segment?

    a. Transport

    b. Network

    c. Data Link

    d. Physical

    A. Transport

12. Windowing is performed at the Transport layer. What is windowing?

    a. A method of buffering

    b. A method of session establishment

    c. A method of flow control

    d. A method of character conversion

    C. A method of flow control

13. The Network layer's primary function is to:

    a. Add MAC addresses to the packet

    b. Establish a communication path to the communication partner

    c. Provide connection-oriented service

    d. Route data between different network segments

    D. Route data between different network segments

14. What are the two parts to a network address? (Choose two)

    a. Source Service Access Point
    b. Host Identifier
    c. MAC address
    d. Network Identifier

    B, D

15. The Data Link layer is split into two sublayers. Name them. (Choose two)

    a. Local Link Control
    b. Logical Link Control
    c. Machine Address Code
    d. Media Access Control

    B, D

16. List the functions of the MAC sublayer. (Choose three)

    a. Unique hardware addresses allow us to switch between different networks and still be uniquely identified.
    b. Provides SSAP and DSAP for passing frame to proper Transport protocol.
    c. Provides error checking through CRC.
    d. Provides an interface to the physical medium.
    e. Acts as a buffer between software and hardware protocols.

    A, C, D

17. List the functions of the LLC sublayer. (Choose two)

    a. Unique hardware addresses allow us to switch between different networks and still be uniquely identified.
    b. Provides SSAP and DSAP for passing frames to the proper Network protocol.
    c. Provides error checking through CRC.
    d. Provides an interface to the physical medium.
    e. Acts as a buffer between software and hardware protocols.

    B, E

18. Which layer is responsible for creating and disconnecting virtual circuits?

    a. Presentation
    b. Session
    c. Transport
    d. Network

    C. Transport

19. Which of the following terms describes the address used at the Network layer?

   a. Physical
   b. Logical
   c. MAC
   d. Host

   B. Logical

20. Place the following in the correct order of data encapsulation for the sending node?

   a. Encapsulates this packet or datagram into a frame with the MAC addresses
   b. Packages it as a message to send to the receiver
   c. Sends the frame across the wire as individual bits
   d. Data encapsulation takes the data from the user
   e. Encapsulates the segment inside a packet or datagram with the network addressing information

   D, B, E, A, C

Chapter 2 Practice Questions

1. When a collision is detected in an Ethernet network, a special packet is sent out. What is the name of that packet?

   a. Collision Packet
   b. Token Packet
   c. Extended Jam Signal
   d. Collision Jam Signal

   C. Extended Jam Signal

2. 10Base5 operates at what speed?

   a. 5 Mbps
   b. 10 Mbps
   c. 100 Mbps
   d. 16 Mbps

   B. 10Mbps

3. The most common type of LAN network today is:

   a. 10BaseT
   b. Token Ring
   c. ATM
   d. FDDI

   A. 10BaseT

4. What are two benefits of using Fast Ethernet?

   a. Cheaper to upgrade equipment
   b. Can migrate into an existing network
   c. Ten times faster than 10BaseT
   d. Uses a token for increase reliability

   B, C

5. Which of the following describes full-duplex? (Select all that apply)

   a. A fast moving four-lane highway
   b. A method of sending data only in one direction
   c. A narrow, one-way bridge
   d. A method of sending data in both directions

   A, D

6. What is the correct order for a node to transmit data on a Token Ring network?

   a. Destination Node receives frame, copies data, and returns frame to sender
   b. Source Node grabs frame and checks to see if it can transfer data
   c. Source Node modifies frame and appends data
   d. Source Node receives frame and releases token onto the network

   B, C, A, D

7. What is the maximum distance of FDDI?

   a. 100 Meters
   b. 200 Meters
   c. 1000 Meters
   d. 2000 Meters

   D. 2000 Meters

8. Multi-mode fiber uses what as its data source?

   a. Laser
   b. LED
   c. Electricity
   d. Radio Waves

   B. LED

9. How is data packaged for transmission over ATM media?

   a. Frames
   b. Packets

c. Cells

    d. Datagrams

C. Cells

10. Which two of the following are needed in a LANE network?

    a. LANE Client

    b. Active Monitor

    c. Hub

    d. BUS

A, D

11. ATM uses a connection-oriented path established by creating:

    a. Virtual Channels through Virtual Paths

    b. Virtual Paths through Virtual Channels

    c. Virtual Tokens through Virtual Channels

    d. Virtual Paths through Virtual Modes

A. Virtual Channels through Virtual Paths

12. If a DAS fails in an FDDI network, what is the result?

    a. There is no effect on the network.

    b. The entire network will crash.

    c. The token will be wrapped around by the upstream and downstream DAS.

    d. The token will be passed through the DAS.

C. The token will be wrapped around by the upstream and downstream DAS.

13. Single-mode fiber uses what as its data source?

    a. Laser

    b. LED

    c. Electricity

    d. Radio Waves

A. Laser

14. What is the term used to describe the node that removes unused frames on a Token Ring network?

    a. MAU

    b. Active Monitor

    c. BUS

    d. Token

B. Active Monitor

15. What device is used to connect nodes to a Token Ring network?

   a. Repeater
   b. DMAU
   c. MAU
   d. LECS

   C. MAU

16. Which of the following describe half-duplex? (select all that apply)

   a. A fast moving 4-lane highway
   b. A method of sending data only in one direction
   c. A narrow, one-way bridge
   d. A method of sending data in both directions

   B, C

17. What is a disadvantage of using Fast Ethernet?

   a. Costs may be higher to upgrade equipment
   b. Can't migrate into an existing network
   c. Slower than 10BaseFL
   d. Uses a token similar to Token Ring

   A. Costs may be higher to upgrade equipment

18. What is the maximum distance of a 10Base2 network.

   a. 200 Meters
   b. 500 Meters
   c. 185 Meters
   d. 476 Meters

   C. 185 Meters

19. A packet that is destined for all nodes on a network is known as what?

   a. Multicast
   b. Unicast
   c. Broadcast
   d. Bandcast

   C. Broadcast

20. What does the acronym CSMA/CD stand for?

   a. Collision Sense, Multiple Access, Carrier Division
   b. Carrier Sense, Multiple Access, Carrier Division
   c. Carrier Sense, Multistation Access, Collision Detection
   d. Carrier Sense, Multiple Access, Collision Detection

   D. Carrier Sense, Multiple Access, Collision Detection

Chapter 3 Practice Questions

1. When segmenting a network, it is essential to:

   a. Limit the number of routers in a segment
   b. Decrease the size of the collision domain
   c. Increase the number of nodes in a segment
   d. Use repeaters whenever possible

   B. Decrease the size of the collision domain

2. Which method of switching has less latency through the switch?

   a. VLAN
   b. Cut-Forward
   c. Cut-Through
   d. Store-and-Forward

   C. Cut-Through

3. Which device works at the Physical layer?

   a. Repeaters
   b. Bridges
   c. Switches
   d. Routers

   A. Repeaters

4. Which two devices work at the Data Link layer?

   a. Repeaters
   b. Bridges
   c. Switches
   d. Routers

   B, C

5. What method is used to prevent bridging loops?

   a. Manually disable the ports
   b. Spanning Tree Algorithm
   c. VLAN
   d. IEEE 802.10

   B. Spanning Tree Algorithm

6. What is the name of the messages that bridges use to communicate with each other?

   a. SPT
   b. SPA
   c. BPDU
   d. MAC

   C. BPDU

7. Which device always works at the Network layer?

   a. Repeaters
   b. Bridges
   c. Switches
   d. Routers

   D. Routers

8. Which method of switching has the best error checking?

   a. FragmentFree
   b. Cut-Through
   c. Store-and-Forward
   d. Cut-Forward

   C. Store-and-Forward

9. You want to place a demand node on the same segment as a resource node. At what percentage of traffic leaving the demand node going to the resource node do you want before making this change?

   a. 50%
   b. 60%

c. 70%

    d. 80%

       D. 80%

10. Which protocol cannot be routed?

    a. NetBEUI

    b. TCP/IP

    c. IPX/SPX

    d. AppleTalk

       A. NetBEUI

11. Which method of switching has a variable latency?

    a. VLAN

    b. Cut-Forward

    c. Cut-Through

    d. Store-and-Forward

       D. Store-and Forward

12. What is the name of the packet that has less than 64 bytes?

    a. BPDU

    b. Giant

    c. Runt

    d. Stunted

       C. Runt

13. Which method of switching can be used with filters?

    a. VLAN

    b. Cut-Forward

    c. Cut-Through

    d. Store-and-Forward

       D. Store-and-Forward

14. What method can switches use to create smaller broadcast domains?

    a. Spanning Tree Protocol

    b. Virtual Trunking Protocol

    c. Virtual Local Area Networks

    d. Routing

       C. Virtual Local Area Networks (VLANs)

Chapter 4 Practice Questions

1. What is the name used for the list of documents that describes TCP/IP in detail?

   a. IETF
   b. ARPA
   c. RFC
   d. DNS

   C. RFC

2. Which order is the correct order (from top to bottom) of the DoD or TCP/IP model?

   a. Application
   b. Network
   c. Physical
   d. Host-Host

   A, D, B, C

3. Which protocol resolves MAC addresses from TCP/IP addresses?

   a. TCP
   b. ICMP
   c. ARP
   d. DNS

   C. ARP

4. Which layer of the DoD model defines flow control and error checking?

    a. Application
    b. Network
    c. Physical
    d. Host-Host

    D. Host-Host

5. Which protocol does the value 17 in the Protocol field of the IP packet refer to?

    a. TCP
    b. IP
    c. ARP
    d. UDP

    D. UDP

6. Which TCP/IP protocols operate at the Network layer? (Choose two)

    a. TCP
    b. UDP
    c. IP
    d. ICMP

    C, D

7. The router will route a datagram after changing which two fields in the IP header? (Choose two)

    a. Source MAC address
    b. Source IP address
    c. Destination MAC address
    d. Destination IP address

    A, C

8. Which TCP/IP protocols operate at the Host-Host layer? (Choose two)

    a. TCP
    b. UDP
    c. IP
    d. ICMP

    A, B

9. Which protocol is the messaging and control protocol?

    a. TCP
    b. ICMP

c. ARP

    d. DNS

       B. ICMP

10. Which of the following is a connection-oriented protocol?

    a. TCP

    b. UDP

    c. IP

    d. ICMP

       A. TCP

11. Which protocol uses the "three-way handshake?"

    a. TCP

    b. ICMP

    c. ARP

    d. DNS

       A. TCP

12. Which of the following is a connectionless protocol?

    a. TCP

    b. UDP

    c. Telnet

    d. FTP

       B. UDP

13. Which protocol is used to transfer files?

    a. Telnet

    b. FTP

    c. DNS

    d. SNMP

       B. FTP

14. Which protocol is used to manage networks with the aid of MIBs?

    a. Telnet

    b. FTP

    c. DNS

    d. SNMP

       D. SNMP

15. Which protocol can be used to log in and configure Cisco routers?

   a. Telnet

   b. FTP

   c. DNS

   d. SNMP

   A. Telnet

Chapter 5 Practice Questions

1. Which method would you use to find all the commands that start with "cl"?

   a. Help cl
   b. Help cl?
   c. cl ?
   d. cl?

   D. cl?

2. What command causes us to exit privileged mode back to user mode?

   a. User mode
   b. exit
   c. disable
   d. user

   C. Disable

3. What ports can a Cisco 2500 series router have? (Choose all that apply)

   a. Ethernet
   b. ISDN
   c. Token Ring
   d. ATM
   e. 10/100 Switch
   f. Serial

   A, B, C, F

4. A user can run any number of commands at the user mode. Which command must be run in privileged mode?

    a. Show version
    b. Show startup-config
    c. Show users
    d. Show interface

    B. Show startup-config

5. The size of the NVRAM is?

    a. 16KB
    b. 32KB
    c. 16MB
    d. 32MB

    B. 32KB

6. Which command will turn on a banner that users will see when logging in?

    a. Banner Welcome to Router 3
    b. Banner #Welcome to Router 3#
    c. Banner motd Welcome to Router 3
    d. Banner motd %Welcome to Router 3%

    D. Banner motd %Welcome to Router 3%

7. What are some of the features that the IOS software can have? (Choose all that apply)

    a. Firewall
    b. Encryption
    c. TCP/IP
    d. IBM Connectivity
    e. AppleTalk
    f. IPX/SPX

    A, B, C, D, E, F

8. Which commands will require a password when trying to enter privileged mode? (Choose two)

    a. Enable password cisco
    b. Enable cisco password
    c. Enable cisco secret
    d. Enable secret cisco

    A, D

9. What command will enter privileged mode?

    a. Press the Enter key
    b. privileged
    c. privilege
    d. enable

    D. Enable

10. What keystroke takes you to the end of the line?

    a. Ctrl-A
    b. Ctrl-N
    c. Ctrl-U
    d. Ctrl-E

    D. Ctrl-E

11. What action does the command "banner motd" perform?

    a. Displays a message when a terminal server logs in
    b. Displays a message when entering privileged mode
    c. Displays a message when logging in
    d. Displays a message after entering user mode

    C. Displays a message when logging in

12. Which command will save you hours of work by saving the configuration to NVRAM?

    a. Copy running configuration NVRAM
    b. Copy run NVRAM
    c. Copy run to start
    d. Copy run start

    D. Copy run start

13. What causes an ambiguous command message?

    a. The command entered does not contain enough parameter information.
    b. The command entered does not have enough characters to differentiate it from another command.
    c. The command entered does not exist.
    d. The command entered cannot be used in the current EXEC mode.

    B. The command entered does not have enough characters to differentiate it from another command.

14. When using a DCE cable to emulate a WAN, what command must you use?

    a. Clock rate 56000
    b. Bandwidth 56000

c. Clock rate 56

    d. Enable clock rate 56000

A. Clock rate 56000

15. Which command allows you to modify the Ethernet port?

    a. Config ethernet 0

    b. Enable ethernet

    c. Interface ethernet 0

    d. Config terminal

C. Interface ethernet 0 (int e0)

16. Which command will show you the same information as the opening boot screen?

    a. Show boot

    b. Show version

    c. Show run

    d. Show start

B. Show version

17. Which set of commands will require a password to log in to the console?

    a. line con 0
       password console

    b. line user 0
       login
       password console

    c. line con 0
       login
       password console

    d. line aux 0
       login
       password console

C. Line con 0 – login – password console

18. Which command will administratively disable an interface?

    a. Shutdown

    b. Disable

    c. No disable

    d. No shutdown

A. Shutdown

Chapter 6 Practice Questions

1. What is the number 11001010 in decimal?

   a. 202
   b. 203
   c. 201
   d. 200

   A. 202

2. What number is 177 in binary?

   a. 10110010
   b. 10100001
   c. 10110001
   d. 10100010

   C. 10110001

3. What command would show you if serial 0 were administratively down?

   a. Show controllers s 0
   b. Show interface s0
   c. Show start
   d. Show run

   B. Show interface s0

4. Identify the Class A address.

    a. 192.168.17.34
    b. 131.15.45.120
    c. 125.76.133.234
    d. 191.234.56.34

    C. 125.76.133.234

5. Identify the Class C address.

    a. 192.168.17.34
    b. 131.15.45.120
    c. 125.76.133.234
    d. 191.234.56.34

    A. 192.168.17.34

6. What series of commands are used to configure an IP address on serial 0?

    a. config terminal
        Ip address 192.168.17.0 255.255.255.0
    b. config terminal
        int s0
        ip addr 192.168.17.17 mask 255.255.255.0
    c. config terminal
        ip addr 192.168.17.17 mask 255.255.255.0
    d. config terminal
        int s0
        ip addr 192.168.17.17 255.255.255.0

    B. config terminal – int s0 – ip addr 192.168.17.17 mask 255.255.255.0

7. What is a Class D address used for?

    a. Assigning IP addresses to hosts
    b. Assigning IP addresses to networks
    c. Assigning IP addresses for multicasting
    d. Class D is not used

    C. Assigning IP addresses for multicasting

8. Identify the Class B address.

    a. 192.168.17.34
    b. 101.17.43.20
    c. 125.76.133.234
    d. 191.234.56.34

    A. 192.168.17.34

9. What is the correct subnet mask for a Class A address?

    a. 255.0.0.0
    b. 255.255.0.0
    c. 255.255.255.0
    d. 255.255.255.255

    A. 255.0.0.0

10. Which statement is correct?

    a. 192.168.17.34
    NetID = 192.168.17.0
    b. 125.73.133.234
    NetID = 125.73.0.0
    c. 191.234.79.65
    NetID = 191.234.79.0
    d. 225.16.54.58
    NetID = 225.16.0.0

    A. 192.168.17.34 NetID = 192.168.17.0

11. How many bits are available for Host IDs with a Class B network?

    a. 8
    b. 16
    c. 24
    d. 32

    B. 16

12. How many bits are available for Host IDs with a Class C network?

    a. 8
    b. 16
    c. 24
    d. 32

    A. 8

13. Which command will start the configuration script?

    a. reload
    b. config script
    c. auto script
    d. setup

    D. setup

14. Which two hosts are on the same segment?

    a. 192.168.1.254
    b. 192.168.2.254

c. 192.168.1.17

    d. 192.168.3.253

    A, C

15. What is the broadcast address for a node 131.15.46.59?

    a. 131.15.46.255

    b. 131.15.255.255

    c. 131.255.255.255

    d. 255.255.46.59

    B. 131.15.255.255

16. Which two hosts are on the same segment?

    a. 191.19.15.255

    b. 191.18.15.255

    c. 191.19.79.202

    d. 192.19.15.254

    A, C

17. Which of the following are considered private addresses? (Choose all that apply)

    a. 11.0.0.0

    b. 10.0.0.0

    c. 172.19.0.0

    d. 162.198.0.0

    e. 16.172.0.0

    f. 192.168.0.0

    B, C, F

18. Which command will set up a second address of 192.168.17.101 on an interface?

    a. Ip address 192.168.17.101 secondary

    b. Ip secondary address 192.168.17.101 255.255.255.0

    c. Ip secondary-address 192.168.17.101 255.255.255.0

    d. Ip address 192.168.17.101 255.255.255.0 secondary

    D. IP address 192.168.17.101 255.255.255.0 secondary

Chapter 7 Practice Questions

1. The subnet mask of 255.255.255.240 can be expressed in CIDR notation as:

   a. /24
   b. /26
   c. /28
   d. /30

   C. /28

2. You have been given a Class C address and need to subnet it to five subnets. What is the correct subnet mask?

   a. 255.255.255.240
   b. 255.255.255.224
   c. 255.255.255.192
   d. 255.255.255.128

   B. 255.255.255.224

3. What is the correct broadcast address for a host with the IP address of 192.168.50.50 using a subnet mask of 255.255.255.240?

   a. 192.168.50.15
   b. 192.168.50.48
   c. 192.168.50.63
   d. 192.168.50.51

   C. 192.168.50.63

4. Which two hosts are on the same subnet given the address of 192.168.50.0/27?

    a. 192.168.50.33
    b. 192.168.50.95
    c. 192.168.50.44
    d. 192.168.50.96

    A, C

5. Which one of the following is a valid host using the address of 172.16.0.0/19?

    a. 172.16.32.0
    b. 172.16.64.0
    c. 172.16.63.255
    d. 172.16.80.255

    D. 172.16.80.255

6. How many subnets are created when using a Class C network with a subnet mask of 255.255.255.248?

    a. 32
    b. 30
    c. 16
    d. 14

    B. 30

7. You have been given a Class B address of 172.16.0.0. You need to subnet it to 14 subnets. Which subnet mask will give you the most hosts per subnet?

    a. 255.255.240.0
    b. 255.255.228.0
    c. 255.255.248.0
    d. 255.255.255.240

    A. 255.255.240.0

8. You have been given a Class B address of 172.16.0.0. You have subnetted it to 255.255.240.0. How many hosts and how many subnets are created?

    a. 14 hosts, 254 subnets
    b. 14 hosts, 4094 subnets
    c. 14 subnets, 4094 hosts
    d. 14 subnets, 254 hosts

    C. 14 subnets, 4094 hosts

9. You have been given a Class C address of 192.168.10.0/28. Which of the following lists a valid host range?

    a. 192.168.10.16 to 192.168.10.31
    b. 192.168.10.33 to 192.168.10.47
    c. 192.168.10.65 to 192.168.10.80
    d. 192.168.10.81 to 192.168.10.94

    D. 192.168.10.81 to 192.168.10.94

10. You have been given a Class C address of 192.168.10.0/29. Which of the following lists a valid host range?

    a. 192.168.10.225 to 192.168.10.230
    b. 192.168.10.233 to 192.168.10.239
    c. 192.168.10.240 to 192.168.10.246
    d. 192.168.10.249 to 192.168.10.254

    A. 192.168.10.225 to 192.168.10.230

Chapter 8 Practice Questions

Use Figure A–1 to answer the questions below.

1. Node A wants to communicate with Node B. Which MAC address will it send to?

   a. 11
   b. 22
   c. 66
   d. 77

   C. 66

2. Node A wants to communicate with Node C. Which MAC address will it send to?

   a. 88
   b. 33
   c. 77
   d. 66

   D. 66

3. What command will show the current routing table?

   a. show arp
   b. show route ip
   c. show ip route
   d. show route table

   C. show ip route

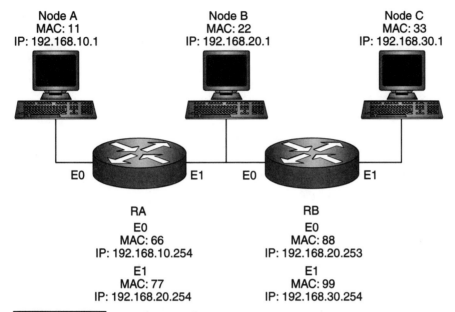

Node A
MAC: 11
IP: 192.168.10.1

Node B
MAC: 22
IP: 192.168.20.1

Node C
MAC: 33
IP: 192.168.30.1

EO

E1

EO

E1

RA
EO
MAC: 66
IP: 192.168.10.254

E1
MAC: 77
IP: 192.168.20.254

RB
EO
MAC: 88
IP: 192.168.20.253

E1
MAC: 99
IP: 192.168.30.254

FIGURE A-1 Sample network

4. Which is the correct route entry for router RA?

   a. ip route 192.168.30.0 mask 255.255.255.0 192.168.20.253
   b. ip route 192.168.30.0 255.255.255.0 192.168.20.253
   c. ip route add 192.168.30.0 255.255.255.0 192.168.30.254
   d. ip route add 192.168.30.0 255.255.255.0 192.168.20.253

   B. ip route 192.168.30.0 255.255.255.0 192.168.20.253

5. Which is the correct route entry for router RB?

   a. ip route 192.168.10.0 255.255.255.0 192.168.20.254
   b. ip route 192.168.10.0 255.255.255.0 192.168.10.254
   c. ip route 192.168.10.0 255.255.255.0 192.168.20.253
   d. ip route 192.168.10.0 255.255.255.0 192.168.30.254

   A. ip route 192.168.10.0 255.255.255.0 192.168.20.254

6. Which is the correct output of the trace program when tracing from Node A to Node C?

   a. 1 192.168.20.253
      2 192.168.20.254
      3 192.168.10.1
   b. 1 192.168.10.254
      2 192.168.20.254

        3 192.168.20.253
        4 192.168.30.254
        5 192.168.30.1

c. 1 192.168.10.254
        2 192.168.20.253
        3 192.168.30.1

d. 1 192.168.10.254
        2 192.168.20.1

C. 192.168.10.254 – 192.168.20.253 – 192.168.30.1

7. Which is the correct command to add a default route?

a. ip route 0.0.0.0 0.0.0.0 192.168.20.253
b. ip route 0.0.0.0 192.168.20.253
c. ip route default 0.0.0.0 192.168.20.253
d. ip route default 0.0.0.0 0.0.0.0 192.168.20.253

A. ip route 0.0.0.0 0.0.0.0 192.168.20.253

8. Which command changes the administrative distance to 100?

a. ip route 192.168.17.0 mask 255.255.255.0 distance 100
b. ip route 192.168.17.0 255.255.255.255 100
c. ip route 192.168.17.0 mask 255.255.255.0 100
d. ip route 192.168.17.0 255.255.255.0 192.168.17.254 100

D. ip route 192.168.17.0 255.255.255.0 192.168.17.254 100

Chapter 9 Practice Questions

1. Which of the following are routing protocols? (Choose all that apply)

   a. RIP
   b. TCP/IP
   c. IGRP
   d. IPX/SPX
   e. AppleTalk
   f. BGP
   g. EIGRP
   h. NSLP
   i. OSPF

   A, C, F, G, H, I

2. Which type of protocol updates its routing tables every update interval?

   a. Link State
   b. Distance Vector
   c. Classful
   d. Classless

   B. Distance Vector

3. RIP and IGRP can be classified as what?

   a. Exterior Protocols
   b. Routed protocols

c. Classful protocols

    d. Link State protocols

C. Classful protocols

4. Which command will list the interval for the hold-down?

    a. show ip route

    b. show protocols

    c. show ip protocols

    d. show hold-down

    e. show ip hold-down interval

C. show ip protocols

5. Which of the following is the term used for a router to identify a network as unreachable immediately upon loss of the path?

    a. Split Horizon

    b. Poison Reverse

    c. Triggered Update

    d. Hold Down

B. Poison Reverse

6. Which of the following prevents routers from advertising routes on the same interface they heard the route from?

    a. Split Horizon

    b. Poison Reverse

    c. Triggered Update

    d. Hold Down

A. Split Horizon

7. Which of the following prevents routers from "flapping?"

    a. Split Horizon

    b. Poison Reverse

    c. Triggered Update

    d. Hold Down

D. Hold Down

8. You have enabled RIP by using the **router rip** command. When you examine the routing tables, however, there is no route information. What other command do you need?

    a. int s0 rip

    b. network 172.16.0.0 rip

    c. network 172.16.0.0

    d. neighbor 172.16.0.0

    C. network 172.16.0.0

9. Which two commands are used to debug RIP?

    a. debug rip

    b. debug ip rip

    c. debug ip rip events

    d. debug ip rip transactions

    B, C

10. Which two commands are used to debug IGRP?

    a. debug igrp

    b. debug ip igrp

    c. debug ip igrp events

    d. debug ip igrp transactions

    C, D

11. Which command will turn off IGRP with the Autonomous System number 101?

    a. no igrp as 101

    b. no router igrp 101

    c. no router igrp

    d. no router 101 igrp

    B. no router igrp 101

12. IGRP can be used to calculate the bandwidth of a network for better route decisions. Which command must be used to configure a serial link correctly?

    a. bandwidth

    b. band width

    c. clock rate

    d. clockrate

    A. bandwidth

13. What command will refresh the routing table?

    a. refresh ip route

    b. clear ip route *

    c. no ip route

    d. no ip route *

    B. clear ip route *

Chapter 10 Practice Questions

1. What command will show the configuration register used during boot?

   a. Config-register
   b. Show version
   c. Show config
   d. Config show

   B. Show version

2. Name two of the pieces of the router architecture.

   a. CMOS
   b. NVRAM
   c. Flash
   d. OS

   B, C

3. What is a disadvantage to using a TFTP server?

   a. It can only run on a Unix platform.
   b. It cannot save IOS images.
   c. It is an unsecured application.
   d. It does not work with Cisco routers.

   C. It is an unsecured application.

4. Which is the correct command to save the IOS to a TFTP server?

    a. copy tftp flash
    b. copy flash tftp
    c. copy start tftp
    d. copy tftp start

    B. copy flash tftp

5. Which is the correct command to restore the IOS image from a TFTP server?

    a. copy tftp flash
    b. copy flash tftp
    c. copy start tftp
    d. copy tftp start

    A. copy tftp flash

6. Which is the correct command to save the configuration file to a TFTP server?

    a. copy tftp flash
    b. copy flash tftp
    c. copy start tftp
    d. copy tftp start

    C. copy start tftp

7. What is the correct command to encrypt passwords when stored in a configuration file?

    a. Password encryption
    b. Service encryption
    c. Password service-encryption
    d. Service password-encryption

    D. service password-encryption

8. What are three methods of configuring a Cisco router?

    a. Autoinstall
    b. Web browser
    c. Autodiscovery
    d. Setup

    A, B, D

9. Which command must be used to set up Autoinstall on a preconfigured router?

   a. Autoinstall address
   b. ip autoinstall address
   c. ip helper-address
   d. tftp helper-address

   C. ip helper-address

10. Which statement is true about lost or forgotten passwords?

   a. The password can never be recovered.
   b. The password can be recovered from a remote site.
   c. The password can be recovered with physical access to the router.
   d. Passwords are reset when the router is powered off.

   C. The password can be recovered with physical access to the router.

11. Which command can be used to tell the Cisco router to boot from the ROM first?

   a. Boot system rom
   b. System boot rom
   c. Boot system
   d. Boot rom

   A. Boot system rom

12. Which command can be used to tell the Cisco router which IOS image to boot from?

   a. Boot system flash
   b. Boot system flash *ios.filename*
   c. Boot flash
   d. Boot flash *ios.filename*

   B. Boot system flash *ios.filename*

Chapter 11 Practice Questions

1. Which command will show the MAC address of the Ethernet interface?

   a. Show ipx interface ethernet
   b. Show ipx interface ethernet 0
   c. Sho interface ethernet
   d. Show ethernet ipx

   B. show ipx interface ethernet 0

2. Which Cisco IOS encapsulation is equivalent to Ethernet_802.3?

   a. Novell-ether
   b. sap
   c. snap
   d. arpa

   A. Novell-ether

3. Which Cisco IOS encapsulation is equivalent to Ethernet_802.2?

   a. Novell-ether
   b. sap
   c. snap
   d. arpa

   B. sap

4. Which Cisco IOS encapsulation is equivalent to FDDI_SNAP?

    a. Novell-ether
    b. sap
    c. snap
    d. arpa

    C. snap

5. Which of the following is a valid IPX address?

    a. 7F00.00.50.04.70.a2.dc
    b. 00007F00.0050.0470.a2dc
    c. 7F0000.500470.a2dc
    d. 0000&f0000500470a2dc

    B. 00007F00.0050.0470.a2dc

6. Which command enables IPX?

    a. enable ipx
    b. enable ipx routing
    c. ipx routing
    d. router ipx

    C. ipx routing

7. Which set of commands assigns the network address of 2FF to Ethernet 0?

    a. int e0
       ipx network 2FF
    b. ipx routing 2FF
       ipx network e0
    c. ipx routing e0
       network ipx 2FF
    d. ipx network e0 2FF

    A. int e0 – ipx network 2FF

8. Which set of commands assigns the network address of 2FF to Ethernet 0, subinterface 1?

    a. int e0
       subinterface 1
       ipx network 2FF
    b. int e0.1
       ipx network 2FF
    c. ipx routing e0.1
       ipx network 2FF
    d. ipx network e0 2FF

    B. int e0.1 – ipx network 2FF

9. Which command will tell you which routing protocols have been enabled?

    a. sho routing protocols

    b. sho route

    c. sho protocols

    d. sho all

    C. sho protocols

10. Which command will enable Cisco routers to perform load balancing?

    a. ipx load balance 3

    b. ipx maximum path 3

    c. ipx load balance

    d. ipx maximum-paths 3

    D. ipx maximum-paths 3

11. Which command will display the detailed information of IPX RIP?

    a. ipx routing activity

    b. debug ipx routing activity

    c. ipx routing events

    d. debug ipx routing events

    B. debug ipx routing activity

12. Which command will display the detailed information of SAP?

    a. ipx sap activity

    b. debug ipx sap activity

    c. ipx sap events

    d. debug ipx sap events

    B. debug ipx sap activity

Chapter 12 Practice Questions

1. What is the correct format for an AppleTalk address?

   a. 200.200.145.31
   b. 45.34.24.23.23
   c. 101.56
   d. 12.3.44.3.3

   C. 101.56

2. Which phase of AppleTalk has a limitation of 127 workstations per node?

   a. Phase 1
   b. Phase 2
   c. Phase 3
   d. Phase 127

   A. Phase 1

3. Which phase of AppleTalk has a limitation of 253 workstations per node?

   a. Phase 1
   b. Phase 2
   c. Phase 3
   d. Phase 127

   B. Phase 2

4. Which phase of AppleTalk allows one zone for the network?

   a. Phase 1
   b. Phase 2
   c. Phase 3
   d. Phase 127

     A. Phase 1

5. Which phase of AppleTalk allows up to 255 zones in a segment?

   a. Phase 1
   b. Phase 2
   c. Phase 3
   d. Phase 127

     B. Phase 2

6. Which protocol is used to dynamically assign an address to a node?

   a. ARP
   b. NBP
   c. AARP
   d. ZIP

     C. AARP

7. What command enables AppleTalk routing?

   a. route appletalk
   b. routing appletalk
   c. appletalk
   d. appletalk routing

     D. appletalk routing

8. What command assigns the network address range of 100–110 to an interface?

   a. network 100-110
   b. appletalk network 100-110
   c. appletalk cable-range 100-110
   d. cable-range 100-110

     C. appletalk cable-range 100-110

9. Which command will show the AppleTalk addresses?

   a. show appletalk addresses
   b. show appletalk interface

    c. show interface appletalk

    d. show interface

B. show appletalk interface

10. Which command will show the ZIT?

    a. show zone-information-table

    b. show ZIT

    c. show appletalk zone

    d. show route zone

C. show appletalk zone

Chapter 13 Practice Questions

1. Which statement about access lists is correct?

    a. All entries in the access list are used.
    b. Only the first entry in the access list is used.
    c. Only the first entry in an access list is used when a match is found.
    d. Cisco IOS places an implicit grant all at the end of the access list.

    C. Only the first entry in the access list is used when a match is found.

2. What is the correct range for a standard AppleTalk access list?

    a. 100–199
    b. 200–299
    c. 500–599
    d. 600–699

    D. 600–699

3. Which of the following access lists will filter traffic from network 192.168.1.0 from reaching 192.168.2.0?

    a. access-list 1 deny 192.168.2.0 0.0.0.0
    b. access-list 1 deny 192.168.2.0 0.0.0.255

c. access-list 1 deny 192.168.1.0 0.0.0.0
    d. access-list 1 deny 192.168.1.0 0.0.0.255

D. access-list 1 deny 192.168.1.0 0.0.0.255

4. Which of the following access lists will filter the entire cable range 20–25?

    a. access-list 601 permit cable within 20-25
    b. access-list 601 deny cable includes 20-25
    c. access-list 601 permit network within 20-25
    d. access-list 601 deny network includes 20-25

B. access-list 601 deny cable includes 20-25

5. What is the correct range for a standard IPX/SPX access list?

    a. 1000–1099
    b. 1200–1299
    c. 800–899
    d. 900–999

C. 800–899

6. Which access list will deny all nodes on all networks from accessing the Novell server on network 500?

    a. access-list 800 deny –1 –1
    b. access-list 800 deny 500 any
    c. access-list 800 deny any 500
    d. access-list 800 deny –1 500

D. access-list 800 deny –1 500

7. Which of the following is the complete access list to allow only host 192.168.17.5 to reach the DNS server?

    a. access-list 100 deny ip any any
        access-list 100 permit tcp 192.168.17.5 0.0.0.0 any eq domain
    b. access-list 100 permit tcp 192.168.17.5 0.0.0.0 any eq 53
        access-list 100 deny ip any any
    c. access-list 100 allow tcp any 192.168.17.5 eq DNS
        access-list 100 deny –1 –1
    d. access-list 100 permit tcp 192.168.17.5 any eq 53
        access-list 100 permit any any

B. access-list 100 permit tcp 192.168.17.5 0.0.0.0 any eq 53 access-list 100 deny ip any any

8. What is the correct range for a standard TCP/IP access list?

    a. 1–99
    b. 100–199

c. 1000–1099
    d. 1100–1199

    A. 1–99

9. What is the correct range for an extended TCP/IP access list?

    a. 1–99
    b. 100–199
    c. 1000–1099
    d. 1100–1199

    B. 100–199

10. Which access list is valid?

    a. access-list 1000 deny 10.0000.0000.0001 0
    b. access-list 1000 deny –1 –1
    c. access-list 800 deny 10.0000.0000.0001
    d. access-list 800 deny –1 –1 0

    A. access-list 1000 deny 10.0000.0000.0001 0

11. Which access list is valid?

    a. access-list 99 deny ip any any
    b. access-list 99 permit udp any any eq ftp
    c. access-list 100 deny ip any any eq ftp
    d. access-list 100 deny tcp any any eq ftp

    D. access-list 100 deny tcp any any eq ftp

12. Which of the following can be used to with the command **ipx output-sap-filter 1000**?

    a. access-list 1000 deny 10.0000.0000.0001 4
    b. access-list 1000 deny –1 –1
    c. access-list 1000 permit 4 10.0000.0000.0001 –1
    d. access-list 1000 permit sap 10.0000.0000.0001 4

    A. access-list 1000 deny 10.0000.0000.0001 4

13. What command can be used to view the access lists of any protocols?

    a. show any access-list
    b. show access-list
    c. show access list
    d. show any access lit

    B. show access-list

Chapter 14 Practice Questions

1. Which of the following are valid serial line encapsulation types? (Select all that apply)

   a. Frame-relay
   b. ppp
   c. Hdlc
   d. Slip

   A, B, C

2. BRI is sometimes referred to as what?

   a. 23B+1D
   b. 30B+1D
   c. 3B+1D
   d. 2B+1D

   D. 2B + 1D

3. What are the correct speeds for the B and D channels?

   a. 64 Kbps/64 Kbps
   b. 64 Kbps/16 Kbps
   c. 16 Kbps/64 Kbps
   d. 16 Kbps/56 Kbps

   B. 64 Kbps/16 Kbps

4. Which set of ISDN protocols is responsible for defining existing telephone networks?

    a. I Series
    b. Q Series
    c. E Series
    d. M Series

      C. E series

5. Which set of ISDN protocols is responsible for defining switching and signaling?

    a. I Series
    b. Q Series
    c. E Series
    d. M Series

      B. Q Series

6. Which set of ISDN protocols is responsible for defining concepts and terminology?

    a. I Series
    b. Q Series
    c. E Series
    d. M Series

      A. I Series

7. What command will show if the ISDN interface and the protocol is up?

    a. show bri 0
    b. show int bri 0
    c. show int isdn
    d. show int isdn 0

      B. show int bri 0

8. Which command will set the ISDN switch type to DMS100?

    a. isdn switch basic-dms100
    b. isdn encaps basic-dms100
    c. encaps isdn basic-dms100
    d. switch isdn basic-dms100

      A. isdn switch basic-dms100

9. Which is the default LMI type?

    a. ansi
    b. q933a

c. cisco

    d. hdlc

C. cisco

10. Which Frame Relay encapsulation type is required if the two connecting devices are not both Cisco?

    a. cisco

    b. ppp

    c. hdlc

    d. ietf

D ietf

11. Which command would show the DLCIs as they have been assigned through Inverse ARP?

    a. show frame pvc

    b. show frame dlci

    c. show dlci

    d. show pvc

A. show frame pvc

12. Which command will establish a static frame mapping from Router 1 (192.168.17.1) with DLCI 120 to Router 2 (192.168.17.2) with DLCI 130?

    a. frame map ip 192.168.17.1 130

    b. frame map ip 192.168.17.2 130

    c. frame map ip 192.168.17.1 120

    d. frame map ip 192.168.17.2 120

D. frame map ip 192.168.17.2 120

Practice Exercise 7.1

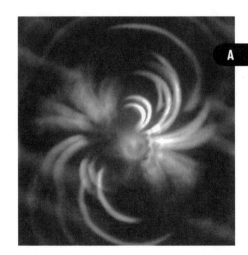

1. You have a Class C address. You need to create 11 subnets. What is the subnet mask?

    a. Class C – 8 bits to work with – 255.255.255.z – 11 SUBNETS
    b. 11 = 1011
    c. 4 Bits
    d. Moving left to right = 240

    Answer = 255.255.255.240

2. You have a Class C address. You need to create 15 subnets. What is the subnet mask?

    a. Class C – 8 bits to work with – 255.255.255.z – 15 SUBNETS
    b. 15 = 1111 => 01111 (Can't have all ones)
    c. 5 Bits
    d. Moving left to right = 248

    Answer = 255.255.255.248

3. You have a network address of 202.17.19.0. You need three subnets now and four additional subnets in the future. What is the subnet mask that should be used?

   a. Class C – 8 bits to work with – 255.255.255.z – 7 SUBNETS
   b. 7 = 111 => 0111 (Can't have all ones)
   c. 4 Bits
   d. Moving left to right = 240

   Answer = 255.255.255.240

4. You have a Class C address. You need a maximum of 30 hosts on each subnet. What is the subnet mask?

   a. Class C – 8 bits to work with – 255.255.255.z – 30 HOSTS
   b. 30 = 11110 (Host bits)
   c. 8 – 5 (Host bits) = 3 (Network Bits)
   d. Moving left to right = 224

   Answer = 255.255.255.224

5. You have a network address of 191.160.0.0. You need a maximum of 12 hosts on each subnet. What is the subnet mask?

   a. Class B – 16 bits to work with – 255.255.y.z – 12 HOSTS
   b. 12 = 1100 (Host bits)
   c. 16 – 4 (Host bits) = 12 (Network bits)
   Moving left to right = 255.240
   1 1 1 1 1 1 1 1 . 1 1 1 1
   128 192 224 240 248 252 254 255.128 192 224 240 248 252 254 255

   Answer = 255.255.255.240

6. You require 20 hosts per subnet using a Class B network address. What is the subnet mask needed?

   a. Class B – 16 bits to work with – 255.255.y.z – 20 HOSTS
   b. 20 = 10100 (Host bits)
   c. 16 – 5 (Host bits) = 11 (Network bits)
   d. Moving left to right = 255.224

   Answer = 255.255.255.224

7. Given the address of 191.15.0.0 and needing 20 subnets, what is the correct subnet mask to use?

   a. Class B – 16 bits to work with – 255.255.y.z – 20 SUBNETS
   b. 20 = 10100
   c. 5 Bits
   d. Moving left to right = 248.0

   Answer = 255.255.248.0

8. Given the address of 202.15.78.0 and needing 20 hosts per subnet, what is the correct subnet mask?

    a. Class C – 8 bits to work with – 255.255.255.z – 20 HOSTS
    b. 20 = 10100 (Host bits)
    c. 8 – 5 (Host bits) = 3 (Network bits)
    d. Moving left to right = 224

    Answer = 255.255.255.224

9. You have a Class A address of 11.0.0.0. You need a maximum of 400 subnets. What is the subnet mask that is needed?

    a. Class A – 24 bits to work with – 255.x.y.z – 400 SUBNETS
    b. 400 = 110010000
    c. 9 bits
    d. Moving left to right = 255.128.0

    Answer = 255.255.128.0

10. You have a Class A address of 121.0.0.0. You need a maximum of 400 hosts. What is the subnet mask that is needed?

    a. Class A – 24 bits to work with – 255.x.y.z – 400 HOSTS
    b. 400 = 110010000 (Host bits)
    c. 24 – 9 (Host bits) = 15 (Network Bits)
    d. Moving left to right = 255.254.0

    Answer = 255.255.254.0

Practice Exercise 7.2

1. You have a Class C address. You need to create 13 subnets. What is the subnet mask? How many subnets and hosts per subnet are created?

   a. Class C – 8 bits to work with – 255.255.255.z – 23 SUBNETS
   b. 13 = 1101
   c. 4 bits
   d. Moving left to right = 240

   Answer = 255.255.255.240
   #Subnets = 2^4 – 2 = 14 subnets
   #Hosts = 2^{8-4} – 2 = 2^4 – 2 = 14 hosts/subnet

2. You have a Class C address. You need to create 14 subnets. What is the subnet mask? How many subnets and hosts per subnet are created?

   a. Class C – 8 bits to work with – 255.255.255.z – 14 SUBNETS
   b. 14 = 1110
   c. 4 bits
   d. Moving left to right = 240

   Answer = 255.255.255.240
   # Subnets = 2^4 – 2 = 14 subnets
   # Hosts = 2^{8-4} – 2 = 2^4 – 2 = 14 hosts/subnet

3. You have a network address of 202.17.19.0. You need three subnets now and three additional subnets in the future. What is the subnet mask that should be used? How many subnets and hosts per subnet are created?

   a. Class C – 8 bits to work with – 255.255.255.z – 6 SUBNETS

   b. 6 = 110

   c. 3 bits

   d. Moving left to right = 224

      Answer = 255.255.255.224

        # Subnets = $2^3 - 2 = 6$ subnets

        # Hosts = $2^{8-3} - 2 = 2^5 - 2 = 30$ hosts/subnet

4. You have a Class C address. You need a maximum of 40 hosts on each subnet. What is the subnet mask? How many subnets and hosts per subnet are created?

   a. Class C – 8 bits to work with – 255.255.255.z – 40 HOSTS

   b. 40 = 101000 (Host bits)

   c. 8 – 6 (Host bits) = 2 (Network Bits)

   d. Moving left to right = 192

      Answer = 255.255.255.192

        #Subnets = $2^2 - 2 = 2$ subnets

        #Hosts = $2^{8-2} - 2 = 2^6 - 2 = 62$ hosts/subnet

5. You have a network address of 191.160.0.0. You need a maximum of 20 hosts on each subnet. What is the subnet mask? How many subnets and hosts per subnet are created?

   a. Class B – 16 bits to work with – 255.255.y.z – 20 HOSTS

   b. 20 = 10100 (Host Bits)

   c. 16 – 5 (Host Bits) = 11 (Network Bits)

   d. Moving left to right = 255.224

      Answer = 255.255.255.224

        # Subnets = $2^{11} - 2 = 2046$ subnets

        # Hosts = $2^{16-11} - 2 = 2^5 - 2 = 30$ hosts/subnet

6. You require 50 hosts per subnet using a Class B network address. What is the subnet mask needed? How many subnets and hosts per subnet are created?

   a. Class B – 16 bits to work with – 255.255.y.z – 50 HOSTS

   b. 50 = 110010 (Host Bits)

   c. 16 – 6 (Host Bits) = 10 (Network Bits)

   d. Moving left to right = 255.192

      Answer = 255.255.255.192

        # Subnets = $2^{10} - 2 = 1022$ subnets

        # Hosts = $2^{16-10} - 2 = 2^6 - 2 = 62$ hosts/subnet

7. Given the address of 191.15.0.0 and needing 40 subnets, what is the correct subnet mask to use? How many subnets and hosts per subnet are created?

    a. Class B – 16 bits to work with – 255.255.y.z – 40 SUBNETS
    b. 40 = 101000
    c. 6 bits
    d. Moving left to right = 252.0

    Answer = 255.255.252.0
    # Subnets = 2^6 – 2 = 62 subnets
    # Hosts = 2^{16-6} –2 = 2^{10} – 2 = 1022 hosts/subnet

8. Given the address of 202.15.78.0 and needing 40 hosts per subnet, what is the correct subnet mask? How many subnets and hosts per subnet are created?

    a. Class C – 8 bits to work with – 255.255.255.z – 40 HOSTS
    b. 40 = 101000 (Host bits)
    c. 8 – 6 (Host bits) = 2 (Network Bits)
    d. Moving from left to right = 192

    Answer = 255.255.255.192
    # Subnets = 2^2 – 2 = 2 subnets
    # Hosts = 2^{8-2} – 2 = 2^6 – 2 = 62 hosts/subnet

9. You have a Class A address of 11.0.0.0. You need a maximum of 200 subnets. What is the subnet mask that is needed? How many subnets and hosts per subnet are created?

    a. Class A – 24 bits to work with – 255.x.y.z – 200 SUBNETS
    b. 200 = 11001000
    c. 8 bits
    d. Moving from left to right = 255.0.0

    Answer = 255.255.0.0
    # Subnets = 2^8 – 2 = 254 subnets
    # Hosts = 2^{24-8} – 2 = 2^{16} – 2 = 65534 hosts/subnet

10. You have a Class A address of 121.0.0.0. You need a maximum of 600 subnets. What is the subnet mask that is needed? How many subnets and hosts per subnet are created?

    a. Class A – 24 bits to work with – 255.x.y.z – 600 SUBNETS
    b. 600 = 1001011000
    c. 10 bits
    d. Moving from left to right = 255.192.0

    Answer = 255.255.192.0
    # Subnets = 2^{10} – 2 = 1022 subnets
    # Hosts = 2^{24-10} – 2 = 2^{14} – 2 = 16382 hosts/subnet

For more practice, determine the number of hosts and subnets for Practice Exercise 7.1.

1. You have a Class C address. You need to create 11 subnets. What is the subnet mask?

    Answer = 255.255.255.240
    # Subnets = $2^4 - 2$ = 14 subnets
    # Hosts = $2^{8-4} - 2 = 2^4 - 2$ = 14 hosts/subnet

2. You have a Class C address. You need to create 15 subnets. What is the subnet mask?

    Answer = 255.255.255.248
    # Subnets = $2^5 - 2$ = 30 subnets
    # Hosts = $2^{8-5} - 2 = 2^3 - 2$ = 6 hosts/subnet

3. You have a network address of 202.17.19.0. You need three subnets now and four additional subnets in the future. What is the subnet mask that should be used?

    Answer = 255.255.255.240
    # Subnets = $2^4 - 2$ = 14 subnets
    # Hosts = $2^{8-4} - 2 = 2^4 - 2$ = 14 hosts/subnet

4. You have a Class C address. You need a maximum of 30 hosts on each subnet. What is the subnet mask?

    Answer = 255.255.255.224
    # Subnets = $2^3 - 2$ = 6 subnets
    # Hosts = $2^{8-3} - 2 = 2^5 - 2$ = 30 hosts/subnet

5. You have a network address of 191.160.0.0. You need a maximum of 12 hosts on each subnet. What is the subnet mask?

    Answer = 255.255.255.240
    # Subnets = $2^{12} - 2$ = 4094 subnets
    # Hosts = $2^{16-12} - 2 = 2^4 - 2$ = 14 hosts/subnet

6. You require 20 hosts per subnet using a Class B network address. What is the subnet mask needed?

    Answer = 255.255.255.224
    # Subnets = $2^{11} - 2$ = 2046 subnets
    # Hosts = $2^{16-11} - 2 = 2^5 - 2$ = 30 hosts/subnet

7. Given the address of 191.15.0.0 and needing 20 subnets, what is the correct subnet mask to use?

    Answer = 255.255.248.0
    # Subnets = $2^5 - 2$ = 30 subnets
    # Hosts = $2^{16-5} - 2 = 2^{11} - 2$ = 2046 hosts/subnet

8. Given the address of 202.15.78.0 and needing 20 hosts per subnet, what is the correct subnet mask?

Answer = 255.255.255.224
Subnets = 2^3 – 2 = 6 subnets
Hosts = 2^{8-3} – 2 = 2^5 – 2 = 30 hosts/subnet

9. You have a Class A address of 11.0.0.0. You need a maximum of 400 subnets. What is the subnet mask that is needed?

Answer = 255.255.128.0
Subnets = 2^9 – 2 = 510 subnets
Hosts = 2^{24-9} – 2 = 2^{15} – 2 = 32766 hosts/subnet

10. You have a class A address of 121.0.0.0. You need a maximum of 400 hosts. What is the subnet mask that is needed?

Answer = 255.255.254.0
Subnets = 2^{15} – 2 = 32766 subnets
Hosts = 2^{24-15} – 2 = 2^9 – 2 = 510 hosts/subnet

Practice Exercise 7.3

Using Practice Exercise 7.1, define the subnet ranges, valid Host IDs, and the broadcast and network addresses for each of the questions.

1. You have a Class C address. You need to create 11 subnets. What is the subnet mask?

> **Answer = 255.255.255.240**
> \# Subnets = $2^4 - 2 = 14$ subnets
> \# Hosts = $2^{8-4} - 2 = 2^4 - 2 = 14$ hosts/subnet
> $256 - 240 = 16$ Range Value

Subnet Range	Host Ranges	Network	Broadcast
NA	NA	NA	NA
16 - 31	w.x.y.17 - 30	w.x.y.16	w.x.y.31
32 - 47	w.x.y.33 - 46	w.x.y.32	w.x.y.47
48 - 63	w.x.y.49 - 62	w.x.y.48	w.x.y.63
64 - 79	w.x.y.65 - 78	w.x.y.64	w.x.y.79
80 - 95	w.x.y.81 - 94	w.x.y.80	w.x.y.95
96 - 111	w.x.y.97 - 110	w.x.y.96	w.x.y.111
112 - 127	w.x.y.113 - 126	w.x.y.112	w.x.y.127
128 - 143	w.x.y.129 - 142	w.x.y.128	w.x.y.143

Subnet Range	Host Ranges	Network	Broadcast
144 - 159	w.x.y.145 - 158	w.x.y.144	w.x.y.159
160 - 175	w.x.y.161 - 174	w.x.y.160	w.x.y.175
176 - 191	w.x.y.177 - 190	w.x.y.176	w.x.y.191
192 - 207	w.x.y.193 - 206	w.x.y.192	w.x.y.207
208 - 223	w.x.y.209 - 222	w.x.y.208	w.x.y.223
224 - 239	w.x.y.225 - 238	w.x.y.224	w.x.y.239
NA	NA	NA	NA

2. You have a Class C address. You need to create 15 subnets. What is the subnet mask?

Answer = 255.255.255.248

Subnets = $2^5 - 2$ = 30 subnets
Hosts = $2^{8-5} - 2$ = $2^3 - 2$ = 6 hosts/subnet
256 − 248 = 8 Range Value

Subnet Range	Host Ranges	Network	Broadcast
NA	NA	NA	NA
8 - 15	w.x.y.9 - 14	w.x.y.8	w.x.y.15
16 - 23	w.x.y.17 - 22	w.x.y.16	w.x.y.23
24 - 31	w.x.y.25 - 30	w.x.y.24	w.x.y.31
32 - 39	w.x.y.33 - 38	w.x.y.32	w.x.y.39
40 - 47	w.x.y.41 - 46	w.x.y.40	w.x.y.47
48 - 55	w.x.y.49 - 54	w.x.y.48	w.x.y.55
56 - 63	w.x.y.57 - 62	w.x.y.56	w.x.y.63
64 - 71	w.x.y.65 - 70	w.x.y.64	w.x.y.71
72 - 79	w.x.y.73 - 78	w.x.y.72	w.x.y.79
80 - 87	w.x.y.81 - 86	w.x.y.80	w.x.y.87
88 - 95	w.x.y.89 - 94	w.x.y.88	w.x.y.95
Etc. - Etc.			
NA	NA	NA	NA

3. You have a network address of 202.17.19.0. You need three subnets now and four additional subnets in the future. What is the subnet mask that should be used?

Answer = 255.255.255.240

Subnets = $2^4 - 2 = 14$ subnets
Hosts = $2^{8-4} - 2 = 2^4 - 2 = 14$ hosts/subnet
$256 - 240 = 16$ Range Value

Subnet Range	Host Ranges	Network	Broadcast
NA	NA	NA	NA
16 - 31	202.17.19.17 - 30	202.17.19.16	202.17.19.31
32 - 47	202.17.19.33 - 46	202.17.19.32	202.17.19.47
48 - 63	202.17.19.49 - 62	202.17.19.48	202.17.19.63
64 - 79	202.17.19.65 - 78	202.17.19.64	202.17.19.79
80 - 95	202.17.19.81 - 94	202.17.19.80	202.17.19.95
96 - 111	202.17.19.97 - 110	202.17.19.96	202.17.19.111
112 - 127	202.17.19.113 - 126	202.17.19.112	202.17.19.127
128 - 143	202.17.19.129 - 142	202.17.19.128	202.17.19.143
144 - 159	202.17.19.145 - 158	202.17.19.144	202.17.19.159
160 - 175	202.17.19.161 - 174	202.17.19.160	202.17.19.175
176 - 191	202.17.19.177 - 190	202.17.19.176	202.17.19.191
192 - 207	202.17.19.193 - 206	202.17.19.192	202.17.19.207
208 - 223	202.17.19.209 - 222	202.17.19.208	202.17.19.223
224 - 239	202.17.19.225 - 238	202.17.19.224	202.17.19.239
NA	NA	NA	NA

4. You have a Class C address. You need a maximum of 30 hosts on each subnet. What is the subnet mask?

Answer = 255.255.255.224

Subnets = $2^3 - 2 = 6$ subnets
Hosts = $2^{8-3} - 2 = 2^5 - 2 = 30$ hosts/subnet
$256 - 224 = 32$ Range Value

Subnet Range	Host Ranges	Network	Broadcast
NA	NA	NA	NA
32 - 63	w.x.y.33 - 62	w.x.y.32	w.x.y.63
64 - 95	w.x.y.65 - 94	w.x.y.64	w.x.y.95
96 - 127	w.x.y.97 - 126	w.x.y.96	w.x.y.127

Subnet Range	Host Ranges	Network	Broadcast
128 - 159	w.x.y.129 - 158	w.x.y.128	w.x.y.159
160 - 191	w.x.y.161 - 190	w.x.y.160	w.x.y.191
192 - 223	w.x.y.193 - 222	w.x.y.192	w.x.y.223
NA	NA	NA	NA

5. You have a network address of 191.160.0.0. You need a maximum of 12 hosts on each subnet. What is the subnet mask?

Answer = 255.255.255.240
Subnets = $2^{12} - 2$ = 4094 subnets
Hosts = $2^{16-12} - 2 = 2^4 - 2$ = 14 hosts/subnet
256 − 255 = 1 Third Octet Range Value
256 − 240 = 16 Fourth Octet Range Value

Subnet Range	Host Ranges	Network	Broadcast
0.0 - 0.15	NA	NA	NA
0.16 - 0.31	191.160.0.17 - 30	191.160.0.16	191.160.0.31
0.32 - 0.47	191.160.0.33 - 46	191.160.0.32	191.160.0.47
0.48 - 0.63	191.160.0.49 - 62	191.160.0.48	191.160.0.63
0.Etc. - 0.Etc.			
1.0 - 1.15	191.160.1.81 - 94	191.160.1.1	191.160.1.15
1.16 - 1.31	191.160.1.97 - 110	191.160.1.16	191.160.1.31
1.32 - 1.47	191.160.1.113 - 126	191.160.1.32	191.160.1.47
1.48 - 1.63	191.160.1.129 - 142	191.160.1.48	191.160.1.63
1.Etc. - 1.Etc.			
255.Etc. - 255.Etc.			
255.176 - 255.191	191.160.255.177 - 190	191.160.255.176	191.160.255.191
255.192 - 255.207	191.160.255.193 - 206	191.160.255.192	191.160.255.207
255.208 - 255.223	191.160.255.209 - 222	191.160.255.208	191.160.255.223
255.224 - 255.239	191.160.255.225 - 238	191.160.255.224	191.160.255.239
255.240 - 255.255	NA	NA	NA

6. You require 20 hosts per subnet using a Class B network address. What is the subnet mask needed?

Answer = 255.255.255.224

Subnets = 2^{11} – 2 = 2046 subnets
Hosts = 2^{16-11} – 2 = 2^5 – 2 = 30 hosts/subnet
256 – 255 = 1 Range Value Third Octet
256 – 224 = 32 Range Value Fourth Octet

Subnet Range	Host Ranges	Network	Broadcast
0.0 - 0.31	NA	NA	NA
0.32 - 0.63	w.x.0.33 - 0.62	w.x.0.32	w.x.0.63
0.64 - 0.95	w.x.0.65 - 0.94	w.x.0.64	w.x.0.95
0.96 - 0.127	w.x.0.97 - 0.126	w.x.0.96	w.x.0.127
0.128 - 0.159	w.x.0.129 - 0.158	w.x.0.128	w.x.0.159
0.160 - 0.191	w.x.0.161 - 0.190	w.x.0.160	w.x.0.191
0.192 - 0.223	w.x.0.193 - 0.222	w.x.0.192	w.x.0.223
0.224 - 0.255	w.x.0.225 - 0.254	w.x.0.224	w.x.0.255
1.0 - 1.63	w.x.1.1 - 1.62	w.x.1.0	w.x.1.63
1.Etc. - 1.Etc.			
255.Etc. - 255.Etc.			
255.96 - 255.127	w.x.255.97 - 255.126	w.x.255.96	w.x.255.127
255.128 - 255.159	w.x.255.129 - 255.158	w.x.255.128	w.x.255.159
255.160 - 255.191	w.x.255.161 - 255.190	w.x.255.160	w.x.255.191
255.192 - 255.223	w.x.255.193 - 255.222	w.x.255.192	w.x.255.223
255.224 - 255.255	NA	NA	NA

7. Given the address of 191.15.0.0 and needing 20 subnets, what is the correct subnet mask to use?

Answer = 255.255.248.0
Subnets = 2^5 – 2 = 30 subnets
Hosts = 2^{16-5} – 2 = 2^{11} – 2 = 2046 hosts/subnet
256 – 248 = 8 Range Value Third Octet

Subnet Range	Host Ranges	Network	Broadcast
0.0 - 7.255	NA	NA	NA
8.0 - 15.255	191.15.8.1 - 15.254	191.15. 8.0	191.15.15.255
16.0 - 23.255	191.15.16.1 - 23.254	191.15. 16.0	191.15. 23.255
24.0 - 31.255	191.15.24.1 - 31.254	191.15. 24.0	191.15. 31.255

Subnet Range	Host Ranges	Network	Broadcast
32.0 - 39.255	191.15.32.1 - 39.254	191.15.32.0	191.15.39.255
40.0 - 47.255	191.15.40.1 - 47.254	191.15. 40.0	191.15. 47.255
48.0 - 55.255	191.15.48.1 - 55.254	191.15. 48.0	191.15. 55.255
56.0 - 63.255	191.15.56.1 - 63.254	191.15. 56.0	191.15. 63.255
64.0 - 71.255	191.15.64.1 - 71.254	191.15. 64.0	191.15. 71.255
72.0 - 79.255	191.15.72.1 - 79.254	191.15.72.0	191.15.79.255
Etc. - Etc.			
216.0 - 223.255	191.15.216.1 - 223.254	191.15. 216.0	191.15. 223.255
224.0 - 231.255	191.15.224.1 - 231.254	191.15. 224.0	191.15.231.255
232.0 - 239.255	191.15.232.1 - 239.254	191.15. 232.0	191.15. 239.255
240.0 - 247.255	191.15.240.1 - 247.254	191.15. 240.0	191.15. 247.255
248.0 - 255.255	NA	NA	NA

8. Given the address of 202.15.78.0 and needing 20 hosts per subnet, what is the correct subnet mask?

> **Answer = 255.255.255.224**
> # Subnets = $2^3 - 2 = 6$ subnets
> # Hosts = $2^{8-3} - 2 = 2^5 - 2 = 30$ hosts/subnet
> $256 - 224 = 32$ Range Value

Subnet Range	Host Ranges	Network	Broadcast
NA	NA	NA	NA
32 - 63	202.15.78.33 - 62	202.15.78.32	202.15.78.63
64 - 95	202.15.78.65 - 94	202.15.78.64	202.15.78.95
96 - 127	202.15.78.97 - 126	202.15.78.96	202.15.78.127
128 - 159	202.15.78.129 - 158	202.15.78.128	202.15.78.159
160 - 191	202.15.78.161 - 190	202.15.78.160	202.15.78.191
192 - 223	202.15.78.193 - 222	202.15.78.192	202.15.78.223
NA	NA	NA	NA

9. You have a Class A address of 11.0.0.0. You need a maximum of 400 subnets. What is the subnet mask that is needed?

> **Answer = 255.255.128.0**
> # Subnets = $2^9 - 2 = 510$ subnets

$$\text{\# Hosts} = 2^{24\text{-}9} - 2 = 2^{15} - 2 = 32766 \text{ hosts/subnet}$$
256 − 255 = 1 Range Value Second Octet
256 − 128 = 128 Range Value Third Octet

Subnet Range	Host Ranges	Network	Broadcast
0.0 - 0.127	NA	NA	NA
0.128 - 0.255	11.0.128.1 - 0.255.254	11.0.128.0	11.0.255.255
1.0 - 1.127	11.1.0.1 - 1.127.254	11.1.0.0	11.1.127.255
1.128 - 1.255	11.1.128.1 - 1.255.254	11.1.128.0	11.1.255.255
2.0 - 2.127	11.2.0.1 - 2.127.254	11.2.0.0	11.2.127.255
2.128 - 2.255	11.2.128.1 - 2.255.254	11.2.128.0	11.2.255.255
Etc. - Etc.			
254.0 - 254.127	11.254.0.1 - 254.127.254	11.254.0.0	11.254.127.255
254.128 - 254.255	11.254.128.1 - 254.255.254	11.254.128.0	11.254.255.255
255.0 - 255.127	11.255.0.1 - 255.127.254	11.255.0.0	11.255.127.255
255.128 - 255.255	NA	NA	NA

10. You have a Class A address of 121.0.0.0. You need a maximum of 400 hosts. What is the subnet mask that is needed?

   Answer = 255.255.254.0
   $$\text{\# Subnets} = 2^{15} - 2 = 32766 \text{ subnets}$$
   $$\text{\# Hosts} = 2^{24\text{-}15} - 2 = 2^9 - 2 = 510 \text{ hosts/subnet}$$
   256 − 255 = 1 Range Value Second Octet
   256 − 254 = 2 Range Value Third Octet

Subnet Range	Host Ranges	Network	Broadcast
NA	NA	NA	NA
0.2 - 0.3	121.0.2.1 - 121.0.3.254	121.0.2.0	121.0.3.255
0.4 - 0.5	121.0.4.1 - 121.0.5.254	121.0.4.0	121.0.5.255
Etc. - Etc.			
1.0 - 1.1	121.1.0.1 - 121.1.1.254	121.1.0.0	121.1.1.255
1.2 - 1.3	121.1.2.1 - 121.1.3.254	121.1.2.0	121.1.3.255
Etc. - Etc.			
254.0 - 254.1	121.254.0.1 - 121.254.1.254	121.254.0.0	121.254.1.255

Subnet Range	Host Ranges	Network	Broadcast
254.2 - 254.3	121.254.2.1 - 121.254.3.254	121.254.2.0	121.254.3.255
Etc. - Etc.			
255.252 - 255.253	121.255.252.1 - 121.255.253.254	121.255.252.0	121.255.253.255
NA	NA	NA	NA

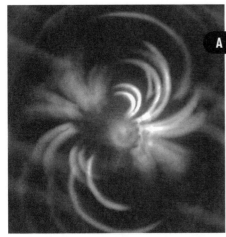

Hierarchical Command Structure

In this Appendix we have laid out the hierarchical diagram of all the commands that have been introduced in this book. This list does not include the arguments allowed for each command. Use the **?** to iterate the available arguments. Note that this is not an inclusive list, which means that Cisco has many more documented and undocumented commands.

To read through this chart start with the login prompt (pressing **<enter>**) and examine the commands available there. If we type the command **enable** then we need to follow the chart that directs us to the A circle. On the next page we will see the A circle and the list of commands now available to us. Continuing in this fashion will show us where we have to be in order to execute certain commands. Some commands have an arrow drawn below them to two or more commands. These are arguments or new commands in the sub-command structure. For example, under **banner** there are two arguments listed: **motd** and **login**. Under the command **router [rip | igrp]** are the commands **network**, **passive-interface**, and **neighbor**. These commands are used inside the router configuration mode.

Remember that each command can be shortened to provide only enough characters to differentiate that command from any other. If we shorten the command too much, we will receive an error message indicating an **ambiguous command**.

To reverse the commands use the **no** keyword with most other commands. For example, **no router rip** will turn of RIP.

Finally, remember the difference between using the **?** character in the command and after a space. We use the **cl?** command to show us all commands that start with the letters '**cl**'. We use the **show ?** (notice the space) to show us the arguments of the **show** command.

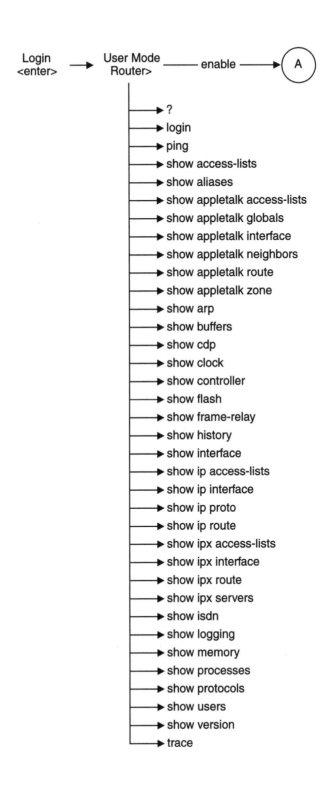

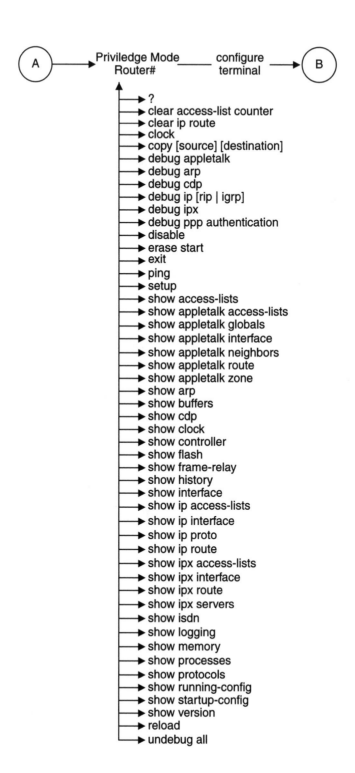

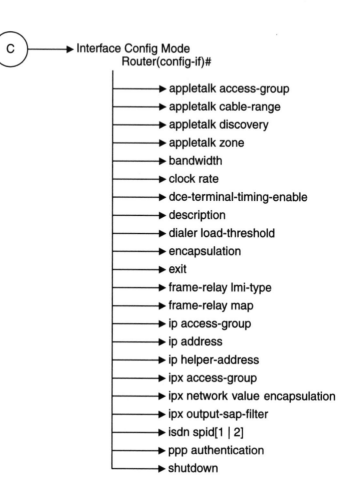

C → Interface Config Mode
Router(config-if)#

- appletalk access-group
- appletalk cable-range
- appletalk discovery
- appletalk zone
- bandwidth
- clock rate
- dce-terminal-timing-enable
- description
- dialer load-threshold
- encapsulation
- exit
- frame-relay lmi-type
- frame-relay map
- ip access-group
- ip address
- ip helper-address
- ipx access-group
- ipx network value encapsulation
- ipx output-sap-filter
- isdn spid[1 | 2]
- ppp authentication
- shutdown

Index

Index

X

Z

LICENSE AGREEMENT AND LIMITED WARRANTY

READ THE FOLLOWING TERMS AND CONDITIONS CAREFULLY BEFORE OPENING THIS SOFTWARE MEDIA PACKAGE. THIS LEGAL DOCUMENT IS AN AGREEMENT BETWEEN YOU AND PRENTICE-HALL, INC. (THE "COMPANY"). BY OPENING THIS SEALED SOFTWARE MEDIA PACKAGE, YOU ARE AGREEING TO BE BOUND BY THESE TERMS AND CONDITIONS. IF YOU DO NOT AGREE WITH THESE TERMS AND CONDITIONS, DO NOT OPEN THE SOFTWARE MEDIA PACKAGE. PROMPTLY RETURN THE UNOPENED SOFTWARE MEDIA PACKAGE AND ALL ACCOMPANYING ITEMS TO THE PLACE YOU OBTAINED THEM FOR A FULL REFUND OF ANY SUMS YOU HAVE PAID.

1. **GRANT OF LICENSE:** In consideration of your payment of the license fee, which is part of the price you paid for this product, and your agreement to abide by the terms and conditions of this Agreement, the Company grants to you a nonexclusive right to use and display the copy of the enclosed software program (hereinafter the "SOFTWARE") on a single computer (i.e., with a single CPU) at a single location so long as you comply with the terms of this Agreement. The Company reserves all rights not expressly granted to you under this Agreement.

2. **OWNERSHIP OF SOFTWARE:** You own only the magnetic or physical media (the enclosed software media) on which the SOFTWARE is recorded or fixed, but the Company retains all the rights, title, and ownership to the SOFTWARE recorded on the original software media copy(ies) and all subsequent copies of the SOFTWARE, regardless of the form or media on which the original or other copies may exist. This license is not a sale of the original SOFTWARE or any copy to you.

3. **COPY RESTRICTIONS:** This SOFTWARE and the accompanying printed materials and user manual (the "Documentation") are the subject of copyright. You may _not_ copy the Documentation or the SOFTWARE, except that you may make a single copy of the SOFTWARE for backup or archival purposes only. You may be held legally responsible for any copying or copyright infringement which is caused or encouraged by your failure to abide by the terms of this restriction.

4. **USE RESTRICTIONS:** You may _not_ network the SOFTWARE or otherwise use it on more than one computer or computer terminal at the same time. You may physically transfer the SOFTWARE from one computer to another provided that the SOFTWARE is used on only one computer at a time. You may _not_ distribute copies of the SOFTWARE or Documentation to others. You may _not_ reverse engineer, disassemble, decompile, modify, adapt, translate, or create derivative works based on the SOFTWARE or the Documentation without the prior written consent of the Company.

5. **TRANSFER RESTRICTIONS:** The enclosed SOFTWARE is licensed only to you and may _not_ be transferred to any one else without the prior written consent of the Company. Any unauthorized transfer of the SOFTWARE shall result in the immediate termination of this Agreement.

6. **TERMINATION:** This license is effective until terminated. This license will terminate automatically without notice from the Company and become null and void if you fail to comply with any provisions or limitations of this license. Upon termination, you shall destroy the Documentation and all copies of the SOFTWARE. All provisions of this Agreement as to warranties, limitation of liability, remedies or damages, and our ownership rights shall survive termination.

7. **MISCELLANEOUS:** This Agreement shall be construed in accordance with the laws of the United States of America and the State of New York and shall benefit the Company, its affiliates, and assignees.

8. **LIMITED WARRANTY AND DISCLAIMER OF WARRANTY:** The Company warrants that the SOFTWARE, when properly used in accordance with the Documentation, will operate in substantial conformity with the description of the SOFTWARE set forth in the Documentation. The Company does not warrant that the SOFTWARE will meet your requirements or that the operation of the SOFTWARE will be uninterrupted or error-free. The Company warrants that the media on which the SOFTWARE is delivered shall be free from defects in materials and workmanship under normal use for a period of thirty (30) days from the date of your purchase. Your only remedy and the Company's only obligation under these limited warranties is, at the Company's option, return of the warranted item for a refund of any amounts paid by you or replacement of the item. Any replacement of SOFTWARE or media under the warranties shall not extend the original warranty period. The limited warranty set forth above shall not apply to any SOFTWARE which the Company determines in good faith has been subject to misuse, neglect, improper installation, repair, alteration, or dam-

age by you. EXCEPT FOR THE EXPRESSED WARRANTIES SET FORTH ABOVE, THE COMPANY DISCLAIMS ALL WARRANTIES, EXPRESS OR IMPLIED, INCLUDING WITHOUT LIMITATION, THE IMPLIED WARRANTIES OF MERCHANTABILITY AND FITNESS FOR A PARTICULAR PURPOSE. EXCEPT FOR THE EXPRESS WARRANTY SET FORTH ABOVE, THE COMPANY DOES NOT WARRANT, GUARANTEE, OR MAKE ANY REPRESENTATION REGARDING THE USE OR THE RESULTS OF THE USE OF THE SOFTWARE IN TERMS OF ITS CORRECTNESS, ACCURACY, RELIABILITY, CURRENTNESS, OR OTHERWISE.

IN NO EVENT, SHALL THE COMPANY OR ITS EMPLOYEES, AGENTS, SUPPLIERS, OR CONTRACTORS BE LIABLE FOR ANY INCIDENTAL, INDIRECT, SPECIAL, OR CONSEQUENTIAL DAMAGES ARISING OUT OF OR IN CONNECTION WITH THE LICENSE GRANTED UNDER THIS AGREEMENT, OR FOR LOSS OF USE, LOSS OF DATA, LOSS OF INCOME OR PROFIT, OR OTHER LOSSES, SUSTAINED AS A RESULT OF INJURY TO ANY PERSON, OR LOSS OF OR DAMAGE TO PROPERTY, OR CLAIMS OF THIRD PARTIES, EVEN IF THE COMPANY OR AN AUTHORIZED REPRESENTATIVE OF THE COMPANY HAS BEEN ADVISED OF THE POSSIBILITY OF SUCH DAMAGES. IN NO EVENT SHALL LIABILITY OF THE COMPANY FOR DAMAGES WITH RESPECT TO THE SOFTWARE EXCEED THE AMOUNTS ACTUALLY PAID BY YOU, IF ANY, FOR THE SOFTWARE.

SOME JURISDICTIONS DO NOT ALLOW THE LIMITATION OF IMPLIED WARRANTIES OR LIABILITY FOR INCIDENTAL, INDIRECT, SPECIAL, OR CONSEQUENTIAL DAMAGES, SO THE ABOVE LIMITATIONS MAY NOT ALWAYS APPLY. THE WARRANTIES IN THIS AGREEMENT GIVE YOU SPECIFIC LEGAL RIGHTS AND YOU MAY ALSO HAVE OTHER RIGHTS WHICH VARY IN ACCORDANCE WITH LOCAL LAW.

ACKNOWLEDGMENT

YOU ACKNOWLEDGE THAT YOU HAVE READ THIS AGREEMENT, UNDERSTAND IT, AND AGREE TO BE BOUND BY ITS TERMS AND CONDITIONS. YOU ALSO AGREE THAT THIS AGREEMENT IS THE COMPLETE AND EXCLUSIVE STATEMENT OF THE AGREEMENT BETWEEN YOU AND THE COMPANY AND SUPERSEDES ALL PROPOSALS OR PRIOR AGREEMENTS, ORAL, OR WRITTEN, AND ANY OTHER COMMUNICATIONS BETWEEN YOU AND THE COMPANY OR ANY REPRESENTATIVE OF THE COMPANY RELATING TO THE SUBJECT MATTER OF THIS AGREEMENT.

Should you have any questions concerning this Agreement or if you wish to contact the Company for any reason, please contact in writing at the address below.

Robin Short
Prentice Hall PTR
One Lake Street
Upper Saddle River, New Jersey 07458

About the CD

The contents of the CD-ROM included with *CCNA Certification* are listed here. Freeware versions of the following tools have been included on the CD. Please note that some of these programs require registration for continued use.

Kiwi's CatTools

Kiwi's CatTools is a collection of useful tools for managing, maintaining, and backing up Cisco routers, Catalyst switches, and LightStream ATM switches. Operation can be interactive or scheduled. The program works by connecting to each selected router in turn via telnet and performing the chosen function. Kiwi's CatTools uses telnet (TCP port 23) only and not SNMP or TFTP as do other network management tools.

Functions include:

- Configuration backup to dated file, notification if a change has occurred since last backup.
- Statistics polling: Interface traffic (Ethernet, Serial, ATM, F/R, CIP) and CPU load.
- Collection and clearing of IP accounting logs.
- Collection and clearing of IP access-list counters.
- IP ARP table collection to maintain a persistent list of MAC addresses versus IP addresses.
- ATM LANE reporting (LES/BUS, and so on).
- Network connectivity testing.
- Switch port enabling and disabling.
- Switch port documentation (Port, MAC addresses, IP addresses, DNS, and VLAN).
- Software and Catalyst module reporting.
- Year 2000 compliant.

The latest version can always be found at www.kiwienterprises.com/download_cattools.com

Kiwi's Syslog Daemon

Kiwi's Syslog Daemon receives standard Syslog messages on UDP port 514 sent from routers, switches, or Unix hosts, and displays the details on the screen.

There are two versions of Kiwi's Syslog Daemon available:

- The NT Service version
- Normal nonservice version

The normal version runs interactively and only operates while a user is logged on to the system. The service version runs as a noninteractive NT service and is started automatically when NT starts. This version does not require a user to be logged on to run.

The Kiwi's Syslog Service Manager program provides the GUI to configure and manage the NT service.

Features (Free Version) include:

- GUI-based (runs under Windows 95, Windows 98, or NT4).
- Visual—you can watch the messages on the screen as they are received.
- Intelligent message forwarding (all or selected by priority).
- Automatic log file archiving (daily, weekly, or monthly).
- Logging to an Access database.

- Alarm notification (audible or via SMTP e-mail).
- Daily e-mailing of Syslog statistics.
- Minimizes to the system tray to avoid task bar clutter.
- Maintains original sender's address when forwarding messages.
- Cool statistics display.
- Y2K (Year 2000) compliant.
- Syslog message buffering so you don't miss a message under load.
- DNS resolution of sending host IP addresses with domain stripping.
- Selectable font and display color.
- NT Service version available.
- Help file included.
- Free to use for as long as you like.

The latest version can always be found at www.kiwienterprises.com/download_syslogd.com

What Is SyslogGen?

SyslogGen sends Unix-type Syslog messages created from the GUI or command-line arguments to a host running a Syslog Daemon. SyslogGen can test a Syslog Daemon setup by sending Syslog messages that have been created by the user from the options available.

The command-line arguments allow the user to specify the receiving host, message priority, and message text. When no command-line arguments are specified, SyslogGen starts in GUI mode, and the user can create a message from the many options provided.

Features include:

- Command line or GUI interface.
  Sends standard Unix Syslog messages or enhanced messages (to Kiwi's Syslog Daemon).
  Fast.
  Simple to use.
  Free—please take the time to register via e-mail if you use this program.
  Can be run from other programs to make them Syslog capable.
  Can fully test your Syslog daemon setup.
- Packet burst mode to hammer the Syslog daemon to see if it can cope under load.

The latest version can always be found at www.kiwienterprises.com/download_sysloggen.com

Platforms

The CD-ROM can be used on Microsoft Windows 95/98/NT.

License Agreement

Use of the software accompanying *CCNA Certification* is subject to the terms of the License Agreement and Limited Warranty, found on the previous pages.

Technical Support

Prentice Hall does not offer technical support for any of the programs on the CD-ROM. However, if the CD-ROM is damaged, you may obtain a replacement copy by sending an e-mail that describes the problem to disc_exchange@prenhall.com.